INSTANTANEOUS PERSONAL MAGNETISM

Combining an Absolutely New Method with The Best Established Teachings or the Past

By EDMUND SHAFTESBURY

INSTANTANEOUS PERSONAL MAGNETISM

Copyright Mind Control Publishing 2010

ISBN -   1453754601
EAN -13 –   9781453754603

THE
TEN GREAT DEPARTMENTS
OF
THIS SYSTEM

I
DEPARTMENT OF MAGNETIC SOURCES

II
DEPARTMENT OF MENTAL MAGNITUDE

III
DEPARTMENT OF THE MAGNETIC EYE

IV
DEPARTMENT OF
INSTANTANEOUS PERSONAL MAGNETISM

V
DEPARTMENT OF MAGNETIC HEALTH

VI
DEPARTMENT OF TENSION ENERGY

VII
DEPARTMENT OF REPOSE AND POWER

VIII
DEPARTMENT OF THE MAGNETIC VOICE

IX
DEPARTMENT OF APPLIED MAGNETISM

X
DEPARTMENT OF MAGNETIC HEALING

THE ORIGINAL SYSTEM

The following facts should be kept in mind by persons using other systems of instruction in the Cultivation of Personal Magnetism :

1. The Shaftesbury System was the first to be issued; and appeared forty-five years ago when there were no other systems in existence.

2. To-day it is the Standard Method, and is so recognized everywhere.

3. It is the only System that is used by the International Magnetism Club, and that has been adopted in schools and various other educational institutions.

4. It is the only System that actually produces lasting results.

5. It is the only System that has helped a long list of successful men and women in all walks of life to acquire a magnetic personality with no failure where its students have been in earnest and ambitious to win the highest goal of earthly existence.

6. Attracted by its success, imitators many years ago began to issue cheap and loudly advertised courses of training, and approached as near as they dared to our methods ; but, for fear of becoming involved in lawsuits for infringement, they avoided all the essential value of our instruction, with the result that they were discredited and all went out of business.

7. Since then similar imitators are likely to appear, with the same inability to guide their students to the successful acquisition of personal magnetism.

8. As personal magnetism is life itself, only the best instruction is desirable. Low priced competitive systems that accomplish nothing for their students are the highest priced in the end. Besides producing failure, they discourage the buyers, drive them away from the study and thereby deprive them of the greatest blessings in life.

9. There is BUT ONE GENUINE METHOD ; it is the SHAFTESBURY METHOD ; long tried, thoroughly tested, and uniformly successful.

GREAT MEN WHO HAVE OWED THEIR SUCCESS TO BOOKS

PITT
owed his success as a statesman to *The Wealth of Nations*, by Adam Smith.

WATT
was started on his way as an inventor by a book: *The Elements of Philosophy*.

MERCER
the pioneer of the artificial silk trade, was stimulated to begin his experiments by *The Chemical Pocket-Book*.

KELVIN
was inspired as a scientist by reading *The Theory of Light*, by Fourier.

LEVERHULME
often said that his career was started by *Self-Help*, written by Samuel Smiles.

FARADAY
was started by a book on chemistry.

ORVILLE and WILBUR WRIGHT
were led to invent the aeroplane by reading a book on gliding, by Lilienthal.

WESTINGHOUSE and FORD
were both started on their careers as inventors by reading magazine articles.

ANDREW CARNEGIE
owed his success to the reading of books, and built 1600 free libraries.

THERE IS NO BETTER AID TO SUCCESS IN LIFE THAN GOOD BOOKS

INTRODUCTION BY THE PUBLISHERS

A PRESENTATION of the causes and progress that have become history in the unfolding of any great movement that has lent itself to the betterment of mankind, is always a source of encouragement and inspiration to a newer generation. To this end we will briefly review the important facts that have been interwoven in the development of the Magnetism Club.

Edmund Shaftesbury to-day is known to about four million men and women who are studying his works ; yet in the forty-five years or more that he has been a teacher, he has refused to advertise his productions ; and it is only at the present time that the publishers who now control his writings have undertaken to invite a larger following by public advertisements. His four million students came from the friends and acquaintances of those who had become students in the same way and who had mentioned these works and spoken of their merits to others. As one instance out of many, a person who owned a copy of this book of Personal Magnetism and who was spending a few weeks at a fashionable summer hotel, left the book on a table for a few days while temporarily absent, and learned that nearly four hundred other guests had obtained the address of the publishers, and had ordered the book. In another case a doctor kept a copy on the table in his waiting-room, and in the course of time more than two hundred of his patients procured the address and ordered copies for themselves.

It is gratifying and also encouraging to prospective students and to those who are about to begin this study, to know that the BOOK ITSELF IS MAGNETIC !

A very capable, clever, successful but strictly honest business man who was told that this system was in itself full of magnetism, refused to believe the claim, and said, " I will pay one hundred pounds to the author if he can induce me to buy the book."—The following questions were put to this business man : " Will you decide the matter as an honest man without any quibble ? "—" Yes."—" Will you take time to read the book carefully ? "—" Yes."—" If, after reading it, you find that its value to you is fully a thousand times more than its cost, will you then buy it ? "—" Yes."—In a short time a cheque for one hundred pounds was his answer.

It is not only encouraging but gratifying to prospective students to know that the book has a most positive and powerful magnetic influence over the lives of those who read or who study its pages.

And this influence is ennobling, uplifting and inspiring.

Edmund Shaftesbury when engaged in his first literary duties as reporter for a great daily newspaper, correspondent for others, writer for magazines, and author of scientific treatises, as well as teacher and lecturer along these lines all of which harmonised in the plan he had in mind, was brought in contact with many great personages, and had the opportunity of analysing the causes of their greatness. No man that ever lived possessed a keener insight into the problems of life ; and we have never heard of any person who was gifted with so great an analytical power of the causes, natural and acquired, that produced the successful people of the world. He compiled for his own use in experimentation and study, private biographies of more than one hundred of the greatest men and women of two generations ago, all personally acquired by actual contact with these people. A few only of these names will be mentioned here, and among them will be included some who were either close friends or students, or endorsers of the training systems created by Shaftesbury.

These names are published for the sole purpose of giving encouragement to new pupils and of arousing in them the latent impulses of ambition to aim high in the purposes of life in the belief that noble examples are truer guides than the allurements of unfulfilled hopes.

To name a few, we find the following great personages among many others :

CHARLES BRADLAUGH, the famous orator of convincing personal magnetism.

JOHN BRIGHT, leading statesman and convincing orator.

CHARLES STEWART PARNELL, for many years a masterful man, and successful leader in the Irish cause.

WILSON BARRETT, regarded in his day as the most magnetic of actors. By his personal magnetism he was able to hold his audiences thrilled until after midnight in his rendition of the unabridged play of Hamlet, which no other actor in our memory had essayed. Mr. Barrett purchased every book by Shaftesbury, and eagerly sought these systems of education on his annual visits to Shaftesbury's native town.

REV. CHARLES HADDON SPURGEON, well remembered as the most magnetic preacher in the last century of English history. By his personal magnetism he built up a following that took him from his humble beginning at Waterbeach to the great Tabernacle where many thousands constantly crowded in order to hear him. Later in his career he organised classes of young men studying for the ministry, and proclaimed the two greatest facts in this profession : first, that the right kind of a prayer is always answered ; and that every successful preacher must develop the power of personal magnetism.

HON. WILLIAM EWART GLADSTONE, the great Prime Minister, whose personal magnetism won for him the highest honours in the gift of the nation. He not only possessed the Shaftesbury works, but, at the solicitation of Queen Victoria, presented her with one of them that she admired. These facts were published at the time.

Other names here listed are but a very few of the many that might be included, but are omitted for lack of space.

BENJAMIN F. BUTLER, of very magnetic personality, in whose office Shaftesbury when a young man spent two years.

JOHN A. LOGAN, an intensely magnetic orator and statesman, as well as successful warrior.

LAWRENCE BARRETT, associated with Edwin Booth at one time.

JOHN B. GOUGH, one of the most energetic of all lecturers and platform orators, a personal friend of Shaftesbury.

CARDINAL GIBBONS, one of the greatest dignitaries of his church, whose personal letter in approval of the Shaftesbury systems was published for many years in a university catalogue.

ARCHBISHOP JOHN J. KEANE, personal friend of Shaftesbury, who nearly forty years ago when at the head of a well-known university engaged him as instructor, and afterwards in an open letter recommended his books, which letter was published for many years.

ALEXANDER MELVILLE BELL, with whom Shaftesbury collaborated in certain writings. His son was the inventor of the telephone.

DWIGHT L. MOODY, the most magnetic of evangelists and yet a quiet and impressive speaker as compared with other orators. He organised great classes of Bible students and young preachers, and extolled the value of magnetism.

BISHOP JOHN PHILIP NEWMAN, the greatest and most magnetic of pulpit orators in his day next to Beecher. He was not only a friend of Shaftesbury, but did him the exceptional honour of seeking his personal instruction.

BISHOP PHILLIPS BROOKS, student of Shaftesbury's works while yet a leader in the Episcopal Church. His approval of these works was published in the form of a letter nearly forty years ago, in which he called them the " new education."

HENRY WARD BEECHER was in the front rank of pulpit and platform oratory in the period in which he lived, and for the successful use of a winning personal magnetism he had no equal. He was pre-eminent in swaying the minds of thousands, rising from one range of magnetism to another ; his genius always rising with him ; for magnetism and genius are inseparable. We have seen him while facing an adverse and hostile audience spend an hour or more in his efforts to get a fair hearing, and eventually end the discourse with the same audience rising and cheering him to the echo. These incidents are stated to make clear the fact that there is such a power as personal magnetism, and that it can overcome all obstacles and break down all barriers. In the years 1875 and 1876, when Beecher was instructing classes in theology in a university attended by Shaftesbury, a strong friendship sprang up between the two, one a world-famous orator, the greatest of his times, and the other a young man seeking the secrets of greatness. From the quiet little prayers at a rude table in a plain room up to the sublime heights of the loftiest oratory, in voice, manner and presence this remarkable man lived in an atmosphere of personal magnetism that thrilled and inspired those who came under its influence ; and, as far as the author of these books was permitted to analyse the sources of this power, it came from a natural possession of gifts that sprang from laws that are within the reach of most men and women.

As we have said, it is our purpose to create in every student of this system the ambition to succeed in life ; and we know the value of high examples and past triumphs. Nothing stimulates the desire to win in the battle of existence so much as the history of past achievements. It is also of prime importance to make known the fact that Shaftesbury created his opportunities for discovering the underlying causes and secrets of success in the lives of great men. By association and study he became eminently fitted to develop just such a course of training as would employ the laws of magnetism in his unfolding of these gifts in his students.

Another fact that is of still greater importance is the reception given his methods by the greatest men and women of his time. It was said of his first edition of the book of Personal Magnetism that, if it were left as by accident in any public place, a single copy would in a few months attract the casual attention of readers, and so bring a demand for a large number of copies, each one of which would exert a similar influence, and this in time would account for the building up automatically of a following of four million readers without a single line of public advertising.

What was the reception given him from the beginning ?

He was overrun with applicants for his personal instruction. Now it is a fact that as much value can be obtained from the books as from personal teaching ; for the latter consists solely of the statement in lecture form of the laws and processes by which personal magnetism can be acquired. He made this fact known ; yet thousands within reach insisted on individual instruction. In his personal teaching he numbered, among others, Cabinet Ministers, Judges, Industrial Magnates, Famous Business Men, Financiers, Members of Society, Lawyers, High Dignitaries of the Church, and almost every class of professional people.

Now we come to the most encouraging fact in this introduction.

Omitting all those persons who came in person to him for lessons, and looking only to those men and women who secured their help solely from his books, we find the following results :

MINISTERS.—Records furnished by persons in a position to know the facts, tell us that up to a recent period, but including the years long gone by, no less than 2781 clergymen of small churches working at low salaries, by the development of personal magnetism rose to eminence, step by step, going from place to place, always up, up, up, improving themselves, doing more effective work, winning greater compensation, and accomplishing greater good in the world. The value of these records is in the fact that these clergymen acknowledge the power of this system of study as the cause of their success ; practically all of them admitting that without it they would still be in the same old rut where so many of their fellow-clergymen have been for a third of a century. And there are thousands of other cases of which we have received no record.

LAWYERS.—We teach that lawyers must win the confidence of the public by strict honesty and fairness of dealing ; must win confidence in themselves ; and then must develop and employ the natural habits of personal magnetism that bring these two influences together ; and on this triple alliance must build the highest efficiency. Reports from 7793 lawyers who began in the humblest station in their profession, and who spent years in the struggle for existence, show that every one of them rose to the very heights of success, hundreds of them becoming great leaders, winning fame and wealth.

DOCTORS.—Every highly successful physician and surgeon needs a large fund of well developed and finely controlled personal magnetism. This is not hypnotism, but is the exact opposite of hypnotism. The latter deadens, depresses, deals with abnormal nerves, and helps only in certain classes of pernicious or vicious maladies. Personal magnetism builds life, is open, uplifting, brightening and cheering. Reports from 12,624 doctors who have studied our works solely by themselves, and who have put them into practice, acknowledge that our system has been one of the causes of their rise out of mediocre conditions to the highest success in their profession. Countless others in the past forty-five years have undoubtedly accomplished great results from the same aid, but have failed to tell us so.

DENTISTS.—The really great dentists of the world have
·fect nerve control—not in their charges merely, but in their
nipulation of the delicate instruments required in doing fine
rk. Here is one letter which is very much like another that
published many years ago : " The book of personal mag-
ism does much more than is claimed for it. In fact it would
; be possible to state its full value, nor a tenth of it. That
nsists that every student shall acquire perfect nerve control
one of its great merits in my profession. Your book has
much improved my skill that this alone is worth many
idreds of pounds to me in increased income." But this is
y an incidental part of the training. Yet there have been
hionable schools for young ladies that have employed this
ise and one other, namely, perfect poise of manner, as aids
an elegant training. Still these are incidentals only.
BUSINESS MEN AND WOMEN.—The law of supply and
nand keeps many ugly-mannered business men alive ; but
a competitive world, where customers may exercise a choice
their dealings, the most effective drawing power is that of
·sonal magnetism, adapted, of course, to the channels of these
ivities. One must know what to use and how to use it in
h division of life. It seems beyond belief that, in the past
ty-five years, more than four hundred thousand persons en-
;ed in business have reported newly acquired success which
y have acknowledged to be due to this study as set forth
the present book and its similar predecessors. And there
, vast army of clerks and employees who have risen steadily
:heir positions, until a great majority of them have become
ployers. Here we have the real value of personal magnetism.
SOCIAL LIFE is a great field for the exercise of the powers
attraction. Men and women have learned that assumed
ietness, gentleness and kindliness are misfits ; they are a
ieer that rubs off when least expected to do so. A young
nan or young man who possesses the actual charm of personal
gnetism, even if poor or less expensively attired than others,
I not be ignored or treated with indifference. This is one of
reasons why certain phases of this study have been regularly
ght in fashionable schools for the training of girls in social
iduct. There is much herein that is sure to benefit any
dent who aspires to social qualities and charming manners,

regardless of the usages of good form which belong to other lines of training, not included in this work.

The present system has for many years been recognised as the standard work of its kind. This prominence comes from its genuine merit as a training method ; its adherence to the practical usefulness of the system ; and to its unfailing helpfulness to every student of its pages. In dealing with hundreds of thousands of students we have never yet met with any totally dissatisfied person.

Having thus set forth the history of this system from its inception and having presented the great names that inspired the author to undertake the formation of a method that was sure to help humanity beyond that of any other influence in life, we will now let him speak for himself in the forthcoming lessons.

One prediction is to be made at this stage :

Since it is true that this book itself is charged with the power of magnetism, we venture to assert that a single reading of its pages will not only draw the reader to it in an inseparable partnership, but will also in itself and of itself have aroused in such reader a very marked degree of acquired personal magnetism. This is saying much ; but wait and note the result.

One reading of this work will effect a complete and revolutionary change in the reader.

The reader hereof will see life differently, will understand life better, will grasp the meaning of countless influences that work for and against success in the activities of existence, and will acquire a keen perception into human nature, and interpret human motives more accurately. If a single reading of this book will accomplish so much, what is to be said of the adoption of the simpler principles ; what of the adoption of the deeper teachings ; what of the absorption of the grand truths that crown the work ?

In these inquiries we are anticipating the lessons that follow ; but it is our purpose to present in intensive form the great powers of the system.

Three great merits have uniformly won success :

1. The lessons meet the mental equipment of the most highly cultured men and women, and yield to them unlimited pleasure and profit.

2. The same lessons are so written and prepared that they can be just as easily mastered by the average man or woman as by the most highly educated.

3. Owners of this system of training very quickly found that they could acquire personal magnetism, and could make practical daily use of it as if it were born naturally in them ; and by its use could achieve the most pleasing and gratifying success in all departments of life.

THE DRIFT OF LIFE
By EDMUND SHAFTESBURY

1. SOURCE OF MAGNETISM.

Sweetly the morning sunlight,
  Climbing the mountain high,
Poured down its gold-beams slanting
  Like a pathway from the sky ;
And along this highway gleaming,
  Came the spirit of one we love :
    Our home to bless
    In this wilderness,
  It came from heaven above.

2. PASSING OPPORTUNITY.

Swiftly the day advancing
  Sped like the sunshine by ;
While the glowing orb of heaven
  Flooded the noon-tide sky.
The rose grew wild on the mountain,
  The bee sipped the honeyed flower,
    And down the vale
    The lily pale,
  Nodded the fleeting hour.

3. LOST.

Gently the evening sunlight
  Touched the horizon's bar,
Reaching the sea eternal,
  Lighting the land afar.
And down the gold-beams slanting
  Like a pathway to the sky,
    On pearls of light,
    Through the gateway bright,
  It passed to the realm on high.

DEPARTMENT OF
MAGNETIC SOURCES

LESSON ONE

THE DRIFT OF LIFE

HUMANITY is hemmed in by so many influences that, from time immemorial, no real effort has been made to gain control of the impulses that run loose in the world. It has been, and still is, easier to let things go as they will rather than exert the will to direct them. But the dividing line between success and failure is found at that stage where aimless drifting ceases.

We are all creatures of emotions, passions, circumstances and accident. What the mind will be, what the heart will be, what the body will be, are problems that are shaped to the drift of life, even when special attention is given to any of them.

If you will sit down and think for a while you will be surprised to know how much of your life has been mere drift.

Look at any created life, and see its effort to express itself. The tree sends its branches toward the sunlight; struggles through its leaves to inhale the air; and, even underground, sends forth its roots in search of water. This you call inanimate life; but it represents a force that comes from some source and goes to some equilibrium.

Man is a higher animal, and animal life is a higher vegetation. There are more millions of flesh cells in your body than your mind could conceive or your pencil could write in figures, yet not one of these cells originated otherwise than in a vegetable, nor could it have originated but for some force that existed in and of the cell itself.

We propose to call this force mere energy, and you may give

it any scientific name you please. It has been named by
various investigators, but the terms used do not help the student
to understand it any the better. In fact, whenever a new book
is written, the author, believing that his invention of a few
hundred scientific words will establish a new science and draw
all students to his feet, loads the volume with long and un-
bearable terms until its interest sinks with its weight. Once
in a while a short, simple word is necessary to the explanation
of a new idea ; but the disposition of scientific writers to invent
hundreds and thousands of long technical terms has loaded
their special literature with an incubus that for the most part
throttles it.

There is no place on this globe where energy is not found.
The air is so loaded with it that in the cold north the sky shines
in boreal rays ; and wherever the frigid temperature yields to
the warmth, the electric conditions may alarm man. Water is
but a liquid union of gases, and is charged with electrical,
mechanical and chemical energies, any one of which is capable
of doing great service and great damage to man. Even ice, in
its coldest phase, has energy, for it is not subdued, nor even
still ; its force has broken mountain rocks into fragments.

This energy about us we are drinking in water, eating in food
and breathing in air. Not a chemical molecule is free from
it ; not an atom can exist without it. We are a combination of
individual energies.

REASON OF UNMAGNETIC CONDITIONS

The plant is a collection of individual energies, without the
power to unite the forces they represent, except in its general
life. Man is a similar collection with the power and sometimes
the habit of so uniting the individual energies within him ; but
he has the possibility of educating and training this power.

If we can be understood at this step it will help along
the work of the present volume both in your understanding
of it and your practice of its exercises. In the first place your
body, whether living or dead, is a collection of millions and
millions of little energies that can never die. In the
second place these energies are separate and individual ; although at times they act in some degree of harmony. In the

third place the human body is a drifting mechanism of life, capable but not accustomed to control the forces within it, except as habit, will, cultivation or special excitement may marshal these forces to the accomplishment of some important end. We are satisfied from many experiments and from the reports of a host of pupils that this power of marshalling and using these energies can be, in every person, cultivated to a high degree. To do so much as this, the pupil must study and practise.

You drift day after day.

The air, sunlight, food and water you take, are agents of a force that comes from the sky and earth. You idly float upon the tide of circumstances to make up your day's life, and the opportunities of being something better than you are drift beyond your reach and pass away.

There are three classes of persons who will undertake the study of this work :

First. Those who, through curiosity, or as incredulous investigators, pursue the study with hesitation and indifference.

Second. Those who commence with enormous zeal and determination to succeed, and devote every spare moment to it for a few days, or weeks, and then suddenly cool off. This is a large class, and they have had their ardour as suddenly cool off in a hundred other undertakings before.

Third. Those who commence deliberately and work and wait patiently, plodding along in the dark for some time ; but persisting until the light dawns upon them. When the light does come it seems to break all at once. They possess that rare faculty called application.

The last-named class will achieve success. The other two will accomplish something of value in every minute they devote to it. Out of the very many exercises of the book *there is not one* which is not of great value. And this value is always practical and useful.

When the subject was first being systematized for study, there was no intention to connect it in any way with benefits to the health ; but it was found that every new habit produced good results in that line. Therefore, while not claiming or laying stress upon the fact, we find the following to be always true of this special training :

1. It promotes a healthy blood circulation.
2. It invigorates the whole body.
3. It builds a good brain-power.
4. It makes perfect nerves, overcoming nervous prostration.

HOW MUCH TIME WILL IT TAKE ?

This is the question that everybody asks. Let it be answered by asking how much time does it take for one who is naturally gifted with personal magnetism to acquire or to hold the power ? It takes no time at all. When the singer whose voice is getting worse is told that there is an artistic position in which the vocal organs may be maintained in order to improve the tones by the mere act of using, he needs no more time to sing with those organs in their proper place than to sing with them out of place. This is the whole secret of magnetism-growth. How long will it take a young lady to write a letter, spelling her words correctly, as compared with the time required to write the same letter, spelling the words incorrectly ?

You will now begin to catch the secret of our course of instruction. Yet some routine work must be done. This will be found to be agreeable and full of pleasant experiences. Our earlier instruction kept the student down to severe labour without much relief, and while the progress was rapid, it has been found that even more speedy results are obtainable by the use of the natural vitality that daily loses itself in the drift of life. Where the waters of Niagara rush to seek their quietude in the volume of the lake below, the building of steam engines where Nature's forces are mightier than man's inventions, would be the adoption of the lesser for the greater. For endless time there has run to waste in that one region more power than was needed to run all the machinery of the country.

In like manner each individual carries in his own body and loses daily through drifting habits more energy than the most magnetic man or woman that ever lived needs to give absolute supremacy to active life. It is true that we can acquire power by building the steam engine on the banks of Niagara, and that the steam so employed is a natural force, as gravity is ; but economy prefers to use the power that is at hand awaiting man's bidding, rather than go to the trouble of generating it in less quantity and energy. The work before us is to acquire the most satisfactory results in the briefest time and with the least effort.

Very recently the author put into practice with novices and others a certain régime which at once gave the most gratifying results in each and every case. It was the first instance in which the energy known as personal magnetism had been brought into active existence at the start.

This present work includes a new method of presenting the same facts and laws that have always existed ; but with this advance in the plan of teaching is found all the instruction from past works. Nothing has been eliminated, while many new aids to this study have been added.

What were mere exercises are now established as daily habits. This renders the study much more interesting and really more effective. An exercise, once it is over, is laid aside. A habit is grafted on the mind and nervous system until it becomes a part of the general conduct of a person.

In the whole scope of the training there is not even the merest influence that does not enter into all other departments of life apart from the development of personal magnetism, as well as involved in it. It so happens that this characteristic is not found in any other line of study ; and the fact that it is so proves conclusively that magnetism is life itself, and its uses are merely forms of existence made still more useful. The reader of these pages should bear this fact in mind, as the most encouraging and inspiring stimulus to achieving the mastery of the subject as herein presented.

An instantaneous subtle influence springs from the first reading of these lessons ; for it bears the message of the greatest law of life, that human existence is a part of the general fund of magnetism that holds sway throughout the universe. This influence is felt in the very unfolding of the facts that constitute these lessons. It is an old saying that declares that " knowledge is power," but it is a true one ; and never was so true as in the present study.

No person can read these pages carefully without immediately gaining the power that comes from knowledge. If adoption and absorption are added to knowledge, the progress is very rapid.

FIRES OF MAGNETISM

W E SPEAK of people as magnetic in a general way. For the purposes of the present volume, we shall class them as having four general tendencies : the light or beautiful ; the mental or thoughtful ; the deep or dangerous ; the rich or luxurious.

Each class is as important as any other. We cannot judge the degree or quality of magnetism by the colour of the eyes, or the general complexion ; but the character of the magnetic fire is more or less influenced by eye-colour.

As a general rule, but by no means a universal one, the dark-eyed person is the opposite of the grey-eyed ; and the blue-eyed of the brown. Brown is the rich verdure of the field over which the blue sky is spread. Grey is the cold zone of the north or the morning sky of the east, set against the tropics of the south or the night-laden sky of the west. Thus the four general classes are the completed horizon, the earth and the empyrean.

Despite the fact that these influences are crossed and counter-crossed even in the same individual, and must be separated and studied apart, likewise in the same individual, there is an under-current of fixed influence belonging to each class. As such we will consider them for the present.

The blue-eyed person, when magnetic, is light, happy, cheer-ful, brilliant, active, quick and even effervescent. The muscles and the blood express the magnetic force within. When unmagnetic, the blue eye becomes cold, the nature revengeful, the plans furtive, and the mind unreasonable in its demands.

The grey-eyed person, when magnetic, is cool, calculating, steady in nerve and unflinching in muscle. He talks but little when a purpose is at stake, and looks you coolly in the eye when you address him. You feel compelled to do all the talking, and he does not assist you by a word or a nod. His face never relaxes into an assent, and so you keep on thinking of new ideas and expressing them, in the hope that you will be rewarded by some show of acquiescence. Meanwhile he is looking you steadily in the eye. A stupid person may seem to do all this, but he does not. Stupidity relaxes the muscles of the jaw and draws down the face into a look of perplexity.

The black-eyed person is both dangerous and deep. The eyes are rarely, if ever, a jet black, unless the pupils are large. The colour, as a colour, is in the iris, or ring that surrounds the pupil. In proportion as the nerves are excited this iris opens, and the cavity behind the pupil shows black on account of its darkness. Nervous excitability and magnetism have been regarded as one and the same thing ; but a black-eyed person in ill-health would have less magnetism than the blue, brown or grey-eyed person. Excitability is generally the sign of magnetic weakness. Self-containment and steadiness of nerve are surer signs of the power. When a black-eyed person is magnetic, the nature, the eyes, the expression, the grasp, the very presence suggest warmth ; when unmagnetic there is a nervous irritability that jars upon the nerves of all who are near.

The brown-eyed person, when magnetic, is affectionate and rich in the expression of energy, but finds it very difficult to hold to a steady purpose, unless fixed habits of life have been educated by circumstances or trained by practice. Brown eyes are akin to black in their deepest hue ; but, embracing a score of shades even to a light hazel, they extend toward their opposite pole, the blue.

The general philosophy of personal magnetism may be summed up in a few outlines that present the theoretical rather than the substantial side of the study.

1. All human beings belong to one of the following inherited magnetic temperaments, or to a blend of two or more of them :

    (a) THE BEAUTIFUL . . . Blue.
    (b) THE COLD . . . . . Grey.
    (c) THE DEEP . . . . . Black.
    (d) THE AFFECTIONATE . . Brown.

The Blue and Grey may blend ; the Grey and Light Brown may blend ; and the Brown and Black may blend.

The Blue and Black are opposites ; the Blue and Brown are opposites ; the Grey and Dark Browns are opposites ; and the Grey and Black are opposites.

2. All spontaneous exhibitions of energy must come from the inherited temperament ; and the degree of that energy and its success in dealing with others depends upon the stage of its development. Circumstances are educators of men and women to a far greater extent than exact training. The so-called gift of magnetism is always the result of some kind of education. It is true that the inherited temperament may be cultivated by exact training such as this volume affords ; but, where we find it in mature life already established, we may suppose that the years past have been fraught with circumstances calculated to bring out the forces within, and to concentrate the individual energies that make up those forces.

3. All deliberate exhibitions of energy must come from acquired temperaments ; or else the deliberation would be unnecessary. It is most curious indeed to follow out a line of investigation demonstrating this remarkable law. The acquired temperaments may be highly cultivated, and are most easily assumed in opposites.

4. The following table gives a list of the simple uses of this energy ; and, if you wish, you may accept the belief that these uses are all unconsciously employed, whether spontaneous or deliberate ; that is, the persons who succeed in managing or controlling others in life's details are unconscious of any magnetic force at work. The cases stated in this table are realities taken from the experience of a number of people, and they represent what is actually occurring everywhere, every day of the year.

> (a) The Beautiful are Muscular.
> (b) The Cold are Mental.
> (c) The Deep are Nervous.
> (d) The Affectionate are Moral.

This table requires explaining or it will be misleading. The beautiful are magnetic in a muscular way ; and only so when they are in their inherited temperament. Now muscular does not mean *big* of muscle but active of what muscle they possess. All beauty is controlled by muscular development.

The flesh is but a mass of very small muscles, as dissection will easily prove. The contour of the body, and all the lines and shapes of beauty are determined by the muscular arrangements of the flesh. The millions and millions of muscular fibres in the fleshy masses of the body are at work concentrating their energies in this temperament when its magnetism is aroused.

The mentality of cold people has nothing to do with the warmth of the body. It is the steady, far-off, cold ray of an unflickering light. It is not excitable or impatient. The brain, and not the muscular system, exerts the temperamental magnetism ; and often with quick, unanswerable blows.

In the nervous temperament, the motor and sensor nerves are all affected. In the affectionate class the moral element predominates ; not as a force of superior morality, but as the seat of magnetic activity. There are good morals and bad morals, and there are moralising natures, and natures easily influenced by motives, good or bad, or by inducements to do right or wrong. All these considerations attach to that class of people who are affectionate in their magnetic temperaments, and their activity is in their moral blends of life. Unless this explanation is early understood, the impression will become fixed in your mind that the moral magnetic temperament represents a high degree of rectitude. It is not true that colour affects the ethical tendencies of the heart.

TABLE OF INHERITED MAGNETIC TEMPERAMENTS

(a)	The Beautiful or Muscular	Is the Inherited Magnetic Temperament of	BLUE EYES
(b)	The Cold or Mental	Is the Inherited Magnetic Temperament of	GREY EYES
(c)	The Deep or Nervous	Is the Inherited Magnetic Temperament of	BLACK EYES
(d)	The Affectionate or Moral	Is the Inherited Magnetic Temperament of	BROWN EYES

INHERITED	ACQUIRED
(a) Muscular (may cultivate)	Mental, Nervous, Moral.
(b) Mental ,,	Muscular, Nervous, Moral.
(c) Nervous ,,	Muscular, Mental, Moral.
(d) Moral ,,	Muscular, Mental, Nervous.

As the truest, fullest type of life represents culture, we would rarely expect to find an accomplished person exclusively in his native temperament.

The distinctions made in this lesson are intended only as interesting reading of the underlying influences that are at work in every life. If they are not understood at first, they will be found helpful after the study has advanced far enough for you to have met all classes of people, and to have learned that no two persons are exactly alike. One of the most pleasing things in this world is the opportunity for studying character and temperament in others. By so doing, you will be acquiring new knowledge, and finding new variations of human experience that, after all, is the best teacher one could have.

Therefore if you wish to plunge ahead with great rapidity, you may defer the re-reading of this lesson until you are drawn back to it by your own magnetism.

Great advantage arises from the practice of making yourself familiar with people ; seeking to determine their powers of resistance to the influence of magnetism as related to the eye-colour. You can easily form the habit of observing the men and women whom you meet from time to time ; learning from yourself the answers to the following questions :

1. Is it true that persons of opposite colour of eyes are more readily influenced by each other ?

2. Is it true that grey eyes are generally studious, calculating and cold by nature ?

3. Assuming that man and wife are more contented if they are interested in the same things in life, does it work out in experience that the best marriages are founded on the union of like with like ?

By securing the answers by your observation of people, you will soon learn to measure them in all other respects.

LATENT MAGNETIC ENERGIES

OF ALL the facts that operate to make our lives doubtful in their success or failure, is the appalling ease with which, on some unforeseen occasion, and in some unexpected and unexplainable manner, we yield advantages that our better judgment should have clung to and held in its keeping. In other words we are not always able to take care of ourselves.

The loss of control is not due so much to our breaking down after a certain amount of resistance, as to our willingness to yield. Often our minds are led to think that it is the right thing to do. Startling propositions contain elements of conviction that rush us to a change of view, almost before we know it. Let us see what these are.

At the present stage of our study we may regard magnetism as a central trunk of influence, having four branches ; each individual being capable of using, as well as controlled by, any one or all of the four, although his or her temperament may prevail in one only. The arrangement is not a scientific one ; but, being correct in fact and illustrating the true relationship of life more accurately than science may do in this part of our study, we are compelled to adopt it.

In every created being there is an aggregation of individual energies left to drift. They furnish the general basis of power. When properly excited they become concentrated and, for a time, are irresistible. So it occurs that many unmagnetic persons are sometimes " aroused," as they choose to call it, and show a force that had never been credited to them.

The energies of the body that arouse magnetism, show themselves very distinctly in one way or another .

The pupil of the eye is not supposed to have colour. It is

a dark hole, and all dark holes show absence of colour, for absence of light can have no other result ; and absence of colour always means the appearance of black. An orator whose eyes were a brilliant blue, addressed an audience with eloquent passion. To the surprise of those who knew him in private life only, his blue eyes had disappeared ; they were displaced by great orbs of black. These friends sat directly in front of him, and were sure of the fact. An actor likewise surprised some acquaintances ; his grey eyes changing to black.

But then the occurrence is a very common one, although it may not be observed as often as it transpires. The pupil of the eye indicates the magnetic condition. When the energy is lacking or is held in abeyance, the pupil is exceedingly small, unless the person is subject to abnormal nervous conditions. The small size of the pupil is due to lack of vitality in the optic nerve and brain as applied to the eye. The most magnetic men we have met were accustomed to carry the eyes as though they were dead ; the fires slumbered, but had not gone out. Blue eyes show a large field of blue when the pupils are contracted. So do grey eyes, or those of any colour. But as the magnetic fire is kindled the field is lessened because the pupil of the eye expands, the aperture is enlarged just in proportion as the energy within takes possession of the orb ; and, under great nervous excitement, the pupil, black, blazing and intense, drives the curtain widely apart until there is no trace of the iris, and consequently no colour to the eye. It is jet black.

Under such circumstances the effect is sometimes awful, especially if the fire is kept within steady control.

Some persons who are able to master the wills of others depend solely on this power of expanding the pupil of the eye. The beholder realises that a change is taking place in the character of the face before him, but he does not analyse its nature. He may be influenced to a degree that leaves him practically helpless, yet he is not by any means put into a hypnotic sleep.

It is not possible to hypnotise a person unless there is a tendency in that person towards catalepsy, which is a morbid condition of the nerves.

You may take lessons, become an expert, and possess the full power, yet where are your subjects ? The healthy man or woman will not permit you to manipulate the senses, nor could you succeed if you were to try. That weakling who is to be pitied because of a deficient vitality is your only prey. The triumph is void of honour. The king has conquered a rag doll. There are schools of hypnotism, but their pupils practise upon cataleptics, upon diseased people, and, after graduation, they are powerless, for they have not acquired magnetism. The latter power is universal. All the world is its teachers, and all the world its subjects.

What the individual is able to find out for himself will not be told him by instinct or Nature. God does nothing for humanity that it is able to do for itself. The life of the race is made necessary, and the impulses of instinct and desire are accordingly given first place in the habits and cravings of the mind and body. With animals below man this rule is reversed. With them, as with man, gain is sought, but for the purpose of maintaining life. Every beast, bird and serpent plays some important part in the plan of existence. Life dies most happily and most easily in the clutches of other life. The bird that must end its days in the slow processes of old age suffers many a month of torture waiting for the end ; but in the jaws of the cat or the fangs of the snake it finds a pleasurable release from the agonies of living ; an enjoyment that is participated in by the victim as much as by the devourer.

To effect this purpose it is essential that the bird should be trapped by a power that paralyses his wings. The chatter of the cat is done to catch the ear, and thence the eye of the bird. Magnetism does the rest. Until the bird sees the expanded pupil of the eye of the cat, it is free ; but after that it is lost. The snake likewise draws its prey by the same law. Fish in the sea are known to hold their victims by a similar use of the eye. The nobler of the savage beasts, such as the lion, the tiger, the hyena, and countless others, are all given the magnetic power as an aid to their purpose of gain.

Ascending still higher up the ladder of animal life we find that the valuable dog and the spirited horse have the same power. Without it the supreme qualities of these better companions of man would be dulled.

In each and every instance where the lower forms of life, or humanity itself, may be seen to give evidence of the power of magnetism, the proof is present in the expanded eye-pupil.

It does not follow that any man or woman can, at will, cause the eye-pupil to expand, but it is invariably true that the normal expansion of this part of the eye is the result of excessive magnetism. The abnormal expansion is due to the nervous powers running wild; the latent energy is let loose and is uncontrolled. One is the valued steed obeying the command of its master; the other is the valued steed running away with its master.

The increase of magnetism leads to the power of expansion; but it does not follow that the power is to be always employed. On the other hand the most magnetic men and women do not allow this power to manifest itself except when they choose to call it into use; they seem to be the very opposites of what they are, for their eyes are apparently lifeless, and even droop like those in a half-sleep. They are in a state of resting most of the time, thus being better prepared for the lightning energy that may be called forth by some special need.

Outward light expands and contracts the eye-pupil; but this is a mechanical action. The cat closes its iris to a vertical line, when it is out in the sun; but let a bird come near by and the iris will instantly give way, allowing the pupil to expand so as to cover the whole area, even in the brightest glare of sunlight. Here we see the inward power outweighing the outward power.

The authenticated cases of freedom from pain while in the clutches of savage beasts are too numerous to admit of question. The hunter who said, "I was quite conscious of the tiger's teeth penetrating my shoulder, but, instead of hurting me, they seemed devoid of pain," voiced the experience of many others. The bird suffers nothing while in the jaws of the cat. Something in the expanded pupils and glaring balls of the captor has lessened the will of the prey, and the sensation of drowsiness that follows may deaden the feeling in the nerves.

The power referred to is not only natural, but is as common as anything in Nature. It is said that a man who faces a wild animal can hold it at bay by a steadfast gaze; yet few persons are willing to depend upon so frail a defence. The statement is correct only so far as the man is able to maintain an energy of power in the eye under the present principle. If the animal magnetism of the beast is of a more enduring quality, the vitality of the man will soon be broken; and this the beast expects and looks for. A quick drowsiness follows, and soon all is over. There are, however, instances well verified where men have not only withstood the gaze of savage beasts, but have actually cowed them by the eye, and this in the haunts of Nature.

The accounts given in this lesson are intended merely to show the fact that there is in every member of the animal kingdom a magnetic vitality that needs only to be aroused in order to manifest itself. Whether it comes as the power to hypnotise or to magnetise makes little difference in the study of the latent force, but does make a vast difference in the use made of it and the results of that use. Instinct teaches animals of prey to overcome the resistance of their prey after the fighting is over ; and the same instinct gives to the victims the relief from all pain as the compensation of Nature.

The fire that glows in the eyes of the aroused animal comes from the same source as the intensity that shines in the eyes of a human being in the exercise of the natural or acquired gift of personal magnetism. But the uses are different, and the results of an opposite nature. The only phase of this animal force that is akin to personal magnetism in man, is in the effort to overmaster an opponent ; but all else is mere hypnotism.

Unless a person is a doctor and has to deal with morbid conditions in a patient, there is never any reason why a man or woman should practise hypnotism ; and there are many reasons why they should not. Imagine a young man wishing to win the affections and love of a young lady friend who did not care for him, and seeking to put her to sleep in order to gain her consent. The whole condition is absurd. Or imagine a man who wishes to sell a piece of land, hypnotising the prospective buyer and so securing his signature to the agreement. In the first place, the thing cannot be done in one case in ten thousand, and if done would not stand the test of a law trial.

Yet on the other hand there are hundreds of thousands of men and women in this as in any large country who are unconsciously endowed with the semi-power of hypnotism ; not one of whom would be willing to have it known that such a power was possessed, nor would it be believed if urged upon them as a fact. We have met in the past forty-five years more than five thousand doctors who possess this power of semi-hypnotism. This profession seems to fall into its use naturally ; and it helps. Almost every patient knows some favourite physician whose voice and touch are soothing and assuring. Such a gift is undoubtedly helpful in curing the sick. Talking with a number of doctors and telling them that they were employing semi-hypnotic methods, they one and all denied it, but we proved to quite a number of them that the assertion was well founded. Other doctors seem to realise that their presence, voice and touch gave relief and confidence and imparted soothing qualities to their patients ; and they agreed that they had known for a long time that this was true. But one doctor said rather earnestly, " I have never put a patient into a hypnotic sleep in my life." Nor had he ; but he had calmed them, inspired them with confidence in him, and had given them relief from pain of the body and worry of the mind. These effects verge closely on personal magnetism, and often merge into it.

Lawyers who tried this semi-hypnotic power over juries or courts would achieve nothing. What helps the doctors would injure the cause of the advocates. Dentists follow the doctors in this line of influence, and business men make use of both personal magnetism and semi-hypnotism in their dealings where they achieve unusual success.

Ministers may become a source of danger if they employ the semi-hypnotic power ; but otherwise if they use personal magnetism. A very remarkable case occurred years ago when some parishioners of a church made in open meeting the charge that was repeated in the papers, that one of the ablest and most successful preachers in the city was resorting unconsciously to the use of this semi-hypnotic power, both in his sermons and in his conversations with the members of his congregation. Following this charge, some reporters attended the church for several Sundays, and found nothing out of the ordinary. The preacher had changed his methods, after consulting with an expert in this line.

After the lapse of several months when the interest had subsided, we visited the city for a series of Sundays in order to hear the minister. It seemed that his voice under certain emotional feelings possessed what is known as HEALING

TONES ; or such tones as a man or woman who is a natural magnetic healer employs in effecting cures of maladies that are not curable under ordinary treatment. These tones are fully described later on in this work. We had several talks with the preacher, and found him to be most sincere in his claim that he did not know he had these semi-hypnotic tones in his voice. We explained to him what they were, how they were produced; and how they differed from the ordinary tones of the speaking voice.

A peculiar fact is that during several visits to the church we had heard these tones and had recognised them, and at the same time had noted the effect of their continual use on the members of the congregation. Of course a drowsy sermon in any drowsy voice with drowsy ideas will induce natural sleep ; but hypnotic tones will not do this ; and as they do not go far enough to bring on actual hypnotic sleep, they bring the hearers into a widely awakened interest in which their thinking powers seem to follow closely the thoughts of the preacher, to go and come with him, and to empty their minds of all else except the offerings of the preacher.

People who recall the great work done by Mr. Moody and who heard him repeatedly, may think that he possessed these tones, and that his success was due to a semi-hypnotic voice. It is true that he came close to this quality of voice, but still employed only his power of personal magnetism for his success.

We have seen an audience contribute five thousand pounds in a benefit meeting, and not for charity, as the result of the semi-hypnotic influence in the tones of the voice. We will learn all about them as we reach later lessons in this book.

The human voice has a number of tones that exert a marked and instant influence over hearers. These tones are quickly acquired, when the way of producing them is understood. One tone may be used by mothers in putting their babies to sleep. One by teachers in securing and holding the attention and respect of their pupils. An entirely different tone may be used by merchants and salesmen in winning success. There is a tone of the voice that arouses instantly the desire of an audience to listen and give absorbed interest in what is said. These are magnetic and not hypnotic.

HUMAN MAGNETISM

HOMER describes the gods viewing the fierce contests on the plains of Troy from the summit of Mount Ida. A later tradition tells of the astonishment of a humble shepherd on this same summit, when he beheld his iron-bound staff leap from his hands and cling to the projecting rocks. History seems clear in pointing to this locality of ancient Magnesia as the scene of the earliest discovery of that wonderful ore or " stone " that would lift a " load," hence called the Lodestone. Very naturally was this force called Magnetism, and the ore a Magnet, out of deference to the place of its discovery.

This may be the very locality alluded to in the Arabian Nights as the Magnetic Mountain, which drew out the iron bolts and fastenings from passing ships, and sank them instantly.

Men were not long in discovering this magnetic iron-ore in other places, and putting it to various tests of usefulness. Chief among such experimental discoveries was the power it possessed of magnetising a needle so that it would always point due North. Even in English annals we find the *sailing stone* mentioned as early as the twelfth century, but it was known and used long previously by other nations.

It seems strange that up to one hundred and fifty years ago men were ignorant of the existence of animal magnetism.

About 1770 a great scientist, Galvani, professor in Bologna, was preparing some frogs to be cooked for his sickly wife. Happening to touch two different metals in contact to certain nerves and muscles, he was surprised to see the frog's lifeless legs resume all the activity of their accustomed motions. Others had noticed this result, but had not been led to investigate its philosophy.

After his death Professor Aldini, a nephew, travelled through Europe proving the truth of Galvani's statements and theories, which had been misrepresented and repudiated.

A favourite experiment of his was to form a battery out of several heads of recently slaughtered cattle, connecting their tongues and ears alternately by wires. The result was always surprising and conclusive. Aldini, among other things, maintained :

" That muscular contractions are excited by the development of electricity in the animal-machine, which is conducted from the nerves to the muscles, without the concurrence of metals."

" That all animals are endowed with an inherent electricity, appropriate to their economy, which, secreted by the brain, resides especially in the nerves, by which it is communicated to every part of the body. When a limb is to be moved, the nerves, aided by the brain, draw some electricity from the interior of the muscles, discharging this upon their surface, and they are thus contracted as desired."

Was it not the shrewd Napoleon I. who said, when he first saw a voltaic battery : " Voilà l'image de la vie : la colonne vertébrale est le pile ; la vessie, le pole positif ; et le foie, le pole négatif."

We know that electricity and magnetism exist in all things. We are assured that its power vastly exceeds our present acquaintance with it. We have also seen that the very air becomes polarised and sets up induction between adjacent bodies.

The human frame is, so to speak, filled and dominated by latent magnetism. Hence the brain, which appears to be the seat of the soul or *ego*, is properly a sensitive electrical condenser, ready at any instant to charge any nerve that they may set their appropriate muscles in action, whenever that *ego* touches the magic *key* which completes the *circuit*.

Thales, then, considering that he lived twenty-five hundred years before our day, was not far out of the way when he said that " electricity is the soul residing in electron."

The latent magnetism of an individual is quickly awakened by the vibratory current of a magnetic person through the action of the voice, eye or touch.

Many persons are afraid to study these subjects, believing that they stand for something that is terrible, some weird power that may be associated with witchcraft. (Hypnotism was un-doubtedly the basis of the old-time witchery, for it has always existed in the world, and been misjudged in every age.)

But personal magnetism has never been in bad company. It has had no unsavoury reputation; but, on the other hand, its work has been of the nobler stamp, and its influence has always tended to make the mind sound, the body whole and the nerves steady. Of all the thousands of pupils in personal magnetism whom we have met, there has never been one who retained the least bit of superstition, nor one who had any fear of ghosts or a belief in them. The brain gets a clear and perfect view of life free from the muddy hues that tinge the meaner nature.

Its very basis is vitality. Life and power grow with the in-crease of personal magnetism. It helps to uplift the weak, whether that individual be the student of the power or the one who is brought under its influence. One magnetic man or woman can wield a vast and inspiring sway over hundreds and thousands of others at one and the same time. Those who are thus dominated are given some of the magnetism of the master power, and the more they are under such sway the stronger they become in mind and purpose. Just the opposite is true of the uses of hypnotism.

Every intelligent reader knows what is meant by the power of personal magnetism, and there are few who cannot at once detect the man or woman who possesses this power. The mere entering of the room, the first steps towards an audience, the first tones of the speaking or singing voice, the touch of the hand, the glance of the eye, or the impress of the fingers on the piano, as in the case of the famous Polish player : these tell in a few seconds the fact that the individual is magnetic. If the gift be natural, then it has come from accidental habits that prevent the constant loss of vital electricity. You will see a self-controlled, easy, but at the same time energetic personality that will attract your attention because of the presentation of these two conditions in one life.

LIFE IS MAGNETISM

THE BODY CANNOT BEGIN LIFE until it first begins to generate magnetism. As has been fully stated in an early lesson, all matter is composed of chemical elements ; and the human body employs fourteen of these elements with one or two present under certain conditions in addition to that number. Each element consists of particles known as molecules ; and shape, formation and construction are given parts of the body by the action of magnetism in the character of cohesion. This attribute could no more exist without magnetism than could the earth remain in the solar system without magnetism. In its absence the body of man would be a mass of dust.

Each particle which is known as a molecule is composed of atoms, and these also are held in the shape and formation of the molecule by the same law of cohesion, without which there could be no chemical elements ; no oxygen, hydrogen, nitrogen, carbon, iron, gold, or other thing. All creation would be alike, and all things as one. Nothing could grow, nothing could live or have shape. Still further analysing matter, we find that the atom is a solar system of its own, in miniature to be sure, but nevertheless just the same kind of a solar system as is that of which our sun and planets are parts. Each atom has its central orb, and around this there fly its satellites in orbits such as we study in astronomy. Each such planet is endowed with magnetism to keep it away from its central sun ; and each such sun is endowed with magnetism to hold to its system every one of its satellites.

Here we find that the basis of all life is magnetism, and that it is also the basis of all matter. Wherever there is matter, there must exist the powers of magnetic influence making life, shaping life, developing all activities of life, and exerting an unending influence in all the operations of Nature. Of such is the body of a human being. Great experts in science say that a single atom, fully developed in the use of the power locked up in it, is charged with so mighty a force that it is capable of blowing up the largest building in the world. We have never believed this statement, but we have seen it repeated many times, and we know that it is believed by abler minds than our own. So what can we do ?

The lesson taught, however, is this : Every particle of the human body is charged to excess and surcharged to excess with active and with latent magnetism. It is everywhere, in the blood, in the organs, in the arteries, in the veins, in the brain, in the membranes, in the nerves, and in every bone and sinew of the body.

Let us see if we can make clear the difference between the presence of a power singly and collectively. This is a most important distinction.

At first we will look into it by using the well-known example of the cell, or the basis of a living structure whether of the animal or the plant kingdom. A cell has its controlling force which is seen as a darker particle generally near one side of the cell itself. This is its intelligent director. This is carrying the secret of the future of that cell. It may be the first cell of a human being ; if so, it will contain the intelligence that will, by being multiplied, build countless billions more cells all like it, which will obey the instructions that are locked up in that first cell, and create the body of a human child. All the future of that child as it grows into a man is contained in the intelligence of that first cell.

The body of the man contains duplicates of the first cell, now given shape and specialised duties, and existing in cell life throughout all parts of the body. This is known as diffused intelligence because it is divided into the multitudes of cells that are contained in the entire organism as units.

There are two great kingdoms in the world :

One is the animal kingdom which includes the human species.

The other is the vegetable kingdom which includes all plant life and all other life that does not belong to the animal division.

The difference between the animal kingdom and the vegetable kingdom is this :

In the vegetable kingdom all cell intelligence is diffused.

In the animal kingdom, cell intelligence is not only diffused, but is also found collectively. Collective cell intelligence occurs in the nerve centres and in the brain. The latter organ in man is an enormously enlarged collective mass of cell intelligence, relatively speaking. In the vegetable kingdom it is not possible to store intelligence in nerve centres, nor in a brain cavity ; hence plants remain plants and are never changed into animals until their cells are taken as food by the latter. But the cells of the vegetable kingdom possess the high honour of being the basis of the body of the animal ; for whether flesh eats flesh or only vegetation, every cell in the animal was once a cell in the vegetable division of life. So the diffused intelligence of the plant world becomes in time the collective intelligence in the brain of man.

By this illustration we come to understand in what way the diffused magnetism of the atom-structure of the human body may become the collective magnetism of man or woman.

It must be borne in mind that every atom possesses tremendous inherent or natural power, due to its magnetism. In the plant kingdom this magnetism is diffused, for which reason there is no collective influence emanating from the tree ; although persons who work out among growing foliage and plants or trees are known to absorb considerable power in diffused form.

In the human body as in animals the magnetism is more or less drawn into central storage conditions. But in all life below man this is an electric and not a magnetic form. In the electric fish this force is concentrated to an unusual degree, considering the size of the organism. In the human species there may be a strong collective force of electricity with an insufficient quantity of magnetism. Thus many persons are found whose bodies are really charged with the fluid known as electricity. The fact is that this fluid is gathered collectively from the magnetism that is the life of each atom, yet it lacks something to bring it up to the standard known as personal magnetism.

We have shown that diffused cell intelligence when brought into a collective condition becomes the brain of animal life.

We have also shown that diffused atomic magnetism when

brought into a collective condition becomes the magnetic power of life.

Personal magnetism is the union of these two conditions ; the blending of the collective form of intelligence with the collective form of magnetism.

From this rather technical, although valuable, exposition of these great facts, we learn that every man and woman is of necessity highly magnetic, although the blending of the two forces into personal magnetism may not yet have taken place.

One further step and we reach the basis of our study.

It is equally clear that every man and woman is naturally in possession of the gift of personal magnetism in latent form. This power exists in fact, but as in a shell, just as the life of the eagle is contained in the shell of the egg. The latter must be broken and the life released.

As every man and woman possesses this power latently, the process of releasing it is necessary ; but when once released it needs only to be guided aright to become effective. When we speak of developing personal magnetism we do not intend to imply that it is to be created out of nothing, for that would be impossible. The word educate in the process of learning, means to draw out, to lead forth, referring to the unfolding of the power of acquiring knowledge. In developing magnetism, it is not created, or made to grow out of nothing, but is released from its latent condition.

There are two processes that may be employed to unfold this power :

One is the use of inciting exercises that stimulate into action the forces that are dormant in the body. This is artificial in its first stages, but if turned into habits of living will in time become natural ; and this change occurs when the exercises have been carried far enough to inspire the adoption of their results as habits.

The other and far better method is that which breaks the shell that obstructs the life within the body, and releases the pent-up power. Then Nature asserts herself, and personal magnetism becomes in fact a gift.

The student should understand the difference between the two processes that are employed in unfolding this power.

Then we meet the fact that there are many persons who are

thus gifted by their own habits of living and habits of using
their powers. Without instruction of any kind, the operation
of certain activities will result in the appearance of this gift.
We have talked with many such men and women. Some of
them have been known to us through a course of years. We
have made a very large collection of little histories covering
such cases, so that we have been able to get at the basic facts
that underlie the acquisition of personal magnetism without
instruction. The results of this analysis are worth knowing.
We refer to men and women who have won great successes in
the various avenues of life, in the professional, business and
social world.

In the first place we are deeply impressed with their perfect
poise whether they were active or were inactive. This condition
they seemed to be cognisant of and they conserved it.

Then we noted a degree of coolness and reserve in the muscular
and in the nervous systems. They did not seem to be unconscious of this condition, for in every case it appeared as if
they sought to maintain it, although this might not always
have been the fact. The same principle was involved as in the
breach of good form which, if it occurred, would have at once
been realised by the parties themselves rather than by
observers. This means that persons who are magnetic solely by
habits of living which have grown up with them, know when
they break any of those habits just as a well-bred person knows
when some rule of conduct has been broken, and will proceed to
avoid it in the future. Thus we see that persons who are well
bred conserve their watchfulness over their own conduct ; and
it has always seemed to us that those who are magnetic do the
same thing automatically.

The third trait that was always evident in this class of persons
was that of high nervous tension held in perfect repose. This
condition was never absent in any of the great men and women
of the past whose lives we analysed from a close personal
acquaintance.

The fourth trait that was found in every one of them was a
certain muscular shaping of the temples which gave to the eyes
a very powerful influence when they were employed either as
accompanying conversation or when listening. This did not
make the eyes either piercing or impressive in the act of being

used ; but there was a subtle quality that we shall explain at great length before this study is ended in this book.

; The fifth trait that we noted differed in its use. At one time it appeared as a form of a living grace that was most fascinating. In other cases it showed itself in the phase of a rugged strength apparently born in ultra grace. But it was not the languid kind of grace, nor the form of ease that suggests relaxing. Life was present in every fibre of the body.

The voice in every instance was very magnetic.

Habits of use had brought this about, for there is no such thing as a naturally magnetic voice in the sense that it came about without some kind of development. People, without knowing it, copy others. A magnetic singer may have a voice highly trained at the hands of a great teacher ; and a hundred admirers among amateur singers may consciously or unconsciously imitate the methods of vocal use, and so come into some of its acquired power.

All human voices are developed by habit or training ; and most of those that are attractive exert an influence over those who associate with the users. Even defects are imitated. We recall the case of a beloved master of a boys' school who stammered, and every boy in the school acquired the stammer unconsciously but in less degree.

The development of the magnetic voice follows an exact scientific process, and can be accomplished with mathematical certainty. It is not a slow proceeding in any event. The reason for this success is due to the fact that exercises may be employed that begin to show results from the very beginning of the training. This can be said also of the development of the magnetic eye. But other branches of the study of personal magnetism require time and patience.

If a person could be constantly in the company of those who were naturally gifted in this power, and who had never been trained or had the opportunity of studying a book method, and such person were observant and disposed to analyse effects and trace them back to their causes, it is more than likely that the power could be acquired by what is called absorption, or the influence of association.

The six traits that we have just described as being evident in all cases of magnetism where there has been no study or training, instead of being copied or absorbed by imitation and association, may be more readily transmitted by study and training, and they are included in the present work ; but only as a part of the methods employed. They are as follows :

1. Perfect poise of manner.

2. Perfect coolness and reserve in the muscular and nervous systems.

3. High nervous tension held in complete reserve.

4. The shaping of the temple formation leading to the development of the magnetic eye.

5. Living grace.

6. A magnetic voice.

As we have said these are only a part of our system of training ; and they are merely reproductions of the unvarying traits that we found in all persons who had achieved greatness through the possession of personal magnetism as a natural gift.

But these same persons had been highly developed in their mental preparations for their life work. Such development never invites magnetism, but is helped by it, and helps it in turn. On the other hand a person who is magnetic without mental preparation is like a powerful motor-vehicle running without driver.

To meet the needs of mental preparation we have included in this work the practice that is designed for arousing ambition and for stimulating the mind, which we have termed Mental Magnitude. It performs the duty of cultivating the thought-processes and of uniting them with natural magnetism.

The work immediately before us then is to ascertain what are the defects and obstructions that prevent the latent magnetism of the body from storing itself collectively in the brain and faculties. These hindrances when once removed will no longer interfere with the development of the power that is sought, and the latter will have free scope to unfold itself in a manner that will leave no doubt of its character and value in life. It is a proved fact that when such power has free scope to unfold itself, it will make the most remarkable progress in its development, and will become then a natural gift, and not an acquired one.

THE VENEER

THERE IS PRESENT in every man and woman enough latent magnetism to give to each person absolute control over all the affairs of life, and to lift such person up to the highest pinnacle of success, if only it were drawn into action and employed in the right way. As long as brain and body are composed of atoms such as we have described, each controlled by a central force as full of energy for its size as is our own fiery sun, so long will every human being hold in latent form at least the potential presence of magnetism. Nor is it a difficult task to develop this power into an active agency, and to use it for the greatest achievements in life.

Every person belongs to one of three classes :

1. The attractive.
2. The neutral.
3. The repellent.

The attractive class possesses qualities that please and win friends, followers and associates, by voice, manner of approach and methods of dealing with them. We do not refer to assumed or transient attractions. A doctor may dress in the height of fashion, be immaculately groomed, employ the most gracious manners, be pleasant and even charming, and yet possess only those attractions that are assumed. On the other hand another doctor may be plain in speech and dress, and yet exceedingly magnetic in voice and methods, winning confidence and reaping success, not so much in money as in curing his patients. The attractions of the first doctor in time pall on one ; while those of the other grow with acquaintance.

A business man may be urbane, unusually polite, full of smiles and kind greetings, and yet fail to impress those who understand such methods. Another business man may be attentive to the needs of his customers, may know what they desire, may find it readily, may discuss with them the questions that pertain to matters in hand, and yet lack the polish of the urbane and gracious gentleman we first mentioned. One may fail to sell his goods as readily as the other, for assumed attractiveness is only a veneer ; and magnetism is abiding.

Therefore by the term attractive in this lesson we mean magnetic.

At the other extreme we find the repellent class. Of every ten thousand persons in this world among civilised nations, only about ten persons are magnetically attractive ; while fully four thousand are repellent ; and nearly six thousand neutral.

Look at a group of ladies in a drawing-room. One always leads all the others in graciousness of manner and winning ways. A few are vivacious, and that is all. Some fail utterly to attract ; or if they succeed in so doing they do not hold what they gain. Some seem to be walled in by a repelling voice, unattractive personality and forbidding indifference. Many are neutral, or lacking in both qualities. This is in the drawing-room where the more pleasing influences should manifest themselves. Out in the great world we find countless thousands of people repelling their fellow-beings, some from causes they do not seek, others from causes of which they are ignorant, and still others by reason of a most lamentable lack of attractive magnetism.

The neutral classes are by far the most numerous. We refer only to magnetic neutrality. Many of them are rich, but wealth is not the chief insignia of success. Many of them are neither rich nor poor, but may be regarded as well-to-do. Many of them are well secured in their places in the social scale, and others belong to the middle classes, socially speaking. It would be humourous were it not pitiable to see many of them trying to substitute some forms of attraction for those that may be lacking. One of the chief defects in these substitutes is that they are employed only in the presence of others. When there are no observers present, the substitutes are laid aside as one would lay by a cloak ; hence they are not natural nor easily assumed. Sunday manners, like Sunday clothes, if worn only occasionally, do not make the lady or the gentleman.

The methods just referred to are employed for the purpose of pleasing or impressing others. In and of themselves they are never magnetic, and therefore do not reach the end that is sought. What we are teaching in this course of training is the development of the genuine power of attraction, that is absorbed as first nature in the individual, that rises with him in the morning, enters into the daily duties, and still dwells within at night, engrafted into his very being. It is a new force, a new form of life, a new birth.

The substitutes for magnetism are many and varied. Those who adopt them do not know for what they are substitutes, but do know that something in some way is lacking in their associations with their fellow-beings. They are told that honey will attract more bees than vinegar, so they indulge in an assumption of smiles, kind expressions, and pleasing ways, in the hope that these will win the goal they are seeking. There are salesmen who are never very successful, although they flatter and praise their prospective customers, and pour out a flood of kindly talk ; while other salesmen possess a subtle, intangible something that convinces and wins easily. We have known commercial travellers who, on making a call, as they term it, are primed with a line of talk that must of necessity bring orders, as they believe, and yet who find themselves held in check by the unbroken refusal of the person they address. They had not learned that talk, while necessary, and ideas, while indispensable, do not arouse an interest in offerings that are not urgently demanded, unless the talk and ideas are mentally magnetic ; for thought may be charged with this power, as well as voice, manner and presence.

We have known of young ladies who have put forth every possible effort to win the affection of men whom they have wished to marry ; and yet who have failed because their assumed attractions did not wear well. The more they were seen and heard, the less grew the charm. Short courtships have been urged in doubtful cases, under the instinctive fear that time and knowledge will erase the veneer of practised smiles and stilted kindliness. The father whose wisdom was of the order of Solomon's, who did not wish his daughter to marry a certain young man, conceived the idea of asking the latter to come and live in the father's family where the suitor could see the daughter daily under the same general circumstances that prevail in married life. The scheme worked. In less than a month the girl was asking herself what there was in this fellow that ever made her want to marry him ; and the young man asked himself a similar question regarding the girl. They parted with a feeling of relief that they had not made the greater mistake of marrying each other.

We shall show that certain supposed attractions bring countless thousands of men and women into wedlock, only to find all too soon that these attractions are a veneer, which, as soon as it wears off, leaves exposed the bare facts of mis-mating, estrangement and divorce.

On the other hand where two persons are drawn to each other by the power of magnetism, they never separate, and there has never been a divorce in any such case. This brings us to the two great facts of life :

1. Personal magnetism is inherent, natural, one hundred per cent real, and one hundred per cent permanent. Once it is engrafted in the life of a person, it remains until death comes, and survives beyond.

2. The substitutes of personal magnetism are transient, unnatural, evanescent and disappointing.

As these substitutes always stand in the way of the acquisition of the genuine power, we shall devote a few pages to the discussion of them. What we seek to teach is the value of the real as against the worthlessness of the veneer.

If you are lacking in magnetism, you will in some form or other become the victim of a veneer. The politician, running for office, shakes hands with you and inquires about your family. That is veneer. The sour girl becomes sweet when she seeks to draw you into her net ; and she assumes what is called a " Sunday Voice " in addressing you ; and Sunday manners with Sunday clothes. Certain salesmen are over-kind, over-pleasant, over-cordial in addressing you. Most lovers employ a veneer in manner, dress and attention. But there never was a veneer that could stand the test of a magnetic power driven against it.

OUTLINES OF MAGNETISM

EVERY IMPORTANT STUDY is built in the form of a structure. Its foundations rest in the bosom of Nature. Its superstructure may rise, part on part, to the topmost section on which rest the spires that point to a power above. Bedded in Nature it seeks the sky. Thus all things proceed. The tree borrows its material fund from the lap of Nature, and responds to the vital forces of the heavens which draw its substance from the ground by the magnetism of the sun. A force holds all things to the earth ; and another force gives them the outstretching arms that seek the Giver of Life.

Magnetism as a study has its basic foundations in Nature. But it rises to the sources of Nature.

It is wholly a subtle and intangible force, yet it is the most powerful force in all the universe.

Beyond this world we find the solar system of which our globe is a part. Beyond our solar system, we discern many other similar systems that unite to form our universe. Beyond our universe, there are countless other universes ; yet they are all bound together by the subtle and intangible force known as magnetism. If this force were absent, all creation would fly apart and be lost in chaos.

The constellations that form our universe are held together by this same force. If it were absent, all the constellations would drift away, or in fact would have been wanderers in space and lost by this time to our gaze.

Our own solar system consists of the central sun, the planets, and planetary orbs that are invisible to the eye ; all held by magnetism to the sun ; all revolving around it ; all repelling the efforts of the sun to draw them into its mass ; and yet all held in leash by the very sun they repel. Were this magnetism lacking, the whole mass would take one of two courses. If the inherent magnetism of the orbs that repel the inviting power of the sun were absent, they would be absorbed in that great fire. If the inherent magnetism of the sun that holds them in leash were lacking, all the planets and orbs would wander off in space, aimlessly and endlessly, with no future except that of frozen ice balls, useless in the plan of creation.

These are the giant energies of magnetism. Yet this force is subtle and intangible.

What we call gravity, for lack of a better name, is the same magnetism. It keeps all things within the embrace of the earth. Without it no living being could remain on the ground. The first step that was raised in walking would lift man from the globe and he would continue to rise until he had met the fate of the orbs that had wandered off into the abysses of space. Every object, animate or inanimate, that moved at all would move off the earth never to return. If you were to rise from a chair you would keep on rising until you reached the ceiling, if indoors, or until you passed out of view in the sky, if out of doors.

All growth in the kingdom of plants, flowers and trees is due to the magnetism of the sun in drawing the material from the earth. If this were lacking, nothing would have life. The needed elements that build the plant or tree are actually lifted out of the soil; while the needed vitality from the sun is actually drawn from that orb, woven into growing things, and eventually stored away in the earth itself.

We have spoken of the universe as composed of solar systems, each with a central governing orb. It was not known until very recently that this form of structure is reproduced in miniature in all substance that is called matter. In chemistry there are more than ninety elements; each element being supposed to consist of a fixed arrangement of molecules, or small particles that never vary their plan of structure unless disturbed by some such influence as radioactivity. One such arrangement results in the element known as iron, another in hydrogen, another in oxygen, another in gold, and so on through all the chemical elements. These molecules are held together in each fixed arrangement by the magnetism called cohesion. If this were lacking, there could be no elements, no iron, no gold, no

4

oxygen, no metals or gases, and no combinations of elements such as sustain life and give shape to all things. Everything would be resolved to dust, or a condition much finer than dust. There would be no animal life, no plant life, no buildings, no tools with which to work, nothing whatever tangible.

Thus we see the wonderful provision of the Creator in giving to all the earth this form of magnetism.

Yet what we call shapes of things are held together not only by this kind of magnetism, but by laws within themselves similar to the laws that govern the universes of the sky. Each molecule which is the basis of an element is itself composed of atoms. While these are invisible, their activities and nature are well known and easily studied. Each atom, once supposed to be the beginning of all things and regarded as holding the secret of creation, is now known to be composed of electrons ; and here we really have the first cause of creation.

Each atom is a universe, or rather a solar system in itself ; it has a central orb or sun, which is an electron ; around which all the other electrons revolve. There is present in the atom the same law of magnetism that holds together the stars and planets.

Our sun is a ball of fire inconceivably hot, shooting forth tongues of flame that extend a hundred thousand miles beyond its surface. The central orb in an atom is relatively active, and possesses the same relative amount of fire, energy and magnetism ; yet a thousand billions of those atoms thus constructed in the form of solar systems could not, if massed together, present enough substance to be seen by the naked eye.

It is of such atoms that the human body, the human brain, the entire nervous system, all the organs, and all the flesh and bones, are composed. The energy that is locked up in a single atom holds enough potential power to destroy the body itself if set free. Every drop of blood is charged with latent and active magnetism. There is no particle of life in a human being that is not a slumbering dynamo.

While electricity and magnetism are not the same, both come from the same source, make use of the same laws, and proceed in the same manner to manifest themselves. The air about us is charged to excess with unlimited funds of electricity and magnetism. If you set up a giant generator in a small room having walls ten feet thick ; a floor of masonry ten feet deep ; and a ceiling overhead made of concrete or stone material ten feet high ; and if you lock up that room with a door ten feet thick, and set the generator working to draw out of the air all the electricity available ; you will never find an end to the flow of current that will supply that engine or dynamo. It will be able to find this power a million years from now. You cannot shut out the supply, exhaust it, or even reduce it. Where does it come from ? How does it get through those walls ?

We have spoken of drawing electricity from the air, as if it were located in the atmosphere. But when a dynamo is placed in a vacuum and set in motion, the flow of electricity is still maintained. This shows that the air is not the agency of supply. There are three oceans by which influences are transmitted :

1. The atmosphere through which the magnetism of the voice is carried in waves from one person to another.

2. The light-ether which fills all space between the orbs of the sky, and through which light waves pass, as well as electric energy.

3. The thought-ether through which waves of thought pass from mind to mind, and which connects life on this earth with all life beyond.

Human magnetism employs all three of these means of communication in the passing of its influence from person to person. But while the waves of sound in the air carry the tones of the voice, and are in that way the agency of the magnetic voice, the actual magnetism is conveyed either by the light-ether or by the thought-ether.

The sound of the human voice travels on air waves at the rate of 1087 feet per second. Light travels at the rate of 186,300 miles per second. Electricity moves at the rate of 230,000 miles per second. Thought is able to reach the farthest orb in space, trillions times trillions of miles, in less than a second ; and yet it moves in waves, uniting not only human beings on this planet, but all beings in the universe.

DEPARTMENT OF
MENTAL MAGNITUDE

THE STOMACH SUBSTITUTE

HUMANITY IS GIVEN FOUR APPETITES ; and in this regard differs from all the rest of the animal kingdom in that they possess only one appetite, which is that of the stomach. An appetite is an inborn craving, not a mere function. It is so strongly implanted in life that it sways all other considerations in conduct and manner of living. More than one-half of the population of the globe are crafty ; by which is meant that they know how to take advantage of the human appetites in order to win their ends.

This craftiness, when it preys upon human appetites and thereby lures men and women into the webbed traps that are thus set for them, takes the place of that noble power known as personal magnetism, and, in combat between the two forces, often wins. We must clear the deck of these enemies before we proceed further, for they are only " substitutes " of genuine magnetism.

The Four Appetites are :

1. The Stomach Appetite.
2. The Sexual Appetite.
3. The Greed Appetite.
4. The Spiritual Appetite.

Humanity possesses all four in the form of controlling influences, while animals possess in fulness only the first : in tage over their fellow-beings, and who, knowing the urgency of the impelling force of these appetites, make use of that knowledge for their own conquests, some of one kind and some of other kinds.

Here we stand face to face with the greatest enemy of personal magnetism.

Here begins the battle-royal of life.

We knew a preacher of great magnetism who was almost always able to achieve whatever success he sought, who had before him a man he was persuading to adopt a new life ; but he found to his surprise that he was losing in the attempt to convince the man, and sought the reason why. A deacon whispered in his ear, " This man is hungry. His stomach has been empty for two days." When that organ was given its necessary supply, the man was open to persuasion ; but the incident shows that the stomach appetite is the strongest of all four in human existence.

Napoleon fed his soldiers liberally before their battles, and gained by so doing. More than this, he conceived an idea that proves the power of mental magnetism, when he gave orders that all prisoners taken from his enemy nations should be well fed at all times, the result being that they preferred to remain in France rather than go back to the mean rations of their own countries. It is related with authority that those who did return under the plan of exchange, and who afterwards fought against Napoleon, surrendered willingly in order to again become prisoners and again be well fed.

Most animals kill for food only, rarely for any other cause unless to protect their young. But they must find enough to eat, and this is the plan of Nature in order to preserve the species. As the pangs of hunger increase, their power of attack becomes more ferocious.

The human race has always been swayed more by the call of the stomach than by any other influence. Crafty people know this fact, and take advantage of it ; no matter how much they may be lacking in magnetism, or even to what extent they may be repellent in this way, they yet are shrewd enough to recognize the fact that men's minds may be reached through their stomachs. Here is a substitute for magnetism that has been employed countless times in order to gain some end.

Every man and woman should learn this lesson. Magnetism is an active, aggressive agency, and should never be kept on the defence. Speaking of mental magnetism as the power of ideas in controlling men and women, or bringing them into accord with the views and purposes of a stronger personality, we find evidences of this influence constantly coming to our notice, and they seem to be unlimited. One such magnetic idea we have mentioned in referring to Napoleon. Here is another that is worthy of adoption : The man or woman who, in the struggle for supremacy with others, is kept on the defensive is always at a disadvantage. Yet the individual who is made use of through any one of the four appetites is decidedly on the defensive. Magnetism must be made aggressive. Therefore it is important that you recognise the nature of the four appetites, and keep your mind alert, or on the look-out for them. In this connection let us see some of the methods employed to reach a person's judgment through the stomach.

All women know that the best way to get to a man's heart is through his stomach ; and this is an old adage. The wife who feeds her husband to his satisfaction is more likely to win his heart and mind in that way than by any other course, if she lacks magnetism. The woman who is seeking a husband, if she is on the way to succeed with some friend whose decision is not yet fully formed, will invite him to dinner and serve him a meal that will linger in his memory.

In society the great allurement is the many-course dinner. In all phases of social intercourse, the stomach, and the mouth that opens the way to the stomach, receive attention. If you make an afternoon call, something goes in the mouth or stomach. If you are to be honoured day or evening, there must be provided things to go in the mouth or stomach. If a great personage arrives in this country, he must be given a greeting in some assemblage where he is fed. A hero from the battlefield, or from the ocean's dangers, is met by a public demonstration ; and, although the hotel at which he is stopping supplies more than ample food for him, he must be fed before a great crowd.

A well-known politician, who recently died, had on his waiting list more dinners and banquets than he could find time to attend ; but he did go to enough of them to ruin his stomach ; and he once said in despair, "If they would only invite me to do something besides eat, I should be a well man." These over-abundant feasts are conceived in a well-meaning scheme of giving pleasure to others and thereby winning their approval. But they are often used directly to win some control over the judgment of others. Men generally are the objects of this kind of feeding. Some are swayed into making decisions through the influence of nicely prepared meals to which they are invited as guests ; but men of magnetism know too well what purpose is in the minds of those who seek to win them in this way, and do not allow a well-fed stomach to control their judgment.

In the old days voters were easily won by the contents of the beer barrel, or the whisky bottle. The candidate for office did not possess magnetism, so he employed a substitute. Millions upon millions of votes have been won by magnetic speakers in their addresses to audiences ; but more millions have been won by the appeal to the stomach. Not only in politics but in every walk in life has the craving of the stomach for drink been made use of by crafty people, in order to win control over those who can be swayed in this way.

To avoid being placed on the defensive through this method, there should be a very clear understanding of the purpose in the mind of one who offers drink, no matter how good it may be in quality, for the disadvantage is of a double nature : First, it places you under some obligation to the one who gives it. Then it reduces materially the power of resistance by making your mind and judgment less clear than it should be in an important transaction.

Study the four appetites. Note them in others. Then take account of stock of them in yourself. Finally analyse the possible motives of people who seek to take advantage of you through them, and cease to remain on the defensive.

Non-magnetic people are controlled by others through the mouth and stomach ; and are even more controlled and deprived of their own magnetism by the cravings of the mouth, which is the gateway to the stomach. Something is entering the mouth through the livelong day : the cigar, the pipe, the cigarette, the chewing-tobacco, the chewing-gum, sweets, soda water, beer, liquor, wine, chocolate, nuts, and three or more meals daily.

THE SEXUAL SUBSTITUTE

BY GLANCING BACK to the preceding lesson we learn that there are four appetites in humanity, any one of which, if played upon, may offset and defeat the power of personal magnetism. These appetites work in two ways. They place their owner in the control of crafty and unscrupulous persons at times; and they bring in financial gains for those who make use of them in the mastery of others. The victims suffer losses that could easily have been averted by the possession of magnetism. They bring rewards to people who know the weakness of human nature.

The advice that has been given in the preceding lesson is to be repeated here. Study the four appetites. Study their power over your mind and life. Be on the look-out for those efforts that sooner or later will be made to place you under the sub-jugation of one or more of them. Throw off the necessity of being on the defensive. Take the aggressive; and this can be done only through the aid of magnetism.

The first of the four appetites is that of the stomach. It would seem as if the injury done to the stomach, by excessive eating or indulgence in things that hurt that organ, would end its cravings at least until it gets back its normal health. But Nature punishes in a mysterious way; for a congested stomach craves stimulants, especially those of the alcoholic kind. A perfectly normal and healthy stomach will not only not crave alcoholic drinks, but will refuse to accept them. In a record of tests in which ten stomachs were found that were in absolutely perfect condition, with no trace whatever of congestion, the admission of whisky that would have been craved by the ordinary stomach resulted in the liquor being instantly vomited up and discarded by Nature. All kinds of cures have been tried to overcome the craving for liquor, and none have been very successful until the method was devised whereby all congestion was removed, and then it was learned that craving for stimulants is the cry of a congested stomach. As doctors declare that a vast majority of all persons have congested stomachs, the widespread demand for stimulants is founded in some reason ; but the desire for stimulants has always disappeared when all congestion has been removed.

Therefore the injury that follows misuse of a natural appetite only leads on to a greater misuse. This is true of the other appetites.

Next to that of the stomach, the most powerful appetite is that of the sex nature. While hunger leads animals to slay, and to make themselves dangerous to other life, it is rare that these lower forms of creation are driven to what is called animal-crimes by the sex impulse. Humanity alone is made slave to this appetite.

It is with men and women a very potent and very effective substitute for magnetism. By the use of personal magnetism a man can easily win the right kind of a woman for a wife ; and if our records of forty-five years are to be believed, not one couple so united will ever be separated either by divorce or unmated temperaments. We know the facts in many thousands of lives and they all concur in the same result.

Not many marriages in every thousand are made by mag-netism ; those that are, never fall apart. It is to be regretted therefore that the true magnet should not bring the man and woman together. The goal is worth the race.

A Judge recently said in his charge to a jury : " It is a fact that more than ninety per cent of marriages are induced by the false lure of sexual appetite." Here is a substitute for magnetism that is at work wrecking lives by the millions. Magnetism unfolds the character and even the soul, and lays bare the truth. It brings forth all the natural good and all the acquired good in man and woman. It builds character on character, goodness on goodness, and worth on worth, and these become fixed and inherent qualities in the mind and heart. On the other hand the sexual appetite, while it draws one person to another, is fleeting on being satiated, and the glamour that it painted with its hopes and promises soon turns to sordid tinsel.

Being easily preyed upon, it is taken advantage of by crafty people for their own ends ; like magnetism it wins what it seeks, but its success is a rope of sand, and its victory hollow.

The horrible side of this influence is that which displays the devil-nature of humanity in its willingness to coin money by commercialising this appetite. Houses of ill-fame are means of making money. White slavery is employed as a means of making money. Paramours and mistresses have lured men of wealth into their dens, because men were not able to resist the call of this appetite.

Wives who possess magnetism need never fear that their husbands will seek the society of other women. This fact has been abundantly proved and can be easily verified. We know of thousands of women who, after marriage, have acquired magnetism, and who by its quiet and undemonstrative influence hold a firm grip over the loyal affections of their husbands, who yield this loyalty willingly and sincerely.

Thus we find that strong as the sexual appetite is, magnetism is still stronger, far more dominant, and always master over these substitutes.

A wanton woman of average beauty is able, by her appeal to the sexual appetite of a man who lacks magnetism, to do almost anything with him if she proceeds skilfully. Great personages have fallen into the clutches of such women, as the court records show. History is full of such examples. In America recently a young woman of more than average beauty poisoned her husband for his wealth after inducing him to make a will in her favour, was tried by a jury of men, and promptly acquitted. She repeated this crime with a second husband in another part of the country, and was acquitted. When she tried it in a different locality a third time, although she actually killed her husband, discovery was made in time to secure overwhelming evidence of her guilt ; and after conviction she confessed to the other two murders. It is a fact that a very beautiful murderess may so addle the minds of the average jurors that they are not able to convict her.

If this is true, what is to be said of the men at large who are constantly being hunted by beautiful girls and women of whom the world is full ?

If jurors are helpless with the law, the evidence, and counsel

uniting to guide them aright, what chance of escape have the
mere men who are allowed to roam at will amid the scenes of
human activities ? _ .

Some people who are sworn to do justice to all very soon
wander from the ethical path of duty if beauty draws them to
itself.

All this is sex appetite.

It is an undue and unholy interest in the opposite sex.
Not all the influence goes to the woman. Not all women who
seek husbands do so because of their desire to be supported.
Many are impelled by their own sex appetite. When this is
normal, and there is genuine magnetism to accompany it, the
combination is ideal.

But fewer men are willing to-day to undertake the hazardous
and expensive experience of wedlock. They are slow to marry.
They do marry in about the same number as always, but they
hesitate before taking the step. To offset this indifference,
women have established several forms of sex appeal ; the most
effective of which is the exposure of the shapes of their legs,
their backs and bosoms. With her attire receding at the upper
and at the lower parts, and the body that in former times was
regarded as sacred, displayed in what is really a vulgar
exhibition, all the power of this appeal is thrust into the gaze
of hesitating man.

Girls and women with decayed tonsils, ulcerised teeth and
blood that is infested with intestinal poisoning, instead of
delicately touching the face as of former times, now plaster on
the paint until Nature resigns and the beauty parlours parade
the scene. The man who marries one of these combinations,
when he awakes in the morning and beholds the facts, becomes
half delirious in the belief that he is passing through some
horrible nightmare.

Many keepers of dance halls, and of cabarets where indis-
criminate dancing prevails, are making money by taking advantage of the sexual appetite of humanity. The majority of
commercialised dancing is a form of assignation. Many public
dance halls are agencies of prostitution. True men and true
women will make use of this pastime as a social function, keep
it within their own set, and place the ban on lascivious contact
such as universally prevails under all other conditions. Boys

and girls in their teens, as well as men and women of all ages
under fifty, drift to the questionable places, drawn by this same
appetite.

In this account we do not intend to criticise dancing as a
social function, conducted as such, nor any friendly use of this
pastime among acquaintances whom one would be willing to
invite into the home as guests.

The strongest magnetic force, taken collectively, is that
of pure home life. Where this exists the world is safe. Where
it is lacking, there the nests of criminals are to be found. The
lure of the public dance hall is rapidly breaking up this influence.
Reports gathered by police departments and by courts show
that a large percentage of the girls who attend such dances
become mothers, with no prospect or desire to marry the boys
with whom they have associated. In one city, in a space of a
year, more than 1400 such girls, many of them not half through
their teens, were ruined ; and all of them ascribed their fall
to the public dance halls and cabarets.

This is all in the name of the sexual appetite. The girls
were excited by lascivious embraces ; the boys and men were
hungry for them ; and the proprietors were feeding their purses
by bringing these two temptations into play under the name of
entertainment and amusement. Many dance halls are equipped
with very small upper-floor rooms. In one hall that was recently
raided, the police found twelve rooms which twelve couples
under the age of twenty years were occupying, having by their
confession awaited their turn with many others ; and this
hall claimed to be conducting a dance to provide entertainment
for its guests.

We have made the assertion that no married person who
possesses magnetism is ever divorced or estranged ; for the
reason that this power is permanent and genuine. It does not
make any difference whether one or both are magnetic. If
either has this quality, it is imparted to the other, for it carries
its own influence to all persons with whom it comes into contact.
We strongly advise that no man or woman consider marrying
unless this power has been acquired and firmly established.

If it is true, as a prominent Judge said in open court, that
ninety per cent of all marriages are brought about by the sex
appetite, then this will account for the innumerable disasters

that follow wedlock. Divorces are common. Separations are more common. Dissatisfied couples are still more common. The claim made by each new couple prior to marriage that in their case there is to be an exception, and that they can never cease to love each other devotedly, has probably been made by every divorced couple before they entered wedlock. More than this they believed it, and think they are to be exceptions of the general rule.

It is claimed that love is blind. --

The spell of the sexual appetite is so great as to be almost blinding. Under this spell Nature makes men and women reckless. Both sexes feel it. Many couples afterwards explain their mistaken judgment by saying that the commonplace of marriage, the disregard of careful manners and careful dress, the gross familiarity, the assumption of ownership and personal claims, as well as the quickness of temper and criticism, bring them out of the dream state, and reveal the realities in their ugly hues. But if marriage had been induced by the attraction of magnetism, as we shall show conclusively in this study, the very things that seem repelling would be regarded as quite the opposite.

That the sexual appetite is nothing but a veneer is proved by the fact that couples who love each other devotedly at one time, develop later on a brand of hatred that surpasses all the firebrands of malice that were ever hurled at human hearts. The sun sets on the newly-weds with a smile and a glow of radiance that promises a happy future. The sun rises on the same newly-weds and scorches their love into a burnt cinder. A single night may make all the difference there is in life. A month may remove all the veneer.

THE GREED SUBSTITUTE

NUMERICALLY CONSIDERED this inborn trait of human nature is fully as much in evidence as any of the other appetites. In fact a great analyst of life has made the assertion that all four appetites, stomach, sexual, greed and spiritual, are divided with an almost equal representation in each, and are all fully taken advantage of as substitutes for magnetism. The latter quality is the power to win ; and this power is invoked by an appeal to the stomach in foods and drink, with marked success, but is not so readily commercialised for profit as are the remaining three appetites. Yet it is as universal as hunger, and necessarily so, for life depends on feeding.

It is doubtful if great financiers or business men can be swayed beyond their judgment in any appeal to the stomach, unless they fall before the temptation of drink. But the great American statesman, Daniel Webster, was easily overcome by drink. Enormous fees in his law practice, in one case reaching twenty thousand pounds, slipped through his fingers into the hands of friends who plied him with whisky ; and just before he took to his bed in his last sickness, he was described by the historian as the most magnificent wreck humanity ever produced. During his last years his whole career was compromised through the same influence. The term vampire that is now applied to women who seek out men of wealth in order to gain by an appeal to the sexual appetite what they could not win by legitimate attractions, recognizes a firmly established profession, and a numerous division of humanity. They could not thrive unless their victims lost the power of resistance.

Greed is the third appetite.

It is not found in any life below man. No animal is greedy, despite the fact that some will store away their supplies for the winter, and others will over-eat at times. But greed, in the sense that it sways them beyond their powers of judgment in securing the existence that has been allotted them, is wholly absent.

This is not true of humanity. Some psychologists claim that greed is a mental disease ; some a nervous disease ; some that it is born of the fear that old age will bring poverty when the earning capacity is gone. It is the duty of this study to guide all its students into conditions of safety in all matters.

Magnetism provides in absolute certainty safety against poverty or the loss of the means whereby to live. It is an old adage, but a good one, which says that every year should find every one in better means. This is one form of mental magnetism, of which there are many waiting to help men and women in the struggle of existence. We will repeat this more prominently :

Magnetism teaches and shows the way by which every year will find every one in better means ; which, being explained, sets up the law that all persons who acquire magnetism become better off financially every year of life. Before this work is ended this fact will be proved over and over again. Then all fear will cease, such as makes people tools of scheming and crafty men, who, like harpies, seek to rob them of their savings.

Every one of the four appetites is a substitute for magnetism.

Every one of them accomplishes exactly the ends that magnetism might accomplish, with the difference that the former bring disaster, loss and suffering, while the latter bring permanent success. The things that are sought by an appeal to the love of food and drink may be better attained by magnetism. The legitimate ends of sex appeal, such as honourable marriage, or appreciation of the attractions of the opposite sex, or the many other goals to which this appetite drives people, may be attained by magnetism.

That men and women are greedy is too widely known to be discussed ; but the knowledge is capitalised to an alarming extent at all times and under all circumstances. The victims of this crafty profession, if fully alert after one experience, learn to suspect everybody and every motive ; and seldom fall again into the clutches of the birds of prey. Ordinarily, however, when a man is once cheated, he gets into another kind of trap that is differently baited. It is the bait that lures him. His suspicions are directed only against the former kind of bait. The following example is a key to some of the methods employed to appeal to the greed of humanity.

A man had been led to invest largely in a certain company, and was told of the earnings of other similar companies that had in fact made their owners very rich. Having the proof of the latter claim, he believed that this new company would be successful ; so he invested, and eventually found that his shares were worthless. / The first bait was the lure of gain or his greed for large profits. He was told that if nothing was ventured nothing would ever be gained. This mental proposition is not generally true. Mental magnetism tells us that if nothing is ventured nothing will be lost. It would have been true in his case at least ; for he parted with more than half his fortune in a venture that was not warranted by his financial condition. If he had kept his money in safe investments at a low rate of interest, he would have had enough for himself and his family to live on during life, with a small but sure annual excess to be laid by under the law of mental magnetism stated on a preceding page which says that with the aid of magnetism every person may be better off financially every year of life.

Figure out these laws of mental magnetism.

Here is a man with sufficient capital to support himself and his family comfortably during life, with a yearly surplus to lay by for the satisfaction of doing it, and without a trace of greed. In his desire to win greater wealth he ventures on a new scheme, and finds himself deprived of half his income and unable to live comfortably. He believed that if nothing was risked, nothing would be won ; but mental magnetism says that if nothing is risked nothing will be lost. The situation we have described has been experienced millions of times ; and men have gone down to the grave with broken hearts because of their greed. Coal mines, gold mines, copper mines, silver mines, oil wells and countless other allurements have brought this disaster to investors who have sought to follow in the footsteps of successful men.

Here is another law of mental magnetism. We have said that such laws are numerous, and that a few of them will meet us in this work, but they in fact are almost unlimited, and have required the publication of a very large work (*Mental Magnetism*) to teach and explain them, which work the author has dedicated to the students of the present work. We must include at this place one of the most potential of such laws as far as guidance to investments is concerned. It is this : Any stocks or shares in any get-rich-quick concern that people are solicited to buy, if one-tenth as valuable as claimed, will be quickly absorbed by men of wealth. They never go begging. There is too much money now invested at three per cent interest and less to remain there if anything of real worth is to be had in place of such holdings.

Let us look at the manner in which a man who has been once victimised, falls a second time into a trap when the bait has been changed.

The man who bought the shares in the worthless company, locked them up in his safe where they lay for a few years when a very impressive gentleman called upon him and asked if he was the owner of shares in that company. He was, and he emphasised the fact with the usual language. The visitor, unruffled, calm as a pond in a dead wind, smooth and convincing, merely remarked that the company was about to begin operations as a great vein had been discovered much larger than the first, and a syndicate of well-known capitalists proposed to buy enough of the outstanding shares to control the reorganisation. But if they could not get a majority of the stock, they would drop the matter. He was soliciting options at a price that was about double what this victim had first paid for his shares. Would he make an option at those figures ? Yes. No delivery was to be made, nor any certificates passed ; merely an agreement to sell at a very attractive figure.

That evening this man was in a jolly mood. Life had turned roseate again. In the course of time a letter that was typed on an engraved letter head, with many names of officials having offices in a suite of rooms in a great building in a great city, was delivered to him saying that the deal might not be consummated, as it was impossible to get enough stock to control a reorganisation ; for holders, hearing the good news, were seeking even higher prices. Also a rival syndicate was bidding more money for the shares. A few days later another man of impressive talking powers called, and stated that he represented the rival syndicate, and offered fifty per cent more for the shares. The prospective victim said that he had given an option to the first syndicate ; but the stranger informed him that the option had a time-limit which had expired. While this conversation was going on, there came a wire from the first visitor, asking that the option be extended for a month under a promise of still better prices. Wishing to be safe the man decided to extend the option. The second visitor went away muttering his disappointment.

The mind of the victim was asleep.

In a few days the first visitor returned and said that his syndicate needed only a small block of shares to have control ; that a certain man held just enough of this stock to meet the requirements ; but could not be given any information from the syndicate ; his shares must be bought by some stranger, and were for sale at the price paid plus interest, which was fair all round. This small block, added to the block already held by the victim, would complete the deal ; and a contract was brought out signed by the officials of the syndicate agreeing to pay for both blocks of the stock, if the victim would agree to buy the second block. Seeing the opportunity to recoup his former losses and to add materially to his capital, the man did enter into this agreement, and did in fact buy the second block of shares, which nearly depleted his remaining capital. But after the purchase, he found himself in possession of two blocks of worthless shares, and never heard again from either syndicate ; nor could he find the office building in which the first one claimed to have a suite of rooms. The bait had been changed, and he fell twice into well-laid traps.

Had this man been a student of personal magnetism, he would not have fallen into either trap ; nor would he have been compelled to face old age broken, disheartened and dependent on the charity of others.

This experience is being repeated times without limit ; and even as we write we are sure that there are millions of men and women who are enduring the pangs of regret and suffering as the result of the greed of others who have made use of their greed in order to rob them of the savings of a lifetime.

Personal magnetism brings complete independence of all attempts to take advantage of the judgment or will-power.

We do not believe that any person who has read this lesson will allow the mind to be clouded, or the will-power deadened by the substitute for magnetism known as greed. It has been our work to teach the methods whereby unnecessary losses are avoided.

THE SPIRITUAL SUBSTITUTE

HERE WE COME TO THE FOURTH and final nature of humanity in earthly existence. If a group of thinking persons were to be asked what of this group is the strongest appetite, the first reply might place the stomach demand ahead of the others. Then as the matter was given more serious attention, the sex impulse would come to the front. Still again there would be many reasons why greed is to be regarded as the most common and most insistent. The <u>fact</u> is that all four are equally distributed in the activities of life.

The stomach appetite is seemingly paramount because the body must live, and to live it must be fed. Yet every body that lives must die ; and as long as death is at one end of life, with birth at the other, so long will the spiritual appetite demand feeding. For this reason, ever since man first came on earth, and has been compelled to face the problems of death, the chief business of mankind has been religion. In the ages of savagery, 100 per cent of all human beings were religious ; what they could not discern they invented, but always in the same way and for the same purpose.

No normal person to-day wishes to die. Nor does any normal person omit the study of the problems of birth and death. Every normal mind thinks of these mysteries, and seeks information at every source where it is possible to attain it. No matter what the result or what the convictions, this normal condition is spiritual.

Every appetite may be taken advantage of by crafty persons, and thus used as means of gain either in money, property, influence or power. In the earliest age of savagery the demands of the stomach and of the sexual nature were held in check and not used as means of gain or greed by superior minds, as is now the case. Nor were there sufficient attractions in greed among the masses to incite the appeal in that direction. This left to the leaders and upper castes the greater field of the spiritual appetite. Influence, power, rule, homage and contributions were the price paid to a select upper class by the terrified middle and lower classes ; nor did the superior minds hesitate to teach and preach every kind of fear based on the mysteries of death and the hereafter, if they could retain their hold on the people in that way.

In every tribe there was the central control composed of priests and teachers and those who shared the spoils with them, and to this centre there flowed an unceasing stream of contributions and homage. These leaders kept the people in a continued state of terror. The images that were worshipped were likenesses supposed to be of the devils that hovered over all living things ; and these were used to supplement the threats and terrors that attended all persons. No matter how much wealth a man had in herds or in grain, or even gold, there was no hesitancy in parting with it when demanded in the names of the unseen gods ; and the spirit of contributions has been kept alive in all the ages that have come and gone. It is only in the most recent times that these contributions made to the churches have been devoted to the uses for which they serve a rightful purpose.

In times past practically no man or woman refused to give freely in the cause of religion, and now a large majority of the people support liberally both the church and the charitable organisations ; for charity is a part of the spiritual nature. Every appetite properly fed, and properly controlled, is a blessing. To give to the stomach the foods that make it a perfect organ whereby it may give health to all the body, is doing the most good in that direction. To employ the sex appetite in the manner intended by Nature, is likewise doing good. Greed when its name is changed to careful saving of surplus earnings, is always a desirable trait. So the support of religion, the support of charity, and the study of the problems of life and death, is fully normal, and most commendable.

It is the misuse of them, the attempt to take advantage of others by crafty minds who know human appetites and their value in securing control over those who are swayed by them, that is reprehensible. How many persons who have just buried their loved ones, are induced when in a state of emotion, to part with their wealth at the solicitation of those who know how to prey on this spiritual appetite ? And how many more persons who themselves had come to their own death-beds, have been induced even while perfectly sane to give their property away in the name of religion ? We are not passing judgment on the matter either one way or the other ; our only purpose being to depict the trait called the spiritual appeal.

The spiritual appetite, as we have said, embraces charity, and it also includes all mystery worship, such as superstition, and the search for occult phenomena. In this free and enlightened country there are millions of people who believe in the existence of the spirit world, and the communication of spirits with mortals. In the name of this belief countless thousands of crafty minds have exacted a big toll in the way of contributions and money. More than two millions believe in theosophy, and several other millions in kindred teachings ; while the Hindoo influence of transmigration, transmutation, metempsychosis and all sorts of happenings after death, has saturated certain sections of this country. Probably all such cults came out of India, and are related. It is predicted that if the prevailing religions crumble, those of ancient India will take their places.

Nearly every man and woman is superstitious ; and nearly all of them deny it. Superstition was once the mother of all savage religion, and it is as natural as any form of the spiritual appetite.

We believe that without a noble religion and without the churches, life on earth would not be worth living ; no person would be safe ; and property would have no value because it would have no protection. In any great city the police department will tell you that religious belief and church influence are greater aids in the suppression of crime than all the laws, courts and police combined. But we accord to every man and woman the full right to believe according to their own convictions.

Our purpose in this study is to show that a power that is inherently good may be used to take advantage of people at times when they are brought into spiritual hunger by public or private calamities, or are swayed by too deep an emotion of fear or dread.

Charity, as we have said, is a part of the spiritual nature ; and knowing this there are countless bodies of organised solic-itors in the name of charity which so follow up the people that escape is not creditable. Most contributors respond in fear of being harmed either socially or in their business. Thus the same spirit of prey is at work in the best of good causes. There are many organised bodies engaged in charity who absorb from fifty to eighty-five per cent of the contributions in their salaries and other expenses. You do not feel as if your money were going in the right direction if more than half of it is spent in collecting and handling it. The question may arise what kind of charity spirit prevails in the giving of funds to such organisations, especially by business men who know full well that omission to contribute would be whispered here and there and may affect their business. Every business man and professional person is known, is listed, and his contributions are recorded and even given publicity. He is therefore more or less compelled to give in self-defence, and not in the true spirit.

Referring again to the uses of mental magnetism as guides in human conduct we find another law helping us through this better influence ; and it is this : The best charity is that which helps men and women to become permanently helpful to themselves ; not that which merely sustains them in a state of helplessness. Teach the true spirit of independence ; give freely of money and time to this end ; and help people help themselves.

In America, surprising as it may seem, there are eight hundred thousand professional and non-professional fortune tellers who employ the so-called visits of spirits from the spirit world to tell their clients what the future has in store for them. It is estimated that of the population of America, numbering possibly close to one hundred and twenty millions, if a census were secured, it would be found that some time in the past or present, fifty millions of them have visited spirit-fortune tellers and paid good money in return for messages from the spirits. The majority of these clients do not believe what they are told. But many do, and are so completely swayed by this belief that they are easily victimised.

A familiar cheat is the spirit-fortune teller in America who charges for general services, but will not accept fees for advice as to how to safely invest money. The events proceed somewhat as follows : The client has money to invest or may have good shares paying low interest and wishes to find a higher rate. The fortune teller goes into a trance and, after some difficulty, figures out the names and addresses of several brokers, some of them well known and reliable, but one in particular is the most honourable and the most honest of them all. His name and address are scrawled on a piece of paper. Certain shares are just ready to rise ; if secured without delay a fine profit will be obtained. No time must be lost. On coming out of the trance the spirit-fortune teller does not know what is written but says that if the spirit told it, there could be no doubt about it. The client is as sure of the honesty and reliability of the advice as that the sun will rise again ; so hastens to the broker who is the most honourable of them all, parts with good money, or with high-grade shares, and buys worthless stock in exchange. This and similar methods of defrauding people who have faith in the spirit world, are robbing them by the thousands in the United States. It is greed making use of the spiritual appetite, and the latter uniting with greed sometimes, but generally seeking only honest investments, though lured into bad ones by falling prey to the power of the spirit appeal.

A person who lacks magnetism allows the mind to enter into a cloud in which all positive thinking ceases, and only the thoughts and beliefs that come from other's minds are active. Suspicion is the only safety-valve left to such persons ; and this trait works both ways : It shuts off the approach of fraud ; and it leaves the mind stalled in the deep woods in every transaction, turning humanity into non-progressive mules. Magnetism quickly disperses the clouds, and life is flooded with the light of knowledge.

LESSON TWELVE

MENTAL MAGNITUDE

WARFARE AND VICTORY are ordained by Nature as means of progress and success. They are as much acts of instincts as are the four appetites. The latter are established so that, when properly used, they may carry on existence in a necessary manner to necessary ends. But as they are essential in life, they are always super-charged with danger. Like electricity, if given free scope, the excess kills. Because of the dangers locked up in the four appetites, we are compelled to carry on a most obstinate warfare against them, and wage it until there can be no doubt about the final outcome. Victory must be assured, and must be permanent.

Until this victory has been achieved, magnetism will be kept on the defensive, and we have learned that any person or cause that remains always on the defensive, is under adverse control.

We have found that it is better to wage the war at the very beginning of this study ; to understand what is threatening success ; to meet the issue manfully and squarely, and to win the greatest victory of life.

The goal of magnetism is to WIN.

If you can win now against these natural enemies, you can win anything in life that you wish. Put this to the test.

There are two classes of enemies working against magnetism :

1. Those that are inborn or natural.
2. Those that are acquired.

When both classes of enemies are overcome the result is natural personal magnetism, or that high grade of power that is called a gift ; and it is always better to possess natural gifts

73

than those that must come from hard lifelong struggle, taking too much time and effort. This distinction is so important that it should be kept always in mind.

The inborn or natural enemies of magnetism are the Four Appetites that we have described. In this lesson our work is to show the way of giving them one great battle and thus secure a victory that will never be wrested from the winner.

It is an old saying and a true one that he who rules himself is greater than he who rules a city. We can extend it to read that he is greater than the grandest king who ever lived. In ruling yourself, you must win over the two classes of enemies ; over the Four Appetites ; and over the foes that you have acquired and taken into your camp as associates. Here we have the story of nations and organisations told over again in tabloid form. Everybody and everything has two enemies, those without and those within. Every nation has had this twofold danger. Napoleon, the greatest master of mental magnetism when in his successful career, made use of another law that served him well. Just as soon as a successful campaign was ended and he had come home to France to give attention to its needs, the usual unrest and intrigue began, and foes within were eating at the vitals of the nation. To offset this he invented stories of danger from foes abroad. The effect of this law is that a threatening outward enemy will cause a disintegrating inward condition to mend itself. Home enemies unite to fight a common cause such as an outward enemy. The plan succeeded even to the end of his reign.

The process we employ herein begins with the overcoming of the outward or natural enemies ; then we proceed to drive out of camp the hidden foes that are lurking there to destroy our newly acquired power.

This lesson we have named Mental Magnitude, or the greatness of the mind as an agent of warfare. The battle is waged in a series of steps. The first step is to recognize the Four Appetites. The second step is to recognize the nature of each. The third step is to recognize the danger attending the activity and control exerted by each. The fourth step is an honest inventory of the influence over your life and habits resulting from whatever control they exercise over you. The fifth and final step is to create within yourself a Mental Magnitude sufficient to completely master the Four Appetites. Let us unfold this method :

1. The Four appetites are the stomach, the sexual, the greed, and the spiritual.

2. The nature of each has been fully explained in the lessons just preceding this ; and they should be thoroughly reviewed.

3. The danger attending the activity of each in its control over you, is indicated very fully in these lessons. What you should do is to make yourself familiar with them.

4. The fourth step is to be taken now, and with it the final step, the creation of Mental Magnitude, or a mind big enough to make you ruler of yourself, and therefore greater than he who rules a city or a nation.

There are several vital laws that are at work in establishing this power and these we will state in simple form so that they may be easily understood :

FIRST VITAL LAW :—Mental Magnitude is a form of personal power that is greater than the combined power of the Four Appetites.

SECOND VITAL LAW :—Mental Magnitude, by enabling a person to escape the attitude of being continually on the defensive in life, which means being under adverse control, brings immediately to every man and woman who acquires this Magnitude the power of personal magnetism as a natural gift.

THIRD VITAL LAW :—Mental Magnitude, working in another channel of influence, tends towards the development of the power known as the control of mind over matter. It is a very great step in that direction.

FOURTH VITAL LAW :—While the control of mind over Matter is now present only as an instinct, and in very crude form, it is greatly increased by the building up of Mental Magnitude in developing personal magnetism as a natural gift.

FIFTH VITAL LAW :—Mental Magnitude is readily acquired and firmly established by the practice of shifting the defensive attitude to that of the aggressive, and thus removing all adverse control.

SIXTH VITAL LAW :—The mental determination acting in any direction, if given sufficient strength, is capable of accomplishing the greatest things in life ; on the principle that what a man determines with all the power of his mind to do, he will do, and nothing can prevent the consummation sought. It is readily seen that we are laying the foundation of personal magnetism as a natural gift.

SEVENTH VITAL LAW :—The simplest and at the same time the most effective method of practising mental determination is had in the system known as the Regime of Mental Magnitude. This will appear in the next lesson.

Books might be written on the subject of the control of Mind over Matter in its now crude form, in which it appears chiefly as visitations of instinct. But what its purpose is, as it now influences humanity, is not known. The familiar example of this crude form is seen in the oft-quoted case of the man who comes home hungry and sits down to a generous dinner, well prepared and highly inviting. He has eaten a part of the meal when a telegram is handed him, which he reads. The blood leaves his face and he is deathly pale, the gastric juice refuses to flow into the stomach and his partly eaten dinner remains undigested. His appetite, which was vigorous, is gone. Yet all that has happened is the intelligence, conveyed to his mind, that he has lost his entire fortune in an unfortunate investment.

His respiration drops to almost nothing ; his heart is barely able to carry on its beating ; and his whole body totters as he proceeds from the table to his room above where he falls upon the bed. It is not difficult to understand why he suffers mental anguish, but why the influence of his mind should control the material body is a mystery. Every function is subjected to the mastery of his thought.

This is only one of many thousands of instances showing that the mind can and does control the body ; or in other words that there is such a thing as the control of Mind over Matter.

It is not alone bad news that will affect digestion. Good news plays its part both ways. Another oft-quoted example is found in the case of a very beautiful young lady whose parents were rich enough to give her all the comforts and luxuries of life ; and who yet fell into anæmic ill-health and could not be brought back to a normal condition. Every possible method and treatment were tried, but in vain. At length her parents began a campaign of discussion and preparation for a magnificent trip abroad, including visits to places that held great attractions for her. Books, pamphlets and folders were read and studied ;

and she was advised to make an itinerary for the journey. Still she did not show any signs of getting better. Then the doctor made the following mental experiment ; consisting of a long letter which he wrote in apparent confidence to her father, in which he said that the young lady was not well enough to undertake so great a trip abroad ; some day she was sure to get well ; but not now ; and the journey must be postponed to a future year. By seeming accident this letter fell into her hands. She read it, and replaced it, and said not a word. But her mind took on at once the mental determination to get well. She resolved to get well. She did get well.

Ordinarily the prospect of a trip abroad or some pleasing venture will increase the health when other means fail ; but such improvement is generally temporary. On the other hands when the MIND sets itself into a fixed determination, real and lasting results follow. This is a well-known law of psychology. Great doctors employ it. The public statement of Thomas A. Edison, who was probably one of the greatest men who ever lived, all things considered, asserts that his grandfather and also his father both died by the determination to do so. We quote here the exact words of Mr. Edison published some years ago in a leading magazine : "My grandfather ate carefully and lived to be one hundred and four. No disease killed him. He was perfectly well up to the time that he died. He lost interest in life. The cells of which his body was composed were anxious to get away. So my grandfather told his children that he was going to his daughter's house to die. He went to her home ; undressed ; went to bed ; AND DIED. There was nothing the matter with him. He was simply tired of life. And my father died the same way. They had found that the secret of long life and perfect health lay in right eating. As for me I eat only because I want to live. As a result my body is not poisoned with decaying, surplus food. My arteries are as soft as a child's."

There are published in books many instances of the power of the mind over the body ; of the mental magnitude that, instead of being swayed and enslaved by adverse control as of the Four Appetites and other enemies, rises superior to them all, and masters them. By this process have come the great men and women of the world.

MENTAL MAGNITUDE RÉGIME

FOLLOWING THE TEACHINGS of the preceding lesson we come to the mental exercises that are prepared for the purpose of developing the power there taught. We strongly advise that the several Vital Laws and all that is said prior to and following them, be reviewed so as to be fully understood, as they are charged with the mission of completely revolutionising your life. Until this study is undertaken, all persons with so few exceptions as to seem none at all, are subject to adverse control, due to the influence of the Four Appetites; and it is here that the battle must be fought and the victory won. Then will come the established habit of meeting all other forms of adverse control, and of conquering all opposing forces whether arising from other persons or from conditions.

Faith in your ability to establish some form of control of Mind over Matter is helpful, but not essential. There are phases of life where the power of faith is very potent, but we do not deal with them. We do not face the excuse that is given when failure comes, that the faith is too weak. Yet we do not undervalue the advantage that comes from its exercise. Our position is this: Mental determination is all-powerful, and when carried forward to a high stage of development it results in a marked degree in the formation of the control of Mind over Matter. This is done by the practice of mental exercises; and these we will give here in their most useful and serviceable arrangement, in the systems known as

MENTAL MAGNITUDE RÉGIME.

This Régime appears in the form of mental determinations made in the first person of grammar so as to bring them home more firmly to the mind of the student.

We deal in turn with the Four Substitutes which are the source of the adverse control that keeps all persons on the defensive and so enables them to cultivate personal magnetism as a natural gift. These are :

1. The Stomach Substitute.
2. The Sex Substitute.
3. The Greed Substitute.
4. The Spiritual Substitute.

The mental determinations are as follows :

1. I will review at this place the lessons that relate to the Four Substitutes ; and I will also review the lesson next preceding this, entitled Mental Magnitude, with especial attention to the Vital Laws therein.

2. I understand what is meant by adverse control which arises from the power of these appetites over human nature.

3. I understand that these appetites are substitutes for magnetism, in that they are employed by crafty persons in order to win influence over other persons, and to gain unworthy ends.

4. I understand that any substitute for magnetism is a veneer and does not bring permanent success.

5. I will not permit my mind to be blinded by the efforts of the opposite sex to influence me through any form of sex appeal.

6. The excessive use of facial make-up I will regard as an effort to conceal a dirty and yellow skin ; and tricks of a similar kind I will look upon as methods intended to mislead my judgment.

7. On the other hand I will give my attention in preference to any one whose complexion is as close to Nature as good taste should permit ; on the theory that good health and cleanliness of blood speak for themselves when allowed to show themselves. This fact I will not forget.

8. I will not be influenced by the appeal to the sex appetite in the manner of dress ; the exposure unduly of the legs and the upper part of the torso.

9. On the other hand I will prefer the person who retains as much modesty as is possible without going to the extreme of prudery ; allowing always for the convenience of dress brevity as a help to activities, but not for unnecessary brevity.

10. I will not engage in any form of dancing that is intended to excite the sex appetite, nor will I encourage any such dancing anywhere.

11. I will do all in my power to aid the law in the suppression of many commercialised forms of dancing, especially of certain types of dance halls, and the cabarets that are places of assignation.

12. If I am not married I will delay that step until I have mastered the study of magnetism as presented in this book, so that the marriage may be made with a view to permanency and happiness.

13. If a woman, I will mentally uncover the veil that obscures the future conditions of wedlock, and I will not be swept unduly into a marriage that may not stand the test of opposing forces coming into conflict when the veneer has been removed. I will look cautiously ahead.

14. I will not permit the need of support, or the appeal to greed to draw me into a marriage that is not founded on a sound basis.

15. I will not permit any improper familiarity with the opposite sex, even under the pretence of affection or love, and I will hold myself aloof until marriage in order that I may retain the respect of the opposite sex, and be held in a higher regard.

16. I am determined not to believe the protests and pretences that are made in order to induce me to change my reserve, nor will I place credence in promises, artificial ideals and gilded hopes of the future such as lure many girls and women into hasty and ill-considered marriages.

17. I will not believe that our marriage is to be the one exception to the usual experience of disappointment and shock when once the illusion has spent itself, and the hard facts of two temperaments facing the crises of the new venture must be met and mastered to avoid the cooling of ardour and consequent estrangement. The future is to be judged by the past.

18. I will not be swept into any hasty marriage by any cause or influence such as drives men and women, and especially young folks into wedlock and its failure ; but on the contrary I will assert my power of mental determination to discover the full effects of the step about to be taken.

19. I am fully aware that Nature, in her scheme of renewing

the species, sets up the sexual appetite in both sexes in order
to hasten forthcoming marriages ; and that fully one-half of
all marriages are caused by the trickery of Nature in drawing
people together and making wedlock necessary ; but I will
avoid being used in this scheme by retaining absolute control
over my inclinations and desires, and keeping safely outside the
limits of temptation.

20. In order to carry out the last determination, I will form
the mental habit of looking with one hundred per cent suspicion
on all questionable or doubtful lures set in motion by the
opposite sex ; knowing that, whatever temporary loss I may
sustain, the future will bring its full rewards in happiness.

21. Assuming that ninety per cent of all marriages are
ill-assorted and wretched, and even when not broken by
estrangement are filled with a lifetime of regrets, I will follow
the later lessons of this book in order to avoid this fate.

NOTE :—In this Régime we have taken the second of the
Four Appetites out of order, as many mistakes due to hasty
action occur following this impulse, and lead to wretched lives
in which the ambition to succeed in other directions is destroyed.
We now proceed with the first Appetite.

22. I will avoid putting into my mouth or stomach anything
that may cause any drug habit, as drugs that stimulate, excite
or distort the nervous activities, make it impossible to develop
magnetism.

23. I will not smoke cigarettes ▓▓▓▓▓ as these are in
most cases charged with some degree of habit-forming drugs,
the purpose being to fasten on the smoker an unshakable
slavery to the habit ; and any form of slavery is an adverse
control that makes the development of magnetism impossible.

24. I will not allow any person to influence my will or control
my decision in any matter by the temptation of drink, which
I know has been used as a substitute for magnetism in order to
serve the ends of crafty persons.

25. I will not allow an appeal to my appetite in any form to
be used to win from me any action that may put me to a
disadvantage in any dealing or matter of importance.

26. I will give heed to the statement of Mr Thomas A. Edison
in the preceding lesson on the subject of eating properly so that
the body may not " be poisoned with decaying, surplus food,"

for I know that there cannot develop in the system the natural power of magnetism when this poisoning is present.

27. Like Mr. Edison I will eat for the purpose of living ; and not live for the purpose of eating.

28. By reference to later lessons in this book I will take advantage of the natural laws of health by putting into my body only the elements that build the body, omitting all things that cannot participate in the building of health and vigour.

29. I will not weaken my vitality by over-eating or over-loading the system even with proper food.

30. I will take advantage of the law that says that a person who eats all that the strength and vigour of the body require and no more, so that he may come away from each meal not fully satiated, but with a small percentage of hunger remaining, will develop a high degree of natural magnetism, while the person who eats to satiation carries a dead and stale condition of the vitality for some time thereafter.

31. In matters where greed may induce others to take advantage of me, I will develop the mental attitude of being one hundred per cent suspicious of all persons and all motives ; believing all persons who are in a position to cause me loss to be one hundred per cent dishonest.

32. I will not allow my judgment of values to be warped by the promise or hope of receiving more than a fair exchange for what I pay in any dealing.

33. I will not cause loss to any person by selling anything at an unfair price, or taking a larger return than is fair to me and to such person.

34. I will not take advantage of the financial embarrassment or distress of any person in order to gain something to which I am not entitled in the fair exchange of values.

35. I will not indulge in the tricks so often used to induce people to buy my goods.

36. I will not sign my name to any blank piece of paper, nor to any written or printed paper having a blank space above my signature ; as safety may be obtained by heavily marking the blank space with ink lines to prevent matter from being written therein.

37. I will not write my name in any album or in any place where, if the leaf were to become detached and were to fall into

the hands of unreliable people, something involving me in obligation might be inserted.

38. I will avoid the trap of writing my name on blank envelopes, especially large ones, under the pretence of being needed for identity, which envelopes could be so cut as to give opportunity for writing or printing a contract, power of attorney or promise that would involve me in a loss.

39. I will not buy or sell any stocks or shares except through a Bank or through a member of a Stock Exchange.

40. I will not endorse a note for another person; nor go on the bond of another; nor engage to stand responsible for another. My duty to my family takes precedence of all such obligations, even for friends.

41. I will not seek a high rate of interest in place of a high grade investment.

42. I will not believe the statement made so often by certain people that they have not had a loss in a great many years. When analysed this claim may be explained to mean anything.

43. I will so manage my savings as to retain at least some part of them every year.

44. I will not follow the suggestion that if nothing is risked, nothing can be gained; but will adopt the better suggestion that if nothing is risked something may be saved.

45. When I have enough of this world's goods, I will not seek an unnecessary excess at the risk of my health, my self-respect or my good name; nor will I sacrifice these at any time in winning a competence.

46. I will not go on piling up a great fortune to be left to those who will not need it.

47. In the uses of charity I will avoid contributing to those organisations whose expenses absorb from fifty to eighty per cent of the moneys collected.

48. I will, whenever possible, make use of the method that helps worthy people to help themselves and thereby become independent of charity.

49. I will not tie up money for inheritance that can be put into use in my lifetime, if such money is not needed by my heirs.

50. No matter whether I am a church attendant or not, I will study the usefulness of the church in the world as the source

of civilisation, the teacher of morality and the only effective agency of law, order and peace.

51. If I do not believe in a Supreme Ruler I will not seek to influence others away from their beliefs, nor will I in any way antagonize those who are sincerely trying to lead moral lives in the name of religion.

52. As belief in superstition is a form of fear, and fear is a serious phase of adverse control greatly interfering with the development of magnetism, I will from this moment on, as long as I live, discard all belief in superstition, and pay no attention to the popular claims of signs good and bad that are attached to various happenings.

53. I will not exhibit a state of mental weakness by entertaining the fear of ghosts, spirits and occult phenomena; remembering that when the world was in its darkest period, all humanity was depressed by this fear, which grows less with the advance of knowledge and intelligence.

54. I will not be swayed in my life by beliefs in supernatural happenings, visitations or spirit phenomena; remembering that men and women who so believe, and who shape the activities of their lives to meet such belief, are always retrograding in their affairs and losing their influence in the world.

55. I will not follow the advice of any person supposed to have been in a trance state; nor will I fall victim to the belief that the person I consult is an exception to the general rule of fraud and pretence.

56. I will not invest any money nor part with any values to any person or for any securities recommended by a fortune teller, or by any person who is supposed to have been in a trance state.

57. As the spiritual appetite is natural and instinctive, inborn and predominant in the world, I will study it and seek to develop it in myself as the associate of that power that brought humanity into existence and that must of necessity direct and control the lives of all men and women who look in that direction for guidance and sustaining help.

58. Recognising the fact that, in this country alone, there are millions of people who firmly believe in the existence of a Supreme Deity, and further recognising the fact that a person who unnecessarily antagonises a great belief always destroys

his influence among his fellow-beings and makes the power of magnetism valueless, I will combine good judgment with discretion in this matter, and respect the opinions of others even though they do not agree with me.

59. Knowing that the spiritual appetite in its best estate is inborn and inherent in humanity, that every normal person is swayed by its instinctive influence, and that character and well-being are greatly benefited and enhanced by developing it to its highest degree as an agency of personal power, I will not neglect this part of myself.

60. In the belief that all persons who are normal possess three great departments of being—physical, mental and spiritual— and that the cultivation of the powers of each will lead to the highest degree of personal influence in life and thereby win the respect and confidence of all those who may come to know me, I will give attention to each of these three departments of my being.

61. As sleep is typical of death, and death is the stimulating cause of spiritual study, I will devote my last thoughts at night to the consideration of my spiritual nature ; and on the following morning I will give my first thoughts to the same subject.

It will be seen that one of the purposes of this system of training is to unfold in each life its all-round nature, on the following principle :

A person who is only developed physically is never magnetic.

A person who is only developed mentally is never magnetic.

A person who is only developed spiritually is never magnetic.

Only the all-round individual is highly magnetic ; all others are one-sided, warped and repellent.

The person who disregards his spiritual character, and who parades his boast that he does not believe in the power that gave him life, soon separates himself from the healthy influence of his fellow-beings, and is pushed to one side in the affairs of this world.

Of course it is a matter of policy to follow the crowd, and there are sticklers for personal pride and courage who think it evidence of a superior mind to declare their antagonism to prevailing beliefs ; and this argument might have weight if it were not founded on conceit and refusal to test the power that is indicated in the items 60 and 61 in the foregoing list ; for countless incidents prove the remarkable increase of personal character and influence following the practice there described.

This system of Mental Magnitude Régime makes a man a real man, and a woman a real woman. If studied in connection with the two final Departments of this book, those of Applied Personal Magnetism, and of Magnetic Healing, but more particularly with the former of these two, it builds a personality that becomes a dominating power in the world. No human being can rise to great heights on nothing but desire and planning ; there must somewhere be the real basis, the solid foundation, the substance, and these come from what will be learned as Values, or units of real worth. There must be the richness of character, of mental development and of actual achievement.

It will be shown in those final Departments that there are three groups of mental faculties : those of the merely physical functions ; those of the reasoning functions ; and those of the inner self, which psychologists to-day term the subconscious group. Magnetism rarely uses any mental groups except those of the last-named faculties, and in all higher-class educational institutions they are being studied to-day under the name of psychology. They present the only part of human effort that may be termed invincible ; and what victories they are capable of achieving will be found stated in the two final Departments of this book.

Some people believe in life after death, and to them the phase of change known as death is likened to sleep, which it is thought was instituted to teach humanity in this life, once in every twenty-four hours, the facts of passing away and of rising again into life. Whether this similitude is warranted or not, the value of the last waking moments at night as the key that opens the secret chamber to the hereafter, or to the knowledge of the life to come, is being brought home to the great experts of the world ; and the most remarkable results are being achieved in making use of the powers that are thus revealed.

It is for this reason that the 61st item of this system of Mental Magnitude Régime has been included in the list of resolves.

DEPARTMENT OF
THE MAGNETIC EYE

LESSON FOURTEEN

MAGNETISM OF THE EYE

A POWER SUCH AS MAGNETISM is acknowledged to be, must have means of use by which its influence may be transmitted to other persons. The greatest and most magnetic of English pulpit orators, Charles Spurgeon, undertook to train young men for the ministry ; and among his most insistent claims was that every man who wished to succeed as a preacher must possess personal magnetism ; and if he lacked it he should acquire it. In America the most successful of evangelists was Dwight L. Moody ; he also taught young men and trained them in Bible classes for ministerial work ; and he made the same assertion in regard to the value of personal magnetism.

Two of the greatest lawyers of international fame were Webster and Choate. Both were magnetic in the highest degree. Choate was called " The Ruler of the Twelve," because he so often won his cases when not opposed by a man possessing magnetic powers as great as his. But when Choate was on one side of a case and Webster on the other side, the real merits won. We have talked often with men who were living during the later years of these two great men. We also have talked with a man who, while of greatly advanced years, was fully cognisant of the successes of both lawyers, and who had been associated several times in cases with Webster. From all we were able to learn, the same traits prevailed with them that we had noted in observing a number of the greatest men and women of our own time.

But the popular idea of the magnetic eye was not manifested in any of these persons. It is true that when aroused to a fever heat of intensity the eye becomes unusually brilliant, and at times has a piercing power ; but this characteristic is not present at any other time. In all other moods the eye is seemingly ordinary as far as the general outward appearance is concerned.

Investigation and study led to the discovery that the power of the eye is not in that orb itself, but in the arrangement of the surrounding parts of the face. Spurgeon in his grandest moments, when he swayed his listening thousands by his voice and action, displayed the strong facial earnestness that gave him an almost sublime appearance. Moody was rarely fervid in a vigorous way, nor would he have been called a great orator by strangers who heard him for the first time ; yet his facial expression that framed the eyes was clearly indicative of the power of the man. Observers who had the opportunity to witness Webster and Choate, agreed that in moments of great intensity their eyes glowed like dark, deep burning coals. An account is given of a conversation between Webster and an obstinate business man who at first refused to accept the lawyer's advice in a certain matter, but who was soon won over by the advocate ; and in this conversation Webster sat with his eyes almost closed. His voice or manner or general presence probably won the day.

These remarks are made to pave the way for a sensible and practical consideration of this phase of our study.

But it cannot be denied that in the process known as hypnotising, the eye is very helpful ; and its use in that operation might well receive attention if this study included that practice. We are dealing with an opposite power. Magnetism wins. Hypnotism defeats the will of another person. A sleep-producing drug puts the subject into slumber, but wins nothing. A bludgeon may do the same thing. Advantages obtained by rendering the subject helpless are a species of robbery. Hypno-tisers cultivate a brilliant and glowing eye by training the nervous system into a high degree of intensity. Any bright object of small size held slightly above the line of vision of the subject, thereby compelling the latter to keep the gaze uplifted until it wearies, will produce hypnotic sleep in a person who can be thus controlled. The eye serves the same purpose.

If there is an advantage in possessing a brilliant and glowing eye, this acquisition may be placed easily within the reach of any man or woman by the tensing exercise of this work. Some women place a few drops of a chemical upon the eyeballs to make them shine and glow ; but the practice becomes hurtful in time. It shows, however, the desire to have brilliant eyes.

The eyes in their size, shape and colour are often called beautiful. Yet the size depends on the iris, as does the colour, and the shape depends on the framing of the eye by the facial arrangement. If you will study the changing moods of a highly-bred cat, you will sometimes note affection, and this will be depicted solely by the positions of the lids. Then surprise will change the entire arrangement of the lids. Mood after mood may follow, each being depicted by the lids and not by the eyes.

Choate said that he never stopped talking to a jury until he thought that the last man had indicated by his eyes that he agreed with him. In those days lawyers were not limited in the length of their address in summing up their cases. We have seen in later days, what Choate saw in his time, in the faces of juries : the turning-point in yielding. Choate once said, " I know how long to talk to a jury. I also know when to stop talking."

The secret is not a great one, although it is important.

A person who holds an opinion opposing you will involuntarily raise the lower lid. This of itself signifies an analysis and scrutiny of your assertions. If the lower lid in addition to being raised is brought in towards the nose, this expresses not only hesitation to believe in your claims, but an affirmative obstinacy which is intended to combat you to a finish, mentally speaking. The mere raising of the lower lid is a normal action ; but when it is both raised and brought inward, it is a concentric and combative action. When the upper lid meets the normal action, it indicates that the mind is at work trying to solve the problem.

The upper lid tells a more common and more easily read story.

If it is lowered and the eyeball is raised to meet it, although not fully doing so, this shows that the mind has ceased to work for the time being ;   and that the speaker whether in the court-room, in the home, or in the office, is not reaching the thoughts of the supposed listener. ⏐ To understand this position, practise looking up to the ceiling, and shutting off the gaze by dropping the upper lid half over the eyeball while keeping the latter in the position of looking at the ceiling.   In any form of con-versation, as well as in addressing a jury, this phase of human nature is always the same.

A magnetic person cultivates the habit of studying the effect of his words upon listeners ;   and the eyes principally tell the facts.

There are several positions of the upper lid with reference to the eyeball that are assumed countless times every day by all persons.   We may list these positions as follows :

The centre of the eye is known as the pupil.

The ring around the pupil is called the iris ;   and its colour gives to the eye the hue that is permanent.

The less the tension, or the calmer the person may be, the smaller is the pupil.   Temperament or heredity, or even nervous disease, may make many changes in this opening. Assuming it to be normal or nearly so, the purposes that control the mind of a person are shown by the lids ;   and the upper lid has the following gamut :

1. If the upper lid completely covers the pupil of the eye, it indicates that the mind is not thinking closely, or may be aimless, or wandering, or sluggish ;   but the principal fact is that such a mind is not being subjected to magnetic control.

2. If the upper lid covers the top half of the pupil, the mind is indifferent.

3. If the upper lid comes down as far as the top edge only of the pupil the mind is attentive.

4. If the upper lid covers half the width of the top arc of the iris, the mind is very attentive ;   and this is what Choate looked for when he was talking to the jury, as he had come to that point where he controlled their thoughts.

5. If the upper lid touches the edge of the iris ring, it indicates that not only the mind is very attentive, but the feelings have been aroused.   This is a double victory.

6. If the upper lid shows any thin line of white above the iris, it indicates that the mind and feelings have been aroused to

an excess, and that the person has lost control of them by the springing into being of some strong emotion such as that of anger, hatred, horror or other mood. It is not a normal condition and should be avoided.

7. If the upper lid shows a wider line of white above the iris, it indicates that the person has become transfixed with fear, horror, insane ecstasy, or other similar mood, such as might occur in the presence of a foe, apparition or wild animal. These two last conditions have nothing to do with the study of magnetism, but are stated in order to complete the gamut and show how clearly the upper lid interprets the state of the mind and the feelings.

The cultivation of personal magnetism includes the study of life in all its moods, and shows the way to read and understand the effects on others of any influence that may proceed from the observer. In other words, the truly magnetic person is able to read instantly the mind and moods of every person he meets. The more one sees of these indications in the faces of others the more confidence will be created in the ability to sway such persons ; and confidence in magnetism is exactly what faith is in religion or in healing.

In a conversation with a very successful financier whose magnetism had given him the leadership in his line of business, we asked the question : " Do you realise that you possess the power of personal magnetism ? " and the reply was made quietly in the affirmative. We then asked, " Without personal magnetism what would be your standing to-day in the financial world ? " The reply was : " I would probably be a ' bucket-shop ' broker." One more question : " What is the most useful phase of personal magnetism as a practical aid to business or otherwise ? " He thought for a moment and said slowly, " The most useful, most practical and most valuable aid to a man in business life, or professional life, or social life, is to know the mind and feelings of those with whom you come in contact ; to be able to size them up as the common saying goes ; to read in their faces what they think and how they feel towards you."

It is by the observing eye that we learn to study the meanings in the faces of others. Nothing is so beneficial to the mind, to the eyes themselves, and to the personal character of the magnetic individual as the practice of analysing the meanings that are written clearly in the faces of people.

Magnetic persons are exceedingly observant.

The habit of constant observation of any details will help to develop what is called natural personal magnetism. Most persons see things in lumps or masses. A non-magnetic person will see a face as a whole ; a magnetic person will see its details. There is a sect in India among the ancient high-class caste that has acquired the highest known form of personal magnetism solely by the process of separating masses into details, and catching the details as separate units, each distinct ; a process that they have trained themselves to develop until it has reached an unbelievably powerful state of control over their fellow-beings.

If you will follow carefully each lesson in this system you will recognise the fact that each accomplishment that is designed to awaken and arouse the latent magnetism of the body, has a wide field of practical usefulness in all other directions apart from the study of magnetism.

This fact applies with direct force to the process of acquiring the power of mental observation of details, in place of masses. The process begins at once to build a mental acumen that becomes a most important weapon in dealing with men and women. As an example of what we mean, let us look back to the preceding pages of this lesson. Ninety-nine persons in every hundred study the normal face as a whole. If there is any mark or evidence of injury, that is seen ; but nothing more than a face in general. There is no reading of the mind and feelings ; no attempt to go behind the mask of the commonplace appearance for the knowledge that is plainly written there. Choate once said to his partner during a resting period in his address, "The fifth man on the back row, and the second man in the front row are not yet with me." After he resumed his address and came to a pause for a drink of water, he said to his partner, "The back row man has yielded ; I have yet to get the front row man." As he spoke he scanned the face of this last juror, and soon read in the fine shifting of a muscle or two the story of his victory.

This is the process of separating details from masses ; lines and fine movements in the face from the general appearance.

MAGNETIC DETAILS

FOLLOWING THE OUTLINES set forth in the preceding lesson, we take up the study of that process which has produced such wonderful results in the manner there stated. It is known as the practice of separating details from masses. The clumsy mind sees everything in a mass or what is called lumping it. There may be directly before us a face that has the story of the mind and feelings behind written in plain characters on its surface and yet the face remains a mystery to the beholder. There is only the thinnest partition between the story that the face reveals of the thoughts and feelings behind it, and the actual reading of the whole mind. In a series of experiments made by us with over two thousand men and women during a period of fifteen years, we found that it was possible for every person to learn to separate details from masses ; that in so doing by reading the face for the thoughts and feelings of a person, in the manner stated in the preceding lesson, the power of thought transference or practical telepathy was instantly developed.

That such a power exists and indicates the purpose of Nature to unfold a higher system of usefulness for the mind than has ever yet been developed, is self-apparent. It should be cultivated.

There are in daily transactions countless opportunities for securing advantage if only we could know the plans and purposes of those with whom we are dealing ; or as a business man said, " if only I could know what is in the other fellow's mind." The power to read aright what is behind the features, is half the battle in magnetism. From an analysis of the methods employed by men and women who have achieved the highest success in the world, it seems certain that they have come into this power as a natural habit.

Some persons are called uncanny who are only trained by their own way of doing things to read and understand faces.

As we have said there is only the thinnest partition between the easily acquired habit of reading faces and of reading the whole mind. It is not a difficult thing to learn or to acquire. It proceeds in two lines of development :

1. Learn what the eyes and the mouth indicate in the fine details of position and movement.

2. Practice the habit of observation of these positions and movements as details in the mass appearance of the face.

We have referred to the eye positions only thus far, using the term eye to include the framework about it as explained in the preceding lesson. Two laws will help us at this stage :

The eye positions and movements stated in the preceding lesson indicate the mental operations in chief, and the feelings as secondary influences.

The mouth positions and movements indicate the feelings in chief, and the mental operations as secondary influences. As the finest shades of movement about the eye tell differing stories of the mind, so the changes of movement and position of the mouth tell different stories of the feelings. In order to be able to acquire the habit of breaking up the lower face into details as opposed to mass reading, it is helpful to learn in a general way the meanings of the changes and positions of the mouth, which are as follows :

1. There are two basic meanings :

2. The first basic meaning is that of the level mouth which indicates normal feelings held in check and good reserve.

3. The second basic meaning is that of the lightly closed mouth which indicates the feelings held in check and good reserve. Thus the combination of these two basic meanings is the highest ideal of character when the mind and feelings are normal. Both basic meanings coincide. If you will study the portraits of fine men and beautiful women you will note the union of these two meanings with variations that do not change them, as when, instead of the mouth being lightly closed, it is very nearly closed, or lightly open. The effect is the same, except that as the mouth opens, the feelings become slightly awakened. The opportunity for shading the meanings is a valuable one in every way.

4. There now enter two new meanings that are based on the level mouth :

5. The level mouth closed in any degree from that of the first position indicates a gamut running from the beginning of slight firmness to that of strenuous determination. This gamut contains at least a dozen degrees in the scale. It is worth studying. You will meet every one of these degrees in the people about you or in the faces of the great men and women of the present and past.

6. Now the meaning shifts to the opposites. The level mouth open in any degree from that of the first position of being lightly closed, to that of being wide open, runs another gamut of at least a dozen degrees in the scale showing the opposite meanings from those of determination or firmness. So intricate are these shades of varying meaning that it is not possible to spend sufficient time to describe them. But the level mouth when more than slightly open indicates that the feelings are being transferred to the care of outside causes as a rule, and occasionally to causes of interest, fear, alarm and even horror set up by one's own thoughts and feelings.

If the level mouth is more than slightly open, something has occurred to take away the determination or the affirmative state of self-reliance. (If the upper lid of the eye falls and the eyeball rises, and the mouth begins to open, the combination is that so often noted when a person needs sleep ; but this is negative, and in the hands of a skilled hypnotist leads quickly to a state of sleep through which the subject passes into another kind of wakefulness attended by unconsciousness of the working mind. This we do not teach but seek to guide our students in the way to avoid it both as subject and manipulator.)

Assuming that the person is to remain awake and alert, the gamut of meanings that run from normal to expanded interest, is one of the most useful of all things to watch and to study.

If you will watch any person who is being addressed, you learn quickly to what degree the interest in what is being said is aroused. If an account of some incident is absorbing, every listener will show not only relaxed lips, but mouths that open gradually to meet the increasing interest. A preacher whose description of some event was greatly interesting noted that every mouth in his congregation was widely open. In another instance a minister who had followed the sea before entering the ministry was fond of depicting a great crisis on the ocean. A flash photograph of his listeners just at that stage where the ship was about to sink unless saved by a seeming miracle, showed every mouth wide open. This same condition appeared at a meeting where the heroic deed of Captain Fry was being told to the audience.

We have seen juries sit with mouths slightly open and as the speech of a certain advocate increased in intensity these listeners gave way more visibly to their feelings.

The main point to be learned is that as the lips separate towards an open position, to that extent the speaker is winning an influence over the person who is listening. To be assured of a victory, it is only necessary that the lips be slightly open ; but in any event the operation of this law is so interesting that its workings are worth all the time given to detect and to understand them.

We now come to two other laws as follows :

7. The lips raised above the level indicate approval or some kindred meaning. The act of raising occurs at the ends of the lips.

8. The lips lowered below the level indicate disapproval or some kindred meaning. The act of lowering occurs at the ends of the lips.

The child who is pleased will begin to raise the ends of the lips. If he is about to cry this condition is heralded by the depressing of the lips. The term approval takes in a large group of meanings but all along the same line, and there is a well-defined gamut of change from the slight raising to the excessive upward position. The term disapproval takes in a large group of meanings ; and there is also another well-defined gamut of change from the slight lowering to an excessive downward position. These gamuts furnish great opportunities for training the mind of the observer ; and the story of success is written in the ability to separate details from masses.

There is no finer education in the world.

Even if it is not to be used in the practice of personal magnetism, it will serve in every department of life as the most practical and useful of genuine accomplishments. The chief power of this study is in the same fact applying to every step of the training ; as aids to the development of magnetism each line of study is important in the highest degree ; and at the same time takes rank as possessing more value in all other departments of life than any other kind of training.

The power to separate the details of the face into their shades of meaning serves in four ways to help the student :

1. It gives him knowledge of what are the purposes, intentions, thoughts and feelings of those with whom he comes in contact ; and this is half the victory in magnetism.

2. It leads close to that subtle power known as telepathy which is a more or less natural gift with the great leaders of the financial, business, professional and social worlds.

3. It is an ever-attendant aid in all other matters that make up the daily activities of life.

4. It gives to the mind the most wholesome, invigorating and stimulating development as a means of preparation for the greatest achievements in the world ; as a result of which the mind grows keener, stronger and far more alert in the exhilarating struggle for supremacy.

These four advantages apply not only to the present phase of this training ; but to all other phases of this system.

By way of review we will note that the mouth has three positions in one line :

Normal or lightly closed or lightly open which is the same in meaning.

Open in a gamut to wide open.

Closed in a gamut to tightly closed.

In another direction we find three other positions :

Level mouth, which is normal.

Raised lips indicating something akin to approval, in a gamut of meanings.

Lowered lips indicating something akin to disapproval, in a gamut of meanings.

Finally we come to combinations as follows :

Mouth level, through gradually wider opening, passing through the meanings of normal, interest, enthusiasm, surprise and astonishment, with intervening shades of meaning all along the way ; and also such indications as are described on a preceding page.

Mouth raised with gradually widening opening, passing

7

through the meanings of normal approval, approved interest, smiling, excited approval, mirth, laughter and finally hilarious enjoyment, with intervening shades of meaning all the way.

Mouth lowered with gradually tightening of the closed lips, passing through the meanings of disapproval, dissatisfaction, discontent, until it reaches the well-known grouch.

Mouth lowered with gradual wider opening, passing through meanings of disapproval plus interest, disapproval plus surprise, and disapproval plus astonishment ; the latter being the well-known expression of horror, and the familiar picture of tragedy ; while its opposite, the combination of astonishment with approval being employed to depict comedy.

It is not our purpose to teach facial expression, nor the painter's art, but to train the eye of our student in the practice of separating details from massed conditions.

The value is not in merely reading faces, but in separating details from masses. The result is a most POWERFUL MAGNETIC EYE.

But we cannot expect any student to jump into the climax of training without passing through the stages that must of necessity precede the end to be attained. For this reason it is important to enter into a line of practice that is of Oriental origin, and that has given to those who have succeeded in it a degree of personal magnetism that is astonishing. In the preceding lesson we briefly referred to this practice. Now that the facial details have been described we will pass into the Oriental practice in the next lessons with a view of preparing the way for returning to this lesson and continuing the work of separating details from masses. The exercises that follow in the next lessons not only develop the power desired, but give the mind a keenness of action that puts it in the foreground of human advantage.

The work now becomes intensely interesting and fascinating.

ORIENTAL SECRETS

CERTAIN HIGH CASTE societies in the Far East conceived the idea that by persistent practice the power of the eye as the source of magnetism could be developed to a degree that made it the weapon greatly to be feared. We are not seeking that end, as we do not think we live in an age when fear should rule mankind. But there are other reasons why the excessive and un-usual power of the human eye should be developed, and these have been fully stated in the two preceding lessons. Behind these reasons there exists still another which has been touched upon in a past lesson and which will be further stated as we proceed; that of the collective generating of the latent magnetism of the body, which can be effected by a number of processes.

The eye has been described by scientists as a small-sized volcano; in most cases latent, quiet, sleeping in its embers, but the centre of the most intensely heated zone, in all Nature, ready to glow when aroused.

What is known as the Oriental Practice is not by any means a new method. It has had uses in other departments, notably in developing a wonderful memory, and in stimulating thought, creating fertility of ideas, building inventive powers and avoiding mental breakdown. None of these purposes will be insisted upon in these lessons, although they will follow natur-ally. The trouble with the minds of unsuccessful people is that they are not alert in a way that wins results. Most of them are sluggish except in pursuit of the needs of the Four Appetites which generally rule mankind. This kind of mental alertness results in placing them under the sway of craftier minds. The field of human activities in other directions is almost unlimited, and in them the powers of mental alertness and keenness are absent.

This explains why most lives are failures.

In the Oriental Practice as it was employed in the Far East, the results hardly warranted the time devoted to it had these people had other lines of usefulness in the world. They were not educated except in religious theories. They were not engaged in anything really worth while in life. Of course this gave them time for their practice ; and led them into methods of concentration that, if their claims were to be believed, gave them knowledge of some of the mysteries of other powers of a superhuman nature. If such claims were in fact true, there was nothing gained by what they acquired.

We are in this world primarily to live the life that is thrust upon us.

No normal human being is a hermit ; hence our duty lies far and wide among mankind. The more people we meet the better it is for us. Interests are interwoven everywhere. Duties involve home and social relations, as well as business, professional and productive activities ; and the practice indulged in by other people who are not so interbound in their duties, does not help us except in the very limited use we make of it.

But any natural and highly beneficial practice that will stimulate the brain into its best uses, and start a new line of habits tending to establish great mental keenness and alertness, will at the same time develop collectively the latent power of magnetism where now it is diffused in the body. Thus the Oriental Practice, kept within such limits, serves a double purpose :

1. It produces, so far as its influence reaches, what is called the Magnetic Eye.

2. It creates collectively a fund of magnetism from the diffused magnetism of the body.

Its direct result in accomplishing these two ends is found in developing the habit as a natural gift of separating details from masses, following the plan set forth in the two preceding lessons ; and based on the two following accepted facts :

1. Persons who do not possess as a natural gift the power of separating details from masses are never mentally magnetic.

2. Persons who do possess this power as a habit, and thereby

as a natural gift, are exceedingly magnetic mentally, and become more so as they put this power into daily and practical use in dealing with other persons.

The method now to be pursued is what is called cumulative.

A process is cumulative, at least in art and particularly in this practice, that begins with the least unit, adds one at a time, and so goes on, always beginning at one. No other plan succeeds in this branch of the training. But few readers will understand what is meant by always beginning with one, or the first unit, or any one unit whether the same is the first or not.

Take a step to an open door leading to an adjoining room ; give one quick glance at the contents of that room ; then withdraw. While out of the range of vision of those contents, mention one article that is in the room. This is the first unit. The same article may or may not be included in the next glance. Go again to the door, look into the room, and withdraw, mentioning two articles in the room. Repeat by taking a third glance, which must be as quickly done as the eye can look. Again repeat by taking a fourth glance, always going out of sight of the room, and name aloud the four articles that are seen in the fraction of a second. Try now to name five articles that are seen at a fifth glance after retiring from the sight of the contents. Then six, and so on until you are not able to add any more.

What is meant by cumulative will now be explained.

After reaching your limit in the number of articles that can be seen in a fraction of a second, rest for any length of time that you may choose. Progress and development take place during periods of rest, but following periods of activity of the mind.

When you feel again an interest in resuming the practice, start with one unit ; not with the number following where you left off. There are two kinds of mistakes that you can make at this stage.

1. The first mistake is to try to see how many articles you can take in at a glance, instead of beginning with one, and adding one at each trial.

2. The second mistake is in not going back over the same ground after taking a rest.

A room in an ordinary house would not contain enough

articles to reach a real test. The mind by the cumulative process will soon be able to include from fifty to one hundred items in less than one second of time. Women train themselves to see in one very brief look everything that another woman has on at Easter time, meaning everything that is visible. In the present style of dress the number of articles is limited compared with those of a generation ago. We once heard a woman witness in court describe an occurrence in which a well-dressed woman participated ; and on being asked to tell what she saw, enumerated twenty-five items worn by the other woman, although she declared that she was passing at the time and did not stop to see all that was happening. She first noted what a well-dressed person of her sex was wearing, and then lost interest in the other matters.

This method of seeing details in mass is of very limited benefit unless it can be made to grow by the cumulative plan.

The Chinese employ the shop-window system, but do not make it cumulative except in the early stages of the training. The plan is to walk along the street past a shop window and to note only one item at first. Then they walk past the window again, and note two items. Then three ; four, etc., and by actual test it was proved that the experimenter, in less than one second of time, could see more than five hundred details and could describe them accurately. Claims have been made that one person reached more than five thousand items. We are willing to stop at a much smaller number ; although what the human brain can be traced to do is unbelievable until known.

The principle involved in the method is all that interests us.

It requires the growing use of the mind as the agent of separating details in the human face, and of reading what is behind those details in the mind ; and for the purpose of highly developing this power, the Oriental Practice is exceptionally valuable.

As personal magnetism is power, first over self, then over all human beings with whom you come in contact, it must follow that the ability to know what is in the mind and purposes of other persons is one of the most valuable and important adjuncts to this power.

GLANCE PRACTICE

U NIVERSITIES HAVE RECENTLY been testing the ability of their students in quick observation. Instead of showing them in what way this acquisition might be developed, they have merely taken them as they found them, and sought to learn how much they had been educated by Nature and past habits of association. It was our good fortune to have studied in the office of a most successful lawyer, a man of national reputation; and we noticed that he was able to read the whole page of a handwritten letter at a glance. He also could read any letter which was upside down, and any printed matter in the same way. Not wishing to intrude by asking questions concerning his personal habits, we refrained from enquiring in what manner he had attained this efficiency; but in later years he gave us the information when he knew we were analysing the methods of successful men. He had trained himself to do these things. They had not come to him naturally. In the midst of a large practice he had found time for this training, and also to memorise many books of the Bible. His memory was so remarkable that he could recall persons by name and circumstances, whom he had met only once and then as far back as twenty years.

The vast majority of people are contented with minds that are developed only far enough to carry on the necessary processes of living and of the chosen vocations of life. But there are vast fields of new adventure.

All these mental acquisitions help each other.

As we have said, we are not teaching memory culture; but if any person desires to acquire a wonderful memory, the

Oriental Practice of the preceding lesson will accomplish this and vastly more.

That practice dealt with the quick use of the eye in separating details from a mass ; and especially in catching every shade of meaning in the face of a person. The present lesson now deals with the catching of a mass of ideas ; but these ideas are really the separate words and thoughts that are expressed on paper. Minds act in several grades of activity. The slow or dull brain gets its ideas very feebly and as the result of effort or waiting. Success is impossible in life under such conditions.

Another brain will grasp a meaning in less time, yet may be very slow and dull. Still another works faster. As soon as we reach the brain that takes in ideas and conditions rapidly, we approach the magnetic power.

Speed may be cultivated, and dull minds converted into alert ones. It is an admitted fact among psychologists and scientists that all human beings, except those who are mentally dwarfed, possess marvellous brain energies that remain more or less dormant through life. Many of these " mind forces " are seen at work in individuals who advance rapidly in the world. The right to accumulate independent wealth belongs to every intelligent being ; but that right is useless in the hands of a man or woman who lacks " Brain Magnetism." Any form of wealth, power, achievement open to you is of little use, if you lack the magnetism to make it yield increased life values.

The test is how much progress a person can make in the following exercises :

1. Take a large sheet of paper, say about 8½ inches wide and 11 inches long. On this sheet print in letters about the size of capitals used on typewriters, about fifteen lines, occupying the whole page. These lines are separated so as not to crowd the vision ; and the words are in letters large enough to be seen readily.

2. Lay this paper on a table, having the printed side facing down. As you approach the table, take the paper in your hand and turn it over, and then turn it back, leaving it there while you sit down at another table and write down as many of the words as you can recall, framing the sentences nearly like those on the sheet that you glanced at as you turned it over. It is best to have the lines that are placed on the paper put there

by some other person so that you may not know what they are. After you have glanced at them during a brief second, and have written down what you saw in that time, you should report to your assistant what you have reproduced. Do so always in writing. The first effort may not be fruitful, depending not so much on the power of your mind as on your experience.

3. Repeat the test in the same manner, and make a separate report in writing of what you have caught by a second glance. This method is to be repeated as on the first occasion until you are wearied. On some other day when you are not mentally tired, repeat it. Do not try to do too much at one time. Keep at it, however, until you can reproduce every idea that is contained in the lines on the paper. That will finish the first stage.

4. After this, have a second piece of paper prepared like the first but with different lines and ideas ; and proceed until you are able to secure at a glance, lasting not more than a second of time, all that is on the paper. Keep a record of the number of efforts which have been required in each stage, and see if you have made progress. Like the game of golf the less times you are compelled to try to reach the end of the course, the more progress you are making. Thus will end the second stage.

5. Now the lines instead of being far apart, making about fifteen to a page, should be placed in the usual distance, making thirty lines on a page. Still the capitals should be employed in this third stage. You will have twice as many lines to see at a glance, and twice as many ideas probably. This stage will take more time and a number more efforts.

6. The fourth and last stage in straight reading at a glance is to be made with thirty lines on a page, and capitals used only when they are ordinarily employed. This means that you are to face the usual kind of typewriting matter. By this time your eyes should have a very keen power, and the lower-case letters should be as easily read as capitals.

7. We come now to reverse reading. This is done by taking a piece of paper of the size stated, and writing in fifteen lines some new matter with which the experimenter is not familiar. This exercise is not glance work, but must follow that. It should not be tried until the four stages are mastered perfectly ; for progress will be very slow until then. In reverse reading, after your assistant has placed the fifteen lines in capitals on the

paper, this is to be left upside down on the table, and turned over when you are seated with the paper placed so that the page itself is upside down. This means that the upper lines are nearest to you but the lower lines are farthest from you, which is the reverse of the usual position. You may take all the time you need, and read aloud every word on the page. This is the fifth stage of this lesson.

8. The next stage consists in placing thirty lines of new matter in capitals on another sheet of paper, upside down as before, and reading it from a reverse position. This is the sixth stage.

9. The next step consists in placing thirty lines in the usual letters including capitals and lower-case letters as in ordinary text, and reading them from a reverse position. This is the seventh stage.

10. Now, instead of using typewritten matter for the lines, cut an advertisement from any newspaper and read it from the reverse position. A very interesting way of doing this is to have your assistant hold the advertisement in the usual way so that he may read it in the proper position, while you are reading it from a reverse position. We have known students to become so adept in this manner of reading that they can repeat aloud every word from a piece of newspaper as freely as if holding it in the usual manner. We have also witnessed races between two persons, each reading at a normal rate of speed, one in the reverse way, and the other in the usual way. This training proves in time to be of the utmost value and highest usefulness.

11. The final stage makes use of handwritten letters, which the expert will be able to read when in the hands of another person who does not suspect that they could be read upside down.

No business man, and especially no financier of large activities nor a lawyer, would wish to make known the fact that they can read letters and documents at a glance when held in the hands of an opponent; but we have seen this done many times; yet if the fact were known these opponents would not only be on guard, but would entertain unpleasant feelings towards those who used such methods. Therefore we are not teaching these things to enable a person to take advantage of others, but to develop in the brain and eye the highest power of magnetism, in order that the expert in these qualities may read humanity as an open book rather than their private papers and letters.

This is a direct source of power.

But sometimes injustice may be prevented by these very methods of catching the ideas that are contained in a letter or document. We were present in a trial where an unprincipled witness held in his possession a paper that contained evidence needed by the other side, but which was being concealed. By chance this witness unfolded the paper and showed it to one of his friends who happened to be in court. The lawyer who represented the plaintiff was able to read any letter or document at a glance ; he saw this paper ; caught its contents ; put the witness in the box, and demanded the reading of the paper. By this means he won a just case, which otherwise he would have lost. We have witnessed many other instances of the usefulness of this accomplishment in securing justice for those who might otherwise have been defenceless.

The eye-power stimulates and fires the brain.

Our main purpose, however, is to train the mind to become keen and alert, and the eye to become powerfully magnetic. When we can do these things by methods that bring other benefits, we feel that the time has been well spent by any student who persists in the practice.

Many enjoyable hours follow.

The benefits are self-evident. That they would be forthcoming is also self-evident. Then another law comes into force that will be fully explained in the next lesson that follows this. It is the law that tells us that an excitant of the eye-power brings to that organ in a collective form a great amount of the diffused magnetism of the body. Here we have one of the most effective methods of building personal magnetism as a natural gift.

What we call exercises soon blend into habits, and from habits come the same natural powers that attend the activities of great men and women.

THE VITAL EYE

WHEN THE FOUR LESSONS that immediately precede this one have been mastered, and not before, the student must put into practice one of the simplest things that could possibly be taught, yet that holds in its little scope the greatest results in any line of training. While it is a simple matter that we now present, it is not the easiest thing to do. No exercises are to be employed; nothing but habits; and these need nothing but attention in order to be fixed and retained permanently. Yet simple as it is, it affects every year of life as long as the person remains on earth. It also affects old age and its unnecessary decrepitude.

Two laws are at work in the face, as reflections of the trend of the mind :

1. When the face drifts into a concentric shape, lack of personal magnetism is not only indicated, but is made so apparent that any person, even a non-expert, may read the fact.

2. When the face drifts away from a concentric shape, the presence of personal magnetism is not only indicated, but the face gradually becomes interesting and attractive to all beholders.

We use the word " drifts " to indicate the tendency of the body to give way to the influence of habits that are both bad and unpleasing. Left to itself it goes wrong at all times.

To use plain language, the face drifts into a concentric shape when its muscles draw towards its centre, not only from the sides, but also from the upper and lower parts. All concentric tendencies of the face denote kinship with the lower forms of creation ; with the beast and the brute. The forehead seeks, apparently, to come down as if to meet the chin ; and the chin seems to rise to meet the forehead. But the most noticeable drifting is that of the sides of the face towards the central line. By this action one, two or three lines form just above the nose between the eyebrows, and we say that the brow is knitted.

When the scalp moves forward towards the eyes, and the eyebrows move upward towards the scalp, the result is a corrugated forehead, in which several lines almost parallel appear. These lines denote some form of weakness, either mental or emotional. Worry gradually raises the eyebrows, and in proportion as they rise the mental condition of worry increases. People who go about constantly with raised brows carry with them the sign of giving way to adverse control of some kind, which is the opposite of magnetism. Likewise the lowering of the scalp indicates some form of trouble.

This part of the face is strongest when the eyebrows are as low as possible without the concentrating of the face between them known as the knitted brows. The combination can be cultivated by care. Often it is the result of weather exposure, and of light shining in the face ; and still more often of a peevish and fretful disposition in which the face is screwed out of shape to suit the character of the moods. These are evidences of weakness.

The scalp has certain muscles by which it can be moved if a person is able once to find them and to start them moving. The temples also have muscles by which they can be moved. These different muscles are constantly employed by persons who knit the brows, and by others who wrinkle the forehead. In both movements, the action is involuntary, but not naturally so. It is made so thoughtlessly.

One of the stimulating exercises is that which knits the brows, bringing them together at the top of the nose, and then unknits them. If you can knit them, you can as readily unknit them. The way of doing this is by the rebound of the muscle. Stand or sit before a mirror for the practice. Knit the brows, and watch them form the vertical lines above the nose ; but instantly unknit them by reversing the direction of the temple muscles. Everybody can do this at the first trial.

The next step is to extend the rebound at every effort. This is done by knitting the brows ; then unknit them in the rebound, making the effort slightly more decisive on each reverse action. Keep on doing this in one or more sessions daily until you can unknit the muscles by a pulling action that stretches the part of the face above the nose into a smoothness that contains no evidence of the vertical lines. Of course this result is not to be reached in a very short time. No matter if it takes weeks or months to be accomplished, its value is so great that it is worth all the time and effort devoted to it.

But very soon the phase called practice will have passed, and the better phase known as habit will be entered upon.

As soon as you are able at will to unknit the brows until the space between them above the nose is perfectly smooth, then adopt this action as a habit following all through the waking hours. Put it into action the first thing in the morning before you rise from bed ; carry it as a companion all day long ; and when falling asleep at night, hold the temple muscles tightly drawn away from the eyes. In this way the concentric tendency is soon destroyed.

The vertical lines between the eyes above the nose may be so deeply indented that they cannot be smoothed out. In this case, massage must accompany the unknitting of the brows ; as the temple muscles pull back from the eyes, rub a cold cream, or better still some cocoa butter against the deep indentations, pressing and rubbing by turns as if trying to iron them out. This massage rubbing is best done in eight directions; right, left, up, down, up diagonally to the right, then to the left, down diagonally to the right and finally to the left. We have seen many cases of very deep indentations completely rubbed out, and that part of the face become smooth and take on the appearance of youth, as if many years had suddenly dropped from the person. In one class, more than two hundred students of more than middle age accomplished this result in a few months ; and several thousand in a single year did so without one failure in their number.

But massage alone will not do the work. In the first place it will not pull the temple muscles back to the positions of youth. Then it will lack the essential benefits of stimulating the eyes themselves.

The crow's-feet or thin lines at the corner of the eyes close to the temples are also eliminated. Thus we get rid of three sets of old-age wrinkles ; the forehead lines, the knitted brows, and the crow's-feet ; all of which accompany old age. Many women make long and painstaking efforts to get rid of these wrinkles by massage and by manipulation in the beauty parlour ; but they never succeed in removing the actual positions of the muscles that attend old age. The old-age positions still remain, and all that massage accomplishes is to cover them over, not eradicate them.

The habit that we teach is the actual condition of YOUTH. We set the clock back twenty to forty years.

Massage is beneficial, but rarely necessary after the face has once been smoothed out by controlling the muscles. Let us see if we can make this clear. In youth the forehead muscles are rarely ever concentric ; if so, they are abnormal and unusual, indicating a morbid mind or nervous system. In youth the temple muscles are never concentric when conditions are normal. In youth the side-muscles at the outer edge of each eye do not close up, as they appear to do later in life.

It is an old law of human nature that conditions that are natural in youth invite the mental and nervous conditions of youth, if they can be resumed. As the normal positions of these three sets of muscles are natural to youth, the reinstating of them invites the mental and nervous conditions of youth. Massage never does this. The plastering on of cream and the creating of a coating of a temporary character on the cuticle itself does not restore a single position of the facial muscles, and does not invite any of the spirit of youth into the countenance. A pupil who has graduated from the beauty-parlour treatment shows an unnatural face, because all the fine lines and delicate lineaments have been obliterated.

There are still other reasons why the muscles must be made to do their own work and to get the face back to the condition of actual youth.

The most recent science tells us that the countless billions of atoms of which the body is composed are charged, each and every one of them, with inherent or native magnetism, the presence of which is necessary to hold together their electrons, and to maintain a sort of solar system in which a central orb exerts an influence over its satellites, and the latter in turn by the magnetism of a force akin to that known as centripetal, keep their distance from the ruling orb. Also we are told that each atom holds a mighty pent-up power that, if let loose, would destroy matter vastly greater than its size. All these engines of force and energy are coming into the body in countless billions daily, serving their mission of making and maintaining life, and passing out to join the great fund from which they were drawn.

All this magnetism is known as diffused power.

It is scattered throughout the body.

This is recognized by all scientists as the basis of a higher use than that which has yet been drawn from it. In order to understand how this higher use may come about, let us review the manner in which the vegetable cell that holds the germ of intelligence is made by Nature to collect these scattered forms of intelligence into a collective mass, which is called the brain, and by which the animal is created from the plant.

In the same way the diffused or scattered presence of magnetism in the countless atoms of the body is drawn collectively into ganglia, or nerve centres, and into the brain or greatest of all nerve centres. When the process of collecting this magnetism is carried forward to greater results, there is present in the body a much more active fund of magnetism. When the collective fund known as brain-power is united with the increased fund of magnetism, the result is personal magnetism.

Any action that will excite the generation of magnetism will increase the stored up fund of this power. Any faculty that is favoured by an exciting cause in this line will be greatly intensified. The human eye is located in the midst of vast funds of magnetism, small as things are considered, but great when related to the uses of the eye. The stimulating of the blood-flow in the direction of the eye will bring countless billions of new atoms to that organ, all of which will contribute their magnetism to it, and so establish the magnetic power of the eye.

The furrowed brow is not attractive and is not necessary.

The knitted brow is not attractive and is not necessary.

THE POWERFUL EYE

SINCE IT IS ACKNOWLEDGED that the methods
of magnetic communication between human beings
are limited to the senses in open expression of influence,
and since the eye is the agent of the most generally used
sense next to that of the sound of the voice, we are giving
the most thorough instruction possible in the development of
the powers of this organ. But, as has
been said in the preceding lesson,
every step in the training has brought
many other benefits than those called
magnetic. The present lesson will
be shown to be the most important example of this fact.

Except where disease or some form of poison has reached
the eyes and produced injury, the loss of perfect sight is always
traceable to a sameness of muscular use, or unvaried activity
of sight.

The routine use of any faculty puts it in a rut, and tends to
make it grow stale. The same uses day after day of the eye
bring about defective sight, and weaken its organic vigour.
Speaking in a general way, the eyeball is nearly round. It is
movable. There are muscles that enable it to move in many
directions ; but they are not the same muscles in every action,
nor are the same muscles always employed in the same kind of
movement, if all their possible motions are used. Thus there
are muscles that enable the eyeball to be pulled to the right ;
others to be pulled to the left ; others to be pulled upward ;
others to be pulled downward ; and also in oblique and diagonal
directions. In a preceding lesson we referred to the meanings of
the positions of the eyelids as helps to a magnetic person in
reading the purposes and intentions of others, and getting close
to the contents of their minds.

In this lesson we seek to develop the studying power of the observing eye, and to enable it to read the plans and purposes of others with greater ease and effectiveness.

In order to do this we propose to draw more blood, more nutrition, and more magnetic energy to the eye itself, by the stimulating action of the muscles that we have described on the preceding page. We start on the basic law that the same kind of routine activity especially of the eyes, will cause them to weaken, to lose their focus, and to flatten. When the eyeball begins to flatten, then we need glasses. When the sight weakens from the constant repetition of one kind of muscular action, the sight grows dim. Here are two distinct results. Dimness of vision is due to the weakness of the eye-power. Loss of focus is due to flattening of the eyeball. The vision is getting worse all the time, just as it would if you were to use glasses that were fitted to your needs, and the lenses were to be changed for those that were flat.

One kind of use of the muscles that move the eyeballs tends to flatten them. This refers to movements of action. But one kind of use of the eyes in reading, or in looking at objects, weakens the eye-power. This fact has been verified in the past five years, and even given prominent attention by specialists of a high order of experimentation, with results that we are to include herein as means not only to strengthen the eye but to add to its magnetic quality for reading the meanings in the faces and minds of other persons. Let us see what they are.

There are nine eye-directions, and these are brought about by the varying action of the muscles. In these activities we overcome the tendency of the eyes to flatten. In fact we have in more than eleven thousand cases overcome flattened eyeballs by these nine movements. We will repeat the causes of eye-flattening again, in order to drive home the importance of this part of the training :

The same routine use of the eyes, which we have called one kind of use of the muscles that move them, leads to flattening and the loss of focus, necessitating glasses to furnish the rotundity that flattening has destroyed. But if the nine muscle-actions are employed either as exercises or as habits, which latter method is feasible in daily life, the eyeballs will be pulled out of their flattened condition ; for the pulling of the muscles in one direction overcomes a part of the flattening, and the pulling of opposite muscles will overcome another part, and so on, making the circuit of movements. But if one direction only is employed in this pulling, the eyeball will be given a bad shape and thereby rendered weak.

Muscles that surround a flexible ball, if all are in turn pulling on the ball, will give it the required or natural shape, exactly the form that Nature intended for it, and gave it at birth. The fact that it is flexible leads to its being flattened by one line of activity in its muscles. It is the all-round activity, exerting its power on every portion of the eyeball, that gives it the natural shape it had during youth.

This part of the instruction has appeared in all the late editions of this book ; and, as we have said, our records show more than eleven thousand cases where flattened eyeballs have had their rotundity restored by the use of the circuit movement which we will present in this lesson. This relates solely to the flattened condition and its cure. / But the other phase of our instruction, relating to one kind of use of the eyes in reading is another thing, and the science and practice that will appear in the next lesson are just being given attention in order to avoid the unnecessary use of glasses.

We trust that you will keep this distinction in mind.

Then also remember that there is a difference between the nine eye-movements, and the nine eye-positions, which we will discuss later.

The nine eye-movements are employed to overcome the flattened condition of the eyeballs, and to restore their natural rotundity. These results take time, but are worth a thousand times more than the cost of this entire study, even if there is no intention of developing eye-magnetism by them.

While there may be many other finer directions of eye-movements than the nine we now present, this number is sufficient for the purpose for which they are prepared. We will describe them as follows :

1. Look straight ahead, neither to the right or left, nor up or down. This is the Number One position. You can stand or sit ; but it is better to be at one side of the room so that you have the whole of the opposite wall facing you. In this case, ascertain what part of that wall, or what object on it, exactly

meets the direction of the eye when you are looking straight ahead, and at something that is in a position level with the height of your eye. We use the word eye as generative, meaning gaze.

2. The second position is on a level with the first, but refers to an object on your left as far toward the corner of the wall as you can look without moving your head. If you move the head at all, the eye loses a part of its range.

3. The third position is on a level with the first, but refers to an object on your right as far toward the corner of the wall as you can look without moving your head. Make the eyes do the whole work.

4. The fourth position is down to the floor directly in front of you and is under the first position. Drop the gaze as low as you can in a vertical direction without lowering the head.

5. The fifth position is down to the floor as far to the left as you can move the gaze, and as low down at the same time.

6. The sixth position is down to the floor as far to the right as you can move the gaze, and as low down at the same time.

7. The seventh position is up to the ceiling directly in front over the first position, as far upward as you can move the gaze without moving the head.

8. The eighth position is up to the ceiling as far to the left as you can move the gaze and keep the head still.

9. The ninth position is up to the ceiling as far to the right as you can move the gaze and keep the head still.

CAUTION.—The first time you try these movements do them only once or twice. Every athlete knows that muscles that have not been used, or if used that have not been given certain kinds of action, will become sore from the strain, no matter how slight it may be. This soreness will lead to a lameness that will be painful. Remember that in the training camps, the managers of athletes insist that they start slowly in order to spare their muscles from pain. In the eye-movements the first few trials should be very limited. After a while, as the atcion is repeated, all danger of soreness will pass.

These are not eye-positions.

The latter will have their usefulness. But for the purposes of this lesson, the muscles must be made to pull the eyeball in all possible directions, in order to bring back its shape in the degree of rotundity intended by Nature.

Movements should be made by opposites.

Thus, beginning at the first position, move to the second, then to the first, then to the second, then to the first, each ten times.

Then move from the first to the third, then to the first, then to the third, each ten times.

Next move from the second to the third, then from the third to the second, each ten times. These constitute the level movements.

Begin now at the fourth position and move to the fifth, then to the fourth, each ten times.

Then from the fourth to the sixth, and from the sixth to the fourth, each ten times.

Then from the fifth to the sixth, and from the sixth to the fifth, each ten times. These complete the lower movements.

Now move from the seventh position to the eighth, and from the eighth to the seventh, each ten times.

Next move from the seventh position to the ninth, and from the ninth to the seventh, each ten times.

Now move from the eighth position to the ninth, and from the ninth to the eighth, each ten times. These complete the upper movements.

It will be noticed that all the foregoing movements are right and left. There are nine others that are up and down as follows.

Begin at the first position, raise the eyes to the seventh, and back to the first, each ten times.

Begin at the first position, move the gaze to the fourth which is directly under it, and back to the first, each ten times.

Begin at the fourth position, raise the gaze to the seventh, and back to the fourth, each ten times. These complete the middle up and down movements.

Begin at the second position, raise the gaze to the eighth, and back to the second, each ten times.

Begin at the second position, lower the gaze to the fifth, and raise it to the second, each ten times.

Begin at the fifth position, raise the gaze to the eighth, lower it to the fifth, each ten times. These complete the left up and down movements.

Begin at the third position, raise the gaze to the ninth, and go back to the third, each ten times.

Begin at the third position, drop the gaze to the sixth, back to the third, and do each ten times.

Begin with the sixth position, raise the gaze to the ninth, go back to the sixth, and do each ten times. These complete the right up and down movements.

We now come to the diagonals, which are the most effective in pulling the eyeball back into its normal rotundity.

Begin at the fifth position, raise the gaze up to the right to the ninth position, then back to the fifth, and do each twenty times ; but do not start any of these until the preceding movements have all been done a sufficient number of times to harden the muscles.

Begin at the sixth position, raise the gaze up to the left to the eighth position, then back to the sixth, and repeat each twenty times, observing the caution just given.

Make your own chart of positions by numbers, which is very easy to do, and place it in front of you for reference. If you do not care to make the chart, then write the following numbers each about two inches apart on a piece of paper :

On the upper row	8	7	9
On the middle row	2	1	3
On the lower row	5	4	6

These numbers placed before the eye will serve in the place of a chart.

After you once learn these movements they can be made at any time and almost anywhere, in the dark as well as in the light. The whole idea is to stretch the eye-muscles, meaning those that control the pulling about of the eyeball, in a series of opposite directions. It may require some time to overcome the flattened condition of the eyeballs, but persistent practice will bring surprising changes and restore the natural shape.

If the necessity for wearing glasses is due, as is commonly the case, to the loss of shape in the eyes, these movements will in time enable the person so afflicted to lay aside the glasses permanently. To encourage our students to engage in this practice, we include in this lesson some statements taken from

of magnetic units, all of which bring to the eye a very great increase of power.

This result is quickly observed.

In this lesson we deal with the eyeball itself as an organ equipped with constructive muscles that are endowed with the ability to change the focus by changing the shape of the ball within itself, as distinguished from the action of the outer muscles that pull it in all directions in order to restore its lost form.

Thus we have three groups of influences working to make the eye a much greater organ in every way.

The present lesson may be omitted if it is too uninteresting, for the development of magnetism does not depend on this practice. It merely is one of the causes that help materially. It does a very useful work in restoring the eye-power of youth and thereby enabling one to dispense with the wearing of glasses.

It also brings a new fire and brilliancy into the eyes, which quickly attracts attention from other persons.

A partial use of this practice, while not doing away with the wearing of glasses, will assuredly save a person from continually increasing the magnifying power of lenses as age comes on. In fact it will avert any further ageing of the vision ; and by partial practice alone.

A successful eye-specialist recommends the practice daily of reading coarse type, and instantly changing to fine type, then back to coarse, and so alternate many times at each session of exercising the eyes. While no results may be noticed for some days or even for a few weeks, in time the eye will become much stronger, and its power and keenness will have increased many-fold.

A climacteric step may be taken now by adopting the tense action of the eye in conjunction with the tense use of the voice. At just this stage will the eye become fired with great fervour, keenness and magnetic life.

Your friends will notice a remarkable change in you.

LESSON TWENTY-ONE

THE FIRE OF THE EYE

AS A FITTING CLIMAX to this interesting and valuable
series of lessons on the power of the eye as an agent
of magnetism, we come to the union of the voice
with the action of the organ of vision. In other words,
the two may at times work together in the uses of the
newly acquired power. What is meant by intensity or fire of
any part of the body is that there is sum-
moned by the act of the will the accumulated fund of mag- netism, and by some
method of use it is given outward mani-
festation. Thus the eye itself may be
fixed upon a person while the whole body is fired with intense
feeling which may be assumed at will, and the eye will
glow by reason of it. Some persons call this glow a phosphor-
escence of the nervous system ; others believe it to be electricity.
It is neither. It is magnetism, which is not electricity nor
phosphorus. We shall prove later that it is pure magnetism.

The facts that are presented in this lesson have been accumu-
lating through many years, although based on experiments
made nearly half a century ago and put to the test in many
ways since, and thus amply proved.

The results have been pleasing and convincing, while highly
beneficial to all concerned.

This glow that flows from the eyes may be increased at will
to almost any condition, after a little practice ; provided all
the foregoing exercises in this section of the book have been
given due attention. It is not possible to jump forward in any
progressive course, and attain results. Each lesson paves the
way for its successor.

In experimenting in a darkened room with this glow of the

eye, we have witnessed lines of fire proceeding far into the room when the eye has been made tense by the will-power.

This glow is never seen in a lighted place for the reason that it is not bright enough ; hence we do not regard it as electric. But the eye itself may be made not only bright, but actually brilliant if the use of it is accompanied by some words that have meaning akin to the position taken by the eye. Most persons who are magnetic show nothing of the kind when they are in a state of normal mental action ; but let them become interested in the achievement of some purpose, and the whole eye-formation changes ; the upper face is different ; and power stands expressed in every lineament.

We therefore refer to the magnetic eye as that organ in a state of action or seeking some purpose. In repose we do not call it the magnetic eye. But these are mere terms that have no real bearing on the power itself.

Any faculty may be made tense by concentrating on it the energy of the mind. Thoughts themselves become fire at times. Feelings are aflame either by design or under great stress. Control them, harness them, drive them, guide them and compel them to do your bidding.

The magnetic eye is always tense.

There is here opportunity for a volume on a single subject. The eye sees and is seen. The sense it embodies is the most important of all. A deaf person can compel the eye to perform some of the functions of hearing, just as a blind person uses the sense of touch with greater delicacy and power. When a person speaks to another the latter gets some of the meaning from the eye. It is not only natural but common to look into the eye to see the individual. All persons in an audience look at the speaker's eye whenever he interests them ; in dull moments only they are attracted to some other part of the body, some peculiarity, or some matter that distracts attention.

The magnetic person generally holds attention by the power of the eye when there is a direct effort made towards one or more others ; but the latter will have no consciousness of such influence. The tensing of the eye comes out of the same power as the touch or voice when either is magnetic. All energy is vibrant. The muscles are controlled by waves of force ; sound is likewise propelled ; so is light ; so is thought ; and magnetism moves by a similar law. Each has its origin, its source of supply, and its method of transfer ; and, above all, each has its kind of pulsation. We never mistake light for sound. When science shall have laid bare the secrets of life it will be known what the difference is between all these energies.

The use of the tense eye changes every part of the face by some strange law of our natures. It also invites a glow into the eye itself that even the photograph will record. This special brightness is due to the electrical energy which is aroused by the tensed condition. This does not arise in the eyeball, but has its origin in the brain, which is the most powerful electric battery of its size in existence ; so that the tensing of the latter organ is the real cause of it. We have for years used a plan of shifting locations which we find to be the best method of tensing the brain and eye. We present this arrangement here in a different light from any elsewhere given. We take the nine locations of the eyes from a former plan, as follows :

8	7	9
up left.	up front.	up right.
2	1	3
level left.	straight ahead.	level right.
5	4	6
down left.	down front.	down right.

The first practice is to look (1) at some imaginary person whose eyes are directly in front of you and on a level with your eyes, adopting a dead-still body all through, but holding the eyes two seconds only in fixed gaze.

From one (1) change to two (2), which means to move the gaze to the left lateral, but do not wink or move a muscle of the face. Hold the gaze at two (2) for the same space of time, two seconds.

Then come back to one (1) and hold the gaze for two seconds.

From one (1) change to three (3), and hold the gaze dead-still for two seconds. So continue through all positions.

While holding the eyes in the positions indicated by the numbers, repeat the following remarks with their full meaning stamped in your tones :

When the eyes are at one (1) repeat : " *I am talking to you and you must hear me.*" Let the voice be low clear and firm, even severe.

When the eyes are at two (2) repeat : " *You cannot escape me.*" The words should be spoken in deep tones as though some person were planning to get beyond your influence. Remember that the face is to remain to the front and no part must move except the eyes themselves.

When the eyes are at three (3) repeat : " *Beware ! Do not make me angry.*"

When the eyes are at four (4) repeat : " *I will not do wrong.*"

When the eyes are at five (5) repeat : " *Get thee behind me, Satan.*"

When the eyes are at six (6) repeat : " *I am stronger than my enemies.*"

When the eyes are at seven (7) repeat : " *Thou God seest me.*"

When the eyes are at eight (8) repeat : " *Right is mighty and will prevail.*"

When the eyes are at nine (9) repeat : " *Angels hold watch and ward over my life.*"

The first few repetitions may be mental, continuing them until the spirit of the sentiment in connection with the positions shall be absorbed, after which it is better to use the voice aloud. Get familiar with the locations as belonging to the sentiments uttered.

In repeating them aloud, speak the sentiment once ; then come back to the central position one (1).

After five days' practice in the above lines, repeat each sentiment five times aloud while holding the eyes fixed in whatever position they take, and go through them all.

After five more days in the last-named practice, repeat each sentiment ten times in the position to which it belongs.

The success in tensing the eyes will depend upon the tone-colour in your voice. An actor could easily accomplish this end at once. You may have to keep at it for weeks, but the power will come sooner or later, and, once come, it always remains.

MAGNETIC EYE OF YOUTH

MORE MAGNETISM is constantly being generated in a young person than in one who is mature or aged ; but vastly more is being lost by excessive waste. For the latter reason we do not think of youth as magnetic. If, however, we can retain the power that the young person develops daily, and turn it to use, we can quickly make ourselves felt in human affairs. But as youth is not able to hold its magnetism, all that we can learn of its abundant fund of vital energy is how it comes about and how to conserve it. On this theory we will take youth as an age and condition of excessive energy, and omit its excessive waste, as applied to the conditions of those who have reached more mature years.

The vitality of youth has often been mistaken for magnetism, but health, vigour and physical power seem to intrude themselves in the place of magnetism and to hold it in check. These qualities are never magnetic.

In a preceding lesson in this Department we have discussed the action of smoothing the forehead, and the sides of the eyes and face, and making this condition a permanent habit. There is a law that is old and yet new. It says : "*Restoring a youth condition will restore the condition of youth.*"

It does not seem to mean much as it is worded. But the term *condition* has two significations. The first is the physical change that is wrought in the body, as where the facial muscles are made to assume the same smoothness as is present in a young person. This is the restoring of the physical condition that was evident in former years in the face. The return of such shape as prevailed at an earlier stage in life, acts upon the mental and psychological nature of the person in such a way as to stimulate the feeling and characteristics of youth. The law is an old one, and has been proved in a number of ways.

If we can bring back the vitality of youth we can bring back the excessive abundance of magnetism that attends youth. Then, instead of allowing it to run to waste, we need only conserve it in order to make it useful.

This facial change has been so thoroughly taught in the lessons of this Department of the Magnetic Eye that we shall not deal further with it.

There are several other influences or conditions that belong to youth that may be restored by very little attention, if only they are known. The next most important is the exciting cause of vigorous blood circulation that exists in the medulla oblongata. As words of this character are not readily understood by the average reader, we will call this little master of life by the name of the Third Brain. It is the upper part of the spinal column. The first brain does much of the voluntary thinking ; the second brain attends to the involuntary life of the body and the muscular system, sometimes obeying the mandates of the first brain.

But life must go on when there is no thinking and no muscular activity ; for the human body must breathe, must carry on the circulation of the blood, and must proceed with digestion, whether of the contents of the stomach or of the intestines. Breathing is always taking place. The blood is always circulating. Digestion never ceases unless the entire alimentary canal is empty, which is very rare. More than half the nutrition that comes from food is derived from the process of intestinal digestion. Patients are often fed by injections at the colon.

This Third Brain attends to all these functions :

> Digestion.
> Circulation.
> Respiration.

We are not intending to teach increased breathing. That is taught in many forms and for many health purposes ; and our students should by this time have established a greater range of respiration. But we are going to show that the influence of the Third Brain, which alone maintains natural respiration, can be employed to vitalize all breathing which mere practice in the exercises will never do. It is not more air that the lungs need, if they are receiving a full supply ; it is vital air that brings new life and with it the magnetism that the body requires.

By reaching this Third Brain with any instrument that interferes with its work as controller of respiration, digestion and circulation, it is possible to immediately stop the heart from beating ; or to stop all digestion ; or to paralyse the lung-action. This has been done, and can be done as often as the Third Brain is interfered with./ In the thinking brain, the pressure on a certain part of the skull, forcing it into the convolutions of that organ, may deprive the person of the power of memory ; or may cause loss of speech ; or do other injury, depending on what part of the brain the injury falls./ So injury or shock of a severe kind that reaches the Second Brain may paralyse the arm, or the leg, or side. Sometimes temporary paralysis is due to a pressure that, if relieved, will cause the return of the normal condition.

Not only does the Third Brain absolutely and completely control respiration, but it controls also circulation and digestion. As we have stated, digestion occurs not only in the stomach, but in the entire canal, including its adjacent parts, and the intricate arrangement of aids that are found near to the stomach itself. Diabetes is caused by interference of a chronic kind with this out-of-the-stomach digestion ; whether by the extreme irritation of too much sugar, starch or other carbon form of food, or by a blow on the back of the neck which has permanently injured the Third Brain which is located there. In fact there are thousands of cases of diabetes arising every decade from blows on the neck, which are cured only by curing the injury at the Third Brain. Worry, which is a mental trouble that depresses all three brains, has caused many cases of diabetes.

Injury to this small Third Brain arising from accident will interfere with one of the three functions. If respiration suffers, then quick tuberculosis takes the victim away. If circulation suffers, then anæmia follows. If digestion suffers, it is generally in the intestinal canal as stated.

We have gone thoroughly into the study of the functions depending on this Third Brain in order to impress on the student its importance in the plan of life. We shall now apply it to the development of magnetism. It does not require an astute mind to see that the involuntary functions of digestion, respiration and circulation are in reality the WHOLE LIFE of the human body ; and that this very small section at the back of the neck that ends that part of the spinal column, plays the greatest part in not only sustaining life but in generating its vital powers, and especially in bringing into activity as well as existence all its magnetism.

But what is to be done about it ?

It is there well encased in bone, and may not be reached except by some fine pointed instrument, or by a blow, or by a strain ; rarely by a fracture, in which case the chances of survival are too small to be considered.

But the entire spinal column, endowed as it is with the controlling power over various parts of the body, which acts as aids to the Third Brain, is composed of small sections, making an electric pile from the base of the torso to the head, charged and supercharged with constantly forming magnetism, and these small sections of bone are tied together with nerves and muscles, and between them are small pads of flexible material ; the whole structure being capable of being bent to the right, to the left, to the back, to the front, and in a vertical direction.

When we bend the body to the right, this column is flexible enough to shape itself into a curve ; and when we bend to the left, the curve is changed to the opposite direction. When we bend back there is a new curve ; and when we bend forward this is reversed.

The boy or girl who is normal is as straight as it is possible to be ; but with reading and leaning over a book or paper, the forward curve begins to show, and the body seems to be bent at the shoulders, until later in life this stooping and the craning of the neck tell the story of advancing age. Yet all persons in the fifties, with few exceptions, are bent at the upper back ; some are bent when much younger ; but no person who is above the age of thirty is free from some shrinking of the spinal column.

The small bones that form the spinal column are cushioned, and so separated from each other. This cushioning and the complex interweaving of nerves and muscles are much more marked at the Third Brain, and the flexibility much more pronounced.

If you will make a mental picture of your torso, which is the part of the body between the neck and the legs, and if you will find mentally the average central line of the torso, you will soon understand what is to follow. Imagine that there is a centre to the neck at its base or where it joins the trunk or torso. Imagine that there is another centre at the lower part of the torso, which centre would be in the middle position between the right and left hips and the front and back. Now imagine that a vertical line runs from one centre to the other ; that it is not only perfectly straight but that it is plumb, or at right-angles with the floor, or parallel with the side wall of the room.

This is the carriage of the torso at all times, if you wish the vitality of youth.

Now we must find two more centres. One is the same as our first, which was at the base of the neck, bringing it in the throat back of the larynx or Adam's apple. The other centre is at the top of the head midway between the front and back and between the two sides. These centres must unite so that a line running between them would be vertical.

Now unite the two vertical lines.

This will make the imaginary line that runs from the centre of the lower part of the torso extend to the centre of the top of the head.

Every curve in the spine, shoulders or neck interferes with the flow of blood and the flow of the nerve vitality or magnetism, through those important controlling agencies of life. You may press against your arm and stop the flow of blood. But you may also press against a nerve in the arm, and put the lower part to sleep. By sitting in a certain position in a chair, as where the front edge of the chair presses against the nerves in the leg, you may put your foot to sleep, and may invite cramp in the legs.

All curves more or less cause similar dangers.

The flow of blood carries new magnetism-forming cells.

The flow of the nerve currents carries the actual life of the body which includes all its magnetism.

Any curvature of any part of the body that interferes with these flows lessens the energy and vitality of the currents so impeded ; as a curvature is more or less a shutting off of the avenues of travel. But the settling down of the bones that form the structure of the spine, and especially of the section known as the Third Brain, will likewise check the flow of magnetic vitality to the functional centres of the body ; such as those of respiration, digestion and circulation.

We have seen several pernicious cases of constipation immediately cured by skilful manipulation of the top section of the spine or Third Brain. There are two great curative professions that employ such methods.

We have seen severe cases of stomach indigestion cured by skilful manipulation of the same top section of the spine.

But some few years ago a very widely known specialist in blood circulation and heart maladies made the assertion that the circulation of the blood was controlled by this top section of the spine to the extent that when sluggish circulation resulted in cold extremities, as of the feet and hands, he could overcome this trouble by stretching the muscles of the neck in such a way as to pull upon the Medulla or Third Brain ; explaining the process by saying : " It requires but slight adjustment of the upper spine to send a very powerful influence to the heart, thereby vitalizing its action and propelling a much more vigorous flow of blood to the feet and hands. This adjustment is made not by another person but by the manner in which the head is lifted. A distance so slight as to be almost unmeasurable will effect such results as we have witnessed."

The manner in which the head is lifted is the key to this process.

Old age brings all kinds of curves to the spine, neck and shoulders. Youth is straight. Age is bent. Some people curve their backs so much when they get old that they must support themselves with canes when they walk, to prevent falling over.

But standing straight is not enough.

The centres that we have described must be kept in mind, and the vertical line must be kept perfectly plumb from the centre of the top of the head to the centre between the hips. · This is the preparation only. But let it be made into a habit, so that whether you are sitting or standing, the centres are maintained in a perfectly plumb line. It is a good habit. Magnetism students, whether they are twenty or a hundred years old, will never forget this vertical line. They will never grow old to the beholder ; nor in their own feelings.

Having learned to acquire the vertical line position, keeping the centre of the head always over the centre of the chest, and never craning the neck, the next thing is the important one ; that of pulling the top section of the spine, the Third Brain, into a stretched position. The manner in which this was done, as explained by the doctor, was to imagine that you could bring the top of the head slightly nearer the ceiling above by raising the head so as to stretch the neck. The new habit then is to keep the centres vertical and to carry the head so that its top seems to be trying to get nearer to the ceiling, thereby stretching the neck muscles, the nerves, and the medulla that controls circulation, as well as other functions.

If you were to be told that stretching the upper spine would stimulate the heart, vitalize its action, and send warming blood to the hands and feet, thereby overcoming their cold feeling, you would not see in what way this action would bring so decided a result. For this reason we have explained it in detail.

But the fact that concerns us is that it is done, and has been done to our knowledge hundreds of times. All that is necessary is to make the neck respond to the effort at stretching.

We are not teaching any exercises in this lesson.

The things we are setting forth are intended as habits.

An exercise takes time.

A habit takes no time at all. You can do things right just as quickly as do them wrong.

If the Third Brain controls the circulation of the blood and gives to its flow a new vitality both of magnetism and of material that bears magnetism in its course, it must follow that it will, in thus restoring the conditions of youth, bring back the excessive power of youthful magnetism.

Like all habits that are taught in this lesson, it is a good one in its influence on the individual in every department of life.

Another habit that belongs to youth and that is lost about the time the man or woman is old enough to vote, is that of avoiding the exhaustion that comes from straining the spinal column, or irritating it. This habit is inborn, but quickly loses itself in the mass of bad methods that attach themselves to the coming adult age. It is that of keeping the strain away from the spine by not using the heels for receiving the weight of the body in walking. No one thinks of doing so when running.

When the act of taking a step is performed by bringing the

weight down on the heel, a blow is struck to the spine that irritates it, and tends to exhaust its magnetism and the vitality of the general body. But it is not only this blow that is harmful ; there is a decided strain put upon the spine that is also irritating and exhausting ; both of which influences quickly sap the system of its stored up magnetism.

· In taking a step, keep the centre of gravity of the torso well forward without bending and without losing the vertical line that we have just taught. This will put the weight of the whole body on the ball of the foot, even if the heel touches the floor first in taking such a step.   When walking in bare feet, the ball, of each foot should touch the ground first, but in wearing shoes with heels, the heel may touch first without any weight going on it, or not more weight than enough to merely support it. Wearing heels that are more than an inch thick, or high, to use a misnomer, detracts from the power of generating magnetism in walking.

This is not an exercise ; it is a habit. It may not be easily adopted at first, but soon you will enjoy it, for it not only does away with the irritation and exhaustion of heel-walking, but on the other hand it stores up considerable magnetism. We know of many cases where men and women could not walk half a mile without becoming tired, who now can walk six miles and feel refreshed in so doing.

Thus far we have found three new habits that, while they generate magnetism, also bring new conditions to the body and improve it vastly.

Another habit that has been much written about must be considered in this training. It is the collapse of the neck and of the vital muscles. When the neck muscles weaken, the head is carried forward. This is a position of age, of feebleness of mind and body, and of exhaustion of magnetism. When the vital muscles weaken, the chest falls in, the heart sags, the stomach drops, and the intestines are lowered.

In women this collapse of the vital muscles brings on prolapsus, which is a never-ceasing enemy of magnetism. It can, however, be cured by vitalizing the vital muscles. This is done not by exercises, but by habits. We have promised not to give any exercises in this lesson, and we are keeping our word. Exercises take time. Habits require no time at all ; for they are merely ways of living. The process by which the collapse of the vital muscles is cured by new habits is as follows :

First, ascertain if your chest falls down when you are sitting. If it does, raise it as high as you can without raising the shoulders, for they must never rise, never be thrown back, never come forward. Keep them in a central position, force them down and raise the chest as high as you can. Then hold it there. Hold it there when you are eating, when you are reading, when you are writing, when you are walking, when you are in train or car, and always everywhere.

In the above manner you can overcome the first collapse of your vital muscles.

Next, ascertain if your abdomen projects forward. If it does, pull it in. Not with your hands, but by its own muscles. If they will not do this, then help them with your hands for a while ; but soon they will be strong enough to do the pulling themselves. Then make them do it. In a very short time, they will attend to this matter as a habit, and that is what you want.

All athletes, all normal young persons, all strong and vital men and women overcome the collapse of these vital muscles. That condition causes old age and leads rapidly to decrepitude besides resulting in badly misshapen bodies and gross appearances, all repugnant to the eye and not creditable to the person so afflicted. We are sorry to say that more than ninety per cent of all persons above twenty-five years of age are victims of collapsed vital muscles.

Thus the good work goes on. These new habits increase the natural flow of magnetism, send much new and vigorous nerve-power to the eye, and so fire it with YOUTH. One of the first results in a better heart-action, and of decreasing irritation to the nervous system, is the brighter and more youthful glow of the eye. As new life comes to the brain and all the faculties, the eye is the first to respond.

By the term, The Magnetic Eye of Youth, we teach that the vital habits of youth if restored and conserved against waste living will give unusual health, vigour, brightness and brilliance to the eyes, which are the gauge that indicates perfectly how much magnetism has been developed in the body.

THE TENSE EYE

OUR FINAL LESSON in this Department of the Magnetic Eye will deal with the organ when under the full sway of great feeling, as distinguished from the sway of the mind. Thoughts move people in one of two ways ; either by the ideas they convey ; or by the feelings they arouse. While the most useful of all displays of personal magnetism come in the convincing force of ideas, the most interesting exhibitions are found in the outpouring of feeling when accompanied by magnetism. We have never yet seen an audience that did not enjoy to the utmost those tense moments when the power of some speaker was brought home to them in currents of magnetism ; not in shouting, or declamation, or physical energy. Some of the greatest victories have been won in quiet tones of the voice ; but not in lifeless ones.

Noise is a physical product, and for that reason is never magnetic. A din, or racket, if prolonged, tends to induce sleep, in the person hearing it. Loud speech must be avoided at all times.

A shouting preacher or declamatory orator may put an audience to sleep if he keeps at it long enough. A quiet voice that has no magnetism may empty a church or hall. It all depends on the presence of magnetism.

What is true in public displays is even more true in the various avenues of life, in business, or home, or professional affairs, as well as in social meetings. The tense voice is far more influential than the loud one.

Before the tense voice can be aroused and used with effect, the tense eye must be developed ; and it is the purpose of this lesson to teach the habit that brings this about. But even such a result cannot be obtained until the conditions of youth that are taught in the preceding lesson are acquired by the formation of the habits there described.

The tense eye comes about from the habit of charging the system with magnetic interest in which both mind and feelings participate. It means that the mind is wide awake, and that the emotional nature is likewise aroused, both uniting to find expression through the eye even if no other faculty than sight participates. By emotion is not necessarily intended the control of the feelings over the mind ; for that is weakness, and indicates that the judgment is being warped by some influence that is driving it from its moorings. Thus the imaginations that bring a mob into existence and dethrone their reason are illustrations of the control of the emotions over the mind.

Just as the human system is a nice balance of acid and alkaline conditions, so the magnetic system of intensity should be a nice balance of feeling and thought. In the absence of feeling, thought becomes magnetic only under the influence of an idea that possesses moving power ; by which is meant the power to win. In other words it is a winning idea. Great men and women rise to this estate who are never emotional, yet are magnetic ; but it requires the element of true greatness to do so. Yet a mind that has once been aroused in these powers quickly forms the habit of creating winning ideas. It then is only a question of acquired habit.

We have met many persons who are overcharged for a time with nothing but feeling. Some lawyers will begin an address to the jury with this overflow of emotion ; but with no winning idea back of it the effort soon falls flat, and the affair becomes ridiculous. But when mind and feeling are both magnetic, that is, when the thoughts are worth while and they are propelled by emotion, the combination is irresistible. The best indication of this nice balance is found in the tense eye ; for it is lighted with the fire of the thought and the fire of the nerves.

In order then to cultivate this brilliant and glowing eye, for it is unusually attractive, the thought itself must be powerful, and the feeling must propel it. One of the best illustrations of this combination to be found in history undoubtedly was the fiery and piercing eye of Patrick Henry, of whose appearance during the heat of eloquence many accounts have been handed down from persons who were present and who faced him as he spoke. Take for instance his defiance of British rule and repudiation of loyalty to the Mother Country when he said : " Cæsar had his Brutus, Charles the First his Cromwell, and George the Third," at which time he was interrupted by cries of " Treason."—" And George the Third may profit by their example. If this be treason make the most of it." As short-hand was not in use at the time, his exact words may not be known ; but ideas are more vital than words, and these were the ideas that he expressed. It is said that his face, which ordinarily was not usually attractive, was lighted up by a fire that shone from his eyes and gave him a godlike appearance.

The student of these lessons has witnessed similar scenes probably many times ; but we quote the foregoing in order to bring home a stirring example of the combination of the most intense thought coupled with the most intense feeling. Yet Patrick Henry did not break down. Had his feelings not been harnessed to his thoughts and made a well-balanced team, he might have broken down, as so many persons do when they give way to their feelings. The evidence of great magnetic power is found in the ability to feel to excess and to hold this pent-up dynamite of force in perfect control. It becomes a beautiful exhibition of human ascendency over the masses.

The quotation we have given above is also intended for use in practice, for the reason that it holds in its few words the most intense thoughts. Try repeating the words a few times, and note the result in your own force of expression. Do not use force of voice ; avoid mere noise. A magnetic thought must live in the mind ; it must make the scenes behind it live again ; it must see with mental vision what it refers to as it is uttered.

All the preceding lessons in this Department of the Magnetic Eye may be given attention at once, or in their order in the book ; but this final lesson should wait on others that follow. As it belongs where it is, we prefer not to move it ahead ; but we advise that it be omitted for a while.

The progress of this study is so interwoven with Departments that claim attention, apparently all at once, that it is difficult to arrange an order of sequence in adopting them. The best plan is to do nothing but read them and think about them, even if this method is never aided by exercises ; for the reading of a thought will often change a whole life. This is merely a suggestion.

In this lesson as in many others we must borrow from lessons that are ahead, and from some that have been given. Thus in order to acquire the tense eye, the youth habits of the lesson just before this will do more than any other influence. Then looking ahead to the Department of Tense Exercises, we find help that is very effective. Also there are lessons in the magnetic voice that possess unusual value. A reading of them will show what is meant.

With these helps, and with a thought that is on fire like the extract from the speech of Patrick Henry, it is a very rapid and easy process to develop the tense eye. The value of this acquisition is that it beautifies the face, gives it an unwonted attractiveness, and makes the eyes brilliant and capable of holding any attention even under the most discouraging circumstances. So important is it that every man and woman should acquire it even if not another thing is learned in this study.

We have seen so many thousands of instances of the use of the tense eye in controlling others that a volume larger than an unabridged dictionary would not hold the histories of them with the circumstances leading up to such use, and the advantages that followed. Later on we will show what can be accomplished in this line of influence. In this lesson it is our purpose to establish the acquisition as a permanent habit. It is one of those things that can never be lost after it has once been firmly engrafted on the nervous system. When you have attained it and have learned to use it, it will always respond to the merest act of the will.

Making use of the helps that are borrowed, as stated, from other lessons and from the careful reading of this whole work, we sum up the lesson by repeating the formula which is as follows :

1. There must be an aroused emotional feeling.

2. There must be a mental control of that emotion.

3. There must be present a great thought driving the emotion as the power in an engine drives the wheels of motion.

The great thought that we have quoted is one of the most vital of all ideas, as it contains a summing up of history in a very few words. When words are barren of ideas they are weak and wearying. When ideas are barren of words they are like jewels in frail settings. The man of few words, if what he says is important, holds more influence over his fellows than the man of many words that clothe the same thought ; but the man of few words that are barren of ideas is dull, stupid and a bore.

Mental vision is the eye of the mind back of the physical eye. Here it is employed to see what happened in history when Cæsar had his Brutus. The whole scene can be made to pass in review in less than one one-hundredth of a second. Then the eye of the mind shifts to another great crisis in human affairs, when Charles the First had his Cromwell. What happened then ?

Now the warning is given that George the Third,—what ?

In uttering these words, the body should remain fixed and wholly immovable ; not a twitching of a finger, nor the batting of an eyelid. Stand facing a mirror, and look into your own eyes until they burn with your gaze, and the reflection burns back to you. Let the voice be low in tone, low in musical pitch, but spoken naturally ; and repeat the words with the vital centres of the preceding lesson and the vital muscles of the same lesson, all in perfect position.

While combining these natural habits as one unit, hold the entire body tense under the instructions given in the Department that is devoted to that subject in a later part of this book.

In one trial you will find that you have tensed your eyes and have given them an unusual brilliance. After a few trials this glow will appear very distinct in a room that is absolutely dark.

One more quotation will be furnished you here in order to fix and complete this study of the tense eye. In the Patrick Henry words we selected the one thought in all history that was most charged with fire. We now pass to the drama and select a thought that stands out as the greatest ever uttered in that profession. It is from the play of *Richelieu*. He was Prime Minister of France, and had for his ward a beautiful girl named Julie. The king desired her for immoral purposes. In that period, any person who was guilty or innocent who was pursued and in danger of being arrested or captured, could secure perfect safety by entering the precincts of a church, as it was dangerous to follow. No soldier dared follow. When the messenger came to arrest Julie and take her to the king, there was no church at hand where she could flee and be safe. So Cardinal Richelieu constructed a mental church into which he thrust her, and thereupon defied the king's officer with the following words :

"She shall not stir ! Mark where she stands ! Around her form I draw the awful circle of our solemn church ! Set but a foot within that holy ground, and on thy head—yea, though it wore a crown, I'd launch the curse of Rome ! "

The mental picture is that of Richelieu in the centre, the king's officer forward obliquely on the right of the Cardinal, and Julie forward obliquely on the left. While he gazes on the officer with tense eyes, he draws the imaginary circle about Julie on the floor without removing his fixed gaze from the officer.

It is an old rule of power in speech that the shorter the words, if they are filled with vital ideas, the more magnetism they convey. In the final or climax part of the above utterance, it will be seen that the last seventeen words are all monosyllables.

Make use of the same directions that we have given for the Patrick Henry quotation, and apply them to the Richelieu quotation. Repeat this in a fixed attitude, looking at the imaginary officer until he seems to stand before you in the flesh, and so proceed slowly, carefully and with the firm determination of mastering both the officer and the king.

Before this book is closed we will show you the many great victories that may be won by the tense eye.

DEPARTMENT OF INSTANTANEOUS PERSONAL MAGNETISM

PREPARING THE WAY

BUSY PEOPLE IN THIS AGE of haste and hurry do not take much interest in a course of training that is founded on nothing but exercises. Such a profession as that of singing or playing a musical instrument will, from its very nature, require long and tedious application to exercises which would not be performed if there were any other way to reach the desired end. Very few young folks like to practise on a piano, or violin, or any other thing hours and hours every week ; and some of them rebel against it most vigorously.

But the woman who has been told that she possesses a charming voice, and that she could earn a living by having it cultivated so that she could sing in public, faces a different proposition. Her name and fame, if not her livelihood, are the goals. She knows from reading and being told that the road to any art is long and time is fleeting ; so she is willing to be taught the many exercises that lay the foundation for a finished voice ; in some cases requiring from five to seven or more years of hard work. With her it is practice, practice, practice. Men singers also must practise long and tediously before they can secure opportunities for displaying their gifts.

Few indeed of the world's vocal artists have leaped out of the uncultured class of natural singers into the accomplished class of successful performers. Art as developed among painters requires from five to ten years of practice, and some after years of experience. Even the prize-fighter must go through a process of training to become recognized as fit for fighting ; and before each important engagement he must again devote weeks or months to renewed training. All sports to-day require some development and some training as may be seen in both the amateur and professional ranks.

When a prospective student of personal magnetism is asked to enter upon this study, he naturally wishes to know what he has to do, and how long he must devote himself to it before he shows results. Before an answer is given, it should be understood that personal magnetism is life itself. It enters into every moment and second of the waking hours of the day and night, and it keeps companionship with every man and woman down to the last days of existence. It is a part of them. It is engrafted into their blood, their nerves, their brain, their thoughts, their activities, and their associations with all other human beings in all phases of life.

A habit is a manner of living.

Personal magnetism is a habit.

Therefore it is and should be a manner of living.

Living includes the expression of thoughts, of feelings, the activities of solitude and of association with others, and the operations of life that are going on within the body and all its parts and functions.

Personal magnetism becomes a vital part of living in all these phases.

Therefore it is not the result of exercises, but of habits.

It is true that there are qualities that may be acquired in shorter time when they are aided by exercises that stimulate them into action ; but the entire scope of the study may be made to include only habits without the aid of exercises.

Nearly every great man and woman has been started on a successful career by reading. Sometimes it is biography ; often other lines of reading. We know of the sailor who found a book that told of the life of a great man ; he left the sea and became one of the most famous preachers of his time. He always said the book did it. We have read of a carpenter who was loaned a book which described the struggles of another great man and his ultimate success ; the tools were thrown aside, and the carpenter entered upon a new career in which he won great triumphs. Henry Wilson, the cobbler of Natick,

Massachusetts, U.S.A., stopped some school children on their way home, and asked them to explain to him the letters of the alphabet. In time he learned to read. He was Vice-President of the United States when he died in 1875. Daniel Webster was loaned a copy of Milton's *Paradise Lost*, and he memorized every word of it. This work led to his desire to know more, and he entered college. But the style and inspiration of Milton followed him all through life, and prevailed in his great orations. It has been claimed that not a single great man or woman has been born great, but that their inherent powers have been stimulated into action by what they have read.

Biography is full of such incidents.

These facts being so, and it being true that personal magnetism is a part of the act of living, the conclusion was not difficult to reach that almost all the help that a man or woman needs in acquiring or developing this power can come from reading a book that presents a complete system on the subject. Exercises may help to hurry the development, but they cannot do more.

Reading alone may accomplish vast results.

Our New Method therefore consists chiefly in showing the way by the instructions contained in the lessons, from which we form the vital habits that bring the results required. But we add all the necessary exercises for those ambitious students who wish to make all the speed possible.

A single idea has inspired many a person.

A word or two may change a habit.

A word or two may completely turn the individual around and face him in the right direction when we see him going in the wrong direction. A very good singer who was too poor to pay for lessons in vocal culture was filling the position of soprano in a city choir, but with poor success. A friend told her that she was trying to make her notes with her throat in the wrong position ; she was told what was correct ; to use a figure of speech, she had been going in the wrong direction, and was turned around and faced in the right direction. A faulty tone is rasping, harsh to listen to, and repellent. All persons, as far as personal magnetism is concerned, are either

    1. Attractive ;

    2. Neutral ; or

    3. Repellent.

Whatever will irritate the brain of another person will irritate the nervous system. A harsh tone or faulty note is irritating. You cannot irritate and attract. But we will see more of this later as we proceed.

The purpose of this lesson is to prepare the ground for the development of instantaneous personal magnetism ; by which we mean the formation of magnetic habits without the trouble and delay of practising exercises. It is easily possible to acquire some useful degree of this power in one day after you have finished a careful reading of the book. Further, it is easily possible to know that you have acquired this first degree ; to be conscious of the fact that you have become partly attractive, less repellent, and have ceased to remain neutral. But you must read every word of the book before you begin the new life, for such it will prove to be.

Read slowly, not in the desire to get through, but with the purpose of understanding every word, every idea, every suggestion. It will pay you to do this. Become a good reader, and you will become a good thinker. Go off by yourself, or else keep the companionship, if in the evening, of some loved member of your family, and read aloud if permitted and desired, or to yourself otherwise. When you have given the first thorough reading of the book your absorbed attention, you will have become worth to yourself fully twenty-five per cent more than you were before. This is gain. It has always been our practice to read an important book twice. If you do this, your gain will be still greater. Then you will be ready for the progress that we call instantaneous personal magnetism, which will begin in the next lesson.

This progress will be so great in a very short time that it will be known to yourself and to others who meet you in the daily activities of life. Let it then be understood that the exercises of this book are designed for those who are exceedingly ambitious, while all others will develop this power by change of habits through reading alone.

IMMEDIATE PROGRESS

HAVING READ SO FAR very carefully and patiently, the student is now to learn what is meant by instantaneous personal magnetism. It means the immediate beginning of its development, the consciousness of possessing it, and the use of it in every phase of life. We have learned that young people generate vast quantities of magnetism, and lose it all by the waste of youth ; or the uncontrolled activities that use up all the dynamic energy of early life in those who are normal. It is the superabundant vitality running itself without a controlling and directing engineer.

This is called leakage.

It is not possible to check it in youth, nor is it desirable to do so. Nature is taking its course.

But this leaking continues into maturity and keeps up the waste without check, although the wastage is far less then, or death would come in the form of fatal nervous prostration. That malady is due to the continued, unchecked loss of magnetism, while neither the patient nor the doctor knows how to stop it. No physician has ever learned how. Medicines, drugs, pills and electric treatments have been tried without success to effect a cure. Change of climate, change of living conditions, change of diet and of habits have been tried, but all have failed. The victim of nervous prostration or neurasthenia goes on slowly to the grave. Magnetism is being wasted faster than it is being generated ; this is the whole story.

It has been proved that if all the abnormal leakage of the body can be stopped, there will occur an immediate accumulation of magnetism. We say of the boy whose vitality is one hundred per cent that it must have vent. If the grown-up person accumulates magnetism, which is the vitality of that age, it may seek opportunities for giving itself vent ; and these come naturally in the prolific thinking of the mind, the thirst for real knowledge in place of sensational news and worthless books; the desire to do something instead of sitting around aimlessly, and the wish to bring light and sunshine into the lives of others who are near and dear to us. Unselfishness takes the place of the narrow conception of duty to those who can be made more appreciative of interest in them.

The possession of magnetism is generally the difference between success and failure. A lawyer who believed in himself and who was somewhat magnetic and knew it, complained that he was not winning his way as he should, and asked why. " You are too fidgety," was the reply. This means that his magnetism was being wasted by useless motions of hands and feet, and of the whole body at times. A fidgety man is unattractive, and all persons are either attractive, neutral or repellent. There never was and never will be a man or woman of fidgety habits who can attract. Here is a double loss. The irritating motions repel of themselves, and they cause leakage as well ; hence such a person fails to get on in the world. A very brief reminder is all that is necessary to cure the fault. In the case of the lawyer, it made so much difference that, when he had caught its meaning, he instantly rectified the trouble, and from that time he became successful. From this account it might seem that this single fault was all that stood in the way of becoming magnetic. It is one, at least, of the many faults.

A woman complained that she could not win friends of the right kind, and was told that she distressed them by using a high pitched voice. This kind of a voice is merely one that makes use of the upper notes such as are found in the musical scale, but spoken instead of being sung. In order to know just what is meant, turn to the Department of the Magnetic Voice and there find the nine pitches with their quotations. Then repeat the quotations of the four highest pitches, or the sixth, seventh, eighth and ninth. Imagine a woman carrying on a conversation lasting minutes or hours and employing no other pitches than one or more of these four upper ones.

It is a well recognized fact that the higher the pitch of the speaking voice the greater the irritation on the ear-nerves of the listeners.

These ear-nerves communicate with the brain centres and

there transfer the vibrations or waves received by the ear. In a high pitched speaking voice as well as singing voice, there are many more vibrations of sound than are found in the lower pitches. Thus a person who avoids the upper pitches and uses the middle or lower ones, relieves the listener of many vibrations in each and every second of time ; and as a person may engage in a conversation that lasts for minutes or hours, the accumulated number of vibrations that are escaped are a great relief to the nerves and brain of those to whom the remarks are made while the conversation is in progress. The woman to whom we refer caught the idea in the briefest possible time, and mended her ways. It required no exercises, no training, no time spent in building up something different from what she was naturally. It was the suggestion that showed her doing the wrong thing, and told her what was the right thing. Then her cleverness did the rest.

Another woman complained that she did not win friends and seemed to be repelling those whom she sought. She was told that she talked too fast and too much. Much as we do not like to say it, no man or woman who talks too fast or too much is magnetic. Here again we see the irritating effect of the accumulated number of voice vibrations that attack the ear-nerves, and through them the brain itself. Many thousands of these vibrations strike small but decisive blows against the ear-nerves and the brain, and it is like so many strokes of a microscopic hammer hitting these sensitive parts. There is a normal rate of speed that is readily made magnetic ; but when you double it, you double the thousands of hammer strokes that are thrust against the brain of the listener, and irritation ensues. It requires a genius of the highest order to speak rapidly and effectively ; and such methods must be varied by modulation of the best quality. Bernhardt could do it, but she had few imitators. Soprano singers need longer periods of absolute silence than others ; and the best of them refrain from using the voice for hours and sometimes days before a public appearance. They talk with pad and pencil.

The woman to whom we referred as talking too fast made an effort to talk slowly, but could not maintain it. Her husband used to sit within range of her vision when they were with others, so that he could signal her to reduce her rate of speed.

But a person who must be coached in this way is hopeless as far as overcoming this fault is concerned.

A minister said that he had no magnetic control over his hearers. We attended his church one Sunday, and the next day told him that he used a monotonous pitch. He did not know what that was. He knew that he was not using too high a pitch, but the idea that, while he kept the pitch down, he made it monotonous was new to him. Anything that is monotonous strikes the brain nerves too often in one way. It concentrates as it were on one spot. The old incident of driving a man insane by forcing him to sit under a tank of water placed above him, from which a single drop fell upon one spot on his head, at the rate of one a second, carries in it the real principle that affects all faults along this line.

If you are compelled to hear one note all the time, the blow falling on the nerves of the brain will make you insane. A very small noise at night, if it is the same all the time, without the relief of variation, will so irritate the brain as to do it injury. A man who plays one tune without change, even if it is melodious and pleasing for a while, will nearly drive every one crazy who is compelled to listen to it. The human brain cannot long endure monotony in any form. There is more insanity among the women of the farms than among those of the cities, because they lead a life of dreary monotony.

It is for these reasons that the minister whom we have mentioned was unmagnetic. He preached along one part of the pitch, even if it were the pleasing part, which is around the middle of the vocal range, known as the magnetic pitch. Relief from this kind of monotony is secured by the cultivation of modulation, or the movements of the speaking voice that employ a variety of pitches for the expression of thought. More than this the really magnetic speakers and conversationalists employ the movements of modulation in harmony with the variations of thought.

This is getting too deep for the ordinary student, and we will pass it on for a later lesson. It involves the finest points in voice training, and is fascinating as well as magnetic ; but it requires practice, and we have agreed to avoid the practice part of our method as much as possible. In the Department of the Magnetic Voice we furnish training that will need some practice ; and this will be fully provided in the latter part of this book.

The point we are making here is that any kind of monotony irritates the listener, and no persons can be attracted to you if you irritate them. This is common sense. The minister learned to use his voice with proper modulation and soon became very successful in his work.

Another man who was in business complained that he seemed to drive customers away, and that his efforts to increase patronage failed at every turn. We studied him from a vantage place in his shop and found that he used his voice with four faults : the pitch was too high, the tones were unvaried and monotonous, the rate of speed much too fast, and he closed the upper part of his throat in talking, making a guttural, barking sound as he spoke.

This brings us to one of the most unmagnetic faults of the human voice ; a fault that repels instead of attracting. When the voice is developed by the drifting methods of Nature, it runs to some kind of faults, just as a beautiful garden, left to the management of Nature, will destroy itself by weeds. Many thoughtless people say they prefer to remain natural than to cultivate good habits, and their argument seems unanswerable, which is : " Nature knows what she is about, and the only proper way of living is to let her do as she pleases." But when this argument is applied to the raising of flowers, fruits or foods, it shows Nature as an unruly impulse in all departments of living things and living organisms. This unruly impulse, when controlling the human voice, brings into it as many faults as it brings into the garden which is left to itself.

There is no vocal fault so common and so almost universal as that of closing the upper part of the throat in speaking or in singing. The skilled teacher of the coming genius of opera attacks this fault first. One of the methods is to place the end of the handle of a teaspoon on the back of the tongue, and so force down the roots of the tongue, with the result that the throat will open in its upper part. Another method that is employed by teachers is to direct that the student swallow, and note the position of the larynx, or Adam's apple, in the throat ; and in tone production keep that organ down where it went in the act of swallowing. This last process may be misleading, for the larynx tries to rise just before it performs the real act of swallowing, and it is the latter part of this act that is helpful in getting the throat open. So another plan was adopted, and it proved a better one. It was that of imitating the gape ; or trying to open the back of the mouth and upper throat as a person does who gapes. This succeeded. When once it can be done voluntarily, which should require but a few minutes of practice, it can be done always at will.

The closed upper throat is an effectual barrier to a decent singing voice ; but it is a common fault in speaking.

It produces voices that irritate and repel in every department of life, and that therefore are non-magnetic.

In a state of Nature this closed position means dislike, and under more pressure it means hatred. It can be seen at once that such a mood is unattractive ; and although it cannot be translated by a non-expert, it is felt instinctively as a repellent tone position. Among beasts it produces the hiss of the cat and all cat-like animals, and the warning hatred of other life below the human species. The growl of the dog has its origin in the same position. Hence to hear it in the voice of man or woman is to feel as if there were more of the growl and threat there than attractiveness. The health of the throat, also, becomes involved in this closed position, for it rasps the membrane, which is very delicate at that place.

This does not imply that every repellent voice is rasping. Any tone that is produced with the upper throat closed is disagreeable, even if it is merely a closed tone. The natural impulse that causes the closing of the throat is born of a dis-agreeable temperament, and this influence is always repellent.

The cure of this trouble is to be found in correcting the throat position in the manner we have described. It is a very quick procedure if our instructions are followed as given. Just as soon as the upper throat is opened, it should be held flexibly open all the time you are talking ; and this applies also to public speaking ; and is absolutely necessary in singing. There can be no real singing voice until this position is acquired and made an easy habit.

As soon as you master this simple matter, you will notice that the character of your voice will at once undergo a change that is revolutionary in its nature. Every harsh and repellent note will disappear. Better volume, which before was wholly impossible, will follow. Then there will be purity, attractiveness and winning qualities to reward your brief effort at mending a fault that stands between you and success in your influence over others. The closed throat fault reacts upon every person who possesses it, and it is present in ninety per cent of all voices. Very few persons are free from it. Hence we seek to eliminate it at once.

The troubles that are cited in this lesson are not all by any means. There are many others, and they must be given consideration as we proceed. Like the garden that is left to the drifting impulses of Nature, humanity collects multitudes of weeds, and also like the garden which is overrun with weeds when left to Nature, humanity needs a bit of cultivating.

Human intercourse is so constituted that the means of communication between one person and another are confined ordinarily to the use of the eyes and of the voice. These furnish the channels for the exercise of the power of personal magnetism.

Incidental to them are the uses of touch and of thought. Luther Burbank by placing one hand on the chest of a person, and the other hand on the back, was able to throw so powerful a current of magnetism into a person that cures were effected that defied all treatments of science or medicine. This is the use of touch.

Ideas are also tremendously magnetic.

But in the wear and tear of life, in the multitudinous activities of the day, the voice becomes the agency of magnetic control in ninety per cent of all communications; and so simple an idea as to allow it to develop itself into an instrument of wondrous beauty by merely adopting the habit of maintaining the open throat in order to give forth pure tones, and of acquiring a pleasing and harmonious modulation in speech, is charged with the potency of a complete revolution of the life-habits of an individual, and this change may begin in a single day.

" FIDGETS "

WE PURPOSE NOW to look ahead and collect in systematic form the causes that militate against the natural acquisition of personal magnetism. They are causes that, once overcome, leave the individual really far advanced in the development of this power. Not all of them can be conquered at once, but from day to day one by one they may be given attention, until all are driven out of life. But no person may possess all these faults. If some are lacking, so much the better. You will have no trouble in recognizing those that handicap you ; nor will you set yourself against trying to drive them away, on the theory that you are exempt when the facts are otherwise. You will be fair with yourself.

All non-magnetic persons lose each day as much natural magnetism as they generate in the act of living.

If they lose more than they generate they die of nervous prostration if this difference is maintained.

The losses occur through what are called leakages.

A leakage in the study of personal magnetism is a waste of natural electrical energy through some fault.

The leakages may be of physical, nervous or mental character.

A physical leakage occurs when muscular energy is thrown away without purpose and without control.

A nervous leakage occurs when some vital energy is thrown away by the erratic action of the nervous system.

A mental leakage occurs when the thoughts persist in exciting the brain erratically, and so exhaust its energy.

GRAND PRINCIPLE

The least magnetic of the so-called non-magnetic people lose each day more vital electricity than is necessary to produce the highest degree of personal magnetism.

The reverse of this proposition is necessarily true, that the conserving of the energy thus wasted would result in the development of personal magnetism of the highest degree. In other words, if all losses from leakage were to be stopped, nothing more would be required. The training and study might cease right at this point. All this is true; but, on the other hand, it must be remembered that personal magnetism, no matter in what degree it exists, is a power only, and that its chief value is in its uses.

In this Department of Instantaneous Personal Magnetism, we have promised to begin the development of this power at once; even on the first day after this whole book has been carefully read through once or twice.

This promise will be kept to the letter. Such development will begin on the first day after the reading is completed; and on the second day there will be more progress; still more on the third day; and so on from day to day until the work of development has advanced to a satisfactory stage.

On the first day a triple combination will do the work in the manner to be stated in a subsequent lesson of this Department. On the second day the same triple combination will do the work, with only one part of the same advanced in order to make due progress. And so on to the end of this Department.

The changing or movable part of the triple combination is the battle with some different form of leakage. This makes it necessary for us at the present time to set forth the groups of Leakages; the first of which is the Physical Group, whereby muscular energy is thrown away without purpose and without control. These are as follows:

I. *The Fidgets.*—These have been referred to in a preceding lesson. Everybody knows what they are. You have seen them in all classes of people, and know the harm they have done in your estimation. Here may be seen your family doctor; suppose he is restless, fidgety and ill at ease. Your confidence in him is weakened; nor do you have to know anything of the rules of magnetism to form your estimate of him. Any man, woman or child can pass judgment in some way or other on the restless doctor. The result is that he loses his clientele. Then failure comes. On the other hand, let him be a stranger, and yet well at ease, free from this fault, and you will quickly be drawn to him. Self-mastery inspires confidence in others, and success is much more probable.

If this restless man should be a surgeon, his usefulness would come to an end at once. How about the dentist ? We recall the case of one who was very much under the sway of this fault ; in the town where he set up practice, he could not make friends in his profession, although he had excellent influence socially and his wife tried to make herself as popular as she could. A wide circle of friends did not create the practice needed. The fault was that he was restless and did not inspire confidence. He brought the matter to our attention. He took up the study of the enemies of magnetism ; overcame his great fault ; moved to a town where he was not known ; and very quickly established a large practice, because he won the confidence of the public.

Thus we see that what is apparently a simple thing, and only a drop in the study of magnetism, is really almost a turning-point in human life.

Now look in the legal profession, and note the calm, cool, powerful control shown by one, and the fidgety manners of another. The brain and judgment are not at their best when the body is leaking vitality. Or look at the splendid bearing of the self-controlled minister, as compared with the smallness of the uneasy, squirming preacher. Many a Sunday have we listened to some man who is addicted to meaningless gestures that are mere motion ; and we have noted that loudness of voice does not hold the interest of the congregation, nor does physical activity of the involuntary kind pass current for earnestness. Such clergymen are numerous everywhere, but we fail to find one who is genuinely successful.

True power is deep. The stronger the feelings, the less should be their outward evidence.

But it is on other grounds that restlessness weakens a man or woman. The constant loss of vitality, flowing out with each involuntary motion, soon saps the force that should underlie the effort of the mind or body.

Then there is still another law at work. Restless people make all beholders uneasy. The jury, the congregation, the school, the friends in a social gathering, the business circles, the patient or client, all are made more or less irritable by being compelled

to watch the restless man or woman. The brain is soon fogged
by such irritability, and a fixed desire to get free from the cause
takes hold of every one. Instead of controlling others, they are
driven away, and after years will hardly serve to regain the
confidence that is thus lost, unless better methods are adopted.

Magnetic people are not restless.

Restless people cannot become magnetic.

Magnetism is a charm, not an annoyance.

Until you learn to hold the body still, as far as involuntary
motions are concerned, you cannot become magnetic. You may
try any and every method you please, but the power attained
will ooze out from the nerves just as a leaking battery will let
its energy escape when subjected to influences that draw away
the fluid that is stored.

Some persons get the idea that all that is necessary to acquire
magnetism is to practise some affirmative exercises. On the
same principle, if you buy the best locomotive boiler, and
puncture it with a hundred small holes, you would deem the
makers of the boiler at fault because it did not maintain its
power.

Affirmative acquisitions in this world must be supported by
attention to negative influences, or the latter will neutralize all
that the former may seek to accomplish.

Habits, good or bad, are quickly formed, and the brain will
execute them. At first it is necessary to study and think of
the many small involuntary motions you make ; but in a few
days you will find the mind performing this duty for you. We
recommend that each student of these lessons ask some friend
to act as a critic. You cannot see yourself as you are seen, and
a critic should mention only your faults. Praise to an ambitious
person makes it difficult to tell the truth when the truth is
most needed. Honest advice is welcomed by the sincere
student.

The value of this lesson in the training of young men and
young ladies can be seen at once. Children are never magnetic,
for Nature encourages their restless activity as a means of
growth. But when they pass the age of fourteen or fifteen, the
strength of youth should manifest itself in a form of demeanour
that assumes to be culture and gentle deportment, although in
fact it is the quietude of magnetism.

Education in schools along these lines is useless until the ages mentioned.

But at that time, and all through the years that follow, it is of the highest importance to train the nerves to steadiness, and the muscles to their voluntary uses only. Mere quietude is harmful. It should be the covering of an accumulated power within ; and, for this reason, the affirmative course of instruction in magnetism should accompany these lessons that are only negative.

This volume must of necessity include both sides of the training. The weeds must be removed from the garden, for nothing will make progress when counter influences are choking out all good impulses.

The removal of weeds is not enough. The destruction of enemies is not enough, either in war or in life. There must be a progressive and aggressive growth of affirmative power.

Nothing is so undesirable as the man or woman who is still or quiet or self-contained because of deadness in the nature, or lack of energy or power. The world is full of such people. Churches, organizations and departments of social and governmental life are already overcharged with dead folks who still live. They are useless and in the way.

Magnetism gives life.

But first it is necessary to make room for that life, and therefore we must continue these lessons with the enemies of magnetism.

It has been said by a very able critic that the best way of overcoming the faults that stand as barriers to self-control is the mental process of " thinking them away." Training is made to take the place of culture, and is then called culture ; but this quality is native only when it becomes a part of the individual, and ceases to be a veneer. Thinking away one's faults produces real culture.

PHYSICAL LOSSES

NOW WE APPROACH a flood of Leakages that come from the losses of muscular electrical energy that is thrown away without purpose and without control. These take place in all parts of the body, and generally at some terminals. What is known as the fidgets applies to the whole body, and in the manner which has just been described in the preceding lesson. Terminal losses are localized and are not as general as the fidgets. The latter attract more attention because they are larger activities. Terminals lose a great amount of vital energy on the principle that they release the power much as points release electricity. We will describe some familiar experiences, in which terminals form an important part with others included.

Typewriting.—It is a well-known fact that more than ninety per cent of all who use the typewriter for any length of time are restless and nervous. Under a system of smooth and easy motion this nervousness may be controlled. There are two kinds of touch for a typewriter : one that resembles the touch of a skilled pianist, and the other that is a succession of pounds with the fingers on the keys. The latter is the cause of loss of vitality. A smooth motion, as is seen in the most skilled piano playing, does not tax the nervous vitality except as all excess of work may weary for the time. Many a young lady has suffered from nervous prostration because of too much work at the typewriter, and doctors are constantly having to deal with such cases. Any jerky movement is harmful to the vitality.

Winking.—We have always attacked this fault first of all : and not until the pupil is able to suppress at all times the habit of moving the eyelids will there ever be a hope of acquiring magnetism. Here is the battle ground for a majority of the readers of these lessons. We are often told that the habit cannot be cured, and our reply is, then give up the study of magnetism. But the habit is being cured every year in thousands of cases, and consequently there is little virtue in the claim that it is a hopeless task to get rid of it in every instance. Attention is the sole method of overcoming it.

Yawning.—This fault is due to a low state of vitality, and the person who is addicted to it is as far from magnetism as the sun is distant from the darkest corner of a cave. It is not only a clear evidence of weakness, such as follows indigestion in nine cases out of ten, or loss of sleep, or wasting of the energy as in excesses of any kind, but is also bad manners and bad deportment. When the claim is made that it cannot be cured, let the usual method of suppressing it be applied. This is to omit every alternate yawn. The cure is complete. Even the loss of sleep and indigestion cannot compel the yawn against that cure. Omitting every other yawn soon reduces the number to less than one in an hour, as the omissions become less and less.

Face Motions.—These are of various kinds. The most common is the action of the lips, and especially of the tongue. These are very small matters, but they have their influence for ill. One of the signs of approaching senility is the habit of constantly moving the tongue against the upper or lower lip, or the lips against the teeth. It is evidence of weakness, and magnetism is a power. Therefore the book of the face should not bear records that are read by people at a glance.

There are other petty physical habits that might be included in the list, but they are generally swept away by a successful contest with those we have named.

While life demands activity, there is a large distinction between regulated power, and force running away with itself. What the will directs increases the power; and what is directed at haphazard is sure to weaken the power.

Drumming.—Some people drum with their fingers; some with their feet. We have known many such drummers, and have never seen one of them who was in the least magnetic. It is not only evidence of Leakage of vitality but of exceedingly bad manners; and persons who are ill-bred rarely get anywhere in the world that is worth while.

Variety when not the spice of life.—To show to what extent non-magnetic people lose their electrical energy, let us peruse the following list :

Fingers.—Not only as drummers on the table or anything handy except an actual drum, do the fingers play their part, but they have numerous other motions. They twirl the moustache, if there is one. They rub against themselves as if brushing crumbs away. They open and shut. They are interlaced at times in a restless manner. They spread themselves. They rub the chin, stroke the face, pull at the ears, caress the nose, and engage in any kind of activity that they can invent.

The cook when making the toast scratches her head with her finger nails and releases a lot of dandruff that otherwise might remain intact.

The embarrassed lover, when trying for the first time to propose to his lady friend, finds a coat button handy for his fingers to work at and eventually to twist off ; and not until he has twisted from their fastenings all but one of the buttons on the front of the coat does she accept him for the sake of saving that final button. On other occasions men finger their coat buttons as a habit and not due to embarrassment.

The number of both sexes who work their toes when the latter are hidden in their shoes cannot be surmised ; but this fault is a familiar one, as all persons may easily believe who know the eagerness of the terminals to throw off waste vitality.

Leg Swinging.—We have seen ladies sitting for an hour or more, some of whom were wriggling the feet all the time, using the hinge action of the ankle for the purpose. The action consisted of pointing the toes towards the ceiling and immediately dipping them towards the floor. This motion they were not cognizant of, but nevertheless it was maintained without cessation. We have seen other ladies and more men who preferred to cross the legs at the knees, swing the whole lower part of the limb forward and back, and sometimes right and left when other persons present were not in the way. A number of these added a special accomplishment by making circles with the toes.

Non-magnetic Positions.—In almost any office, you will note the customary position of the body of the male clerk who is sitting at the table or desk. He is slouched down far into his

11

chair, his head is lower than his feet, and the latter are resting on the table or desk.

Most chairs are uncomfortable. They compel the person who would use them for resting the upper part of the body to lounge in them in strained positions even when merely sitting. The common illustration of this fact is seen in the straight backs of some church pews and of some drawing-room chairs. The cure of this fault is to ignore the back and allow the body to rest itself only as far as its sitting posture is concerned. After standing until you are weary, or after walking until any kind of sitting support is acceptable, you are glad to get even a box or log to sit upon, and may exclaim, " How delightful ! " yet the box as well as the log is without a back and you never notice it. The support of the back is not required in most cases until the body has been sitting too long ; then, instead of rising on the legs as ought to be done, the custom is to shift the support from the sitting posture to that of leaning back against something. When this proves too monotonous, there is always an inclination to lean farther back, until the hammock or the lounge is wanted.

During this process of wearing out the vital forces, the body is getting more and more tired. It becomes a refreshing relief to be able to lie down, and to thus employ the faculties in reading or studying. This tired-out feeling is seen in offices and other places where men and young men lounge into easy attitudes until they are seen with feet on the table, and their heads far below a normal relative position.

Where the circulation of the blood is interfered with, the vitality is low. When the back receives any support the heart lessens its efforts to push the blood through the body. Remove the support from the back and the heart will do much more vigorous work. Now stand, and the heart still increases its activity ; and this increase is very marked when you walk, and quite energetic when you run, showing a steady, proportionate effort of this great organ of life to keep pace with the demands of the muscular system.

The more you rest, the more you will require rest.

The more you favour the back muscles, the more you will feel inclined to do so.

The more you sit with raised feet, lowered head and resting back, the more you will want to do these things.

The more you lie abed, the more you will have to lie in bed.

The less you stand, the less you will be able to stand.

The less you walk, the less you will want to walk, except in certain abnormal instances where the deadness of the muscles rebels and a few minutes' walk is refreshing ; but the weariness afterwards will make you declare that you will not give way to such indiscretion again. Then, awaking to the fact that you are muscularly lazy, you try to atone for years of weakness by a few days or weeks of exercise, with the result that you break down the exhausted tissue and do yourself a permanent injury. Habits should be changed slowly if they affect the body or any of its faculties. Immoral habits may be changed by moral surgery, and haste never makes waste.

Another straining position is that which lets the chest fall down on the stomach. It ought to be trained out of all children from the first years of their schooling. This almost universal fault is the first step in consumption. Bold as the declaration may seem, we nevertheless make it, that you will not find consumption or its symptoms in a man or woman who is free from this bad habit. The fallen chest is weakness itself, and the heart is crowded and checked in its work. The raised chest compels the heart to do more work ; its blood is drawn with remarkable energy all through the interiors that feed the lungs, and the vitality is such that the germs of tuberculosis could not long live there. You who would like to do good in the world, take this one proposition into the lives of all men and women, into homes and into schools, and note how a small principle will revolutionize humanity.

One fact is not generally known ; it is this : The upper lungs never receive air from an ingoing breath, but always from a repressed, energetic out-going breath, as when it accompanies some physical effort, or is forcibly discharged through the partly closed mouth. This effort should be tried occasionally.

NERVOUS LOSSES

LIFE IN THE HUMAN BODY on the animal side is physical, nervous and mental; not meaning that animals are mentally endowed, but that man is born in the animal kingdom with these divisions of his being. We have discussed in the preceding lesson the losses that occur by Leakage in physical activities. We now pass on to nervous wastefulness. A fidgety person may or may not be nervous. Nearly all nervous persons lack the fidgety faults. They may be very calm and self-contained until some little thing happens to startle them. In fact, they force themselves to be calm as much as possible, knowing the likelihood of flying off their nerves, as they term it, at almost nothing.

Some men and most women scream at the sight of a mouse, spider or snake. The calm judgment of the mind would show the folly of such giving way to this nervous weakness; for a person of high intelligence would not find anything to cause fright in any of those objects of creation. One such experience drives out more vital energy than can be stored in three days.

Sudden starts.—These are trifles in themselves, but they work havoc with the nerves, and what lowers the tone of the nerves will always lessen the magnetism.

Sudden Stops.—These may apply to the whole body or to any part of it. They are quite frequent as we will see a little later on in this work.

Trembling.—This is not the shaking of fright, so much as the unsteadiness of hand which many persons allow to fall into habits of senile weakness early in life.

Sighing.—This is due to a low state of respiration. It denotes that the nervous system is out of order. Like yawning, it will disappear as the affirmative lessons of this course of training are put into practice.

Short Breathing.—This is a habit distinct in itself, and grows if left to itself. It invites the open mouth breathing which is injurious to the health. All usual respirations should occur through the nostrils. Magnetic people breathe deeply and never pant.

Halting Speech.—Strange as the assertion may seem, it is nevertheless a fact that not one person in two hundred talks or speaks without halting. The usual expression when the halt comes is *uh* as a little observation will prove. In speaking formally at meetings, or even in businesss conversations, the habit is very prevalent. The cure of it is to speak smoothly by direction of the will.

Rapid Talk.—Vehement and earnest delivery in speaking, or in conversation, is one thing ; but the habit of rapid talking is quite another. Vehemence generally helps to increase magnetism, if the body is tensed and free from the enemies to which we have referred. ; but rapidity of talk is one of the quickest methods of destroying vitality. Nervous prostration is the penalty of the man or woman who talks much and talks fast.

We know of many cases where persons are all tired out after an afternoon of gossipy talk. Recently our attention was called to a woman of great wealth who said that she would give a liberal reward for some treatment that would check her nervousness and loss of vitality. In looking into her habits, we found that she was an incessant and rapid talker. Not wishing to offend her, we outlined a course of conduct that required four weeks of silence. She was told that she must use pencil and paper for all her communications she wished to make ; and to appease her curiosity we showed her a letter from Patti, the English prima donna, in which the latter spoke of her habit of always refraining from conversation, and using paper and pencil, during the days preceding her engagement to sing at night. When Patti adopted this plan for the purpose of saving her voice, she found that it saved her vitality as well. The four weeks of silence resulted in a complete cure of nervousness and low vitality. We do not recommend silence in ordinary cases ; but we do suggest that those who talk much cannot become magnetic.

The orator of greatest powers is always a man of few words

when not engaged in speaking. The same is true of the actor.

There are many reasons, mostly of policy, why a person should be addicted to few words. Total silence may seem like shyness, but a moderate degree of this quality is helpful to any man or woman. As a rule, the less you talk, provided you talk some and talk sensibly, the more you are respected ; and the person who is able to command respect has easy sway over others in the use of magnetism.

A person sits in a hall or church ; some one drops a book ; the former gives a general start of the whole body, sighs, leans back and suffers from the weakness engendered. In that one motion of the body a great volume of magnetic vitality leaped forth.

A person is walking upon the street ; a friend comes up from behind and slaps him on the back ; he jumps, catches his breath, turns pale, and is soon himself again, but weaker.

A woman thinks she sees a mouse in the room. With one involuntary recoil she shrinks backward. The magnetism so lost will not easily return in a week.

Something occurs to attract the attention. A jump is made from the chair to the feet. Vitality is lost.

A touch of the finger against something hot causes a sudden movement of the arm and upper body backward. Life is thrown off in such action.

We might cite thousands of cases, all of which depend upon the element of suddenness resulting from whatever may startle. Is it possible to conquer such tendencies ? Yes, there is no person of a reasonable degree of intelligence who will not become supreme monarch of himself if he sets out to do so and has a system of training to guide him to success. Who is more nervous than a very nervous woman ?

A Mrs. Brown was moving about the house one evening, having got into her night attire ready for bed. A lady relative of about her age was in another room similarly attired ; she followed after Mrs. Brown, making no sound whatever, came up to her and laid her hand upon her cousin's shoulder. Mrs. Brown gave a start that took her a yard or two before she stopped. She collapsed with weakness. A year later the same thing occurred again, except that her husband was the offender.

He came up behind her with noiseless steps and laid his hand upon her shoulder, thinking that she knew he was there. She was more startled than before and became weaker.

Under the advice of her doctor, who was a student of our system of magnetism, Mrs. Brown took up the study of self-mastery. In three months she conquered her great fault. One night after twelve she arose from her bed in the dark and proceeded to get a drink of water in an adjoining room. Her husband was awakened, got up, followed her noiselessly and they met in the dark. Mrs. Brown writes as follows : " I did not know he was awake. I had no idea that he was coming into the room. His hand was outstretched as if feeling his way along in the dark. It was a cold hand and laid itself on my face. I was as much surprised as if I had been touched by a corpse fresh from the grave. A year before I would have screamed, jumped and no doubt fallen into a dead faint. Since I began the study of magnetism I have learned to hold my nervous system as solid as a rock. I have schooled myself against everything." Her case is cited as one of a large number of persons who have acquired the much-coveted one of self-mastery.

The very same movements that demagnetise when made involuntary, will develop magnetism if done under the control of the will or if accompanied by internal energy.

A very good illustration of the losses that occur from sudden starts and sudden stops, may be seen from the action of water on an object ; if the latter is made to stop with a quick action the water will be thrown off ; and the same is true if it is made to start suddenly. A quick stop of a train may throw a person forward off the seat. A quick start of a carriage may throw a person backward.

Magnetism is a force that is likewise thrown off by sudden starts, stops and jerky motions. To overcome this, unless you think of the fault by mental attention, it is a good habit to be acquired by utilizing the motions of each day's activities in the practice of starting and stopping all movements easily and smoothly. In so doing, your general carelessness, and perhaps awkwardness will wholly disappear, and so add to your power of attraction.

MENTAL LOSSES

PHYSICAL AND NERVOUS Leakages have been discussed in the two last lessons, and we now come to
the third part of human existence and find losses
flowing out of the magnetic fund of the mind as freely
as in the other divisions of life. These are not so easily
mended, although they do great harm in lessening a person's
influence in the world. Physicians say that more vitality is
lost and more injury is done to the system by means of mental
waste than in any other manner. This waste takes place in a
number of ways, and has two results :

1. It lessens the energy of every part of the body—mind,
nerves, the functions of the organs, the power of digestion, the
power of accurate thinking, the respiration and the circulation.
It can be seen that it invades the duties of the Third Brain as
well as its own. This result is called self-injury.

2. By its various exhibitions of weakness and defects, it
invites the ill opinion of all persons who meet or associate with
those who suffer such losses. This is called the inability to
gain or hold the confidence of others ; a quality that is absolutely necessary in any kind of effort to succeed in life.

Mental losses are double acting, a danger that is charged at
both ends and that weakens the person who is the victim of
them, and repels others.

These losses are caused by some form of mental exhaustion,
or a set of influences that lead to such wear and tear on the mind
that it becomes a difficult task to control self or others.

The most dangerous and at the same time the most prolific
cause of mental exhaustion is WORRY. There are two kinds :

1. WORRY from causes that arise in the activities of life.

2. WORRY that is a mental disease.

The subject is almost unlimited, and all we can do is to

suggest the methods that have been employed successfully in the past to combat this trouble. A small library of books might be written about it.

It is not at all difficult to ascertain what are the causes that arise in the activities of life. These can be learned by the careful plan of listing them as they become evident. From reports sent us in the past forty years, we found the average number to be in the neighbourhood of six ; the least to be one, and the greatest to be twelve ; that is, there were a number of causes at work to create worry. Half the victory is attained when you know what these causes are and can put them down in writing to be seen and studied. We have found that they all disappear under the training of this book taken as a whole ; for that is one of its great purposes.

But worry that is a mental disease is like cancer in the blood ; it is there to stay for a while, and can be eradicated only by a strong uphill fight that, if waged in the right and by the right weapons, will bring victory. As that subject is not a part of the proper study of personal magnetism, but is a disease, all we can do is to express a willingness to make suggestions by written correspondence if the student cares to send a letter of inquiry to the publishers whose address is on the title-page of this book.

Melancholy is a mental waste that not only destroys the person's vitality but deprives him of the good opinion and confidence of others without which there can be no successful association with them. For this and the next trouble, a perfect remedy is found in the Régime of Mental Magnitude which was presented in an earlier lesson of this volume. The next trouble referred to is known as

Pessimism.—This is the opposite of optimism. We have known of many men and women who have built up very successful systems of personal magnetism instinctively by employing optimism in combination with some method similar to that set forth in the Régime of Mental Magnitude. Optimism without the steering hand of good judgment and common sense is mere gush ; and there are men and women who pour out this kind of nonsense in the presence of their friends and acquaintances with no gains whatever unless some of these persons are themselves weak-minded. This effervescence is generally followed by periods of reaction in which melancholy prevails.

However, the misuse of a good thing does not put the latter in disgrace.

The quickest way to accumulate personal magnetism, if a person wishes to secure results *the very first day after this book has been read* through in the manner we have stated, is to turn your mind into that of an optimist ; but to be sure to harness it to the Régime of Mental Magnitude so that its work may be successful from the very start.

Do not go to the other extreme and overdo it. Do not gush. Do not be flowery, as Scrooge said to Marley's ghost. Remember that optimism not given magnetic power by the Régime of Mental Magnitude is a mere veneer, and can be seen through by any keen mind. Your mind should be keener than the keenest mind you meet in the battle of life.

Discouragement is another waster of magnetic energy. It is always traced to the inability to see opportunities for advancement in one's progress through the world ; or, if seen, to be made to recognize the state of unpreparedness to take advantage of them. Such persons suffer the most acute mental reactions.

Youth is the time for making preparations for success ; not for wasting the valuable hours. And the same law applies to middle life and any age in one's career. The man who when in middle life was not able to read or write, and who afterwards employed every spare moment in educating himself and rose to the office of Vice-President of the United States, might have lived and died a devotee to idle pleasures and frivolities. To conquer discouragement it is necessary to move on in life. This means to spend less than you earn ; to add every day something of real value to your stored knowledge, and fit yourself for contact with people who are worth knowing. Five minutes a day will in time give you control over those awful errors in speech that keep you down to the very dregs of existence. Five minutes a day will in time make you a decent speller and decent grammarian ; yet bad spelling and bad grammar are the greatest barriers to progress in the business and social world. These are examples selected at random of some of the ways in which you can move on.

Surface Thinking.—Magnetism is the power of purpose intensely willed and carried to execution by the faculties. It is of necessity an act of the mind, as well as of the heart and nervous forces. Its enactment is planned in the brain, and the method of accomplishing the end sought is built in the thinking powers.

The surface brain is a natural condition that allows the individual to enjoy much thinking without carrying the burden of thought.

The magnetic brain is deeper, and it becomes mightier as the depth is sounded.

Surface Thinking includes : Light reading, novel reading, newspaper reading, games, play, puzzles, cards, social intercourse, and many kinds of activities that do not come under the class of work or study.

These are mental desserts. The purpose of any dessert is to balance and give variety to the serious, the useful and the heavier duties of life, no matter what Department is included. It is true of the stomach. It is true of the mind. A rich man can afford more desserts than the poor man, but the latter is blessed with his limited purse, for desserts weaken when they are out of balance.

It is arranged by Nature that the mental desserts shall affect only the surface brain, as we call it in popular language. The purpose is to call the blood and activity from the deeper portions of the mind, and such relief is often a blessing. But there are useful ways of establishing the balance between the two brains.

A person whose duties are mostly muscular is relieved by mental efforts of any kind.

A person whose duties are mostly mental is relieved by muscular toil or exercise.

In other words the sedentary person may seek variety in any use of the muscles, and the toiler may seek change in any use of the mind.

For the toiler to seek his relief in mental desserts is to throw away the greatest opportunities he has of becoming a successful power in the world. He needs relief, but he will get it even in the hardest study. Why, then, should he use only the surface of his mind ? History is full of instances where men who have worked with their muscles have also carried on the heaviest studies in the intervals, with the result that when their faculties were ripe they leaped into power almost at a bound. But there is not a single instance in all history where the toiler has become useful in life, when he has turned from his labour to seek relief in mental desserts. This one fact speaks volumes.

It should find deep root in the lives of those who wish to rise from their humble stations. Let it be remembered that the greatest men and women of the past have come from the humblest ranks ; but they have obeyed this instinctive law of life.

Personal magnetism is not an empty acquisition. It is based on something real ; not on sham and pretence. The more you acquire in the mind, the more accomplishments you cultivate in the faculties, the greater will you become when these qualities are harnessed to the power of controlling your fellow-beings.

By another law of balance, the realm of mental desserts is also the only realm of worry, apprehension, fear of the future and gloomy forebodings of all kinds.

The woman who deems life made for mental desserts is the most wretched of all creatures ; despite the effort she makes to establish the contrary belief in her friends. Her smiles are forced. She is burying under a mountain all those better gifts that God has placed in her charge, and she repays the trust by reading novels, playing cards, devoting her time to play or amusement and much worrying, with an ever-growing dislike for the sweeter and more serious things of life. It is surface thinking and the use of only the outer layer of the mind. Like the stomach that feeds on nothing but desserts, there comes a weakening and breakdown, a nervous unrest, or a tendency to hysterics, or other cloud upon her existence. She sees all the weakness of others, even in her own family, and they make her unhappy, all the while longing for some excitement and some form of stimulant in her pleasures, until at last her soul passes over to the morbid chasm.

Mental desserts have their time and place, but nobody can afford to make them the chief meal of the brain.

The millions of young men, and the countless thousands of grown men in this country who hate any form of mental action except desserts, are playing into the hands of those who pursue the laws of Nature for more useful ends.

That vitality which is magnetic and which gives to each person the power to rule self and others, springs from the deeper uses of the mind than the surface. It is for this reason that few persons have any real mastery over themselves. In fact it is so hard to put down temptation that few care to essay it. The cravings for each and every kind of harm are so supreme in these weak lives, that vices are always on the increase.

Surface thinking is a petty matter. The sensations of the press, the love for gossip, the criticism of neighbours, the reading of magazines, the perusal of novels, the study of puzzles, the playing of cards and other games, the idled hours in social affairs, the worship of fine attire, the fascination for races, for gambling and for games of chance : all these call into action the surface brain and weary the deeper mind by their effervescence. Most of them are harmless as far as actual injury is concerned ; but they deprive the better faculties of their part in the plan of existence.

There can be no magnetism where there are only mental desserts to base it upon.

The athletes that win the great contests are not fed on pie, cake, pastry, ice-cream, or sweets. Such a diet would at once place them beyond all hope of even entering the tournament. In fact, the rule is the opposite, for all desserts are denied them during the long period of their preparation.

We have often been asked to outline for the ambitious young man and woman, and the adult as well—for no person is too old to study, and student life makes all young again—some studies that are most useful and that arouse the powers of the deeper brain ; and we append our usual list at this place :

As thought lives in words, and as the great people of the world have been masters of words, we advise every ambitious person to learn the synonyms of English, the shades of meaning in English words, and their representative words in some other language, notably Latin. This is an interesting line of study, and soon becomes quite fascinating.

The greater the number of words that a person is able to use intelligently and with shades of meaning, the greater the power of mind and thought that will be developed.

GAINS WITHOUT WAITING

DELAYS IN THE ACQUISITION of a power so valuable as that of personal magnetism should be avoided because of the fact that much time will be lost in coming to results that will bring gain and advantage to the possessor of this gift. Time is passing and the years will not wait on any unnecessarily slow process in these efforts to move on to success. We have tried to make it clear in this system that the magnetic power is a natural part of the human body and its faculties. Thousands of men and women have possessed it by the manner in which they have lived ; and this has been their only training, but it has been training nevertheless. They say that experience is a teacher, and probably the best in the world ; but it is a teacher ; and its pupils are those who have been bright enough to shape their lives to its instructions.

Since the power we are discussing is a natural gift, whether acquired by experience, or habits of living, or as the result of suggestions and directing guidance, or stimulated by exercises, it still remains a natural gift, and as such may be drawn into the activities of life from the very start ; to-day, some of it may be acquired and recognized ; to-morrow, more of it ; and so on without limit, for it is limitless in its scope ; being life itself it is as far-reaching and all-embracing as human existence.

You can learn to drive a car in one lesson, that is, a little way, and farther in the next lesson, and so on. But you should read up on the subject first. We ask only that you read this book through as the beginning. Take time for it. Read carefully, slowly, understandingly. Then review the interesting parts ; omitting the exercises that come in the latter half of the volume. Then give a third reading to the Régime of Mental Magnitude, as that furnishes the completed combination that makes this power, as has been stated, a unit of all the operations of the human organism.

The body is composed of material from chemical elements ; and these are made up of molecules ; these are built of the combination of atoms ; and each atom is composed of electrons that are in the same kind of motion that prevails in our solar system, with a central sun, and revolving planets. Thus the material of which the human body consists is, in the ultimate analysis, nothing but electrons, and all of these are generators of magnetic energy. This is the material body.

Each cell in the body holds its intelligent centre, and when these are brought together in masses, the result is the creation of the brain.

The electrons of the body hold magnetism in a diffused state ; and it is part of life to collect them in nerve centres or ganglia, and in the brain mass. But it is easily possible to increase these almost without limit ; and an increase if it is not wasted by the faults and Leakages we have described becomes magnetism.

Personal magnetism is a combination of Mental Magnitude and the generated magnetism of the body.

These reasons are given here to show why we wish you to read the Régime of Mental Magnitude at least three times before beginning the actual work of developing this power as a means of winning success in life.

Another bit of advice is added here. Read three times the lesson in the Department preceding this which is entitled the Magnetic Eye of Youth. We wish you to assume at once as a new and fixed habit the control of the vital muscles, the control of the chest, the control of the vertical carriage of the head and body, and the control of the facial contractions. All these influences make or mar your immediate success. You will now have as the basis of progress :

1. The careful re-reading of the book.

2. The adoption of the Régime of Mental Magnitude.

3. The control of the vital muscles, the vital centres and the facial contractions. After the reading of the book has been concluded, the last two items will require only a few minutes and this we call

THE FIRST DAY.

But the day's advance does not begin until after the reading is completed and this must be remembered.

The next step is to retain what you have acquired to begin with, and to add the study of the Mental Losses, in the preceding lesson, ending with the fixed purpose to acquire optimism of the right kind. That lesson will tell you what is the right kind. This we call

THE SECOND DAY.

Progress of a marked and distinct kind has been made by the reading of the book ; more progress has been made by its review ; and still more progress has followed the mastery of the Régime of Mental Magnitude and the control of the vital muscles, the vital centres and the facial contractions. But very decided progress attends the adoption of the right kind of optimism. You will recognize your very sudden acquisition of personal magnetism ; and there will have gone out from you a certain subtle but very distinct power which will reach others and be felt by them without their knowing how it came about. Unconsciously there will be paid you both respect and attention, and you will rise in their estimate of you. Yet this is only the end of the second day.

Now you must adopt one of the dead-still positions that are taught in a later part of the book. It is not an exercise, but a habit. Keep all that you have acquired in the first two days, and add some dead-still positions as stated. This we call

THE THIRD DAY.

Next you are to add one of the tensing habits taken from another Department of the book, while retaining all that you have acquired. This we call

THE FOURTH DAY.

Now you add another of the dead-still positions ; keeping all that you have acquired ; and this we call

THE FIFTH DAY.

When we say that all you have acquired is to be retained, you must remember that whatever becomes a habit takes no time to use. It is not an exercise. It is a way of living.

THE SIXTH DAY requires attention to the Physical Losses that are described in one of the lessons of this Department. Select any one loss that you find of sufficient interest to be discarded, and eliminate it from your list of Leakages.

THE SEVENTH DAY is to be devoted to the elimination of another Physical Loss.

THE EIGHTH DAY brings the study of the Nervous Losses ; and one of these should be overcome.

THE NINTH DAY deals with another Nervous Loss.

THE TENTH DAY includes consideration of a Mental Loss.

THE ELEVENTH DAY brings in another of the dead-still positions, to be selected by you. Bear in mind that each day's addition is to include all that has preceded. This may seem difficult, but it is very simple when actually put to the test.

THE TWELFTH DAY adds another tensing habit.

THE THIRTEENTH DAY deals with another Physical Loss.

THE FOURTEENTH DAY deals with all the remaining losses, Physical and Nervous and Mental ; thus ending them at this time. If they cannot be overcome so readily, devote further days to them after this list has been ended.

THE FIFTEENTH DAY adds one more of the dead-still positions.

THE SIXTEENTH DAY includes another of the tenso habits.

THE SEVENTEENTH DAY adds one more of the dead-still positions.

THE EIGHTEENTH DAY includes the tense walk.

THE NINETEENTH DAY goes back to the lesson in the Department of the Magnetic Eye, under the title of the Vital Eye, in which the Temple Generating or the Temple Pulling habit is taught ; and that habit is now to be fixed for permanent use in developing the magnetic vitality of the eyes and face, as well as brain. It is to serve a most important mission in your life.

THE TWENTIETH DAY deals with the three middle pitches of the speaking voice, called the fourth, fifth and sixth pitches. Begin now to practise using them in conversation of all kinds, whether at home or in other places.

THE TWENTY-FIRST DAY introduces the use of the tense eye as taught in the Department of the Magnetic Eye.

THE TWENTY-SECOND DAY takes up the subject of mental determination which is to play so important a part in Applied Personal Magnetism and in Magnetic Healing. At this

12

time we can only consider the beginning of it, for it will require weeks or months to fully unfold its possibilities, which are really unlimited. Mental determination is a power that is given to magnetism from the brain ; and, when developed, is capable of accomplishing any purpose in life that can be accomplished. It cannot do the impossible ; but, before these lessons are ended, we shall show you that it can come close to this achievement. It can come close also to the age of miracles when brought up to its highest standard.

Mental determination is founded on the fully developed magnetic powers of the body, the nerves and the brain. Without all the magnetism that comes from these sources, it would fall short in its work. For this reason we will only start its work at this place. It is both interesting and valuable.

The only part of this study that we will introduce here is a simple quotation that is intended to serve as an exciting influence in firing the mind to secure its ends. This quotation comes from the play of *The Merchant of Venice*, and is a demand as well as expression of purpose made by Shylock who, on finding that he is entitled by law to a pound of flesh from the enemy to whom he made a loan, purposes to enforce the terms of the bond in order to cause the death of the man he hates. Therefore when he is offered more money than is due him, in place of exacting the penalty, he insists on the latter. With fist clinched, he stands facing the Judge, and says :

" I will have my bond."

You are to repeat this with body tense, and dead-still, holding the fist of the right hand forward and about on a line with your hip, with the tones of your voice subdued but very firm. On the first repetition, place the emphasis on the word bond. " I will have my *bond*."—On the next repetition, place the emphasis on the word will. " I *will* have my bond."—On the next repetition increase the emphasis on the word will without raising the voice. " I WILL have my bond."—One more repetition with the emphasis made still stronger on the word will. " I WILL have my bond." But be sure not to raise the voice. It is this increase of power by the mental force that takes the place of noise-force, that develops the mental determination. It is a law of magnetism that any increase of the will-energy that can be made without requiring the aid of the physical tones or physical body, will very speedily develop mental determination.

The wonderful part of this determination is that it exists just as strongly when no sound is made by the voice and no words are expressed as with such sounds and words. Now the final repetition is to be made silently but with tense fist and dead-still body. Speak the words mentally only, but look at the imaginary Judge. If he were living before you we guarantee that he would know your decision without your uttering any spoken words. This is the beginning of the subtle power that is able to sway men and women and to win its way in the world. When we come to the Department of Applied Personal Magnetism, we will find inspiring opportunities for carrying on this development in a variety of uses that show that its value is greater than can be told in words.

In this Department of Instantaneous Personal Magnetism, we have shown the way to come immediately into this power, and to recognize your possession of it. The probability is that you have advanced fully one-half of the journey in these twenty-two days. That is, you are now fifty per cent or more developed as a person of magnetism. This is a quick work. The rest will be easy, but you will not advance so rapidly. Nor would you wish to do so, for there is a pleasure and fascination in pursuing these studies ; and to have them come to an end too soon would leave you missing them as you would miss a beloved friend.

If you have not advanced half-way at the end of these twenty-two days, the reason will be that you have not followed the suggestion made, especially as to reading and re-reading the whole book carefully before starting the first day. Then there may be the reason that you have not given full attention to the different requirements. Other students have made the progress that we have indicated ; you are fully as bright as they are, and perhaps you have skimmed over the suggestions and instructions, expecting they might be adopted with very little attention. If we are right in this surmise, then we feel sure that you will repeat the twenty-two days, and proceed more carefully and studiously.

DEPARTMENT OF MAGNETIC HEALTH

LESSON THIRTY-ONE

FOUL HABITS ARE REPELLENT

THERE ARE TWO KINDS of health; one of the general body including the flesh, the nerves and the brain; the other relates to the electrical vitality which is allied with the sources of magnetism such as are described in this work. It is never a fact that mere physical or mental or even nervous health brings magnetism into use; for there may be a dozen counteracting influences that offset what is gained. There are robust farmers and robust city dwellers who seem to possess perfect health, yet who are lacking in personal magnetism. Any student of this book will see why they are not gifted with such power.

On the other hand there are persons who seem very frail who are quite magnetic. So there is another basis of success other than mere health of the body and its parts.

But it is true that anything that saps the vitality prevents the accumulation of magnetism; and PAIN of any kind is one of the greatest enemies in this line, for it is exhaustive of nervous and magnetic energy.

We have never seen a person who was suffering from the toothache who had any magnetic control over others. This affliction not only saps the vitality and draws away its vigour, but sets up a still more dangerous enemy in the shape of irritation.

Whatever will irritate a person, whether in physical pain, or torture of the nerves, or mental aggravation, will rapidly reduce magnetic power. This fact is known to most persons who are crafty, who take advantage of it to destroy the coolness and calm demeanour that are so attractive in an opponent. It requires skill of personal management to ward off the attempts of another to irritate you; but this is generally mental irritation. Pain from toothache racks the nerves, if severe; and vitality flows out of the body faster than it is generated.

We have never seen a person who was suffering from headache, or rheumatism, or neuralgia, or neuritis, or other acute malady, who was magnetic at such times; although they might have been highly so when conditions were normal. We recall on one occasion hearing Beecher say in private that his last address was a failure because at the time he had a most painful attack of indigestion; and his hearers must have wondered why he was so stupid; yet under ordinary circumstances his personal magnetism exceeded that of any public speaker of his times, and his control over audiences was almost unlimited.

Pain.—It is one of the axioms of magnetism that anything that saps the life out of the nervous system is sure to demagnetise the body, which means that no person can hope to acquire power when the avenues of escape are as great as the opportunities of acquisition. Pain is the surest and quickest of all enemies. It wearies mind, nerves and flesh. A boil will lower the tone of the system through its exhausting influence, as also will toothache, a headache, rheumatism, or any kind of physical torture.

How to get rid of these enemies is easily answered. A boil is not so great a problem, for the cure and the prevention are both at hand. The same is true of headaches and rheumatism. The toothache can be stopped in most cases by extraction or by treatment. But, whatever the cause, and whatever the remedy, the principle remains the same—there can be no magnetism where there is pain.

There are several reasons why bad teeth should be treated. One is that they generate pain, and so sap the vitality. Another is that they send into the blood and into the general circulation of the whole body a virulent poison that affects the brain, the mind, the heart, and especially the nerves. One tiny drop of this poison contains billions of bacteria, and these spread far and wide in the blood and do injury that until recently was unaccountable. This injury may prove to be neuritis, or rheumatism, or neuralgia, or brain taint affecting the processes of thinking and even the criminal nature. Therefore the most sensible thing a sensible person can do is to get rid of the teeth if there is no other remedy.

But there is a still more potent reason why decayed teeth should not be allowed to remain in the mouth. The odour is offensive to those who must come in contact with the breath from such poison. In addition to this odour which is due to the height of neglect in personal care, every exhalation carries out upon the air millions of floating bacteria from open rottenness both in the teeth and tonsils. Speaking of the modern insanity known as " flirtation parties " in which painted girls with bad tonsils, decayed teeth and intestinal poisons saturating the breath through blood circulation, kiss and are kissed by boys and young men with bad tonsils, decayed teeth and intestinal poisons saturating the breath through blood circulation, a physician says : " From knowledge obtained in a professional way it may be stated with certainty that ninety-nine per cent of these young people are foul physically, no matter what they are morally." Such conditions are repellent, and therefore there is no hope of magnetic attractions in them, and they grow up as hopeless in after-life as now. They furnish the common herd, without which there would be no chance for ambitious people to rise in the world.

We have been informed of many cases where men with decayed teeth have been rejected by women who were repelled by this foulness. We have heard of many cases where women with decayed teeth have been unable to attract and win men worth having. Foulness is unmagnetic and therefore repellent. People with more desire for wasting their money in frivolities than for making themselves attractive, go through life losing friends and opportunities because of decayed teeth ; and we have had information covering thousands of cases to the effect that chances for getting on in the world and winning greater rewards in every way, financially and otherwise, have been lost because of the stupid refusal to spend some of their earnings in getting cleanliness of the teeth, while they waste it for doubtful forms of pleasure. They injure their health, lose friends, lose respect of decent people, and lose opportunities for bettering their financial condition. Only recently have we learned of the case of a very brilliant young man who was in line of advancement where his salary would have been a thousand pounds a year; and, instead, he was discharged. We asked the employer why this was done, and was given this reply: "He had been with us seven years. Our manager suggested to him that, as he had to meet many people, he should have his teeth looked after, and he told the manager that he had not employed a dentist at any time in his life and he did not intend to begin now. So we let him go. Since he has gone the air in the office is not as foul as when he was here." It is a fact that one person with ulcerated or decayed teeth can send out into the air of a large room a very offensive odour.

Hence it is easy to see why ambitious persons will fail in life, even if capable and efficient. Another employer said: "There always comes the time when one or more of our employees may rise in their positions, and one or more may be dismissed. Personal habits or neglect have much to do with promotion and demotion."

The tonsils, when decayed, generally discharge pus in small drops from their pores. This pus, although very small, contains billions of bacteria, which spread rapidly as they enter the circulation of the blood. In the "flirtation parties" it is estimated that practically every one taking part in them has pus oozing from the tonsils; and this pus works its way to the lips and is transferred to the co-kissers; but in eating food or in drinking water or other liquid, the pus mixes with it and enters the stomach. Congestion in the stomach is fertile soil for germs and poisonous bacteria, and the rapidly spreading cases of ulcerated stomachs will be the result.

Under such conditions magnetism is impossible.

Personal neglect is always unmagnetic, even if it did not lead to disease and loss of vitality.

Any influence that tends to bring genuine success is an aid to magnetism; and it is a fact the odour of a bad breath is sending more men and women into the ranks of failure than any other unpleasant habit. The people who can help them, avoid them as much as possible.

WANTON LOSSES OF VITALITY

HABITS GOOD AND BAD play an important part in making or ruining vitality. One person keeps himself at the point of exhaustion in certain indiscretions, and goes through life an under-dog; he never chooses to save his energy, and so blames the world because it owes him a living, and does not give it to him. There are men and women who are careless and defiantly negligent of their health, in the conceit that they are hardy and can endure any exposure. Here is a fine young man being buried who went out the other day in a chilling rain with no protection against outdoor conditions; he plunged from a warm house, without overcoat, and in three hours was brought back home suffering from chills which developed into pneumonia. Obstinacy is the exact opposite of mental magnetism. Most of the bad judgment in the world is due to obstinacy; and a large proportion of deaths are the result of this defect of the brain.

Here is a woman who is clad in her indoor clothing standing at the outer door, saying a long and oft-repeated good-bye to a lady friend who is dressed for the chilling blasts and who does not mind standing there indefinitely. She lacks the judgment to leave promptly; and the woman whom she is saying good-bye to does not like to hurt her feelings; so she contracts fatal pneumonia, and hurts the feelings of husband and family. Any exposure that will end in death will surely weaken the energy when it does not kill.

Wet Clothing.—Electricity, which is the basis of magnetism, is just the same in a human body as it is in a storage battery or along a wire. Dampness is a good conductor, and will lead it away from its centres. When the clothing is wet, the body drops many degrees in vitality, as most persons find out when it is too late. The same is true of damp or wet shoes. The same is true if you sit on the ground, or stand in damp places, or in any way connect the warm skin with the great fund of outer moisture by carelessness.

Thin Shoes.—We had intended to omit this enemy, because there is such opposition everywhere to the wearing of heavy shoes. But the fact may as well be stated that thin shoes bring the vital nerves of the feet so close to the ground that dangers ensue from wearing them. One of the severest critics of a prominent statesman spoke of his shoes and boots as being heavy enough for a giant. Bonaparte made it a point to buy the heaviest shoes for the feet of his soldiers, as he found it saved them the disorders that arise from marching too much in damp places. His soldiers were less stricken with bowel troubles than any armies ever known. In the Great War thousands of men died of bowel weakness. Sickness kills twice as many men as the shots of the enemy.

Standing on cold ground, or damp ground, or walking on wet or even damp ground, with thin shoes is one of the surest means of getting the body out of order, to say nothing of the loss of vitality that affects the generation of magnetism. This fact has been verified by a large number of experiments, and cannot be challenged.

Excitants of Appetite.—No greater mistake can be made than that of exciting or tempting the appetite with something that is abnormal. Nature furnishes excitants that are wholly within reason, but man seeks to improve on her efforts by perverted creations, such as spices, rich gravies, condiments, pastry, and almost anything that may be craved by abnormal tastes.

Much that grows in the lap of earth is poison. The products that are safe to take into the system are very few, compared with those that are death-dealing or poisonous. Therefore the fact that Nature produces them is not proof that she produces them for the human family.

The test of value is found in an analysis of the body itself. A certain number of chemical elements are required and their combinations are known to a certainty. Anything else is foreign and therefore an injury.

In many hotels gravy is bought from gravy manufacturers, who produce it by the hundreds of barrels. Analysis shows that it is not suited to the human body. This is but one of hundreds of things that people are compelled to eat who live away from their own firesides. The art of seasoning, flavouring and enriching worthless foods is now such an exact science that the expert chef, who does not want his employer to look into the kitchen, can take the carcass of a cow that died of tuberculosis, allow it to become badly tainted with decay, as was proved in a recent number of cases, then cook it so as to conceal the taste, dress it with gravies, and pass it before the banquet board as a delicious viand.

Most people eat too much. This being true, the safer way is to eat only the foods that are known and recognized, and discard all others. We know that it is unpopular to teach plainness of diet, but we feel warranted in saying that vitality and magnetic energy are weakened by rich foods, and by the tempters of a false relish. The nearer we can come to plain eating, and not much of that, the greater will be the powers of life.

Indigestion.—It is hardly necessary to speak of this fault, after all that has been said. But it is a fault, rather than a malady, just as a headache or toothache is a fault. What can be prevented or removed cannot be termed a malady. Indigestion is either blind or acute. The latter is felt after eating, and may abide for hours or days. Blind indigestion is not felt at the stomach, and leads persons who eat harmful foods to exclaim that they agree with them, for no unpleasant results are felt at the stomach. They do not take into consideration the rolling of the intestines, the weakness at the heart, the yellow bile in the face, and the bad breath ; so they go on eating the things that keep the vitality low.

As all life, both magnetic and physical, comes from the nutrition that makes the body and its parts, the first great battle at this stage of the course is to fight down and entirely remove all traces of indigestion, both acute and blind.

Carbon that has been turned into a poison by a chemical action is found in all conditions and almost everywhere. Its presence in the breath that passes from the lungs is easily detected, for it will extinguish burning carbon, and where carbon will not burn life cannot exist. It is also present in all newly made bread, cake, and most of the eatables that are fresh from the oven. It is the essential power in making dough rise.

It is found in all soda-water ; and there is no drink so vicious as that which contains gas of carbon. It is found in all charged waters of every kind. It is the sparkle. Champagne is based almost wholly upon carbon gas for its quality. Wine, beer, cider, soft drinks, and all ferment are filled with this poison.

It is liked because it has the bite, the snap, the sparkle, and much of the scrape that throats long for. One of its great offices in sickness is to cleanse down the stomach after the mucus of an outraged gastric juice has been collected there, clogging it to excess. The gaseous fluid cleanses it, just as a file will clean the teeth, or sandpaper will remove dirt from the face. Many doctors recommend plain soda, or other form of carbon gas ; and what wonder is it that nearly every person who has taken it has had appendicitis ? The latter malady is so much on the increase to-day that it may be called the forthcoming epidemic of civilisation. It is due to the loss of the fine surface membrane of the intestines, which opens the way to the vermiform ; and this is the first result of too much carbon gas.

Neuritis is also becoming epidemic. It is due to the taking into the stomach of elements that are not assimilated by the system, because they are not food elements. More things that are not foods are eaten to-day than those that are foods. Yet they pass as foods, and are found on every menu and in most homes. These tax the vitality because they not only do not furnish nutrition to support it, but require a great and wasteful expenditure of power to dispose of them and get them out of the body.

Sickish Diet.—This does not mean sickening diet, but it is intended to include diet that gives mere pleasure and no strength. It costs a large fund of vitality each day to digest and throw out of the system the excess of food that is generally taken ; and when this excess is of the sickish kind, there can be no energy to be added to the storehouse of magnetism.

The plainer the food, the greater is the energy and the vitality of the body. It is, however, a hard doctrine to preach, for there is a universal craving for carbon in one form or another. Some like their carbon in the shape of sweets, some like it in cake, dessert, puddings, pies, doughnuts, fats, butter, cream or alcohol. The last named is almost pure carbon. When a person likes alcohol, there is less liking for sugars and fats, for the result would be disease.   One form of carbon is interchangeable into another.   Sugars everywhere make alcohol.   Starches everywhere make alcohol.   Starches make sugar.   Rich gravies, icecreams, butter, cakes, sweets, and all the things that please the palate, are carbons, and their own element could have passed easily into alcohol.

The child is born with a craving for carbon, and the mother's milk is therefore much sweeter in sugar than the milk of the cow whose young is destined to eat hay and grain.   The human craving increases as years are unfolded, and no parent can ignore the demand of Nature.   The absence of carbon means the absence of magnetism ; while the excess of it means the burning out of the fires.   Nothing will burn that is not carbon.   This craving allows the palate to pass on to the stomach almost anything that has carbon in it, and the result is the eating of much that is sickish in its nature, such as cakes, pastry, icecream, new bread, gravies, patties, crisp fried and baked foods and many things that tax the energy of the nervous system in the effort to drive it out of the body.

We were at one time invited to sit upon the platform in a great hall where one of the most magnetic speakers of his times was to make an important address.   He was a man who was known to possess what is called natural personal magnetism ; having come by it through habits of life that tend to develop it.

Just before he appeared for the introduction, he made the statement that he had eaten an evening meal that contained too many rich foods ; his stomach was uneasy, as he put it.   A sickish taste was in his mouth.   Eructations of gas troubled him.   He said, "I generally eat sparingly before speaking to the public, and only the plainest foods.   Now, to oblige a very kind hostess, I am not feeling as well as I should."

The speech was a failure ; he did not evince any magnetism ; and he made the apology to the audience that he came there in poor health.   Magnetism requires a sensible diet.

ARTIFICIAL MAGNETISM

THE WANTON LOSSES OF VITALITY that were discussed in the preceding lesson were those that related to physical losses. There is another class that may be called hygienic, because they relate to the loss of health, and consequently to the weakening of the sources of magnetism.

Ice-Water.—The use of ice-water if taken slowly and allowed to warm in the mouth, a little at a time, will not do injury to the health ; but the pouring of a half-glass or more at one time into the stomach will quickly decrease the action of the heart, check respiration, contract the stomach so that it will force out some of its contents undigested, and lessen the magnetic heat of the nervous system. We recall several cases where speakers were deprived of their usual magnetic powers by drinking ice-water just before making their addresses. One of our students, a lawyer of national reputation, wrote the following assertion in a letter to a friend which was forwarded to us for criticism : " I have had success in my trials whenever I have held magnetic sway over the court. I have learned that food and drink have something to do with magnetism. I am fond of ice-cream when I am heated, and often partake just before going to court in the afternoon. I have noticed that my vitality is less and my magnetism is very much impaired for speaking after I have taken either ice-water or ice-cream, or any chilling food or fluid." The experience is a common one if care is taken to watch results.

Excess of Water.—This is injurious just before an attempt to use the magnetic powers. The best time to drink water is when the stomach is empty. Thirst should not invite great floods of fluid to the stomach. The more water one drinks in the course of twenty-four hours, if taken in small quantities at a time, the

189

better will the machinery of the functions do their work. This method of drinking prevents the stomach from carrying more water than the blood can take up, and hence it is not harmful.

There is a widespread belief that the use of stimulants will develop magnetism. They burn up the magnetism in the body, and during the very brief period of this burning, they seem to set free the power they are destroying. This is wholly artificial and wasteful, for every reaction leaves the person weaker than before the taking of the supposed aid.

That is a stimulant which seeks to make some foreign matter do the work of Nature, and arouse a failing power or bring to life a dead vitality. Tea, coffee, alcohol, and the many concoctions that are sold as hot winter drinks or cold summer beverages, are indulged in, with the result that the fires of magnetism are burned out. There is much discussion on both sides of the question, some persons claiming that stimulants are necessary. The author can speak of his own experience, and say that he has never used tobacco, tea, coffee, alcohol, or stimulant of any kind since he was born. He can also speak with authority of many persons who have held magnetic sway for decades, and who have not used any of the things named.

A very important law of life comes into play in this attempt to substitute the artificial for the natural, and it is this :

Nature will not carry on the process of generating vitality, energy or magnetism while some foreign agency is employed as a substitute for that purpose.

The same law is seen at work in the supply of natural heat. The warmer the room in which you live, the less heat will be generated in the body ; the colder the outside conditions, the warmer will the surface of the body become. If you toast your feet, as the saying goes, over a grate, or at a stove, or supply artificial heat, Nature will not develop as much natural heat within the body. In a person of normal health, the best way to get the feet warm is to bathe them in cold water, wipe them very dry, then bathe the upper part of the chest in cold water. The feet will be in a glow in a short time, and will remain warm. The quickest way to get confirmed cold feet is to form the habit of warming them at some stove or heater that furnishes artificial warmth.

This law runs through everything.

In the study of magnetism, no greater mistake can ever be made than to seek power through stimulants ; for the best stimulant can do nothing more than burn up in a more rapid manner what power is already on hand. Some speakers get so far down in vitality that they can do nothing until they take whisky or other stimulant ; but their fires are soon burned out, as has been proved in hundreds of well-known cases. The magnetic speaker or actor needs no fluid in the mouth from the time he begins until he is done. The few exceptions to this rule are in cases where careers of usefulness are on the wane. Two generations and more ago the three most magnetic men alive were Daniel Webster, Rufus Choate and Junius Booth. Not one ever used water or fluid of any kind during a public effort ; there was no pitcher and glass on the stand to supply them with moisture. All three were great because of their excess of magnetic vitality, and all three have left names that will live for ages. Yet Webster and Booth, in later life only, were victims of the alcohol habit ; but not one of them made any fame during that period. Booth had achieved all he was capable of during his years of ambition, when he wholly ignored wines and liquors, as his son, Edwin, has so well stated. Success turned his head, and his career was erratic and downward. Yet he was not a drunkard.

Webster was not a drinking man during the years that he climbed to the pinnacle of success. He was afraid to touch any beverage that was not *clear, cool water*. Success and acceptance of social attentions dethroned him ; and in the latter years of his life, when his work was done, although he was only in the early sixties, he stood before the public " a failure in every department of life," as one of his greatest friends has declared in a printed work ; and he was later on described as a magnificent ruin.

Magnetism brings success. Success brings social attentions.

Rufus Choate was a man of the highest morality in personal habits. He had but one love, and that was triumph in his profession. He worked himself into a state of nervous collapse, and then became an excessive tea drinker. But his work had been accomplished long before he took up this habit. The tea broke down his health. He ignored all laws of diet and soon his stomach was a wreck. Death came to him while yet in the prime of active life. Many young men have been misled by the statement, so often made, that Choate's magnetism was the result of his tea-drinking habit ; and we know of men who have sought the power by the use of this beverage, and have wondered why it failed them.

In our efforts to ascertain the facts, for facts are very important in this study, we at first were led to believe that Choate built up his magnetism by tea. Many experiments with scores of men proved that no one else could do the same thing. We left no stone unturned to get at the true origin of the story that has so often been printed to the effect that he was an inveterate tea drinker all his life, and we found no proof of that ; nor did his historian have any proof of it except the well-known fact that he drank tea to excess in the latter part of his life ; and only when his health had begun to fail did his friends and relatives know of the habit. His favourite beverage in the first forty years of his life was water.

No grander example of magnetism was ever seen than that displayed by John B. Gough, who was personally known to us for many years. After he had discarded his early alcoholic habits, his power developed, and not before. For all his years of public triumph he used chiefly cold water as a beverage. One man who had attended him on his tours for eight months stated in the most positive terms : " I have not missed a meal during all this time, having been at the table with Mr. Gough day in and day out, three times a day, and having partaken of his lunches when the regular meals were not to be had. We were companions in eating. I personally know that no fluid passed his lips except cold water. He had used coffee and tea, as he told me, but only in small quantities. During the severe tax of a prolonged lecture tour he depended solely on cold water. I am told that, later in life, he used both coffee and tea in moderation, but not when his health was at its best. Plain food and cold water gave him his best powers." Gough once made the assertion that he could get along on a diet of bread and water and yet maintain his public work.

THE MAGNETISM OF HEALTH

MANY PEOPLE LIVE TO EAT and there are some who eat to live. Several principles are involved in the matter of eating. Dieting is the employing of that restricted line of foods that are necessary in order to cease irritating the body so that Nature may get a chance to repair the injury that has been done by improper foods. While many maladies are set in motion at the beginning by attacks by bacteria, it is well known that no bacteria will be able to secure a hold in the system until improper foods have prepared the soil for them to feed upon. No infectious or contagious diseases can get a start until improper foods have preceded them. Even inherited taints and maladies will be held dormant and will never appear until the blood has been poisoned by improper foods.

This then brings us to the consideration of what are and what are not proper foods.

Our reason for discussing this subject here is that magnetism cannot be generated to any appreciable degree in any body that is subjected to the irritation set up by congestion of any organ or membrane. Nothing so quickly saps the vitality as irritation. It is a form of torment ; and the soil that invites bacterial diseases is the one great cause of irritation. Being derived from the use of improper foods, our present study must deal with them.

The husband whose digestive system has been subjected to the torments of badly cooked or wrongly selected food, and whose nerves are wild with the suppressed agony of blind indigestion, cannot exhibit for his wife that fondness and affection that is expected of him when in normal condition. Nor could he exercise the power of magnetism over any one. We were told by a man of unusual magnetic power that when he called on his sweetheart to propose to her, an undigested dinner was crying for relief, and his stomach was filled with a thousand little devils all shrieking with pain, due to his indiscretion in eating, and his efforts to win the approval of his lady-love were a dismal failure. The conversation was as follows, as reported by the lady and confirmed by the man :

He (taking her hand).—I have something to say to you this evening that I have been wanting to say for a long time. Can you guess what it is ?

She (demure).—I am sure I do not know what you mean.

He (placing one hand over his heart ; but the hand slips down to his stomach).—I have a feeling for you here.

She (watching his hand).—Where ?

He.—Here. Where else should it be ?

She.—Are you ill ?

He.—No. What is the matter with you. Are you nervous ? I am trying to tell you how much I love you.

She.—But you are so restless that you annoy me. I have never seen you this way before.

He.—I am in pain. I thought it was a heart pain, but it must be that darned dinner I ate. My stomach is full of dancing devils.

She.—I do not like your language. You would have sworn if I had not been here. Now is it not true that if I were out of hearing you would swear with your indigestion ? Tell me the truth.

He.—You bet I would.

She.—And if we were married would you not swear before me under the same circumstances ? Do not conceal the truth.

He.—A man who is being tortured as I am would not be half a man if he were not capable of swearing. I am a whole man when it comes to indigestion. Will you marry me ?

She.—Why should I ? You are not attractive when you do not swear, and you would be less than attractive when you compelled me to listen to your profanity. If we are not married to each other, I can dismiss you when I wish, which I could not do after marriage.

He.—You then refuse me ? Do you dismiss me ?

She.—I think it best that you go at once and see a doctor.

In this case all semblance of personal magnetism had been lost in the pain of indigestion.

The cause was improper food.

The rule of proper food is this :

Eat only the elements of Nature that are required to build the body and all its life, both nervous and mental. Any food that contains elements not required by the body and its life is foreign to it ; hence is a poison, and sets up intestinal poisoning.

The rule of the proper preparation of food is this :

It should be eaten in a state that retains its elements in their actual value ; and no process of cooking should change such condition or value.

DIGESTION takes place as follows :

Forty per cent of all digestion occurs at the stomach ; and sixty per cent of all digestion occurs below the stomach, including the intestinal canal.

Active indigestion takes place in the stomach. Acute indigestion is a dangerous form and may cause the heart to stop beating. More than one hundred thousand people die every year from acute indigestion ; but the lesser form known as active indigestion is almost always curable, although very exhausting and weakening. Blind indigestion occurs after the food has left the stomach, and lasts much longer than the active form. It is not painful but sets up a state of restlessness, nervousness and irritability ; but because it is not painful, the condition is misunderstood by people who, when not feeling distress at the stomach, come to believe that they can eat anything with impunity. " Nothing I eat ever hurts me," says the man or woman who is highly nervous and irritable.

They will not tell the truth.

Not one person in a thousand, except doctors, knows that sixty per cent of the nutritive value of food is extracted from it by the process of intestinal digestion. Yet it is a matter of common knowledge that, when a person's stomach will not receive food, the nutrition is given in the form of injections at the lower end of the intestinal canal. Life has been supported in thousands of cases by this method of feeding. Any food or liquid having an odour that is so injected soon comes to the breath ; as when onion juice or peppermint water, or some other thing is forced into the colon ; showing that the contents of the intestines enter the circulation and are carried to all the organs, as well as to the brain, and even to the skin.

The blood is no better than the contents of the intestines.

There are two classes of foods :

1. THE PROPER FOODS. These give magnetic health.

2. THE IMPROPER FOODS. These destroy magnetic health.

If only the proper foods are eaten, the development of vitality and electrically charged energy is a very rapid process.

When the improper foods are eaten they produce in the blood and in the tissue of the body, including flesh, nerves and brain, the soil that makes disease possible, and without which soil no disease could ever enter the body.

Improper foods also cause intestinal poisoning, and this foulness attacks every part of the body. It is one of the causes of rheumatism, neuralgia, and neuritis. It is the sole cause of the catarrhs that infest the membranes, especially the catarrh of the nose and throat which repels many a friend and defeats many an effort to win the respect of others. No person wishes to fall in love with a catarrhal individual ; for the mucus and phlegm are not only infectious but have an offensive odour. If there were no intestinal poisoning, there would be no catarrh ; and if there were no improper foods eaten, there would be no intestinal poisoning.

A familiar affliction that is due solely to intestinal poisoning is the collection of dandruff in the scalp, and also scalp disease. There has never yet been discovered a remedy for these troubles until the source was discovered, and it was found to be the contents of the intestines flowing into the blood. Skin maladies also have their origin here. All these defects stand in the way of success through magnetism ; as falling dandruff, sore scalp and blotched faces all repel friends and followers.

Another affliction that repels friends and associates is that known as BODY ODOUR. Both sexes suffer from it. We have met daily for weeks and months women and girls who were employed as clerks, who were troubled with arm-pit odour. We have known society women of the highest refinement who have applied to us for a remedy for the latter offence. They had tried all the advertised cures, but with no success whatever.

Painting the skin under the arm-pits with a semi-varnish stopped the pores and nearly caused cancerous growth, but was stopped by advice of physicians.

There exists but one remedy.

It is to prevent the poisons from the foul contents of the intestines entering the circulation of the blood, and thereby coming to the arm-pits.

In hundreds of cases this remedy succeeded, and has never failed in any instance. By choosing proper foods the blood is cleaned, and the circulation is sweet and free from all odour.

The skin becomes fair, pure and of fine texture. This shows in the face, and quickly relieves women and girls from the necessity of heavy painting. Very recently a man who believed more in natural than in artificial beauty and colouring, and who knew that what is called love is not so permanent a quality as respect, abiding admiration and deep appreciation, resolved to choose a wife from among more than two-score lady friends, and devoted himself to the study of the face and its natural health and colouring, discarding those faces that were submerged beneath coats of paint through which he could not see the texture of the skin. He succeeded, and is now happily married. Natural colouring that indicates fine health is attractive.

The teachings of this and similar lessons refer to those aids to magnetism that serve to attract instead of repelling people. It cannot be denied that, in spite of these personal disadvantages which we are discussing, there are men and women who are magnetic because of the possession of accumulated nerve fire driving forth ideas from a fertile brain, and stirring into action many thousands of followers by this direct power. But close association with persons whose bodily conditions are offensive serves to ostracise in time the people who would otherwise have been greatly admired and respected.

Nor does mere health bring the power of controlling others. To be useful in this way it must be actually charged with those inherent forces that we are teaching in this system. Like all attractive qualities it is a splendid help to magnetic supremacy.

FOODS THAT ARE MAGNETIC

EVERYTHING THAT IS CALLED FOOD appears in one way or another and in one place or another in the experiences of humanity ; but it may surprise most readers to know that a majority of the things eaten are not even food but merely furnish the soil that invites disease, and more than this, they furnish repellent conditions that cause people to lose their best friends at times and to lessen their influence in every walk in life. When man came on earth he had no one to tell him what to eat and what not to eat ; nor had he the experience of his predecessors in testing out the value or danger contained in the things that were found growing about him. He had to try them for himself. If he survived they might be safe. If he died, some one of his family might have learned why. If he lived and suffered, he might have guessed what hurt him. It took time to learn all about foods, and the time has not yet expired. In the next lesson you will see what has yet to be learned in this line of experience.

In the preceding lesson you will find the great truths that arise concerning food selection ; and the damage that is done to health, influence and life by the use of improper foods ; and we advise you to re-read that lesson as you have the book open close to it now. It tells you vital things of the greatest importance. In the present lesson we intend to furnish a list of the foods that are proper and that establish magnetic health, at the same time overcoming the extremely disagreeable conditions that may make a person repellent instead of attractive.

The following list contains foods from which you may select what you prefer. It is not necessary to use them all or even a half or a third of them if you do not care for them. What will appeal to one person will not be liked by another. The list is large enough to admit of selection and choice. Some persons use but few things in their dietary ; we do not expect any one person to use all we hereby mention.

THE MAGNETIC FOODS

1. ALMONDS as a nutritious dessert ; and ALMOND COFFEE. This is the king of nuts, and the best of all nut foods. It is rich in several of the special elements that are difficult to find in other foods. But almonds are never beneficial unless they are chewed into a fine meal ; or else so ground before being eaten. The habit of chewing roasted and salted almonds after a meal is the best of all aids to digestion, the making of pure blood, and the bringing of a fine complexion into the face and clear vision to the eyes ; providing other Proper Foods are eaten at the meal. No other nut can approach the almond in these qualities.

ALMOND COFFEE is used in place of the ordinary coffee. It is made from almonds that have been roasted to a dark brown, then ground in a coffee mill such as is found in all homes. After grinding, they should be pounded in a mortar or on a board into a fine meal. They are taken in a cup of hot milk. The heating of milk pasteurises it, and if it is allowed to get cold it loses its vitamins ; for which reason pasteurised milk is not beneficial compared with raw milk. Re-heating pasteurised milk will not restore the vitamins. But heating raw milk to any temperature and using it while hot or very warm will not lose these qualities. Therefore in almond coffee, raw milk should be heated as hot as coffee usually is when served, and enough of the almond meal put in it as may suit the taste of the person. It should be well stirred not only when put in the milk, but re-stirred in drinking it, so that the meal may be thoroughly mixed with the milk. It is a deliciously nourishing drink, with no bad qualities and plenty of good ones.

2. APPLES.—These should be sweet or mild, and should be perfectly mellow before cooking. They are best baked and eaten with cream or milk, and sweetened if desired. Apples should not be eaten on an empty stomach, and are best as a dessert.

3. ARROWROOT well cooked.—A side dish only.

4. ARTICHOKE.—A vegetable of light nutrition.

5. ASPARAGUS.—This is an ideal vegetable either in seaso or canned.

6. BARLEY.—This is best used in the small form, called pea barley, and is most readily suited as one of the ingredients c soups or stews.

7. BEEF.—This meat if desired is the most nutritious of a foods of the animal kingdom. It should be cooked slightl underdone ; and is to be preferred roasted. Tough beef is nc very beneficial. Steer meat is, of course, the best of all. Bee broth, beef juice, and raw scraped beef spread on hot toas and well salted, make good foods.

8. BEETROOT.—These should be young. They can be bough at almost any vegetable market, and the smaller sizes ar lower in price and make better food. If so bought or raise in the home garden they should be canned for winter an eaten freely.

9. BREAD that is not new. All hot white flour products ar harmful, and so is fresh bread.

10. BUTTERMILK.—This is a medical food, which means tha it is not only nutritious but has a decidedly curative value. I makes new blood quickly and helps to repair diseased organ But it is a mistake to drink it. The best way is to sip it slowl alternating with other foods.

11. BUTTERED TOAST.—Old bread should be toasted an when hot should be buttered, and eaten before it gets cold.

12. CAKE.—If plain and not rich, any cake may be eaten a any meal.

13. CAPON.

14. CARROTS.

15. CELERY.—This may be eaten raw with salt, or cooked i any form. It is also used raw in salads. As a *purée* it make a valuable evening first course.

16. CHERRIES.—These should be perfectly ripe, mellow an sweet. Avoid the small ones that are coloured red with coal-ta dyes.

17. CHESTNUTS cut partly open and boiled or roasted.

18. CHICKEN.

19. CHICKEN BROTH.

20. CARP.

21. CLEAR SOUP, or bouillon.

✓ 22. COCOA, if pure ; or cocoa shells.

23. CODFISH, fresh. Avoid all other forms of this article.

24. CORN, green in season.

25. MEAL.

26. CRACKERS of the bready kind.

27. CREAM.

28. CREAM CHEESE if made at home.

29. DATES.—These are the most valuable of all the food-fruits. They can be eaten in any form ; but cut up in milk they are very beneficial as a part or all of a breakfast.

30. DOUBLE-BAKED BREAD ; meaning old bread that has been sliced and again baked in an oven, and laid away for use. Broken in milk, or toasted and buttered, it is wholesome.

31. EGGS.—These may be taken raw or lightly cooked, or boiled two hours, and eaten with butter and salt. If not boiled two hours, they should be merely made hot in the water, or what is called soft-boiled. The two hours of cooking alters their character and renders them digestible and highly nutritious. Never eat them fried.

32. FIGS.

33. FLOUR from whole wheat. Remove the coarse bran by a sieve ; and use three times as much yeast if bread is to be made, as for white flour. It is best served as a boiled pudding or mush.

34. HADDOCK, fresh.

35. HALIBUT, fresh.

36. HERRING, fresh.

37. HOMINY.—This should be long cooked. It is a better food than white flour, which causes constipation.

38. JUNKET ; a light food for weak stomachs.

39. LAMB ; if young and not cooked to a hard, dry mass.

40. LENTILS.

41. LETTUCE.—This exceedingly valuable vegetable may be eaten raw, and in this state it may be made a part of a salad. Or it may be cooked, and in a *purée* makes a splendid first course for an evening meal.

42. MACARONI, or spaghetti, or the like.

43. MACKEREL, fresh.

44. MILK.—The best form is in the raw state when handled cleanly. Pasteurising takes away much of its value. Certified raw milk is merely a notice to the public that unclean farmers and milkers have been watched some of the time. Pasteurised milk is notice that dirty milk, or possibly dirty milk, has been cooked to cover up the dangers coming from dirty milking. As milk is the basic food of all peoples of all times and ages, a public official should be appointed in each community to see that this, the most vital need of life, should be made safe and avoid an excess of cost for cleanliness that takes more money out of the people than the Income Tax

It should be understood that pasteurising does no harm if the heat can be retained, or the milk when hot sealed up in proper containers. But when it becomes cold in the air the vitamins are lost. If you heat raw milk remember to use it before it gets cold, either at the table, or mix it in some ingredient like a pudding, which will prevent loss of vitamins.

45. MILK TOAST. Or cream toast.

46. Moss, Irish, Iceland or any sea moss. It is a light food.

47. OATMEAL.—This should be cooked three hours, or better still all night in a fireless cooker.

48. OLIVES ; not when ripe.

49. ONIONS.—These should be eaten boiled, never raw or fried.

50. OYSTERS ; always cooked, preferably in stew, or fancy roast, or steamed, or scalloped ; never raw, nor fried.

51. PARSNIPS.

52. PEAS.—These are good food in season, and also tinned.

53. PIGEON, young.

54. POTATOES, white.—The best way to prepare white potatoes is to bake them ; next to boil them. They are good scalloped, or sliced and cooked in a pan with milk. Avoid fried potatoes. Chips have caused many deaths from indigestion. Very new white potatoes are indigestible, as their starch cells have not been developed. Old waxy potatoes are injurious, as are those with green on the skin.

55. RAISINS.—Use the seeded kind in preference to the seedless, and avoid dried currants. Seeded raisins are very nutritious.

56. RICE.—Get the unpolished kind which is for sale everywhere.

57. RYE.

58. SAGO.

59. SOLE, or any good fresh fish.

60. SPINACH in milk, cream or butter dressing.

61. SQUASH, or pumpkin.

62. SWEETS.—White or brown sugar is essential to the health. Maple sugar is not so good, but may be used. Honey is the best of all sweets. Molasses is very useful and very nutritious, besides containing valuable salts, which are also in brown sugar. The juice of cornstalks will not digest, but passes through the system unaltered. Bought sweets are not always safe, and must be excluded from this list.

63. TAPIOCA.

64. TOMATOES.—These contain malic acid, citric acid, and some of them a small amount of oxalic acid. But if used sparingly, as in *purées*, they may not do harm to a system that is not afflicted with rheumatism, neuralgia, neuritis, or headaches.

65. TROUT.

66. TURBOT, or any good fresh fish.

67. TURKEY, if not too expensive.

68. VEAL.—This meat is a poison to some persons, due to its being too young. From a calf six months old it is safe ; and the older the calf the better is this meat as a source of nutrition.

69. VEGETABLES.—These may include almost everything that is raised, if not cooked by frying. Lettuce and spinach lead in value as food and for vitamins. Cabbage, turnips, parsnips, carrots, celery, beets, green peas fresh or tinned, green beans fresh or tinned, limas, string beans, and others are good food. But avoid radishes and cucumbers, as both set up intestinal indigestion and poisoning, and hold a large mortality list.

70. VERMICELLI.

FOODS THAT DESTROY MAGNETISM

KNOWLEDGE OF THE VALUE or non-value of the things that enter the human system has come from the experience of the past, from sickness and death that have followed, and from analysis of their contents. No thinking person can get away from the conclusion that, when it is known that the body requires about fourteen to sixteen elements in about seventeen chemical combinations, the daily use of double that number in about eighty chemical combinations is the actual cause of the sickness in the world, and of the suffering and premature deaths that fall to the lot of misguided human beings. Here are the latest facts :

1. Inherited disease and blood taint remain dormant in the body until improper foods excite them into action.

2. All organic maladies are impossible until improper foods poison the blood.

3. All bacterial diseases are impossible until improper foods furnish the soil in which they live and on which they thrive.

4. Improper foods cannot be digested, and therefore their poisons generate the intestinal foulness that is a prolific cause of neuritis, neuralgia, rheumatism, headaches, bad breath, heart disease, kidney disease, blood pressure, all catarrhs, body odours, and deranged mental and moral natures.

Experiments made by governments and various hospitals and other institutions for the purpose of discovering the causes of crime, insanity, and moral taint, have traced one line of causes directly from intestinal poisoning arising from improper foods and drinks. In fact some cases of insanity have been cured by changing the diet ; and there are other cases where the criminal nature has been overcome by diet alone.

Irritability is the most potent foe of magnetism ; and there is no form of irritability so acute as that which arises from intestinal poisoning.

This poisoning sets up a malady that doctors say now prevails among 990 persons in every 1000 ; that of congestion of the stomach and of the membranes. This results in irritability and loss of magnetism. The brain is surrounded by three membranes in layers which control all the thinking processes, all the moral standards and activities, and all the criminal instincts. These membranes become quickly congested following the use of improper foods, for the blood that supplies the brain with the fluids required in all thinking activities, is loaded with intestinal poisons, and we cannot expect accurate thinking, good judgment, high moral standards and obedience to law from a flow of blood that is charged to the limit with the foulness of the intestines. Here we find the explanation for the lack of common sense that incites men and women, and to-day even girls and boys, to become carousers, drinkers, law-breakers, libertines and abject fools by the millions, indecent in talk and conduct, flippantly boastful of their disrespect for all that is right and noble, defiant of correction or disapproval, sneering at home, love and life, scoffing at parents and religion, and dancing attendance on every devil pleasure as the only influence in life worth following. Their blood, brain and moral nature are fed by poisons. When you see a person who is willingly and boastfully breaking the law of the land ; who is indulging in night frivolities at the expense of health and decency ; who is ready to slap in the face the mother who gave her best years in caring for her family ; who thinks, talks and dreams in terms of lasciviousness born of nasty methods of dancing, who guzzles beer until the eyes are bloodshot and the head reeling, you are witnessing the natural and logical effects of a perverted nature that comes from blood saturated with intestinal poisons.

The proper foods properly prepared and cooked, perform their mission in the body, and develop no foulness whatever in the intestines. While more than half of the nutrition that sustains life must come from intestinal digestion, it is all cleanly and pure under the foregoing circumstances. This is due to the fact that the body requires only fourteen or fifteen elements, and when these are supplied, the demands of life are met ; but if you send down into the system a mass of things that the body cannot use in its maintenance they cannot be assimilated, and must be made war upon, fought out and eliminated ; all of which takes vitality away from the other functions of the body.

In other words, if you omit the improper foods you will have pure blood and will become immune against disease, suffering, irritability and the losses to magnetic power that attend these afflictions ; and you will add other advantages that are of still higher value than any of these blessings.

THE NON-MAGNETIC FOODS ARE

presented here in alphabetical order ; and it must be remembered that some are totally foreign to the needs of the body ; others are partly so ; and others directly poisonous in a form that slowly and insidiously undermines the health, bringing on those hidden diseases that do not give warning until it is too late. There are also included some proper foods that are ruined or partly so by bad methods of cooking. In the following list will be found a few things that readily change into poisons in the body, that otherwise would be nutritious.

1. BACON.—This is recommended by doctors because of its carbon ; but it does a vast amount of injury in spite of that fact.

2. BAKED BEANS.—For a labourer with iron-clad digestive powers this may furnish a stand-by for hours after being eaten ; but for the purposes of this study, it is a wrong food.

3. BEANS, dried.

4. BREAD, new.

5. BISCUIT, new or hot ; and hot or new rolls.

6. CABBAGE that is old and fibrous. New, young and tender cabbage is the opposite of the old and tough kind.

7. CAKES that are rich, or that contain spices, citron or dried currants.

8. SWEETS not home made. Some shop-bought sweets are harmful, being made partly of bad grease, imitation sugar, coaltar dyes for colouring, and in many instances of impure chocolate. There are no doubt a number of shop-bought sweets that are wholesome.

9. CHEESE ; except home-made cream cheese.

10. CHIPS, whether potatoes or other kinds.

11. COFFEE.—The kind that is now sold is much more poisonous than the kind formerly obtainable. In any event it is not a food, nor does it contain any of the elements needed in the body. Use almond coffee instead.

12. CORN FLAKES.

13. CORN CRISPS. Or any crisps. They are not food, and even if they were made of corn grain, they are not properly prepared as food.

14. COCOA-NUT.—This is a food in the lands where it grows, with its milk and fresh meat ; but in our clime it is indigestible.

15. CRANBERRIES.—Here we have a much advertised article that has no food value, and that does great injury to the blood.

16. CRISP surfaces of meat or anything else.

17. CUCUMBERS.

18. CRABS.

19. CURRANTS, dried.

20. DOUGHNUTS.

21. DRESSINGS, if rich or not simply made.

22. EGGS, fried.

23. FRIED food of any kind.

24. FISH, fried.

25. FRUIT CAKE.

26. FRUIT PUDDINGS.

27. FISH, smoked.

28. FISH, salted or pickled, dried or cured in any way.

29. GOOSE.

30. GRAVIES.

31. HAM.

32. LARD, including all substitutes.

33. MARMALADES.

34. MEATS, smoked, pickled, dried, salted or cured in any way.

35. MINCEMEAT.

36. NUTS of the oily kinds. Almonds and chestnuts are the best.

37. ONIONS, fried or raw.

38. OYSTERS, fried.

39. PASTRY, patties and the like.

40. PEAS, old.

41. PEANUTS.

42. PEANUT butter, peanut lard, etc.
43. PICKLES.
44. PIG'S FEET.
45. PEPPERS.
46. PORK.
47. POTATOES, fried or crisp.
48. RADISHES.
49. RHUBARB.
50. RINDS of oranges, lemons, etc.
51. SAUSAGE, and all ground-meat mixtures.
52. SAUCES.
53. SHRIMPS.
54. SPICES.
55. STRAWBERRIES, gooseberries, currants and crab apples.
56. SWEETBREADS.
57. SWEET POTATOES.
58. TEA.
59. TERRAPIN, or any sea scavengers, including lobsters.
60. TURNIPS when old and fibrous.
61. VEGETABLES when old and tough.
62. VINEGAR, and all things mixed or dressed with vinegar.
63. YAMS.
64. VISCERA or entrails, sweetbreads, kidneys, brains, hearts and hoofs including hoof-made gelatin, and gelatin made from glue elements. These things, also tendons and muscles, appear in sausage form, and in meat breads and meat cheeses, as well as other mixtures, and should be avoided as the worst of enemies as they contain the dead within the dead.

The foregoing list is formidable and will not meet the approval of people who like the things which we discard, and who do not like to be told what they should eat. But there is behind this list more than forty years of experience and test. There is a difference between a chemical test and a living test. One tells what a food might be, the other tells what it is from its effect on human life. For instance, chemistry tells us that soap fats and axle grease are rich in calories and vitamins ; experience says they are suited to the inhabitants of the Arctic Zone, but would kill people in our part of the world.

We are closing this part of our studies which have thus far dealt only with the formation of HABITS.

The book might be ended at this place, and the pupil would have advanced far into the development of the power which is being taught. It requires but little impulse to set in motion the agencies that bring to men and women a vastly increased magnetism with all the advantages that accrue with it. But we are going on to great achievements.

The next step will be to develop *Magnetic Energy*. When this is accomplished, the final process is to acquire the permanent use of it. While all these processes are going on the pupil is growing healthier, heartier, more manly and more womanly in a physical sense ; the nerves and brains are reaching a state of vigour that can be obtained in no other way ; and existence at once assumes a loftier bearing suggestive of the old-time belief that humanity has kinship with the angels.

Thus this study becomes the most important in life.

The work thus far is not difficult, nor will it consume time or attention to the detriment of other duties. The progress to be achieved will keep pace with the regular work and thought of the day, and not intrude upon them. A man may take a smile to his office or his toil, and it will accompany him in his round of duties ; not displace them. The common query is, how much time must be devoted to the practice of the lessons in personal magnetism, and the answer is in the form of another question, how much time will be required to do the same thing correctly that you are now doing wrong, as for instance to walk or stand with the weight on the vital part of the foot instead of carrying it on the heel. The substitution of one way for another does not take time ; it calls for attention at the start.

We therefore conclude that no extra time is to be demanded by the lessons thus far given.

Having finished this part of our study, we are now ready to enter into the affirmative accumulation of the fund of power from which personal magnetism is developed. With the enemies out of the way or reduced, the work of forging ahead into new fields of discovery and accomplishment will be surprisingly fast. The gradual unfolding of the latent energies of the body and mind will be as marked and pleasing as is the life that is founded upon power attained by inheritance or gift.

The wonderful sea or ocean of communication that surrounds

14

all human beings is worth the cost of time and effort required to thoroughly investigate it. Its waves beat now upon your unconscious brain : let us learn to recognize them, to interpret them and to set our influence at sail upon their unbeaten tracks. In so doing we shall learn what mind and soul are, what God is, and what place each one of us occupies in the plan of earthly existence.

With power of magnetism there comes a clear light that breaks into the windowless haunts of others' minds, that shows defects and flaws in the plans and purposes of our fellow-beings, and gives the power and the right to uplift and ennoble the lives that drift in weakness through a storm-tossed gulf.

While mystery and fascination both play upon the imagination, the new world of fact will resolve every grade of influence into fixed currents of energy that obey a system of laws ordained for the benefit of humanity.

We are now ready to enter the fields described.

Before doing so we must repeat what has been insisted on many times in this study, that all exercises may be omitted and the student of these pages will make rapid and permanent advances into the realms of this power ; so marked in fact that those who know and see the reader of these lessons in daily life will note the changes for the better in every respect.

In our former systems the greater part of the training consisted of exercises ; these are now retained ; but each and every one of them may be omitted and yet great progress will result. But the exercises serve to bring a higher degree of power very quickly ; after which they merge into habits. Both methods combined make a very fascinating study.

DEPARTMENT OF TENSION ENERGY

PHYSICAL TENSING

HAVING COMPLETED that part of this study that deals exclusively with habits, we now approach a part that requires some attention to exercises with the ultimate object of forming a new set of habits, and thus leaving the work for the future as the adoption of a method of living rather than a system of development. By so doing we shall be able to acquire magnetism as a natural gift and not the result of artificial attention to the causes from which it sprung. Tension energy is found in all persons who are magnetic and successful, whether they have been taught or not. It is an essential part of the power, and is never absent from its use. Therefore if we were to omit it we would leave the student only partly provided with the means of winning success.

Tension of the muscles is a setting of them for some great physical effort.

As all muscular action is impelled by the nerves, it follows that muscular tension has its origin in the nerves.

Tension energy, as the term is used in this study, relates solely to the setting of the nerves for some great effort, not muscular, but nervous.

In muscular tensing, which is common and necessary with any athlete, the nerves send forth their command in one impulse for each setting.

In tension energy, which is necessary for the expression of the power of magnetism in any form, there is no setting of the nerves, but an increasing flow of nervous force, beginning small and proceeding by building on itself as it is used. This distinction, while seemingly technical, is so important it should be understood, and for that reason we will repeat it in another way. Take the following description as a further example.

If you set the muscles for some great effort you tense them all at once for the degree of effort at hand. If greater demand is to be made on your muscular power, you set them at still greater tension ; but each setting is fixed for the time being.

On the other hand, if you wish to give expression to some magnetic power instead of muscular power, you do not set the nerves, but you start them on the way to flow with greater force as your magnetic uses of them grow in life and vigour. The flow INCREASES as it takes place.

If the flow were to start at a fixed limit, it could not increase unless more was required of it ; in which case it would be a series of jumps.

It is the INCREASE in vitality during any tensing progress that generates magnetism. Thus a magnetic person is always improving his power instead of using it up. Here again is another important fact.

Believing that you have not yet grasped the meaning of these distinctions, we will offer you a very familiar illustration in the shape of an exercise, by which we will show the value of increasing the flow of vitality in place of setting its tension to start the action.

Get a small part of a broom handle about six inches long. Hold this in your right hand. Shut your hand over the stick as tightly as you can. This is a muscular setting of tension, and has no value in developing magnetism. If you were to hold a full length broom handle in both hands, and some one were to try to take it from you, you would grasp it with both hands and with the muscles set. They are thus tensed, but the tensing has no value. It is never true that muscular or physical power develops magnetism. On the contrary it offsets it, and tends to decrease its growth.

Returning now to the six-inch length of the stick which you are holding in your right hand, instead of grasping it tightly, take hold of it as lightly as you can and retain it. Here the hand is relaxed. Now add the least bit of power to your hand as you hold the stick. Then gradually and slowly add more, not by a series of increases, but by a smooth flow of additional force ; and keep this going as long as you can do so, without reaching that degree of grasp that is required for muscular tension.

When the increase in nervous flow approaches the force used by the muscles, stop. Never go as far with the nerves as the muscles go in their tension. This margin leaves the flow wholly nervous.

Now it is this INCREASE in the nervous flow and the margin that is left, without reaching a muscular climax, that generates magnetism. And it generates it rapidly and in great quantity. The question arises, have you caught the meaning and the importance of this distinction ?

The principle of life cannot be explained, yet it is a process constantly generating the magnetic power. The author has known of many persons who have so mastered the exercises of this series of lessons that they could easily feel the life principle at work within them. This has proved the seat of life to be co-extensive with the brain and the organs enclosed within the walls of the chest, the spinal column and the diaphragm. Physiologists who analyse this agency will at once comprehend the deeper questions of life.

GRAND PRINCIPLE

Tense conditions magnetize.

It is the central law of magnetism. In the first place, it is necessary to understand what is meant by the word *tense.* The dictionary very nearly expresses it when presenting the definition as *not lax.* It is also called *rigid,* or possessing the power of firmness. In this study the meaning of the word *tense* is this : *The power or condition that exists when any part of the body is passing from a state of laxity to a state of rigidity.*

It is the opposite of *laxity.*

It is not *rigidity.*

In a condition of laxity the muscles are devitalized or devoid of life expression. In a condition of rigidity the muscles are set ; the work is done ; the end is attained. Nothing is going on at the time except that the nerves are holding the muscles in place just as a man might hold a stone on a wall. To make this matter clear several principles must be presented at this place and discussed together.

GRAND PRINCIPLE

Setting the muscles produces muscular energy only.

We see illustrations of the various uses of the muscles in the way calisthenics are performed in classes, as much in the high schools as elsewhere. When the movements are languid, we call the muscles devitalized or lax. You may try these and see what is meant : Stand ; raise the hands to the shoulders ; shut up the fingers lightly, half clinching the fists. Extend the arms slowly in the front, oblique front, lateral, and other directions, and back a few times, keeping the motions as languid as possible, and in every sense lazy. Then do them rapidly but lazily. You see it does not make much difference what degree of speed you use, if the muscles are lax.

In such manner are most of the exercises, calisthenics and other movements performed in schools and under the direction of teachers of physical culture, and the time is more than wasted. Lax movements and lax conditions produce weariness. Lax walking is the cause of exhaustion. Like begets like. It is not good logic to suppose that a muscular action can originate of itself ; if it can, why will not an amputated arm act as well by itself as when it has life to move it ? Or why does an electric current cause a detached leg of a frog to move its muscles ?

There must be energy behind the motion, or it will have no vitality, and the nearer we get to the condition of energy the farther we go from the tendency to weariness and exhaustion. For this reason any lax movement is a detriment to the vitality of the body ; it is plain to understand that it loses its own stored up force without having it replenished from the source of supply. Therefore, lazy walking, or lax walking, to use a more polite term, is wearying. Therefore, also, the lax manner in which gymnastics, calisthenics and physical culture movements are performed destroys all their value and even detracts from the condition of the body prior to their employment.

This is why so many hundreds of thousands of persons fail to get benefit from the most valuable of all means of health.

If the growth of the muscular strength is what is sought, this end is to be attained under the present grand principle. It is by setting the muscles that we make them strong. The attempt to hang by the arms from a horizontal bar without setting the muscles will tear away tissue that is necessary to health. Pulling in the same way is injurious. But just as soon as the muscles are set, the tissue is protected and vitality supplants laxity. Any experienced person knows what we mean. The method by which strength is attained is found in this law ; yet nothing but muscular strength comes from such practice. The facts may be concisely stated as follows :

1. Lax movements weary and exhaust.

2. Set movements strengthen the muscles.

3. The continual use of set movements leads to stiffness and awkwardness, unless relieved by counter-movements. The farmer and common labourer never make use of the counter-effects ; their bodies lose their graceful shapes ; they are strong enough, but never graceful or magnetic. It is almost always possible to find grace among skilled artisans.

Thus we see the importance of tensing for all uses. Nothing can be accomplished with the muscular system, either for exercise or for work, unless it is tensed when it is employed.

But while there is a side relationship between such tensing and that employed for the development of magnetism, it does not generate the latter. It is the setting of the power that defeats its use in magnetism work. What is needed is a progressive increase of tensing for the latter purpose. Being progressive it is developing, and while developing it builds as it progresses. This progress is what we are seeking.

A person who works without tensing the muscles is doing worthless work.

One who exercises for health without tensing the muscles is doing worthless exercise, and useless physical culture.

But these matters belong to the physical side of life only.

NERVE TENSING

OUR PRESENT LESSON brings us to a discussion of the power that develops magnetism collectively from the diffused state in which it exists in the body. The latter, as has been stated, is composed of chemical elements which are created by the formation of molecules through the law of cohesion into fixed combinations, each remaining the same unless affected by some such law as radio-activity. Each molecule is made of a certain number of atoms; the kind of element depending on the number of atoms in each; although the claim is being made that the number of electrons in each atom determines the kind of chemical element. In any event it is said to come down to electrons as the basis of all matter, and all else. These being wholly electrical it follows that the human body is a composite organism consisting of nothing but magnetic forces.

Each unit is capable of developing a tremendous force in and of itself.

As the human body is made up solely of electrical units, and as the magnetism that is everywhere present in the body is diffused, it follows that some agency must be invoked to bring these diffused forces of magnetism into mass-control; and the natural agency is the power of tensing the nerves, as distinguished from tensing the muscles. We have seen that the latter must be tensed either for work or exercise in their lines; so the nerves must be tensed, but in a wholly different way, in order to develop magnetism.

GRAND PRINCIPLE

Magnetic tensing is the transit from laxity to rigidity.

The tensing is not the laziness of devitalization, nor is it the stiffness of rigidity. In other words, it is not a condition of rest or of fixed strength, but a process of change. It is the progressive increase of energy. The process is one that may be easily understood. When nerves and muscles are lazy, they depend upon no supply of power from the vital sources of the body. When they are set, they are held by a fixed degree of energy, which is alive but not progressive. When the muscles are taken from a lax condition to one of strength, but not allowed to reach a limit or to become set, the nerves are kept in a progressive condition. This ever-changing effort makes a continual demand on the source of supply, and the creation of energy is the result of that demand.

There can be no growth of vitality where there is no occasion for its use. Nature ordains that a demand shall be necessary to create a supply. The same law holds true everywhere. The muscles will not grow at all if they are not used. Being used, they break down their tissue ; the blood is excited towards this breakdown, and it leaves its nutrition to repair the waste, a thing it would not do had there been no effort, no breakdown, no waste.

The only process by which man is able to generate electricity within his body is by tensing. This consists in many ways of using the body. We see the most noticeable examples of it in persons who appear before audiences to speak, sing, act or otherwise hold the interest. They are more readily observed, more readily singled out, and we find their actions more generally understood. A person possessed of magnetism does not tense and set the body all at once, for, if he were to do this, the influence would soon be gone.

We recall hundreds of cases of lost magnetism owing to this mistake. Here is a lawyer, young and inexperienced ; he rises to address the jury on an issue of great importance ; he is full of his case ; his magnetism springs from eye and voice and bewilders his listeners in the opening sentences ; he does not begin easily increasing his energy gradually, as one of skill in the magnetic art would be sure to do ; he plunges into the case with pent-up power blowing off all its steam on the first words ; he holds all hearers in thralldom ; then, in five minutes, he feels that it is all gone, and the interest flags. His case is lost. He wearied the jury. He commenced like an Alexander and ended like a tired child. When his magnetism was blown off in the first few minutes all his zeal, his earnestness, his power had to vent itself in force ; he shouted and gestured vehemently ; having allowed his magnetism to escape, he wearied the jury .

Many and many a speaker has told us that this has been a common experience. They did not know the cause or the process of the loss, but they knew that they began with a magnetic charm and soon felt its collapse ; then how empty and hollow the voice sounded. Speakers who know nothing of the technical laws of magnetism are obeying those laws on the negative or the affirmative side ; they are failing or succeeding by them. To commence any effort with a full head of energy means a blow-off, and no opportunity is afforded for generating the power, for there is no tensing.

All greatness is plain, simple, humble and quiet in its intro-ductory efforts. This allows opportunity for tensing, for growth, for an increase. Whether a conversation, a transaction or a speech, it is to be likened to movements of the arm, thus :

1. When the lax arm and hand are pressed forward and back as in calisthenics, no energy is expressed, and this would represent the indifferent speaker.

2. When the fist is held tightly clinched in the movements, the physical and noisy speaker is represented.

When each motion of the arm begins languidly and energy is called in gradually and increasingly instead of all at once, the magnetic speaker is represented.

It is worth one's while to watch such a person, whether speaker, actor or conversationalist. Let us look at the first named, the speaker. He steps forward on the platform, calm and easy. The audience may be regarded as strangers to him, or he to them. What will his effort prove to be ? We cannot tell as yet, for we know nothing of him by reputation or experience ; but the student of magnetism may detect in his repose and coolness the evidence of a magnetic power yet to show itself. This, however, may be born of stupidity and cheap conceit. A few minutes of time will tell ; for, if he is of the latter mould, the moment he attempts to warm up he will evince nervousness, and he will warm up suddenly.

He proceeds as easily as he began, but he has not displayed

any evidence of the great orator. To be sure he speaks fluently and steadily, if somewhat slowly. His language is interesting ; it shows thought, care in preparation and a belief in its declarations. The audience listens well. They really know that it is not above the average quiet efforts of oratory, but it seems smoother and pleasanter. They like it. They feel that it is going to be more interesting ; that something greater is at hand. The very atmosphere seems to contain that information.

Soon the interest deepens. It appears to be in the facts presented, but the voice and manner present them so pleasingly that the audience would rather hear them than read them. Now the student of magnetism notices that the eyes of the speaker have darkened ; no one else pays any attention to the tiny fact. The grey, brown, blue or hazel has not changed, but the pupil has distended, and this always appears black. Then the student of magnetism, sitting on the platform or in the front row, has observed that the body of this speaker, untrained in the art as he probably is, has changed ; the chest is gradually, very slowly indeed, solidifying ; it is full, large and firm, but motionless ; the arms no longer hang devitalized, nor have they suddenly become rigid. The shifting from the easy repose of the opening lines to the energy that follows has been imperceptible to everybody except the keenest observer. The speaker is not only holding his magnetism, he is collecting more, generating it rapidly by slow tensing ; and soon it is felt in his voice.

Every ear is attentive. Little by little, unconsciously to the audience, the speaker has increased the tension of every part of his body and of every faculty. He himself may have no knowledge of it, for he may not think of it, but the fact exists in him as in all magnetic persons, that there can be no increase of power unless it is accompanied by a corresponding increase of tensing. How was this fact ever seized upon for exercises in this art ? Simply because it was universally noticed that all men and women who were possessed of personal magnetism were always in a tensed condition while under perfect control.

THE TENSE TOUCH

LITTLE BY LITTLE we have approached this the most important part of our work; and we will now proceed to enter into the depths of it in order that the progress may be marked and decided in its benefits. We strongly advise that you read again the two preceding lessons in order that this subject may be well understood; and also to help you obtain the utmost advantage from the present and coming lessons. Learn what tensing really is when applied to the development of magnetism.

By the present use of the word we refer to that quiet form of increase in the development of energy that never reaches its limit of power. It is gentle, but not lax. It is firm, but not set. Between the extremes there is opportunity for a long range of increase without too great firmness. If we can make this clear we shall be able to get you started right in the present period; and that will mean much to you.

We have met students who have failed, and we can always tell in advance why they have failed. A gentleman called upon the author some years ago and said, " I have not made as much progress in the development of magnetism as I ought, although some of my friends have done remarkably well." We replied, " It is possible to write down the cause of your failure before you explain anything in detail," and we wrote and sealed a brief statement which we gave him. Then we asked him to perform the tension movement a half-dozen times. This he did. We said, " The cause of your failure is in that envelope. Open it." He did so, and read, " You tense too suddenly and reach the limit of force. Both these faults or either of them, will stop all progress."

A tense condition of any faculty supplies energy, but it must have the power of magnetism back of it, just as a live electric wire must have a battery or generator to supply its force. It could be alive and yet weak. Tensing calls into action the magnetic stores of the body, even increases them, and co-operates with the dead-still processes in producing both quantity and power.

GRAND PRINCIPLE

The magnetic touch is always tense.

The first test of a person of magnetism is in the hand. If it is cold there is either a withdrawal of vitality for the time being, or the individual is lacking in magnetism. Warmth alone is not sufficient. It is necessary, but not all that is required. When you clasp the hand of one who possesses this quality, the effect is not marked in any way except by a slight muscular interest. The tight grasp is set and valueless, while the lax touch is dead. No one likes to take a cold and flabby hand.

There are men and even women who delight in hurting the hand by giving a tight squeeze every time they welcome an acquaintance. This is physical, and not in good taste. To set the muscles for vigorous pressure is just as far from mag-netism as is the lax hand which weak persons adopt from necessity. Marital affection is the quickest generator of magnetism, in a temporary way, that is known. Even the ancients, four thousand years ago and less, knew that warm lips and warm hands were two of the evidences of love. Nature ordains this to be so, for she compels the two sexes to attract each other, and gives them the power to win, to enchain, to enthrall, in order that the race may be perpetuated. Yet in many cases this is a blind magnetism. The loveless hearts, or those that never felt the power, are non-magnetic.

The delights of friendship are generally thrown away by impetuous or careless individuals. What is the use of grasping the hands as if they were tools of ice, or setting them as in a vice ? Neither gives pleasure. One is affectation or weakness ; the other is physical and emotionless. The true lover never hurts the hand of his sweetheart ; the latter never gives the light grip. While timidity may vibrate the hand and make it tremble, there is a series of finer, inner waves of pulsation that are in no way related to the former, just as the ocean may roll and toss in a storm, while its billows transmit the vibrations of sound and the still tinier pulsations of light, all at the same time. The feelings in a human body are variously expressed, but the magnetism of love always tenses the body and proves itself in touch, voice and sight.

If in your own life or in the experience of others you wish to know the truth, and separate the real from the sham, apply this rule, and watch the results. When the hands clasp each other weakly, there is a negation of the avowals that have been uttered by the tongue or pen ; when they are set in their clasp, there is the affirmative evidence of pretence, the attempt to seem in earnest. If love—genuine, honest love—prompts the greeting, the touch is at first as light, but soon holds the hand in a slowly increasing pressure that never clasps tightly. The interchange of opposite magnetic currents is the most delightful sensation in the world. It is because of this great law of human life that the book of _Sex Magnetism_ has been written. It has done, and is doing to-day, more good than any other work or school of special education, for which reason it should be placed within reach of all persons without cost but under proper conditions.

As we write there is an old couple, as they call themselves, although the man is not sixty and the woman not much over forty, sitting in a room across the way watching the November fires die in the western sky. They hold each other's hand as sweetly as the tenderest lover of nineteen ; none too old to evince the keenest interest without impetuous display. Look at the maiden and her fiancé ; they meet and greet with a handshake that is perfunctory because they may not be altogether alone. But when time and place are theirs they yield to each other a far different tribute ; it may be the good-bye of the evening, or the more prolonged farewell of the visit. Their eyes meet with deeper glance, moist with fervour ; large, full eyes charged with the expression of kindred emotions. They know instinctively that the lips are the agents of speech, that words are idle vows, but that the tokens of speech coming from the very source itself are deeds of exchange that may be impressed with the seal of approval ; and, in a delicacy of approach that drifts like a golden vapour nestling against the silvery moon, he bends over the uplifted face, while a pressure of the arm obliterates their identity, and the crimson bloom mounts her fair cheeks and paints roses in a garden of lilies. The cold lipped reader of this page will shudder at our description and think it strange. Without magnetism there is no sentiment in life, no poetry, no sweetness, no charm, nothing but the plainness of mechanical existence.

There is no better way of developing the power of magnetism than in the touch of the hand through the ordinary greeting. Avoid the two extremes. Remember that the lax hand is worthless, and that the set grasp is insincere, if not an automatic fault. Do not think that mere firmness is all that is required. Tensing is an increasing approach to a rigidity that is never reached when the increase cannot be maintained, a limit is found and that is non-magnetic. Nothing better indicates progress than this power, and progress never stands still. It is in the first delicate growth toward firmness that the body, the arm and the hand evince magnetism. Experiments can be made all day long with decided results. It is hardly necessary to add that nothing unusual in your conduct should attract attention, for it would at once end the usefulness of the practice.

By this is meant that any form of practice should be so conducted that it will not be noticed by another person. But there are phases of your life that will command the interest of others ; and these relate to your general changes from what you were to what you have become. Thus the person of a month ago is now so much improved that others mentally comment on the fact. An employer said of his clerk, " Something has happened ; a new personality is evident." The young lady in society of a short time ago is not the young lady of to-day. But no one has seen the transformation taking place.

All these methods may be adopted as habits. They will require attention to begin with, but this will soon blend into the ordinary occurrences of the day, and will take no time after they are well established.

THE TENSE VOICE

STILL ADVANCING in our study, we come now to the consideration of the chief avenue of communication between human beings, which is the speaking voice. Perhaps ninety per cent of all communication is made by the sounds of the voice, when magnetism is employed. It is true that a letter may be magnetic, but only through what is known as mental magnetism ; and printed words may in the same way hold power over a reader. There is a very large Department of this book that is devoted to the Magnetic Voice ; but as we are dealing with tension, we are including the tense voice in the present Department. It will make the Voice lessons so much easier to master.

GRAND PRINCIPLE

The magnetic voice is always tense.

Magnetism, exerted through the voice in speaking and singing, is so very important an accomplishment that we devote one entire Step in this course to the subject. Here, we briefly sketch some phases of the use of magnetic voice.

There are three general classes of voices : the flat, the tense and the emotional. The first is the common sound which is everywhere heard, from the simplest remark up to the vigorous tones of the market-man or the wearisome orator ; a mere mechanism of sound. Flat voices are never tense, never vibrant, never possessed of feeling ; for which reason the street vendor would never succeed in the lecture field ; and for which reason also the vast majority of public speakers, preachers, advocates and others fail who might be great if they had the enterprise to get better delivery.

In daily conversation this flatness of sound is the universal experience. When a voice tires you, the cause is easily ascertained. No tense voice is ever wearisome. Some vibrant voices are. Some emotional voices are. There are so many characteristic classes of sound vibration involved that the subject seems endless. Sound itself is a wave-force, but when kept within its own range it is always sound. It is possible to add other vibrations to it. Even the church organ is given a tremolo that corresponds to the same action of the singing and speaking voice ; but this is neither evidence of tenseness or of feeling.

Many persons wonder why the piano or the organ yields a more impressive sound under the touch of a genius than when the amateur manipulates it ; and why at times the expert is more skilful than usual. Technique and finish are factors of importance, but there is the indescribable something that cannot be accounted for by any rules of execution. It is magnetism. But how can magnetism affect a musical instrument ? Is the latter not a mechanical affair that is what it is made to be, a mere tool ? Yes, but so are the vocal chords of the throat. So is everything ; bones, flesh, muscles, nerves, all are parts of a machine of matter. Behind the material is the soul, the vital-spark, the magnetic quality. So when the gifted musician touches the keys of the musical instrument this quality lives in the vibrations of a tense hand, waves as small as light-pulsations that go out into the air and awaken a harmony in all other life.

But they are felt by all who hear them.

If your voice is flat it can never be magnetic ; and the first step to be taken is towards the destruction of the flatness. This is done by the adoption of the tremolo in all degrees of coarseness and fineness ; an old attempt to substitute the appearance for the reality. The throat tremolo is used much in musical training, but it is not natural. Emotion springs from the diaphragm, a large muscle situated at the base of the lung cavity and just above the stomach. To find this muscle, place the fingers over the stomach at that place where the apex of the rib-arch is found. It is at the highest part of the abdomen and the lowest part of the chest, at the soft bone.

When you cough the diaphragm jumps up and its edge gives a leap forward. This can be detected by the fingers. Now take a deep breath, place the palm of the left hand on this
15

edge of the diaphragm and the palm of the right hand over back of the left hand. Pronounce the sound " oo " as long as possible, while shaking the lower chest with the rapid action of the hands. This will make the tone shaky. It is the only natural tremolo, for the diaphragm by its vibrations produces laughter, gladness, joy, grief, sorrow, weeping, crying, hysterics and every mood known to the human heart.

This class of vibrations is divisible into a hundred or more grades. The usual series in the study of expression embraces ten only and they should be fixed in the voice by practice. After the hand has caused the tremolo, the next step is to produce it without the aid of the hand. Prolong the sound " oh " instead of " oo " with a decided tremolo, and keep at it until it is very easy to say such sentences as the following with ease : " Pity the sorrows of a poor old man," " Oh, the long and dreary winter " ; " Dear master, I can go no farther," and the like. When this can be done the next step is to increase and decrease the range of the vibrations ; that is, to make them wider and narrower at will. The doing of this is of the utmost importance and is not an easy task.

We recommend that you make a gamut of the tremolos, from one to ten. Take a large piece of brown paper and a heavy pencil. Across the top make a wavy line, about ten inches long and two inches wide, and mark this the tenth degree of the tremolo. Under it make another wavy line ten inches long ; but with waves only an inch high, calling it the ninth degree ; under that put another wavy line, three-fourths of an inch high, as the eighth degree ; then under that put the seventh degree, which will have waves a half-inch high ; then the sixth degree, with waves three-eighths of an inch high ; then the fifth degree with waves one-fourth of an inch high ; then the fourth degree with waves one-eighth of an inch high ; the third degree with waves one-sixteenth of an inch high ; the second degree, with waves one-thirty-second of an inch high, and a straight line for the first degree, representing a flat voice. The rule of practice is to begin at the middle degree and increase, then decrease in turn. It will be seen that the scale of increase is not regular. When the finer tremolos can be used at will it is necessary to exclude the plain ones. A plain tremolo is one that is audible ; it expresses emotion rather than magnetism. A concealed tremolo is one that is present but not noticeable. It attracts no attention as a wave-action of sound, but it affords an easy transit to a tense voice. To develop the latter we advise the foregoing practice, and then the use of the sentences given in connection with the tense eye under the following methods.

The purpose of cultivating these fine and indistinguishable vibrations is to destroy the flatness of the voice, and to prevent the building of the voice of an auctioneer or mere shouter, such as we often hear in public addresses. This is one purpose, but not the main one. The waves must be too fine to be noticed. As soon as they are given the intense power that belongs to the magnetic voice, their real value will be recognized. There will be no more indifferent listeners anywhere.

In order to produce the tense voice, assuming that you have acquired the fine vibrations as stated, develop the tense chest according to the practice that will follow in this Department, and associate with it the tense eye as taught in the Department of the Magnetic Eye in the early part of this book. You are then ready to graduate from this lesson of the tense voice. We repeat here some quotations that are useful. Let each one be spoken easily without raised pitch or loudness of tone ; keeping the chest tense and the eye tense :

" I will have my *bond*."—Emphasize the last word.

" I WILL have my bond."—Emphasize the second word.

Repeat this quotation now with the hand becoming gradually tense as it closes in firm determination.

" Civilisation on her luminous wings soars phœnix-like to Jove." Repeat this with raised eyes tensed, chest tense, vibrant voice, and right hand raised over the head. Repeat twenty times each day until the power that is sought shall be recognized by you as having come into the voice.

In this connection review all the lessons of the Department of the Magnetic Eye, and read ahead the remaining lessons in this Department.

THE GREATEST POWER IN LIFE

NOTHING IS SIMPLER than forming tensing habits, and blending them into the various activities of life. The only difficulty arises in learning the difference between setting the muscles and tensing the nerves, as both processes seem associated in part at least. The distinction has been made clear in the preceding lessons, thirty-eight and thirty-nine. They should be carefully reviewed. If the purpose is to exert muscular strength, a firm preparation for that effort is necessary, but that kind of effort never develops magnetism.

The latter comes from the progressive increase of nervous effort, beginning with the lax or relaxed condition, and gradually vitalizing the nerves in any part of the body. It is better always to devitalize the part that is to be trained ; then slowly vitalize it. This change is seen in the tensing of the hands. Try at first with one hand, the right. Relax that, so that it is devoid of any power. Slowly vitalize it by closing the fingers ; but closing them is not enough ; add vitality as you close them, but add it gradually to avoid setting the muscles.

Another way is to shut the fist tightly and yet relax it so that there is no vitality in it ; then slowly add vitality. In the first case you closed the fingers at the same time that the tensing was going on ; closing and tensing together. In the second case, you closed the fist first, and afterwards slowly tensed it.

Any increase of vitality by the process known as tensing that does not go far enough to set the muscles, draws magnetism from its diffused or scattered state in the body to the nerve centres and to the nerves that are being tensed. This has always been Nature's way, and there is no other method that is natural. In these lessons we are simply copying Nature.

A test of whether you are actually tensing instead of gradually setting the muscles is found in the following experiment. Learn first to relax or devitalize. Relax the hand. By this is meant that all muscular effort has gone out of it ; the fingers may be shaken about like so may limp rags.

The test is made by maintaining that relaxed condition of the hand while tensing the whole arm from the shoulders down to the wrist, and there ending the tensing effort. In other words you cut off the vitality at the wrist, holding it in the arm. When you can do this you will recognize what is meant by tensing ; for it is not possible to set the arm muscles while the wrist is devitalized. The test is so valuable that, if you can meet the requirements, you will quickly be able to generate an unlimited amount of magnetism throughout the whole body.

Next after completing this test, you may proceed rapidly with the rest of the body. But first carry the test to the left arm and hand after finishing with the right ; and then make yourself so skilful in the action that you can at any time on a second's notice repeat the performance with either arm.

Repeat these conditions with the right leg and foot ; relaxing the latter until it is devitalized, then while maintaining that state tense the whole leg. Transfer the test now to the left leg and foot, and keep practising until you are an expert at it.

The neck must receive attention now. Before making the experiment at that part of the body, look back to the lessons of the Magnetic Eye, in which the vital centres are explained. To sum them up briefly, all that is necessary here to say is that the centre of the top of the head, the centre of the neck, the centre of the chest and the centre of the hips, all must be in a vertical line, one above the other, as if a plumb-line had been dropped down through them. Stand and sit always with these vital centres maintained. It means a great deal to you eventually ; besides which it is the only natural position that indicates vigour, strength, mental power and magnetism.

We have witnessed many episodes in human experience, and we have never seen any exhibition of magnetic power that was not accompanied by the maintenance of these vital centres. More than this, it means better health, better form, better physical appearance, and the status of youth ; for the man or woman who always maintains the vital centres in the vertical line, will never take on age.

Having learned this, now try to tense the neck, not by setting the muscles, but by slowly calling nerve force into the support of the head. Do not forget that, in an early lesson, it was shown that the third brain controls all the vital functions of life ; that, after the vital centres were discovered and kept constantly in their vertical line, the attempt to force the top of the head a half-inch nearer the ceiling by lifting the head so as to pull at the muscles of the neck, stimulated the circulation of the blood, one of the most noticeable effects being the warming of the feet and hands by this increased excitement of the function of circulation ; and that respiration was increased to a wonderful degree, thereby bringing new life into the blood and helping the development of greater magnetism. We have said that all magnetic people have warm hands and feet.

Following along this same line of experiment, we learn to tense the neck while at the same time stretching it all we can, even if less than one-hundredth of an inch, by trying to raise the top of the head in the direction of the ceiling above.

When this double practice has been developed to a proper degree of efficiency, the results will be wonderful. They will surprise you. Many of our pupils have expressed themselves as believing them to be uncanny. One of the greatest psychologists now living witnessed these experiments, and became so interested in them that he set about practising this double action, which he mastered in a few days. He said of the results : " The stretching of the neck pulls on the spine, pulls on the muscles and nerves that are meshed about the medulla, and excites enough flow of vitality to that locality to stimulate it. So delicate is it that the influence of the weight of a feather reaching it would excite it to greater activity. But it would not need any appreciable excitement to make it accomplish wonders. We know that the touch of a needle-point on certain parts of the brain would produce mountainous results, if that term is allowable. So the pulling of the neck muscles in an upward direction may do as much. But in addition to this is your tensing, which in and of itself is a wonderful reproduction of Nature. The two combined are capable of exerting unlimited powers. Then will follow the psychological value of the combination, and you have the most powerful agency in life transforming the body into a dynamo of energy. I have never seen its equal."

This medulla or third brain, is the top section of the spinal column, and while it controls and directs all the vital functions of the body, it also throws a powerful flood of magnetism into the brain itself when these double experiments are made. Do not treat this part of the work hastily. If you will take time for the study and practice of this combination, we promise that you will meet with a degree of success in this and other lines that will astound you beyond all words of description.

Having mastered the above combination which stands out as the greatest aid to human power ever known, you are next to develop the tense chest.

GRAND PRINCIPLE

The tense chest generates vital-magnetism.

To the man or woman who would become magnetic in the shortest possible time this principle is most important, for it is most helpful. It is not enough that the vital organs be raised and maintained ; that is of inestimable value, but the life itself of the chest and all its contents must be kept energized. This does not mean that the chest is to be set or strained by muscular effort, for that will lead to no good.

Direct the mind as closely as possible to the *inner* portion of the chest, keeping the outward part immovable. Think of a point as near the centre as possible. Make the whole internal portions tense, and as gradually as possible. It will be some time before this can be accomplished. The nerves and not the muscles are, in fact, exercised by this process.

A magnetic person can in an instant generate, also, a heat within that can be felt very distinctly, giving a glow of warmth, that is transmitted by the vibratory process through the eye, voice or touch to any person within reach of these.

When the voice is impelled by these influences it becomes an agency of great power.

THE GREATEST ENGINE OF VITALITY

W E NOW COME to the pleasantest part of the instruction in this line of study, which is called tense walking. In order to know the exhilaration of the habit, we must learn to develop a knowledge of the great engine of vitality, which in medical books is called the diaphragm. It is a large and wide muscle, constituting the entire floor of the lungs or roof of the stomach. It reaches from one side of the body to the other and from the front to the back. The ancients taught that here was the seat of the soul. But it is merely the great engine of vitality.

It is full of mischief, and can play many pranks. If, for instance, it gets fast in its upward movement and will not go down by its own impulse, the result is that you will have the hiccoughs. We were called at one time to visit a person who had suffered from this malady for two days and no doctor could relieve him. We showed him in ten minutes how to take in more breath than he had been inhaling, increasing this intake with each respiration, and as soon as he was able to take in a fair amount of air, the diaphragm was forced down to its place, and the hiccoughs ceased at once. We have known this method to be employed successfully many times. It is valuable in mild cases when a person wishes to get rid of this troublesome condition. Its cause is merely a raised diaphragm that will not go down until the lungs are filled with air, and the breath held for a short time.

The act of sneezing is interesting as showing the relationship between the nerves, the third brain, and the respiratory function. If you have a grain of dust in the nostril, it will tickle the nerve there ; this nerve will communicate with the medulla, or third brain, which is the top section of the spine ; and as this third brain controls the organ of respiration, that muscle which is called the diaphragm will suffer a quick paroxysm, with the result that it will rise with great suddenness, hurl the breath out through the nose or mouth, and produce what is called the sneeze. This sneezing is frequent in colds or hay fever ; and we find that over half all such cases are due to false sensations which may be controlled.

Another set of caprices that this great engine of vitality indulges in is called mirth, and it has many varieties. If a young man says something nice to the girl who is just blooming into society, her diaphragm will respond with rippling waves of action, the result being that she will giggle. Mild forms of mirth are caused by the same organ. There are twenty different kinds of laughter, each requiring a different throbbing action of this organ that rests at the base of the lungs. Actual laughter of the robust kind is merely the very large motions of the same organ. In hysteria the whole trouble arises in this diaphragm, whose powers are then running wild like a motor vehicle plunging ahead uncontrolled. As laughter is exactly the same action as weeping, the sounds emitted by the person who is indulging in hysterics are as often laughing tones as crying ones. Some people weep with joy ; others laugh with joy. When a child is crying, the transition from weeping to laughing cannot be recognized without seeing the face.

When a person weeps the corners of the mouth droop ; these pull on the tear sacs, and tears flow. Laughter that is attended by the drooping mouth is prolific of tears. Hard crying, yelling, or bawling, is a form of shouting that can be turned to loud laughter in less than one second of time. Of course the emotional mood controls the result ; but the diaphragm does all the work in any case.

When you pant, it is the diaphragm.

When you gasp in horror or otherwise, it is the diaphragm.

When your attention is concentrated on any idea, this organ of respiration almost stops its action.

When your mind and thoughts are wholly absorbed in something, this organ of respiration CEASES ITS ACTION COMPLETELY. This cessation has been known to last for minutes and then to be followed by a minimum of breathing, thus lowering the vitality and endangering the heart and general health. This cessation has been caused countless times by giving rapt attention to what is being said and done ; and it accompanies any attempt to hypnotize a person ; therefore it is important that you practise the teachings of this lesson for warding off all outer influences, no matter of what character.

A lowered diaphragm develops magnetism naturally.

A raised diaphragm depresses life, weakens health, and destroys magnetism.

In hypnosis it is raised.

In rapt attention it is raised.

In hysterics it is raised.

In hiccoughs it is raised.

In giggling, simpering and suppressed or abnormal levity it is raised.

When another person is holding any kind of control over you, your organ of respiration, the diaphragm, is raised.

In fainting the diaphragm is raised.

In illness it is raised.

In death it is raised.

In any condition of the mind that transfers the full attention to something, such as a game of gambling, or of chance, as of cards, this organ is raised in the same position as in death.

For these reasons and because such condition depresses life, weakens health and destroys magnetism, it is important that this fault should be overcome by the formation of a new habit. This is accomplished by the following practice :

1. Learn to recognize the location of the diaphragm. It is the floor of the lungs, and is to be found at the top of the abdomen above the stomach, at the arch of the front ribs, where the soft part of the abdomen joins the bones. Place the tips of the fingers of both hands at this part, and cough. As the diaphragm does all the coughing, it will give a series of jumps when that action is going on. Try one big cough, and note the way in which the diaphragm gives a big jump. Snivelling is caused by small jumps of the same organ.

2. Next exhale all the air from the lungs, then inhale as much as you can, and hold the breath for one second. After a rest, repeat the whole process and hold the breath two seconds. Then exhale as before all the air from the lungs, after another rest ; breathe in all you can, and hold the breath three seconds.

3. After another rest exhale all you can, then inhale all you

can, hold the breath for four seconds, and tense the locality of the diaphragm, which is done by directing attention to it as the breath is retained in the lungs. This tensing is best done by attempting to spread the lower chest as far to the right and to the left, as well as in front and back, as is possible. This is called expanding the diaphragm. When this organ is raised it is contracted; when lowered habitually it is expanded. It is able to carry on the process of respiration in the lowered position, despite the fact that it rises for exhalations and falls for inhalations. But there is a vast difference between a rising and falling diaphragm in a raised position, and a rising and falling diaphragm in a lowered position.

4. As soon as you are able to master this habit, adopt it always. This means to keep the locality of this great engine of vitality both tensed and expanded. You will soon find yourself a very much changed and improved person with new courage, new confidence and new powers.

5. Combine the tensing and expanding of the diaphragm with the very excellent practice of tensing the chest. Both are related, and should work together.

Remember that in tensing and expanding the diaphragm and also in assuming the positions just described, the abdomen must not be allowed to protrude. If you are over-large in that section, this lesson will slowly but very gradually reduce you there, for it gives to the body its most beautiful and graceful shape. Persistent attention, however, is necessary.

These exercises are in use in institutions that have purchased this system of personal magnetism for the purpose of imparting health, vitality, grace, freedom from awkwardness, and beauty of form and action to pupils who have sought the best refinements of the body. They destroy all bad developments, ill-shapes and evil habits of carriage, and overcome flat chests, fallen shoulders, spinal curvatures and unattractive positions.

But these advantages are incidental only.

TENSE WALKING

PERHAPS THE MOST pleasing and exhilarating of all habits is that of the tense walk. It combines the tense eye as taught in the Department of the Magnetic Eye, the tense neck, the tense diaphragm and the tense chest. These seem like a ponderous combination of new habits to be learned and acquired ; but they fall into place naturally and simply in a very short time. They hardly involve as much work as would be needed to master a few lessons on the piano. When once adopted they come about as habits just as easily as the habit of good manners may be acquired in any one line of conduct.

Tense walking is a rapid generator of magnetism.

Here we have the most wholesome and healthful of all exercises, and the one that is most easily adopted, for all persons who hope to possess vitality in a strong degree must depart to some extent from a purely sedentary life, and walking is common to all.

We have watched those women who, as queens of their homes or in the fashionable drawing-rooms, take leadership because of that commanding charm which the world calls personal magnetism, and they have never been the weak affecters of dignity, nor the set muscular types of strength ; but they always have shown unmistakable evidences of the tense character. We have closely studied many a speaker who has aroused his audience to the highest realms of pleasure and enthusiasm by the same quality ; and we never yet have seen one who did not gradually become tense as the magnetic vitality grew and increased. We have observed the men and women of the great activities of life, as they were engaged in the commonest duties, and the same law held true. Even in walking they are different from the lax and lazy, on the one hand, and from the stiff and muscular, on the other hand.

There are two kinds of magnetic walking ; the plain method is that of easy and gentle tensing ; the beautiful method is that of alternating tenseness and release. Both are very valuable as means of culture as well as of development in vitality. The reader of these pages who is able to adopt as the fixed habit of life either one of these two styles of walking, has already gone a long way toward victory in the present study ; for the practice of such walking is like an electric generator that is always creating the needed power. Habitual tense walking takes the place of nearly all other practice in this period. Continue with it the two other great exercises, and you have

THE MAGNETIC TRINITY

1. Maintain vital organ muscles as a permanent habit.
2. The tense chest as a permanent habit.
3. Tense walking as a permanent habit.

And the advantage is that they do not require a minute of time, nor take you from the regular duties of life.

The tense walk is acquired at first by comparisons. The beginning of the practice is in the lazy walk, which represents the languid condition of the body. This is always wearying. The next effort is to take rigid steps, allowing the knee to spring back with firmness as the weight comes wholly on each leg. Then increase the speed a little, and avoid springing the knee fully back. Here we have an excellent example of tensing in walking. To set the muscles firmly on each step will accomplish the same results provided there is not great rigidity ; and this permits of slow walking. Rapid lax walking is injurious to the nervous powers. Rapid set walking exhausts the muscles. Rapid tense walking is midway between the two, and is highly beneficial to the health and nervous system. Let some form of tense walking be made a habit.

TENSE AND RELEASE

The most beautiful and most valuable type of walking is that which embodies the same practice as is seen in the tensing of the arm preceded and followed by laxity ; each change being gradual. To do this in walking the whole leg is devitalized as it becomes free after the weight leaves it ; and is tensed as it again assumes the weight ; each action being gradual, although done quickly. When properly executed the walk has every appearance of being unstudied and easy ; although a crude experimenter would make it laboured and unnatural. There is nothing gained by lifting a free foot tensed ; and the more this walk is considered the more natural it seems. A compromise is secured by the following method :

Walk slowly and firmly with a tension in both legs, made stronger on each alternate leg as the body passes the weight over it in walking. Thus it will be noticed, that, while the tension is to be kept great during the entire exercise, it becomes greater while the leg carries the weight of the body, as is done in every step. The will-power should be kept constantly on this slight increase of tension at these times.

When several weeks have been spent in this practice, the habit should be formed and applied permanently to everyday pedestrianism. It then, of course, becomes more rapid, and varies itself with the circumstances attending each mode of walking.

A magnetic person is known by his walk.

At first the new method may seem awkward, but when it has become a habit, it is the most graceful carriage of the body known.

This line of development, like all else in the study of personal magnetism, brings with it every kind of advantage, even if the specific purpose of the instruction were not sought. It proves that what is acquired for establishing a personal attainment, if it becomes useful in every phase of life, is a part of Nature's purposes and plans to better humanity.

But the present Department of tensing stands in the foreground of value and importance, as it brings results rapidly and they are absorbed into permanent habits. One of the most skilful, successful and wealthiest psychologists now living has said of our present line of instruction :

" Any person could safely offer the sum of £1000 to any man or woman who failed to acquire magnetism by the tensing methods alone ; and these are but a contributory part to the magnificent system which they serve."

DEPARTMENT OF REPOSE

THE FIRST VICTORY

EVERY STEP IN OUR PROGRESS becomes more and more interesting and important, if such can be the case where every part of the work is of the highest value. In this new Department we have used the term REPOSE in place of the former title of dead-still practice ; but either will suffice. It is necessary to offer the explanation that by repose in this art we refer to life that is not wasting itself ; not to the absence of life. The more life that is present in the mind and body, and the greater the calmness in the process of thought and the power of the body, the more value there will be in such repose. Here we must contend with and defeat the greatest and most common foe of magnetism, the loss of vitality.

General restlessness is the most frequent cause of leakage of vitality.

A person is generally restless who is uneasy, fidgety, squirming, or in any way addicted to irritating activity. This cause of leakage is not the same as that known as nervousness, or depressed nerves, or prostration of the vitality.

If there were no enemies of magnetism in the human body, there would be no case of nervous prostration, no case of neurasthenia, no case of depressed vitality, and no case of mental exhaustion. All these ills are direct results of allowing weeds, which we call enemies, to enter and to remain in the habits of life. Thus, without intending to deal with matters of nerve-health, we find the study of magnetism the most important cure of such maladies.

When once you have concluded that such a man or such a

239

woman whom you meet or see from time to time is magnetic, you will soon discover a train of facts, not one of which would have attracted your attention unless brought before your mind for the purpose of analysis. These facts are always the same, no matter who the man or woman may be, if the charm of personal magnetism be present. As they always agree, there must be some natural law at work producing them, and at the same time producing the power known as personal magnetism.

We recall several friendly interviews with Hon. Henry W. Grady, the great orator, many years ago. Not only in his public work, but in private as well, he gave unmistakable evidence of the possession of personal magnetism. There was a charm in his voice, a charm in his step, a charm in his presence, a charm in his methods of execution. The more he undertook, the better he did it. The more he engaged in broader activities of life, the greater seemed to be his hold upon his fellow-beings. In youth and young manhood giving no evidence of unusual ability, he unfolded his usefulness just in proportion as he unfolded his magnetism. He drew men to him. They liked to receive orders and suggestions from him. They enjoyed the work of carrying out the grander thoughts which grew upon his mind as he extended his efforts on behalf of his country.

There is no doubt that in his case the fame he acquired and the following secured were due wholly to the magnetism that grew as he added years to his career.

Now, while some would regard him as a nervous man, he was not a restless, fidgety, squirming or uneasy individual. His nervousness, if it could be called by that term, was the presence of power.

But the very first thing that attracted attention, when one came into the room where Mr. Grady was standing or sitting, was his total lack of restlessness. If there were twenty men present with him, and all were standing, he would attract attention by reason of his superior physical quietude ; provided, of course, the mind were making the analysis. If there were a dozen, or dozens of men and women present, and all were sitting, he would be the first to win approval from the critic who was seeking proof of the first cause of magnetism.

Yet not one person in ten thousand would be able to analyse this difference or explain it.

This freedom from restlessness is not the stiffness of a person of awkward carriage who braces himself into a fixed position and resolves to maintain it or die in the attempt. Relaxation is the basis of ease, polish and grace ; but it must be the relaxation of power, not of laziness. It must be the flexibility of great nervous tension, and not the deadness of the grave. These ideas will be worked out as the later steps are taken in this study.

An engine may lack fuel and have the repose of emptiness ; or it may contain tremendous power and be calm in its repose, or smooth in its action.

We were so much fascinated in our youth and earlier manhood with the consideration of the traits of magnetic people, that we carefully inquired into the private lives of some of the leading men and women of this country ; always seeking to ascertain if it was true that there were uniform habits that accompanied the power known as personal magnetism. How we succeeded is a matter for the public, but how we secured the evidence may or may not interest the students of this book. We have all along laid down the general proposition that any sincere and earnest man or woman who seeks information for proper ends can very easily gain admission into the private lives of great men and women.

When the author was sixteen years of age, two of his works had been published. They attracted some attention, and this alone was helpful in making acquaintances. Not long after that he established and published successfully a periodical which also proved helpful. Still later he allied himself with some newspapers and their editors, and served in the capacity both of contributor and reporter. These offices gave him the right to create new acquaintances. He was personally known to a number of the most prominent men and women at a time when the country was rich in the fame of such personages. Later on he was identified with lecture work, employing such speakers as Phillips, Gough, Beecher and others, all of whom were most gifted with the power of personal magnetism. He knew in other ways such men as Brooks, Newman, Sumner, Conkling, Grady, Edwin Booth, Wilson Barrett, Lawrence Barrett, and scores of others, all of whom were successful because they were magnetic.

Not one of these great men possessed the power of hypnotizing. All were successful in the highest degree. Not one was in the least impressionable under the efforts of a hypnotist. The uniformity of these facts shows conclusively that personal magnetism is in no way associated with hypnotism.

But it is also true that not one of these men, nor any men or women who have ever been magnetic, was addicted to the fault of general restlessness ; at least not as long as life was successful in each individual case. We recall that, during the last years of the career of Lawrence Barrett, when a certain malady depressed him, he became quite nervous, and restlessness was seen at work undermining his power. But such an exception proves the rule.

Apply this fact to any phase of professional or practical life that you please, and note the result.

It must be remembered that a magnetic person must attract, and therefore must be attractive. The fidgety and restless person is not only unattractive, but is repellent. In addition to this disadvantage, there follows the loss of vitality from the body which is carrying away with it the magnetic power that is necessary for success after the repellent influences have disappeared.

This is the first victory.

A fine illustration of the efficacy of this power of repose, under great pressure of energy held in bondage, comes from the testimony of a man of world-wide reputation who undertook the study of this system for the sole purpose of overcoming his almost uncontrollable temper when angered. He says : " I learned from your book that perfect repose counts most value when the whole body, mind and nerves are aroused to a fearful power. That described me when I was aroused to frenzy by some person whom I hated. I kept myself in perfect repose ; but I looked, thought and felt daggers. I was ready to explode, but was as calm as a summer zephyr. I learned the secret of life."

CALMNESS

HAVING ACHIEVED THE FIRST VICTORY by the resolute determination to put an end to leakage and restlessness, it will be possible now to take up the affirmative lines of practice in substituting repose of power in place of loss of energy. Examples are always helpful in acquiring an understanding of the meaning of a great proposition. These examples are seen in everyday life about us. First let us recall a case in court where we witnessed the conduct of two opposing counsel.

1. One was active, full of life and movements—"smart," as they termed it. He got excited when he became earnest. He tired his listeners and beholders.

2. The other was calm and solid as a fixed rock. Not one waste motion escaped him. When he spoke his voice was full of a pleasant vigour and accumulated feeling that held all listeners spellbound. He commanded respect. When he became earnest his calmness was so intense that it seemed a disappointment that he should stop at all. He was never fidgety, never got excited, never hitched and halted in his words. He won the case. Such people are rare. How we respect a lady or gentleman who can show such self-control !

This brings us to the consideration of dead-stillness in the presence of others. The quiescent condition is not magnetic stillness ; it is always rest or stupidity, never repose. That is, it is not called repose even if it is absolutely still or dead. There must be the magnetic life of the live engine, with the calmness of conscious strength ; the power of the full-developed energy without waste of force. When you have such vitality, not physical but nervous, then you are ready to put dead-stillness to practical usefulness. Look at some examples of it.

Standing before a vast mob that threatens to demolish a great city with the growing vengeance, a nervous man calls, shouts and gesticulates, all in vain. His wild antics exhaust themselves upon deaf ears. Another man, his eye fixed with earnestness, steps forward upon a balcony, looks calmly into the heart of the assemblage, never moves a line of his face, raises his hand for attention, and stands like a statue while the fixed gaze holds the eyes of all the multitude. He makes no sign, expresses no appeal with voice or glance ; shows no mark of anxiety on his face, does nothing to ask for silence, and there he stands a volcano of pent-up energy under absolute control ; and it is true that his perfect stillness gives him his magnetism. The attitude tells the complete story of the situation ; a man of heroic purpose determined to become the master of that mob.

This is life. It is also an actual incident. It tells the story of life. What good would shouting do ? What would be the use of frantic appeals, prayers, entreaties, threats, stormy passion or plaintive coaxing ? How may persons would have thrown themselves into a paroxysm of action, from the sternest command to the most intense soliciting, in the effort to still the mob ? Yet there was but one kind of person who could succeed in the attempt, and that was the dead-still individual ; one who could gaze calmly into the angry faces and assert his superior power. One by one they looked upon him and came to recognize his god-like bearing ; their voices were lost in their eyes ; a feeling of approaching silence began to travel across the crowd ; it deepened ; the man stood like a rock, yet alive to the highest degree ; the shouts died away ; all was as quiet as the grave ; and in the hush of that solemn stillness his every word was heard and absorbed. One man had mastered many thousands.

A well-known business man of great coolness and magnetism, took his accounts home one night for the purpose of looking over them. He had a sum of money with him, of which a desperado had knowledge. It was the hour of midnight ; stormy without and lonely within. The man sat at his desk writing, and thought he heard the sound of steps in the adjoining room which was dark, although the door stood open. He was a man of mag-netism as we have said. One of the essentials of magnetism is coolness ; coolness to an extraordinary degree. The person who gets excited, who shows fear, who trembles, who quails before anything, is to that extent lacking in this power.

Coolness can be acquired. We have had letters from nervous persons who have said they were incapable of becoming cool ; and yet they conquered the fault as soon as they began to develop magnetism. From the very fact that nervous motions cause a rapid loss of vitality by throwing off the energy of the body, it could at once be seen that the absence of coolness would amount to a loss of control over another person. The man referred to was of the combination required to cope with the burglar. The following conversation is substantially that which took place :

" Come in."

The burglar resolved to kill the merchant if he resisted ; and although he was surprised at the announcement, he entered the room, levelled a revolver at the head of his victim, approached him and said :

" I've got you."

" Eh ? "

" I've got you."

" Sit down."

" No, I won't. I'm here for business. I've got you."

" Eh ? "

" You're mine. Now give up."

" Isn't your language a little peculiar for a professional burglar ? "

" Well, that's my look-out. Give me that money or you're a dead one."

" The money is all right. I give lots of money away without being asked for it. I don't mind the money. I have plenty for my own use and to give away. I don't like the tone of your voice."

" That's all right. Be quick now. I'm here to do a clean job."

" What will you do ? "

" I'll kill you if you move."

" What good would it do you to kill me ? You would hang for it."

" Hang nothing."

By this time the merchant, who had kept his eyes fixed on

the burglar, found a slight evidence of quailing in the latter. From that moment he was sure of the result.

" You will certainly be hung. Do you see that button ? "

" Yes."

" Do you hear the sound below ? "

" Police ? "

" Give me your revolver."

The man is now serving a term of imprisonment.

Coolness with magnetism are sure to conquer all things ; and these two qualities belong together. The more of one you get the more of the other will follow, provided the coolness is not of the blasé, cold-blooded type of stupidity. Remember that the engine must be alive with power.

A speaker stands on the platform delivering his speech. He is languid, gentle, quiet, cool, collected, effeminate, weak and yet free from nervousness. He lacks the energy of a thoroughly live man. There are no fires in the engine ; hence the quietude of the body.

Another speaker stands on the platform delivering his speech. He has vitality enough, but it leaks out at all sides. His head beats the emphasis of his ideas just as nearly as all readers' and speakers' heads do. His eyes are unsteady, looking in every direction without power of expression. He steps about, shifting his weight every minute or two, now advancing, now retiring, now going across to the right or the left, and never standing still very long at a time. He brings the upper half of his body forward and bends to give emphasis to a supposedly strong idea, doing this several times a minute. He gestures in every sort of way, but contents himself to do finger movements in the absence of the full-arm action whenever the thought is not weighty enough to admit of gesticulation. Soon he has exhausted all that stock of energy that would have gone to produce magnetism, and he now finds that he must make up in the physical what he lacks in the magnetic, and he shouts and pounds.

Another speaker, the rare kind, the individual with the greatest degree of honesty because he has the conscience to equip himself for his profession, stands on the platform delivering his speech. He is cool, not because he is weak, but because he knows that great truths require all the power a man possesses to give them full weight of utterance. He stands still. When there is cause for action of the whole body he steps forward with a single movement as a stately ship might swing from her moorings, not as a fidgety orator might jog about over the platform. His head is not bobbing up and down, right and left, to the rhythm of his words, as is so commonly the case with speakers. He keeps his head erect upon his shoulders, strong, powerful, energetic, but in perfect repose. This is what excites the admiration of the audience.

Few men and few women carry their heads in magnetic poise. When weak it falls forward, or is inclined to the right or left, or is tilted back ; while the person of magnetism is of easier and yet more solid poise. There is no setness, no stiffness about the neck ; but there is firmness and certainty of carriage that denotes the presence of power. To be still does not require that one be stiff ; the stillness of death holds that quality. We wish the stillness of life. When the ordinary person is told to straighten up, to remove the lines of weakness, he has no other recourse than to the lines of hardness, and the latter is worse than the former. Magnetism steers us clear of these extremes.

The third speaker of whom we spoke was magnetic. He had cultivated the body and all its faculties. He knew the value of repose, of dead-stillness, as he stood before his audience. The vitality that another might have thrown away in useless action he kept in storage to be dealt out as he chose. His gestures were inclined to assume the character of attitudes, for he presented as much versatility in his physical portrayal of his thoughts as did any of the other speakers ; but he preferred the gesture of the outstretched arm and expressive position of the hand rather than the swinging motion so common to others. Why is it that nearly all speakers believe that motion expresses more than attitude ? Does the blow dealt by the hand hit anybody in a gesture ; and, if not, why are the uplifted arm and clinched fist not more expressive of the meaning of a blow ? The speaker seeks to illustrate this thought. He cannot reproduce life by acting its details. He cannot fire a gun when he tells of a killing. Repose in the attitude of description is always more effective and far more beautiful than action that never comes to a position of meaning.

A lawyer who holds mastery over himself at once wins respect. He does not fly up out of his chair to shout his objection to the judge. If the interests of his client demand that he make objection he can always be heard, and the more dignified he is the more likely he will be to get a full hearing. Judges admire cool, self-possessed lawyers ; they dislike the active, nervous fellows who try to carry everything before them as by storm. The cool lawyer is most powerful in handling witnesses, for he thinks more rapidly and carries more trains of thoughts than the excitable lawyer.

The habit of walking to and fro while speaking is the result of nervousness, and is very taxing on the vitality. It occurs before juries and before audiences generally. Some men walk up and down, striding from place to place as though the action were impelled by a special degree of interest ; but if you will take notice of the successful, the brainy, the magnetic lawyers, and orators generally, you will find them keeping closer to a given spot. It is true that action arouses latent magnetism ; but when it is aroused, it should not be wasted and thrown away wantonly.

There is no more interesting study of human nature than that which is devoted to watching people about you, and seeking to apply some of the laws of life to their habits and methods of handling themselves.

A new phase of the study of personal magnetism is called the Comparative System. It is employed by those who wish to make the greatest progress in the least amount of time and with the least effort. It has been used with great success by a number of keen-minded persons, and seems to have been invented by a man of unusual magnetic power for his individual advancement.

The value of the Comparative System is that it requires no time whatever, and no practice. It is simplicity itself. All that is needed is to watch other people, and study their various mannerisms and defects of handling themselves ; and compare each action and each defect with yourself in the same line. Thus, how does such a person sit, stand, walk, talk, move about, exhibit unrest or lack of control, and so on ; and what of these defects, if any, or merits if any, do you possess, comparing each and every detail ?

LESSON FORTY-SIX

CALM ENERGY OF POWER

OUR NEXT STEP brings us to the consideration of
perfect calmness of body and mind while charged
with tremendous energy; the power to think great
thoughts and not to let them run wild with the emotions;
the power to hold great determination and not lose any of its
force in wasted action. Can you imagine a perfect machine
that has been built for the execution of the most delicate
and at the same time the most useful movements; a machine
that does what it was made for, and nothing else; a machine
that never loses any motion in the midst of those that display
its efficiency? Every detail of its work has a purpose behind it.
If it were permitted to perform other details, some of its
power and much of its usefulness would be wasted.

In like manner it must be remembered:

1. That there must be the energy of a strong life within.

2. That there must be no action without except what is
needed for the expression of the life within.

The practice introduced in this chapter is of a mixed character.
We prefer, wherever it is possible, to use the necessary events
of the day as means of progress, rather than dry exercises. The
child that grows up to manhood or womanhood, and becomes
magnetic without practice, is in fact always practising. The
nervousness, the activity and vigour of youth are all evidences of
extra vitality with which young people are supplied; the excess
being intended by Nature to carry the child through the perils of
early life, for statistics as well as circumstances conspire to its
cutting off. Out of that turmoil of activity a few come to the
settled repose of stupidity which has but little life within; and
a rare few attain magnetism by natural processes.

But how?

Who told them that a live soul, a throbbing, pulsating life

within a body, when held compressed by the other forces, became intensely magnetic ; that the use of the inner power through the controlled channels of expression increased that magnetism ; and that waste action or lost motions sap the fountain and spend its wealth ?

No one ever proclaimed these things to them, perhaps, but some genius whose presence they could not discern whispered the secret to them; and they, all unconscious of the fact, became experts in the art of self-composure. Or it may be that a keen judgment told them that persons who cannot sit still or stand still are less capable of impressing themselves upon their fellow-beings than those who retain all their vigour while commanding its use. At any rate, the person who is naturally magnetic possesses the same traits as those who have acquired the power. The possession has come through the same processes.

What may be practice to you is habit in another. There are not two royal roads to the same palace in the study of mag-netism. It is by conserving the energies of life and increasing them that the results are attained. These things are done by habit in one case ; and by practice in another ; but they are identically the same. While the work of the present chapter may be called practice, we are endeavouring to set it forth in two classes :

1. In the habit of persons who are naturally endowed with personal magnetism.

2. In dry practice.

If you adopt the former without the latter, it will suffice, provided you are able to make the easier and more natural methods count as effectively as the dry practice. The latter has the merit of being speedier and more certain.

Newly acquired habits soon become second nature.

What you decide to do regularly in the daily routine of action, will grow upon you and soon attend to its own performance. If it were not for this quality of the human mind, we would all be helpless. Parts of the body may be trained to take up these secondary habits and carry them on in many diverse ways at the same time ; as is specially noted in the case of the musician. No person can play the piano until the fingers have acquired the habit of travelling over the keys with accuracy of touch, a thing that is impossible for may weeks or months.

By and by the ten digits of the two hands are able to perform ten different duties, all exact, and at the rate of hundreds per minute. Then comes the time when the habit of playing is so well established that the eyes need not see the keyboard ; the mind can measure it through the hands. The church organist operates the many keys that are made for the hands, as well as a number of pedals for the feet.

One of the charms of second nature is in the fact that a new habit does not bother the mind when it is correct in its operations, but does bother the mind when in error. Here is a person who has spoken bad grammar for years in ignorance ; he learns the rules of grammar, soon applies them, does so with accuracy for weeks until he finds himself speaking correctly as a second nature, and thereafter he has no knowledge that he is following the rules. Being adopted into his life they demand no attention from the mind. But here comes the wonder : When he speaks correctly he is not aware of the fact ; yet let him make an error and his mind will recognize it at once.

In stronger force the same law holds true when personal habits are involved. The faulty attitude is overcome by practice and disappears ; if there is negligence the breach is noticed at the time, but the continual doing of what is one's regular way is never recognized by the doer of it. It is the error, the exception, the break in the habit that arrests attention. When an attempt to establish dead-stillness as a second nature has been persisted in for a few weeks, the whole nervous system will take it up and adopt it as a habit. Then, when some breach of this occurs, the mind will have knowledge of it.

Dead-stillness requires perfect calmness of the mind and emotions.

When the mind is excited, the body as its agent loses control of itself to some extent. The emotions or feelings go much further, for they unbalance both mind and body.

We know of nothing more important in this or in any other study than that the mind should always be calm. Even if the muscles must give way to their proneness to move constantly, or the nerves twitch, the brain which is the engineer should never under any impression show excitement, nor should the emotions control the mind or body.

A calm mind is a successful mind, if the calmness is one of strength, not exhaustion. Many little laws come into play at this juncture ; not broad enough to be called principles. We will state them :

1. The muscles of the body, by constant involuntary motions, may waste the vitality without involving the action of the mind.

2. The nerves of the body, by constant twitching, may waste the vitality without involving the action of the mind.

3. Dead-stillness as practised in this book, will overcome both faults and lead to the accumulation of magnetism.

4. The excitement of the mind may or may not involve the action of the muscles or of the nerves. It generally does affect them seriously.

5. The excitement of the emotions may or may not involve the mind, muscles and nerves. It is almost certain to affect the mind, unless the person is of strong magnetic self-control.

6. It is a test of power to be able to separate the thoughts from the face.

7. It is the best test of power to be able to separate the emotions from the mind ; thence from the face and general body.

8. The practice of dead-stillness as given in this book will accomplish such results.

Napoleon could make his face like marble if he chose. He never allowed his nearest friend or closest counsellor to know what was passing in his mind, or what effect any news, good or bad, really produced on him. He retained that placidity of countenance that told nothing. Apart from his occasional periods of anger, he was a man of dead-stillness ; an engine of tremendous power held in control. His magnetism was most powerful. By it he held men of treachery under sway of his will ; he inspired his soldiers to deeds of frenzied heroism, and overawed his opponents in diplomacy.

Bismarck, Gladstone and all great men have separated their emotions from their minds, and both from muscles and nerves ; so that passion never intrudes itself unbidden.

9. Mental and emotional excitement may be concealed by

controlling the muscles and nerves, even at times without possessing much magnetism ; but it requires the highest degree of this power to prevent the voice from betraying the excitement. It is dead-stillness in full earnestness.

Practise dead-stillness all day long. Use all parts of the body that are required in the performance of any duty ; but do not allow a single action otherwise to escape. It will take no time. You will be all the stronger for it. If need be, have some friend watch you to give advice as to any escaping motions. Make everything count.

The parent can always control the child, and without unkindness, by the perfect power of absolute repose of all parts of the body not needed in use ; the steady glance, the placid face and the calm control of mind and body. No child, however fractious, can resist this influence if backed by the magnetism that such calmness will generate.

The school teacher is able to control the most unruly of scholars by the conditions just stated. We could devote hundreds of pages to reports from teachers confirming the irresistible force of dead-stillness when alive with magnetic energy.

The same results are everywhere reported. There is no reason why you should not be master of those with whom you come in contact.

However, all such control requires tact. It is the one key of success in life. Tact unlocks all the doors in the hearts and pockets of your fellow-beings. It wins friendships without ostentation, and secures wealth without wrong.

It makes but little difference how much magnetism is born in us or later cultivated, if we have no tact we cannot suitably use it. There are to-day living in obscurity great men and women who need only this one power to develop them. They have aspirations and longings for a proud career, a noble future, but have no tact. Could we go among them and bring them out by teaching them how to come in contact with the world, we should find Shakespeares and Miltons, Whitefields and Spurgeons, Websters and Clays, Garricks and Goughs, where now we see but the yearning for greatness stamped upon the face.

The cultivation of tact and the cultivation of personal magnetism go hand in hand.

LESSON FORTY-SEVEN

EXPERIMENTS

A FEW PLEASING TESTS arranged for the purpose of hastening the progress of the student will be welcomed as a diversion. While they are highly beneficial they are not very difficult unless your nerves are shattered by bad habits or ill-health. If they are repeated a number of times they will begin to grow easy, as has been often declared by those who have tried them.

FIRST EXPERIMENT

Take a sheet of notepaper, neither too stiff nor too thin ; tear it in halves ; hold one-half of it in the hand by placing the thumb and two fingers at the lower corner of the paper, holding the hand about a foot from the chest, and the elbow away from the body. The entire arm must be free—that is, must not touch anything, nor have any means of support.

If a mirror is convenient it is well to locate some fine spot on the glass (if it has none, place an ink spot there), and hold the paper so that the upper opposite corner from that in the hand shall be on an exact line with the eye and the spot on the mirror. Hold this for twelve seconds, and note the deviation of the corner of the paper from the spot. If there is no deviation, you are ready to undertake the second experiment. If there is, you should practise this until you can prevent any departure, however slight, from the spot indicated.

SECOND EXPERIMENT

Take a large sheet of writing paper, tear it in halves, and hold it in the same manner as in the first exercise. Persist in practising until there is no deviation even of a hairbreadth. Do not be discouraged if it requires patience. The left hand

254

may be employed about one-quarter of the time, or *vice versa*, if the pupil is left-handed.

THIRD EXPERIMENT

When the last exercise has been mastered, the pupil may take a sheet of the larger size foolscap paper, tear it in halves, and continue as before.

FOURTH EXPERIMENT

When the third exercise has been accomplished, the pupil may take an entire sheet of foolscap paper, and, without tearing it, open the whole sheet and hold it by the lower corner, having the thumb and two fingers upon as small a portion of it as possible. The paper must be just stiff enough to stand alone. Making a hollow curve diagonally across the centre will aid in keeping it stiff.

Be sure that the elbow has no support and is extended from the body.

FIFTH EXPERIMENT

Fill a large wineglass two-thirds full of water ; take it at the small part just above the bottom, by the thumb and first finger only, and hold it for thirty seconds on a level with the chin, the elbow being away from the body and the whole arm free. The water must not shake or even tremble. Rest.

Hold it in the same way, employing the thumb and second finger only, for thirty seconds. Rest.

Hold it in the same way, employing the thumb and third finger only, for thirty seconds. Rest.

Hold it in the same way, employing the thumb and little finger only, for thirty seconds. Rest.

Your patience will be sorely tried.

But after several efforts you will suddenly find yourself mastering the experiment with unexpected ease.

These experiments will seem to make you " nervous " ; you will say that instead of making you control yourself better they irritate and vex your nerves. So it will seem at first, and likewise at all times when your leakage is going on rapidly. This apparent "nervousness" is really the rebellious leakage being checked. It dislikes to be stopped. A "nervous" person wants to let the leakage go on until complete prostration ensues.

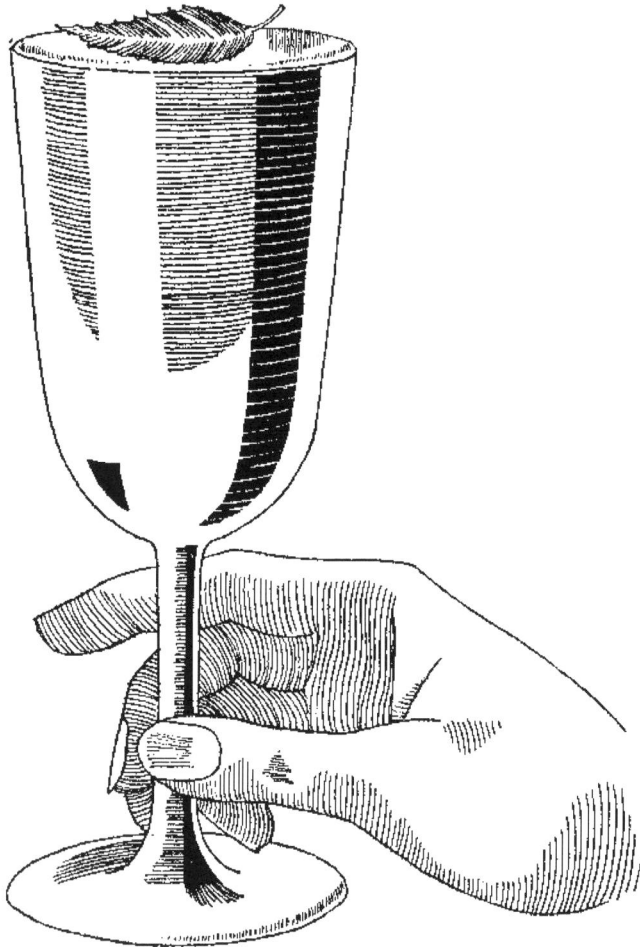

FIG. 1.— FLOATING THE ROSE-LEAF.

There is a temporary agony in the checking of the outflow of this vital force. While the loss is going on the person walks and moves about, swings the feet or twitches the hands, tears paper, fingers some button or watch chain, gets in a rocking-chair sometimes, and shows every manner of restlessness. The downhill grade has begun.

To check it at first is to make the person suffer. Yet the great men and women of the world have somehow learned to stop this waste. Those who want to achieve greatness, or even wish to learn to control others, must endure the suffering.

In conversation with those who have been magnetic and have been successful in life, it was learned that every one had made some effort to check this waste of vital force. Not one knew the principle involved, and not one had the advantage of any guide or help ; and, stranger yet, none knew that any other person was endeavouring to reach the same result. Such conversations proved that our great men and women do more for themselves in private than the public suppose. Some of their efforts are often simple, child-like, and even ridiculous. Yet they accomplish great ends.

You who give up now would better cease to hope for much in this world in the way of commanding talents.

FIG. 2.—EXTENDING THE FLOATING LEAF.

17

Take a large wineglass (not a tumbler) even full at the top with water. Place the bottom in the flat palm of the hand and hold the same at arm's length. The water must not be allowed to spill or even shake or tremble. The other hand may be tried occasionally. Then procure the aid of a friend who is to give you two wineglasses of water, one in each hand, the water coming to the top and slightly rising above the edge. Hold these in the two hands out at arm's length for thirty seconds, without the slightest tremor or shake of the water.

You will not be able to do this at first, but perform it daily for a month, and you will be surprised at the result. If you give it up before the full design is effected you will yet learn what patience is, and patience helps to overcome the erratic action of the *vital-force*.

The fact that the water trembles or overflows at the top need not discourage you. We are constantly receiving reports from our members who have failed utterly and have given up all hope of accomplishing anything in this practice. One says :

"The water shakes out and spills. I can no more do that exercise than I can jump over the moon." And we reply, "Oh yes, you can. The very fact that you cannot do it is proof of the need you have of it."

No one need fail ultimately. All can do it in time. Those who have given up completely have in most instances, come back to the practice, drawn by the fascination of it, and they have succeeded in the most difficult of all experiments—the great Rose Leaf Test, which is now for the first time made public, although we have given it many times to our private pupils. It will be presented in the next chapter.

The wineglass experiments have great value in bringing the nerves to absolute perfection. They are tests that never tell an untruth. The nerves may be alive, jumping, irregular, erratic and out of normal health, while it is possible for a person of strong will to keep all the muscles dead-still. So we see that the present experiments reach a condition that may always escape the previous exercises. They give smoothness to the flow of the nerve-currents ; they tone down the irritated fibre ; they do for the direct electric system of the

FIG. 3.—RAISING THE FLOATING LEAF.

body what dead-still practice will do for the muscles.   Experience alone can show great benefits.

DENTISTS

Many of our pupils have been dentists.   They of all persons require not only muscular dead-stillness, but nervous dead-stillness, and these experiments have so qualified them for exactness of movement and delicacy of touch that their skill as well as their income have been greatly increased.   The sensitive spot on a tooth is often very small ; a careless or uncontrolled movement of the hand would cause severe pain to the patient. The dentist who allowed a drill to slip and penetrate the flesh of the cheek, coming through on the outside of the face, would never have had the accident had he been a student of magnetism, and his patron would not now be disfigured for life. The person of steady nerve will, if the instrument slips, not allow it to pass an eighth of an inch in any direction.

While in a large room try to follow with the steady eye a line on a height with the head, or if there is no line, then an imaginary one, first from left to right, and reverse. Do this slowly fifty times each way. The eye must not move by small muscular jerks, but very smoothly and slowly. It is not easy to do, and to do well. Do not wink while doing it.

If outdoors, try it by following a horizontal line of mortar on a brick building, or the joints of a wooden one.

To those to whom the object of the foregoing experiments may not seem clear, it will be necessary to say a word :

The pupil is asked to remember that the *vital-force* is the life of the body ; from it is generated the Magnetism which controls others. It is constantly being formed, and some portion of it is constantly in motion. It propels the action of the involuntary organs by the decree of its Maker, and without the direction of the human will. The heart circulates the blood ; the diaphragm attends to the breathing ; and the stomach propels itself during digestion ; and thus the trinity of life's movements, without each and all of which life itself would cease, may be traced to the action of the *vital-force*, and through that to some power beyond.

But here the line is drawn, and one of the Principles of Personal Magnetism is called into requisition :

" No movement of any voluntary muscle of the human body must be made unless directed by the will."

The voluntary muscles are those whose motions may be operated by the conscious being.

They should never move involuntarily.

Leakage occurs in the following ways :

1. By unsteadiness of the hands, arms or body.

2. Twitching of the eyelids, or constant winking.

3. Drumming with the fingers after the habit has been formed, or with the feet.

4. Sighing.

5. Yawning.

6. Wakefulness.

7. Swinging the arms, hands, legs, feet, head or body.

8. Rocking, after the habit has been formed.

9. Restlessness.

10. Twitching of the fingers, or any movement of any part of the body during embarrassment, or while speaking or being spoken to.

11. All kinds of embarrassment.

12. Awkwardness.

13. Shorter exhalations (in point of time) than inhalations.

14. Stammering and stuttering.

15. Lack of fluency in speech where it cannot be attributed to want of words or ideas.

16. Allowing the ankle to be turned or a strain to be put upon any muscle by an uneasy standing position. Never have the foot on its side. Never twist the body.

Who are exempt from all these ?

The cool, determined, successful, magnetic people of the world.

STILL LIFE

OUR course of training now leads us into new fields of practice, although what is presented in this chapter rests upon the previous lesson with a wide difference in the way of tests and results. This must be clearly understood at the start, and we will state that the work previously presented has been designed for two specific missions :

1. To bring the muscles to dead-stillness while the life within is most energetic.

2. To bring the nerves into perfect smoothness while the life within is most energetic.

Statuary work is the combination of the two. In the practice of muscular dead-stillness it is allowable to express life in any form and to use any muscles that are needed. The experiments given in the preceding chapter, called mechanical exercises, are for the nerves alone. This distinction must always be understood. Now we unite the two and produce statuary effects.

The definition of a statuary position might be one that embraced the power of complete imitation of a statue. To be sure such training is properly included in other lines of culture. The woman who was told by her husband that she was so restless and uneasy all the time that he was constantly irritated by her presence, did not leave home and go back to her mother ; she quietly studied forms of expression and learned grace and particularly statuary attitudes. Then she was no longer restless and nervous. A home that might have been broken up and joined the long list of disasters due to *incompatibility of temper* became the bulwark of love. Let husbands and wives do everything possible to retain the home before giving up and separating. If we have no other crown to wear, we are pleased to know that our efforts in carrying the study of magnetism into home-life have saved many men and women from the misery of failure in marriage. We know that over ten thousand couples are living happily together at this time, who would have been divorced but for this very study. Husbands and wives who are magnetic never quarrel.

This fact is easily proved.

The statuary exercises of this chapter are not difficult to undertake. If you are capable of interest in anything you can go through all the requirements with relish for the practice. The fact that they are not easily mastered does not render them uninteresting or hard to try. They are not everything in this study, but only a part of the general structure. In many cases to be able to perform one or two perfectly might be sufficient. Others wish to take them right through without omissions.

As a good student studies all his life, so there must be a constant use made of the principles involved in this chapter, as long as the student lives. The exercises may be abandoned in a few months after they have grown into habit, but do not abandon the results they produce. The dead-still attitudes concentrate the electrical or static forces, giving them an opportunity to accumulate while Internal Energy is going, and by a change of the static into the dynamic form of electricity, intense Personal Magnetism is developed.

Then new habits follow.

Students have to grow into this power ; they cannot jump at a bound. After the force has commenced to grow it can be kept growing for many years, just as a child grows into manhood.

The pleasantest period of one's study of this art is when he or she experiences the consciousness of the presence of a new power within, the Internal Energy. We would gladly lead the student to that happy condition by a flight to the mountain-top, avoiding the toilsome plodding through the valley, if we could, but we cannot. Patience is a test of character ; you must have character enough to be patient as you go slowly through the tedious drill of this chapter.

Later on we shall commence the formation of Internal Energy. Then the two means of development will work together. For the present we shall introduce exercises that open the way to those that are to constitute the main practice in this chapter.

First Step—Sitting Still.

The movements which lead to the sitting position and those which lead from it are elsewhere described, together with the principles underlying them. This exercise deals only with the attitude of sitting.

FIRST DAY

Attach to the wall or to some object directly in front of your chair on a height with the eyes, a watch having a second hand. If you do not possess this article, mental counting must be substituted ; that is, count silently one to each second, as nearly as may be estimated in the mind.

Sit down. Take as easy a position as possible, without supporting the back.

1. Looking steadily at the watch (which must be on a level with the eyes), try to avoid winking for *five* seconds. Rest a few seconds.

2. On resuming you may take the mind from the winking, and think exclusively of the fingers. Look steadily at the watch for *five* seconds and be sure that no movement of the fingers takes place. Rest a few seconds. Do not hurry, as it will cause a loss of time and labour.

3. Resume and look steadily at the watch for *ten* seconds, without allowing the eyelids to move in the slightest degree. Rest a few seconds.

4. Resume and look steadily at the watch for *ten* seconds, without allowing the fingers to move in the slightest degree. Rest a few seconds.

5. Resume and look steadily at the watch for *fifteen* seconds, eyelids dead-still as before.

SECOND DAY

The student must now rest until the next day, and then he must repeat the foregoing five exercises.

THIRD DAY

On the third day he may continue the Dead-Still sitting

positions as directed below, arriving at the tenth exercise on that day.

6. Resume and look steadily at the watch for *fifteen* seconds, fingers dead-still as before.

7. *Twenty* seconds, eyelids dead-still.

8. *Twenty* seconds, fingers dead-still.

9. *Thirty* seconds, eyelids dead-still.

10. *Thirty* seconds, fingers dead-still.

FOURTH DAY

11. *Thirty-five* seconds, eyelids dead-still.

12. *Thirty-five* seconds, fingers dead-still.

13. *Forty* seconds, eyelids dead-still.

14. *Forty* seconds, fingers dead-still.

15. *Fifty* seconds, eyelids dead-still.

NOTE.—When the eyes begin to water, continue only five seconds after the unpleasant feeling begins. Do not keep too long at one time on the eye movements. Judicious practice will strengthen the eyes very much.

16. Continue in this way until you can go to *eighty* seconds, fingers dead-still, and eyelids as long as possible.

17. After a few days' practice, you will be ready for this and the next exercise.

18. Look steadily at the watch for *one* minute, not moving a muscle of the body, and keeping the mind upon the feet, and especially the toes. The extremities of the body, the fingers and the toes, and the eyelids are the first parts to show *nervousness* or leakage. These must be watched at all times during the day, as well as in these exercises.

19. Look steadily at the watch for *one* minute, keeping the mind upon the *entire body*, being sure that no motion of any kind occurs in any part. This exercise should be performed daily as long as the person lives. The good that grows out of a long continuance of it cannot be estimated.

NOTES.—*All the foregoing exercises refer to the sitting posture, the back being unsupported at the time.*

It is better to have the light behind you.

The watch may be four feet away unless you are near-sighted.

The following exercises will add to your stores of magnetism, through the principle of Still Life.   Practise these as opportunity permits.

Second Step—Lounging, Dead-Still.

20. Take a sitting position, allowing the body to fall into a lounging attitude of perfect ease ; hold this position without a movement of the fingers, toes, arms, eyelids or head.

Maintain for *two* minutes, watching some object steadily.

Third Step—Standing, Dead-Still.

Arrange a watch, as in the first exercise, on a height with the head and as far away as the hands can be easily seen.   In standing, allow the arms to hang at the sides as dead weights. If all muscular tension is taken out of them they will hang easily and properly.   The weight of the entire body should be borne on the balls of the feet, the heels merely touching the floor.

Make this position natural.

21. Stand for *thirty* seconds, fixing the mind upon the eyelids, fingers and toes.   Do not move any of these a hairbreadth.

22. Stand for *thirty* seconds, fixing the mind upon the entire body, and draw in full and very long and deep inspirations, exhaling when necessary, all without the slightest swaying of the body or rocking to and fro, or movement of any voluntary muscle.   It is a good idea to keep the chest fully extended and immovable and the shoulders down, but not back.

Do not assume an unnatural attitude.

Gradually increase these periods until you can stand for *sixty* seconds under the conditions named.

23. Stand for *ninety* seconds dead-still, as to every voluntary muscle of the body ; the hands at the side ; the second and third fingers of the right hand touching each other very lightly ; the same as to the left hand; the eyes looking fixedly at some object.

This exercise is so important that it should be practised every day during life.

Fourth Step—Frozen Movements.

24. Stand for *one* minute with the entire body dead-still, and the arm raised so as to allow the wrist to rest lightly against

the body, near the hip, and a little in front. Either arm will do. Do not move the eyes or lids, or any muscle of the body.

25. Advance to a table, place the first finger of the hand very lightly upon it, and look steadily for one minute at some fixed object ; the whole body being dead-still. As the first inclination to move will be at the fingers, toes, eyes or eyelids, all these points of *leakage* should be guarded.

This watchfulness will soon become a habit.

It is not intended to include Sunday in the practice days, although the better habits of life should prevail at all times.

Fifth Step—Statuary Positions.

The normal positions just taken are very exacting in their requirements, and must tax the will-power of the student to a great degree.

To stand still, however, is not sufficient. This calmness, this repose of conscious strength, becomes the highest type of manhood and womanhood when carried into the activities of life. Excitement is weakness ; calmness is strength ; energetic repose is grandeur.

Think what all these mean.

In after years make it the chief element of your daily habits to adopt the principles involved in these exercises. For instance, when irritated remain perfectly calm, when nervous or fidgety be absolutely in repose, physically and mentally. When others address you adopt the manner of one who is not easily embarrassed or moved by the remarks or actions of another.

Learn the art of perfect self-control. Do not be afraid to look another in the eye ; to remain passionless when others are excited ; to turn every disturbing influence into an idle wave battering hopelessly against the strong wall of calmness that hems in and protects that sacred essence of being, your personality.

This is the secret of personal magnetism ; and it is a secret that all great men and women have acquired.

THE GREAT ROSE LEAF EXPERIMENT

This has never been published elsewhere, but the author has for many years given it as an exercise to his most accomplished students, and it has been the means of affording both pleasure and gain in the control of the nerves. When done in class it is attended by so much enthusiasm that the energy is not lacking within. We think greater progress is made from books ; and the expense of many guineas for class lessons, or for private instruction, may be avoided. The present edition of this book is intended to do away with all need of such lessons.

The Rose Leaf experiment should not be attempted until you have graduated from the preceding stage, as time will be lost otherwise. It consists in filling a wineglass with water, while holding the wineglass in one hand, the arms being free from the body. When the wineglass is full to the top, by the law of adhesion it will hold about an eighth of an inch more. To pour this on requires very great steadiness of nerves. Then the wineglass must be set down upon the table and a rose leaf

Fig. 4.—Swinging the Floating Leaf.

taken up and floated on the top of the water, without jarring any of the latter from the glass. Thus the one hand will move while the other is held still, and neither must be affected by the other. If a leaf is not easily obtainable for this test (as would be the case in the winter-time), a piece of waxed paper usually will do, bending up the edges to prevent it lying wholly flat upon the water.

Now comes the test.

When all this can be done easily, the wineglass with its extra water and rose leaf must be held out half-arm's length, or about twelve inches in front of the chest, for one minute. Rest.

Next hold it out full-arm's length in front of the chest. Rest.

Reverse by taking the leaf away, pouring the water away, changing hands ; then, holding the wineglass in the other hand, fill it full as before, and extra full also, to which the rose leaf should be added.

With hands reversed as just stated, hold the wineglass out in front of the chest half-arm's length. Rest.

Next hold it out full arm's length for a minute in front of the chest. Rest.

With the wineglass full as stated, and the leaf floating on top, pass it to the other hand, then back again. In class work we used to pass it from pupil to pupil until some one spilled the water ; then we would begin over again.

FIG. 5.—LOWERING THE FLOATING LEAF.

A very difficult task is to pass the wineglass from the hand to the table, then from the table to the floor and back again. A stooping position tests the smoothness of the nerves as much as anything can do.

The wineglass is then raised to various heights and positions.

When connected with much muscular effort, these smooth-nerve tests do not always accumulate magnetism, although they tend that way. When associated with tensing they never fail to develop magnetism rapidly. When done with flabby life of the body, they are neutral, and have no value except to teach control. When done with energy within the chest, they quickly accumulate magnetic power. As we have said before, they are not all.

Other helpful tests are as follows :

1. *Dressing.* Put on a coat or jacket without the loss of any motion small or great. The fidgety person will have trouble in finding the sleeve-hole, or something will hitch. Even the buttons must go into place with ease and smoothness. Wherever the coat may be in the room, lift it from its place, put arms in the sleeves, and button it ; all to be done smoothly and easily.

2. *Shoes.* Put on your shoes that lace, inserting laces in eyelets, avoiding the loss of any motion, however small. When this is done, unlace them. Do not use force. Every movement must be smooth and free from hesitation.

3. *Books.* Take a book from a table, open it at any page and turn ten leaves forward. Close the book, place it on the table, and again take it up with the other hand. Open it, turn ten pages forward ; shut it ; open again at another place, and turn ten pages backward. No leaf must be missed, no motion must be lost, and every detail must count some value. This is a very difficult thing to do successfully.

As irritability destroys magnetism, the purpose of smoothness in the above exercises is double. There must be gentleness of action and placidity of mind in every detail. That which would ordinarily cause you to scold must be welcomed as a test of your perfect self control.

DEPARTMENT OF
THE MAGNETIC VOICE

QUALITIES THAT WIN

W HEN ONE PERSON is said to be more magnetic than another and thereby secures some influence or power over the other person, there must be some means of communication between the two in order that the stronger personality may be conveyed and express itself. This fact makes it necessary for us to consider how many such means of communication exist, and what they are. We know that all methods of conveying such influence are of wave character; but the results and not the processes are of the most importance; and these will claim our attention. The recognized means of communication between human beings are as follows :

1. The Eye.
2. The Voice.
3. The Face.
4. The Touch.
5. The Presence.
6. The Thought.
7. The Feelings.

The first of these has been very elaborately discussed in an important Department of this book. Later on, in Lesson Forty, the tense action of the voice was taught. At this place we will take up the other powers of the voice, and unfold another important method of development founded on the practical usefulness of this means of communication between human beings.

Of course something cannot be evolved from nothing. For every value in life there must be somewhere an equivalent. Voices are trained for singing, and it is a matter of common knowledge that they may be vastly improved for speaking and especially for conversational uses. In addition to these attainments, there can readily be built a number of leading qualities, which we call magnetic for the reasons to be stated and explained.

THE MAGNETIC VOICE

Must Please * * Attract * * Win * * Hold

"To Please."—Not one voice in a thousand is pleasing. It may even be said that not one in ten thousand is capable of giving genuine pleasure to those who hear it. The first great step is to find out why the voice is not pleasing, and then ascertain the way by which it can be made a source of pleasure to others.

"To Attract."—Having accomplished the first great step in this work, the power of a pleasing voice to attract others should next be acquired. As this has been done many times in the past by the method taught in this book, it is certain that it can be done again in every case where the student is determined to achieve so great an end.

"To Win."—It is our creed that there is nothing worth while in this life unless it can win. We all wish to win the respect of others ; but that is not enough. Our character and personality should be lovable ; our social relations sincere and estimable ; our business dealings of the highest standard ; and our habits cleanly and pure. But, added to these traits, there should be constant activity of the most useful kind and a steady mental improvement. These bring social and financial success in many lives ; yet they may fall far short of winning true success if the voice be repellant, as it is in most men and women. There are many instances where a magnetic voice has won the greatest degree of success in life, in spite of almost everything else being absent that should make a person attractive ; because the voice is the one greatest agent of communication. But let a magnetic voice be coupled with all the other splendid traits, and success is more than doubly assured.

It is grand to win friends. It is grand to win social distinction. But the burdens of life are many and are heavy, and it is necessary to win the means of support, and the bank account that shall stand between old age and want when the days of activity are over. If, therefore, the magnetic voice can be turned to substantial earnings, it is one of its legitimate goals. This course of lessons shows the many and wonderfully varied ways in which such earnings are made possible.

1. A clergyman can increase his salary and accomplish vastly greater results in his profession.

2. A lawyer can increase his income in his office practice and in his work before judge and jury.

3. A physician can increase his earnings and his influence over his patients for their good.

4. All professional men of every grade and rank can attract greater patronage and win larger earnings.

5. All business men can double in a short time their effectiveness.

6. All clerks, salesmen and all employees who deal with others, can rise in value to their employers and secure better compensation.

7. Friends and social advantages are more readily won by a magnetic voice than by any other power.

8. School teachers can add to their value by their better control over their scholars and by their increased skill in teaching.

" To Hold."—There are persons who possess what seem like pleasing voices, who cannot hold their power over others. There is something in the voice that tires after a certain time. The ability to please, to attract and to win, should be supplemented by an enduring magnetic quality that never is lessened. This comes best from training.

A few advance thoughts will be in place here :

1. Mere sound is never pleasing. Most voices are far from pleasant. They serve for a while as a means of communication in business or social use, then the hearer is glad when they cease.

2. Some voices are considered pretty and even beautiful that soon tire the listener. Ninety-nine persons in every hundred use

18

the same part of the vocal scale when they converse. Now, suppose you have a friend whose voice is actually rich, and she sings always on one note ; or suppose you have a musical instrument with the most beautiful tone ever produced, and it is played on one note all the time ; can your brain long endure that sameness ?

3. A voice must not only be pleasing, but there must be brought into it a subtle quality known as magnetism, in and of itself. That which is magnetic is more than pleasing ; it must attract, win and hold. We heard a lawyer speak for an hour, and everybody was exhausted ; as he had tired them out, and had weakened their vitality by the strain necessary to follow him and understand what he had in mind. On the other hand, we listened to another lawyer who was defending a hopeless case of great moment, and he talked all day. There was never a moment when any listener was tired of his voice. He knew when he had won his case, and not till then did he cease talking.

4. Above all, there must be naturalness in the voice. A musical instrument is not natural, although it may have fine tones. The kind of magnetism that will serve on the stage, will not do in oratory, nor will either kind do in business or social usage. The thoroughly flexible voice responds readily of itself to all the operations of the mind and heart, and thus it becomes natural. Flexibility, therefore, must be acquired to a very high degree of efficiency ; and the time spent in such acquisition will be more than amply rewarded.

5. In securing perfect flexibility of voice, this faculty comes, incidentally, in its natural gift of reproducing any sound that can be made in nature ; not always with the force of the latter, but in all other respects in the exact likeness.

WINNING AND LOSING

MANY INFLUENCES contribute to the making of a winning voice ; and many more detract from its value. In this lesson we shall discuss both classes of influences ; for we can learn more by looking at what should be avoided at times than by dealing only with the qualities that are desirable. To know what is wrong is half the battle. Then to know how to remedy the wrong is another step in the progress to be made ; while the climax is reached by the actual process of effecting the remedy.

"THE MEANING"

Cold type does not express the meaning.

It rarely does this. Any line can be rendered by some person in an ordinary manner and seem to have but little thought in it. Some other person will make it full of meaning. But a man or woman with a perfectly flexible voice will make the thought stand forth in a most amazing power, and the tones employed may be quiet and wholly unassuming.

What does the following statement mean :

" The man would have died if you hadn't cut his foot off."

You can read it in such a way as to make the man alive ; or in such another way as to make him dead ; and it certainly is important to know which fact you desire to convey. There is a great difference between a living man and a dead man.

Put your mind behind the words and think that the man is alive.

Think that the operation saved his life. Think that, if the foot had not been cut off, he would not have lived, but would have died because the foot was left on. In so thinking, you will do something more than emphasize the word *died* ; the flexible voice will not depend wholly on emphasis. The object point

275

of the voice is the word *died* in the reading, " The man would have *died* if you hadn't cut his foot off." Try it fifty times or more until you are able to read the thought that he is alive.

Now try to execute him.

This is done by the human voice. Think that the man died. Think that he would have died anyway. Think that the operation of removing his foot was of no avail ; that he was sure to die anyway ; and that he " would have died if you *hadn't* cut his foot off."

After making your voice perform this execution, repeat it fifty times, always on the same man. Repetition gives a flexible voice. If you can read the above skilfully so as to make the man alive or dead at will, you are then well advanced on your way to a successful attainment in this course.

If you cannot do this, then call in some friends to help you solve the problem. But if you can do it fairly well, keep on the practice of repeating until the meaning stands out more and more day by day. No one is perfect in such practice.

" THE INTENTION "

In the preceding lesson we have dealt with the meaning. Now we seek to read the purpose or intention of the thought. Imagine yourself seated in an outer room, and that in the next room there are two persons—one a wife, the other a husband. The wife says to the husband :

" *Will* you ride to town to-day ? " What does she intend ?

But instead of putting it that way, she says :

" Will *you* ride to town to-day ? "

Does not the first inquiry clearly indicate that she desires to know whether any one is going to town to-day ? And does not the second inquiry take it for granted that some one is going, but is *he* the one ?

Instead, however, of either inquiry, suppose she had asked :

" Will you *ride* to town to-day ? " Would not the intention shift completely ? Someone is going, and you are the person ; but *how* will you go ? The town is two miles away. Will you walk, ride or fly ?

Another meaning is brought out in the following question :

" Will you ride *to* town to-day ? " You sometimes go into

the town, or as far as the town ; and often go in that direction, and not *to* the town itself.

Here is still another intention :

" Will you ride to *town* to-day ? " This asks whether you are going there, or elsewhere, perhaps into the country.

There are six words in the sentence. One remains to receive attention.

" Will you ride to town *to-day* ? " Here the purpose shifts in the most startling manner from the other five intentions. Is to-day the time of your visit to town ?

The acute thinker will note that, when one word is made to carry the idea, all the others are taken for granted. This is a very important fact. In court a witness is held accountable for all ideas so taken for granted ; and, as every man and woman is likely to come to the witness stand some day, it is well to know to what extent the human voice is committing its owner.

Thus, when the wife asks : " Will you ride to town *to-day* ? " she may not think that she is assuming as admitted truths all the other facts suggested in the sentence ; but she does so in her form of inquiry.

If the husband were to enter the room and say to his wife, " I will *ride* to town to-day," he would know, or ought to know, that she understands that he is going, that his visit is to be to the town, and to-day is the time, as well as the other minor ideas to be as stated ; but that he will not walk, as he has decided to *ride*.

Here the meaning changes with every repetition.

But the real object of this lesson is to teach you to form the habit of expressing exactly what you have in mind.

The voice becomes natural and flexible by specific practice. Thus, if you were to repeat each of the above inquiries fifty times, or a total of three hundred times, you would find your voice much improved in its powers of expression. What you can do once, or a few times, is merely what you are in the habit of doing all the time. To grow more and more expressive, is the chief object of vocal practice. Repetition does wonders. Great actors have been known to repeat a single line many thousands of times, and so they have become great in so doing.

Repeat. Repeat. Repeat.

" THE PLEASING VOICE "

Not more than one voice in a thousand is pure in its mechanical quality. Some musical instruments, by wear and tear, develop what is called in art a *mongrel tone*. A dog that is neither one thing or another in breed is a mongrel ; and when it is mean in its habits and nature it is known as a mongrel cur. Such a dog does not appeal to the best tastes of the community.

The human voice is constantly subjected to influences that destroy its purity of quality. The singer knows, or soon comes to know, that the everyday habits of life take the value out of the voice ; and so there are exercises that restore the purity of the quality. Some musical instruments have exquisitely beautiful tones. Some horns of gold alloy are exceedingly rich in tone-value ; some of silver are almost as rich ; some of brass are more blatant ; and so the quality follows the metal. On the other hand, there are methods of construction that help make the tones richer. The sounding-board of a piano has much to do with the excellence of the sounds to be produced. All other parts exert some influence. The instrument that to-day attracts by its fine tones may in the course of time give forth a sound like an " old tin pan." The same deterioration that takes place in a piano is certain to occur in the human voice.

That the latter is rarely ever found in a pure quality is a well-recognized fact.

The vocal cords are made rough and coarse by the use of vinegar, acids, spices, tea, coffee, tobacco and alcohol. Excessive meat-eating generates a poison in the blood that reaches the throat in its circulation.

Inhaling through the mouth is the most injurious of all habits. It is always better to breathe in through the nose. The outgoing breath does not affect the vocal cords. Mouth-inhalation brings dust and germs to the throat, and also chills its walls ; these combined influences often introducing contagion into the system.

The larger the lung capacity becomes, the more readily the vocal cords will respond to any method of improving them. Therefore, deep breathing daily is necessary to voice development.   This may be done without interfering with other duties. You must breathe all day long, and it takes no more time to breathe deeply than in the usual shallow manner.

" THE PURE VOICE "

If you have absorbed the lesson next preceding this, you may go on with the work of securing a vocal quality that is called pure.   In so doing, you drive out all the accumulated roughness and crudeness of years of growth.   Just think of the value of a musical instrument, the notes of which are clear, sweet, rich and pure.   Listen to the piano that sounds like an " old tin pan " and compare it with the new piano every tone of which pleases because of its mechanical purity.

A simple exercise will bring vast results.

Learn what the vowel " ah " is and how and where it is made. We have been told that it is the most open of all sounds.   This really means that it can be readily made the most open.   In fact, it is possible to make it with the lips almost closed.   It is possible to make it on the front of the mouth, at the lips, on the tongue or in the throat.

If you make it on the lips, your voice will not improve, for lip sounds are never pleasing.   The vocal cords are in the throat, in what seems to be the bottom of the throat-well. Imagine the throat to be a deep well, and that you are to produce the sound from the lowest part of that well.   Open the mouth at the lips, at the tongue, in the middle, at the back of the palate, and deep down in the throat.   Then say " ah."

The latest and most approved method of voice production is that which starts the tone in the deep throat and projects it at the front upper teeth.   This quickly leads to purity and clearness.   The process is as follows, and, if duly employed, the results will soon be marvellous :

1. Utter the sound " ah " in the manner just stated, and try to make it as clear as possible.   Think of the place of origin which is always at the bottom of the throat-well, and at the same time think of the point of attack which is at the front upper teeth.   Keep these two locations always in mind. Never release your attention from them.

2. Having mastered the two points as just stated, and having

made yourself capable of executing the tone as required, try to prolong the sound of " ah " for five seconds. In doing this, depend on the expert acuteness of your ear ; for your ear will tell you what character of tone your voice is producing. Your ear is to be your mentor, your guide, your dictator ; and you must encourage its good work.

3. Listen to the tone you are producing. Is it getting clearer ? If so, then prolong it for ten seconds by your watch.

4. Then prolong it for fifteen seconds.

5. Then for twenty seconds ; and so keep on, adding five seconds at a time until you are able to prolong a good tone for sixty seconds in one breath.

6. When you rest, start over again with five seconds. Never, after a rest, try to see how long you can maintain a tone. always begin with five, then let the breath out, inhale, and go to ten seconds, and so continue. The real progress comes in the habit of beginning over with five seconds. It would be a waste of time, or nearly so, to try to go a long period, say twenty or more seconds, at the start. Build up, five seconds at a time, and progress will be rapid.

7. The ear is to detect the growing purity of the voice. That will soon find improvement, and then it must insist on the continued bettering of the tone until it rings true and clear as a flute note.

The pure voice in a man is a resonant, clear, beautiful tone, suited to the manliness of the individual ; while in a woman it is free from any of the blemishes that mar a perfect voice. It is not confined to one part of the vocal range, but sustains the same quality in each and all of the pitches. It is sometimes attained, and very speedily, by the process of elimination. This means to first get rid of the throaty character by learning to open the throat to its full capacity, thus allowing the tones to come through to the front upper palate. Another fault to be eliminated is that of unvocalized air passing through the mouth mixed with the tones. This occurs in both speaking and singing, and is called partial aspiration. The ear can detect it and lead to its disappearance. The nasal twang can be likewise overcome.

ROUNDING THE FLAT VOICE

A VERY LITTLE CHANGE determines the difference between the good and the bad, and often turns a losing existence into a winning one. People who are compelled to get their living by their voices, and who find themselves failures in all their efforts to make progress towards success, are sometimes turned around and made to face in an opposite direction; and what was repellent becomes attractive. Flat voices under all circumstances are repellent; round ones are always attractive. The reason lies deep in the meanings of Nature. Flat voices express dislike, hatred, disapproval, suspicion and irritability, with many kindred moods. You can readily see that such voices are not likely to win friends, sell goods, secure contracts, or draw victories out of efforts at any form of speaking.

"THE FLAT VOICE"

Few persons realize that the voice is either round or flat.

As the voice is produced by the vocal cords which are located in the throat, the character of the tone must of necessity depend on the shape of the chamber through which it is compelled to pass; the throat giving that shape just as the musical instrument determines the character of the sound that is developed in it. A trombone emits a tone quite different from the cornet or the flute.

By changing the shape of the throat and mouth, a nasal effect is produced that often causes laughter or ridicule. By other shapes the throat is made to give out a guttural growl which disagreeable men are too often guilty of; or hard, distressingly crude tones that repel. Yet these same throats may be so shaped that in time their sounds will be pleasing and even beautiful.

The two great divisions of the shapes of the throat are :
1. The flat.
2. The round.

Every time you swallow, you assume a flat throat ; and, as you swallow hundreds of times a day, you are constantly training the throat to take on its flat shape.   Habits are the great master of the voice.   Nature employs the same throat for eating as it does for singing.   The act of eating is more important than that of singing ; but persons who live to eat, instead of eating to live, lose much of the real pleasure of existence.

In swallowing food, it is necessary that the throat shut it off tightly and send it down to the stomach by a slightly convulsive action which produces the flat shape at the location of the vocal cords.   It is this bad shape that all singers and most speakers of ability train themselves to overcome.   It is very easily changed to the proper condition with a little practice.

" PRACTICE ! PRACTICE ! "

It is not necessary to practise much.

Nature sets things right very quickly.   Habits take a long time to make them wrong.   It is knowing how that counts.

One minute a day will keep the voice in fine shape after once you get it so.   But do not be ashamed to practise.   All great singers look after their diet, their daily habits of living, and their little tests of vocal condition.

No great orator ever became great unless he practised. Most of them discovered instinctively the need and the way of practising.   Demosthenes probably invented his own scheme, but history is very clear on the point that he did spend time in making his voice right.   The same fact is shown in other biographies.   Patrick Henry made use of every empty schoolhouse he could find ; and Daniel Webster, by the testimony of Edward Everett and others, built up his voice by practice. All the great men of this art of speaking have been willing and glad of the opportunity to practise.   It is the little men who are above it.

Hon. Roscoe Conkling had one of the richest and most pleasing voices we ever listened to.   When he died, no one knew the combination to the lock on his safe.   " Did he have

any favourite word ? " asked the expert. " Yes," said a
young man in the office, " I have often heard his voice ring
out on the word Rome, when he was alone in this room."
The word *Rome* furnished the key to the combination, and
the safe was quickly unlocked.

History and public as well as private biographies are full of
incidents connected with the practice indulged in by great men
to keep their voices in good shape. It pays. It even pays for
the salesman and the clerk ; for improved voices mean better
work and more effective results. A pleasing voice, even though
quiet, draws people ; while crude, harsh, flat voices repel them.
Add to the pleasing voice the charms of personal magnetism
and there is no better investment in the world.

" ROME ! ROME ! ROME ! "

All natural habits are good or bad.

The drift of things, left to themselves, is to the bad.

What is called a natural gift, is an accidental drift to the
good ; often stimulated by ambition or earnest effort.

Any drift can be cultivated. That which is cultivated, if it
coincide with a natural drift to the good, is as natural as if it
had come about of itself. True art everywhere is a cultivated
drift toward the better things ; and, the more it coincides with
Nature, the greater is the bond of union between the cultivated
and the natural gifts. In fact, that which is cultivated is far
more valuable, because it outlives the accidental drift of habits.

Between the flat voice, which is the drift to the bad, and the
round voice, which is the voice of art and cultivation, there
is as much difference as between a golden-toned piano and an
old tin box. People who meet those they seek to impress have
enough instinct to drop the flat voice and assume the round
tones in part—although in small part. This proves that effort
is able to control the character of the voice even among persons
who lack all desire for culture. What has been called the
" Sunday voice " in a preceding lesson, is an example of what
instinct may accomplish. The woman who would employ the
flat voice that her family hears constantly to a visitor for
whom she had great regard, would utterly fail in making
herself pleasing. She would repel.

Women often wonder why the men who attracted them before

marriage are so quickly tiresome after the honeymoon is over. Wives maintain their " Sunday voices " for a longer period after marriage than men do theirs ; but it is all over sooner or later, and the dreadful commonplaces fill all their hours together. Once in after years the husband has the old kindness in his manner and tones, and the wife says : " Harry, your voice sounds now as it used to sound when we were engaged."

Why go through life with a flat voice ?

While habit and special effort will make it partly round at times, art alone can fill out the full quality. Short cuts in art are as good as long and expensive journeys.

The quickest way of reaching the round voice is to practise with the word so constantly used by Conkling : " Rome ! Rome ! Rome ! " Not he alone, but many others have employed the same word. It was the favourite tone of David Garrick, the greatest actor of his day.

" MAKING RAPID PROGRESS "

It is possible to do a right thing wrong.

Any person can speak the word " Rome " with a flat throat. But it is such a word as will respond more quickly to the attention of the mind than any other that can be found.

The mind and the ear should be combined ; or, in other words, the mind should give constant attention to the ear, so that the latter may note the right utterances. The voice is ready at all times to obey the ear and mind, if both work together.

Of course a round tone is made by a round throat. But there is no necessity of going through a long period of practice to learn how to make the throat round. A " yawn " will do it at once, if a person is able to yawn or imitate the action of yawning. The process consists in lowering the " Adam's apple," or vocal box of the throat, which always goes way down during the yawn, and rises way up during the swallow.

Yawning is not a good habit to establish, but all singing artists have been compelled to use it to start with ; then, when once the open throat is secured, the muscles will repeat it afterwards as desired. If you have ever noticed any great singer, you will at once recall the position of the throat.

Any sound of " O " will tend to make the throat round in shape. Any liquid word containing " O " will do likewise.

" Lo " is a liquid word. So is " Mow." So is " No." So is
" Ro." So are words made of these consonants : as " More,"
" Roar," " Lower," and others. Words containing " M " and
" N " tend to free the voice from the offensive twang called
the nasal defect. " R " tends to make the tongue flexible as
it is a tongue consonant of the liquid kind. Hence there is no
word quite as good as " Rome " for practice. The word
" Roll " is used a great deal by actors and singers and orators
in their private practice which they carry on in their room ;
but it lacks the resonant value of " Rome."

It does no real good to utter the word " Rome " without the
aid of the ear and the attention of the mind. The latter should
make sure that the throat is in the open position, as its first
duty, and that the sound is pure and round ; while the ear
should note the various kinds of tone-characters produced, and
select that which is most pleasing. Friends often meet for
practice and mutual criticism, and as this is the most important
culture in human life, it should be given first place over all
other duties.

Like a beautiful flower garden that is capable of bearing
exquisite gems if kept in a condition of culture, but that goes
to rank weeds when left to itself, the voice responds to careful
attention or drifting neglect, being the agent of the mind, the
heart and the soul in their communication with humanity.

" THE UGLY FLAT TONES "

A badly shaped musical instrument will emit badly formed
and unpleasing tones. A flat throat is badly shaped for song
and speech. It is the result of natural drift. A bad disposition
accentuates the flat voice. In fact, humanity, like the canine
species, is disposed to growl at things it does not like. You
are so used to hearing the growl and snap, in various degrees,
that you pay little attention to them, although they instinctively repel you when you are able to get away from them.

If you are a clerk or employee, you would prefer to work for
a man who has a kindly voice rather than for one who closes
his throat into a guttural tone. If you have read the story of
" Christmas Carol," by Dickens, you will recall the kind of man
Scrooge was, as therein depicted. Dickens, himself, when
giving public readings, used the flat voice in very close form

for the character of Scrooge, until the change had come over
the tight-fisted man ; then the kindly tones fell from a beauti-
fully rounded voice.

We have had many reports from gramophone records of the
utterances of men and women whose dispositions have not
been pleasant, and who have therefore developed the flat voice
in excess, which means that the throat comes closer together
in the act of speaking. These tones are very near to the
growl of a dog, which is made with a flat shape of the throat.

If you can speak as many persons about you speak, and will
take the trouble to reproduce their tones, you can carry them
into the growl without much change of throat.

When people disapprove of some act of their fellow-beings,
the throats are closed flat, and the tongue was made flat also,
thus throwing forth the tones of dislike, the same as the cat
does when it is in an ugly mood. The growl of the dog and
the hissing of the cat, are both made with flat throats, and
evince a hateful disposition at the time.

In art, the hiss in a tone is called aspiration, and the growl
is called guttural. You will hear them both, in one degree or
another, all about you. For purposes of imitation, they may
be learned and used ; for they will help you to avoid them if
you are able to make them and drop them when you like.

But it is a good rule to never misuse the voice ; always keep
it in its pure qualities ; and let the ear determine the presence
of defects. In cultivated voices for singing, the teacher first
uses his ear to detect faults ; then tells the pupils to keep
alert in the same manner so that they instantly recognize and
avoid them.

MAGNETIC MODULATION

HERE WE COME to what is considered the most beautiful and at the same time the most effective use of the speaking voice. In song the beauty and power depend on the variation of notes in the musical scale, combined with arrangements of time, force and other qualities, all of which are useful in the speaking tones as well. Every departure from a monotonous tendency in speech is a relief to the listener ; and when the changes suit the meanings of the thoughts, the effect is more than doubly attractive.

" MEANING OF MODULATION "

The word modulation in speech means variation in pitch, although it may be made to include change of force and time in utterance.

But the chief and important meaning of modulation is variation in the *pitch* of the voice.

Most persons who try to give an off-hand definition of *pitch* call it force. It has no relation to loudness or softness, or any of the uses of force, but applies wholly to range of voice, up or down, in the musical scale. Thus a tenor has a high pitch voice ; and if he converses in the same general part of the scale that he uses in singing, he will talk in a high pitch. The bass singer generally talks in a low pitch. Those who sing in the middle part of the vocal range, or scale, talk in the middle pitch. It is proper to say that you pitch the voice high or low ; but it is not proper to say that you pitch it loud or soft. In the roof of a house the pitch is the declivity or steepness, not the strength.

" TIRESOME VOICES "

Nature gave to every man and woman a two-octave speaking range, and even greater range than this can be cultivated, and is cultivated year after year by thousands.   Yet most men and women use in conversation only a small part of one octave, and generally only one note.   There are millions of one-note talkers in the world, and they wonder why they are not attractive in business or socially.

Even a beautiful voice that is used on one note, or on only a few, will tire.   The human brain will not long endure peacefully the constant hammering at one kind of sound.   The nerves rebel.

If you have a fine piano and strike one key all the time, how long will your neighbour put up with it ?   One refrain has driven people crazy.   Not long ago a man rushed out of a house with a smoking revolver having killed a girl who was playing a few bars of a strain that she had caught and sought to fix. No mind is wholly sane and sound, and it is not difficult to make it lose its self-control.   Nature steps in and relieves the brain from monotony by sleep in a majority of cases ; and this accounts for the ease with which monotonous preachers will put a congregation into a state of slumber or close to it.   But what can be said of the calling of the man who will thus fail in his great work ?

All about you are one-note speakers, or one-note talkers, and they are failures.   We have rescued many of them in the past twenty-five years, and we hope that these lessons will rescue thousands more.   The human voice has the greatest opportunity of all the faculties, and is the most used, but the worst used.

One note is the climax of monotony ; but even two notes will not give relief; nor will three or four.   If Nature provided fifteen or more, let them all be developed into actual use. Some singers who are able to exceed this range in song, talk in a monotonous pitch when they converse, showing that the mere possession of a large range is not enough.

" RANGE OF VOICE "

The term *Range of Voice* is well understood to refer to the compass or extent of pitch. This by some authors is divided into registers, and called the Upper, Middle and Lower.

The Upper register is said to embrace the highest third of the vocal compass of a thoroughly developed voice.

The Middle register embraces the middle third.

The Lower register the lower third.

The highest third, sometimes called the head register, indiscriminately, is best represented by the vowel sound of E, as in the word *meet.*

The middle third, sometimes called the throat register, is best represented by the vowel sound of Ah, as A in *father.*

The lowest third, sometimes called the chest register, is best represented by the vowel sound of O, as in *roll.*

These divisions may be mental ones, at least, and will somewhat assist the pupil in practice.

The development of pitch is absolutely necessary to the singer, and to the reader or orator it is an exceedingly valuable acquisition. Many singing voices are developed by the exercise of this book, yet nothing of the technique of music is here attempted. A person may be ignorant of music and remain so, yet understand, perform and master all these exercises. For speaking and reading it is not necessary to preserve minute distinctions of pitch or be musically exact.

" DEGREES OF PITCH "

Voices limited in range will not be able to make the divisions given in this exercise ; but persistent practice will soon show great improvement. Those who understand music may make the nine pitches one whole note apart, if their vocal range admits of it, or a half note apart, if very limited in compass ; or a note and a half apart if the range is comparatively extensive ; or two whole notes apart, if possible.

Rule.—Arrange the pitches so that their range, from the very highest to the very lowest degrees, may be a little greater than the ability of the voice to produce, and then work to produce them perfectly.

THE NINE DEGREES OF PITCH

No.	Description.	Expressional meaning.
9	Extremely high	Very excited.
8	Very high.	Excited.
7	High.	Enthusiastic.
6	Rather high.	Rather serious.
5	Middle.	Calm.
4	Rather low.	Rather enthusiastic.
3	Low.	Serious.
2	Very low.	Very serious.
1	Extremely low.	Profound.

"MEANING OF PITCH"

Every part of the vocal range has a meaning of its own, as will be seen in the following :

QUOTATIONS FOR PRACTICE IN THE NINE DEGREES OF PITCH

No.	Description.	Quotation.
9	Extremely high.	" I repeat it, sir, let it come, let it come."
8	Very high.	" Three millions of people armed in the holy cause of liberty ! "
7	High.	" The sounding aisles of the dim woods rang."
6	Rather high.	" With music I come from my balmy home."
5	Middle.	" A vision of beauty appeared on the clouds."
4	Rather low.	" Friends, Romans, countrymen ! "
3	Low.	" And this is in the night, most glorious night ! "
2	Very low.	" Roll on, thou deep and dark blue ocean, roll ! "
1	Extremely low.	" Eternity ! Thou pleasing, dreadful thought ! "

An extra No. 9 pitch may be made by crying " Boat ahoy ! " holding the last syllable as long as can be done easily, as " Boat aho——y ! "

An extra No. 1 pitch may be made by pronouncing the word " Swear " in a deep, sepulchral tone, as described in the next exercise.

Incessant practice in the quotations will accomplish more in cultivating a wide and extended range than would seem possible. The *Rule* must be observed strictly.

" HOW TO PRACTISE "

Some years ago a prominent man came to us, having been sent by a famous teacher of singing ; the purpose being to extend his range of voice. He could sing in about an octave and a half, and the teacher had exhausted every method to increase his range.

At the same time a politician came to us who had almost no range at all; his voice being pitched on the note above the middle, and remaining there during his entire efforts at speaking.

To both these applicants for lessons, we gave the following rules of practice. The singer in the course of time acquired a full octave beyond that which he possessed when he began the exercises in range that are given here. The politician acquired a two-octave range, and was constantly re-elected for sixteen years. He connected himself with our institution as a result of his interest in the good work being done.

The practice consists in speaking, not in singing, each quotation of the table in the preceding lesson.

Begin with the middle, or fifth quotation. Say the words, " A vision of beauty appeared on the clouds," in the easiest pitch in which you can speak, and make it conversational in style. Say this a number of times, always aloud, but not loudly.

If you have a piano or musical instrument nearby, find how many notes you have in your voice, and speak the above quotation in the note that is about midway between the highest and the lowest.

Then speak the next quotation below the fifth, which will be as follows : " Friends, Romans, countrymen ! " This should be given in a rather serious vein, and the pitch should be close to the middle, but not quite up to it. Follow with the next quotation, " And this is in the night, most glorious night ! "

giving the words in a pitch lower than the fourth. Then proceed to the lowest pitches in turn. After this, repeat the fifth, " A vision of beauty appeared on the clouds," in the middle part of your range, and then take the sixth, and so on up to the top or last one, which is the ninth.

It is first necessary to establish the nine degrees of range, then to extend them gradually as practice gives you great security in the production of them.

" THE LOW NOTES "

The higher the pitch rises, the more vibrations there are in a second of time. These occur at the vocal cords. The lower the voice descends, the fewer are the vibrations. These relieve the ear and brain of the listener ; for which reason the magnetic tones are more often effective in the low notes than in the high ones.

After acquiring the number one pitch of the table of range as given in these lessons, try to drop below that by speaking the word " oh " and then the word " swear " in a still lower note. These words suit the effort. Imagine the throat to be a very deep well, and in that well utter the word " awe " very solemnly a number of times, trying to get it lower each time. All three words help, but some voices respond better to one word than to another.

THE CONVENIENT LOW NOTE

In the low register of the voice there are some notes that are weak, especially the extremely low ones.

Constant practice on the lowest note of the voice that can be made easily will soon result in the next note below it acquiring strength and fulness by sympathy, owing to its proximity to the note that is being used so much.

The note next below, then, will be the " convenient low note." This should receive the attention of the student just as soon as it is full and strong. Remember to wait until the fulness has come to it through sympathy, not to force it.

When the new " convenient low note " has been practised for months as its predecessor was, it in turn, by sympathy, will cause strength and fulness to creep into the note next below, and so on down the scale the voice will extend itself in range.

MODULATING MOVEMENTS

EVERY VARIATION in the voice, whether in conversation or address, is a relief to the ear nerves and brain nerves of the listeners ; but when the variation expresses the meaning of the thought or the feeling behind it, the effect is more than doubly pleasing and attractive. Few persons know these facts ; and we have never known a man or woman who came by this practice naturally or as a habit. Like accomplished singing, it is one of those things that must be taught as a form of culture, producing in speaking and in conversation what is known as the cultivated voice.

The attractive voice must be :

1. Natural.
2. Modulated.
3. Flexible.

Commonplace thoughts should not be declaimed nor rendered in a bombastic style. When your thoughts, whether of your own composition or coming from other sources, are commonplace, the natural style is conversational.

Very often lofty thoughts are clothed in simple forms, and rare beauty dwells in ordinary words. We here give an example of this complex composition ; but nevertheless it is much more effective and carries the impression of naturalness if rendered in a purely conversational tone ; just as if you were in the same studio with the artist trying to describe your mother to him.

> " Oh, if I could only make you see
>> The clear blue eyes, the tender smile,
> The sovereign sweetness, the gentle grace,
>> The woman's soul, and the angel's face
> That are beaming on me all the while !
>> I need not speak those foolish words :
> Yet one word tells you all I would say :
>> She is my mother."

Commonplace thoughts may be lofty, like the foregoing ; and as such they may be given the dignity and value they demand, even in ordinary conversation.   In an address or recital, speech or reading, this natural style is most agreeable and pleasing.

But it should be coloured with true feeling.

A modulated voice is one in which there is a constant departure from a monotonous pitch, or avoiding too much closeness to one of the pitches as scheduled in the preceding lesson. The table of the Nine Pitches furnishes the working material for an immense amount of practice and development in many departments of vocal training ; therefore it should be not only well memorized but kept at hand ready for use whenever called upon for service.

Everybody knows, either through experience or instruction, the havoc that is wrought upon the nerves of listeners through the lack of modulation in conversation or speech.   A trained voice is not only able to produce the needed variations, but knows how to make them coincide with the meanings in the thoughts and in the feelings.   Wonderful as the voice is, the power of expressing meanings in the movements of pitch is still more wonderful.   These meanings may be summed up as follows :

UPWARD MOVEMENTS

1. Thoughts or feelings that tend towards uncontrol move upward.

2. All forms of excited interest tend upward.

3. Tendencies to lightness or frivolity tend upward.

4. Sympathy, gentleness, tenderness and similar moods move upward.

5. Beauty, exaltation and triumph move upward.

6. Inquiry, doubt and insincerity move upward.

7. Weakness moves upward, including servility and obedience.

The Sound of the voice, as well as the vibration, determines the character of the thought or feeling.

DOWNWARD MOVEMENTS.   The following take downward modulations :

1. Decision, strength, command, conclusion.

2. Discouragement, surrender, and similar moods.

3. Sublimity of statement.

4. Disobedience and surly moods.

5. Reply and certainty of assertion.

6. Self-control.

7. Weighty and serious thoughts.

8. Superiority.

In the natural use of the voice all modulating movements undulate, which means that, instead of a steady rise or fall, they rise and fall back and forth on an upward movement, and fall and rise back and forth on a downward movement. This fact would have been discovered by any person in practising.

The following is an upward modulating movement :

" He that formed the eye shall He not see ? "

Begin at any part of the scale of Nine Pitches which may be found in the preceding lesson, and rise naturally in the inquiry. Repeat until this movement is easily made.

Here are two quotations from *Hamlet* :

" Hold you the watch to-night ? "

" Armed, say you ? "

Other quotations that exemplify the laws for upward movements are as follows :

" Dear master, I can go no further."

" Insects generally must lead a truly jovial life."

" This our life, exempt from public haunt,"

" Finds tongues in trees,"

" Books in the running brooks,"

" Sermons in stones."

" And good in everything."

The first of this group depicts weakness ; the last six depict beauty ; and all require a general modulation upwards, not in steady rises but in undulations.

The next group requires falling modulations :

" Stop, I command you."

" Life is a shadowy, momentary dream."

" The dizzy train reels as it swoops down the mountain."

" Conscience does make cowards of us all."

It is not at all difficult to find quotations that meet the requirements set forth in the early part of this lesson ; and it is a very excellent mental exercise for the student to do this, as the practice will cultivate discernment.

One of the best examples of an undulating, modulating movement is the following quotation from a speech of Patrick Henry; and accounts of his style made by witnesses who were present agree that he used his voice very much in the following manner :

" Shall we acquire the means of effectual resistance by lying supinely on our backs and hugging the delusive phantom of hope until our enemies shall have bound us hand and foot ? "

The quotation contains four divisions.

Each division is a movement upward in the following manner approximately :

" Shall we acquire the means of effectual resistance," starting in the lowest pitches and gradually rising for about three or four pitches.

" By lying supinely on our backs," starting about the third pitch and moving upward for three or four pitches.

" And hugging the delusive phantom of hope," starting about the fourth pitch and moving upward for three or four pitches.

" Until our enemies shall have bound us hand and foot," starting at about the middle or sixth pitch, and moving upward as high as the voice will run.   Having practised these movements many times, the final process is to blend the whole quotation as one piece of dramatic inquiry.

Double movements are very pleasing, and can be selected freely by any student.   Here is one from *Richelieu* :

" I have re-created France."

The words, " I have re-created," are given a decided upward action, and the word " France " falls.   This is a double movement.

Perfect freedom of choice is allowed any student in making these modulating movements, provided their meanings are sustained under the laws stated in the early part of this lesson.

FLEXIBILITY consists of mental colouring and of magnetic colouring.   It impacts to the voice an inexhaustible richness and a most exquisite beauty.

MAGNETIC COLOURS OF VOICE

PERHAPS THE MOST DELIGHTFUL and at the same time the most satisfying of all studies in voice, whether for conversation, reading or speaking, is that which deals with the effort to develop changing colours in the tones, and to recognize them as they appear. When one tone differs from another, there is magnetism in it ; when you yourself can recognize the fact that one tone differs from another, then you are conscious of the presence of magnetism ; for no voice, except one that is magnetic is able to make its tones change their colour.

"TONE COLOUR"

In more than ninety-nine per cent of all people, the great defects of voice are :

1. Monotony of pitch.
2. Flatness of tone.
3. Lack of flexibility.
4. Absence of colour.

Even a beautiful voice may be uninteresting after a few utterances.

Colour of tone is the presence of feeling in the tone.

Persons are often unable to give expression to their real feelings from lack of colour-development in the voice. For instance, a voice that has never been employed, except to express the merest commonplaces of life, would find it impossible to put any other colour into the nobler or more beautiful thoughts, unless a systematic course of practice, like that given in these lessons, should be adopted.

Without colour all expression is mechanical and artificial. It is art without nature. Yet by the rules of art we can dive down into the hidden recesses of Nature, and bring to the surface her most precious secrets ; then, by practice, adopt and wear them as our own, for they are ours by heritage.

Our purpose is to provide a series of exercises for acquiring all the colours of the voice, by special practice, until they become natural.

Having said this much, we now invite the student to commence the most fascinating practice known in the art of expression. It is well to keep a record of the number of times each colour is repeated, for all practice counts something, even if but once a week or month. It is only after repeated trials that the ear begins to recognize the real colour ; it may not be until after hundreds of repetitions that the colour will be recognized ; but when it comes, as come it surely will, a delicious feeling of pleasurable satisfaction is experienced.

While these lessons are not intended to include instruction in singing, hundreds of singers with colourless voices have applied for them during the last twenty-five years and have been greatly benefited by them.

All persons who speak, read, converse, or sing should develop tone colour.

" TONE COLOUR EXERCISES "

The feelings are many, and their colours should be made to harmonize with them. The greater number of colours you acquire, the more magnetic will be your voice.

Some colours are easily developed. They happen to coincide with your common moods. Others must be brought into your voice by placing your mind and feelings in the realm of existence that the thought seems to describe or indicate. Make no two colours alike.

(Only the words in quotation marks are to be coloured. Colours that seem alike are quite different.)

1st Colour.—*Mild Determination.* Colour words : Impossible ; cannot.

" It is impossible, I cannot."

2nd Colour.—*Strong Decision.* Negative. Colour word : Not.

" I will not."

3rd Colour.—*Strong Decision.* Affirmative. Colour words : Will ; bond.

" I will have my bond."

4th Colour.—*Surprise.* Colour words : Gone ; married.
"Gone ! to be married ! "

5th Colour.—*Wonder.* Colour word : Wonderful.
" Oh, a wonderful stream is the River Time ! "

6th Colour.—*Amazement.* Colour words : There ; look ; steals.
"Why, look you there ! look, how it steals away ! "

7th Colour.—*Beauty.* Colour words : Heaven ; thick ; patines ; bright gold.
" Look, how the floor of heaven is thick inlaid with patines of bright gold."

8th Colour.—*Grandeur.* All the words are equally coloured.
" Roll on, thou deep and dark blue ocean, roll."

9th Colour.—*Pride.* Colour words : Inch ; king.
" Ay, every inch a king."

10th Colour.—*Arrogance.* Colour words : Like ; myself.
" I have no brother, I am like no brother, I am myself alone."

11th Colour.—*Defiance.* Colour word : Defied.
" I tell thee, thou'rt defied."

12th Colour.—*Dignity, Grave.* Colour words : God ; come.
" Sir, before God, I believe the hour has come ! "

13th Colour.—*Dignity, Earnest.* Colour words : This ; self ; true ; any.
" This, above all, to thine own self be true, and it must follow as the night the day, thou canst not then be false to any man."
The foregoing sentiment builds a very magnetic voice.

14th Colour.—*Courage.* Colour words : Free ; host ; liberty ; man.
" Now, my brave lads,—now are we free indeed ! I have a whole host in this single arm. Death or liberty ! We shall not leave a man of them alive ! "

15th Colour.—*Affection.* Colour words : Wear ; core ; heart ; thee.
" Give me that man that is not passion's slave, and I will wear him in my heart's core, ay, in my heart of hearts, as I do thee."

16th Colour.—*Greeting to a Friend.* Colour words : Glad ; twenty ; years.
" Well, Tom, I'm right glad to see you ! It's twenty years since last we met."

17th Colour.—*Greeting to Country.* Colour words : Crags ; peaks ; again ; you ; still.

> "Ye crags and peaks, I'm with you once again.
> I hold to you the hands you first beheld,
> To show they still are free."

18th Colour.—*Coldness.* Colour words : Unwelcome ; extend.

> "Sir, you are unwelcome here ! I do not wish to extend our acquaintance."

19th Colour.—*Indignation.* Colour word : Leave.

> "You may leave this house."

20th Colour.—*Shame.* Colour words : Shame ; blush.

> "Oh, shame ! where is thy blush ! "

21st Colour.—*Anger.* All the words are equally coloured.

> "What do you mean, sir ! "

22nd Colour.—*Caution.* Colour words : Hush ; silence, word ; word ; lives.

> "Hush ! Silence along the line there ! Not a word—not a word, on peril of your lives ! "

23rd Colour.—*Descriptive.* Variable colours.

> "From dumb winter to spring in one wonderful hour,
> From Nevada's white wing to creation in flower,
> December at morning tossing wild in its might ;
> A June without warning, and blown roses at night."

24th Colour.—*Faith.* Colour words : Youth ; bright ; no.

> "In the lexicon of youth, which fate reserves for a bright manhood, there's no such word as fail."

One of the greatest actors of the last generation repeated this 24th colour 20,000 times aloud.

25th Colour.—*Longing.* Colour words : Long ; better ; striving ; heart ; me ; alone.

> "I have another life I long to meet,
> Without which life my life is incomplete.
> O better self, like me, art thou astray,
> Striving with all thy heart to find the way
> To mine ; seeking, like me, to find the breast
> On which, alone, can weary heart find rest."

26th Colour.—*Hope.* Colour words : Hope ; angels ; away.

> "Ah, well ! for us all some sweet hope lies,
> Deeply buried from human eyes ;

And, in the hereafter, angels may
Roll the stone from its grave away."

27th Colour.—*Solemnity.*   Colour word : Eternal.

" Oh, thou eternal one ! "

28th Colour.—*Dark Intensity.*   All the words are equally coloured.

" Thou sure and firm-set earth, hear not my steps which way they walk."

29th Colour.—*Sublimity.*

" But thou, most awful form, risest from forth thy silent sea of pines, how silently !   Around thee, and above, deep is the air, and dark, substantial, black—an ebon mass. . . . But when I look again it is thine own calm home, thy crystal shrine, thy habitation from eternity."

30th Colour.—*Contempt.*   Colour words : Loathe ;   scorn ; taunt ;   fight.

" I loathe you in my bosom, I scorn you with mine eye !
   And I'll taunt you with my latest breath, and fight you
      till I die."

31st Colour.—*Threatening.*   Colour words : Pray ;   remorse, accumulate.

" If thou dost slander her, and torture me, never pray more ; abandon all remorse ;   on horror's head horrors accumulate ! "

32nd Colour.—*Hate.*   Colour words :   Hence ;   Satan ; behind ;   go ;   hate ;   despise.

" Hence !   from my sight !   Thou Satan, get behind me ! Go from my sight !   I hate and despise thee ! "

There are a few other colours such as a tragedian would use on the stage, but they are not suited to this work.

Charles Dickens, in his readings, employed all thirty-two colours which are given in these lessons.

When once a colour is developed in the voice, it never leaves it, but flows naturally with the tones at all times.   This makes the voice natural and never artificial.

It can be seen at once that such a voice can never become monotonous or repellent.

VOCAL QUALITIES

FEW PERSONS KNOW what is meant by qualities of the voice, and still fewer persons ever make use of them. All conversations are carried on in the same uninteresting flat tones, which soon tire even those who employ them. We now approach the study of those tones that reflect the real soul and character behind them. The mouth and throat are given the power to change their shape, and thereby change the nature of the tones that are uttered. Earlier in these lessons we learned that when the upper throat is nearly closed, the tones are flat and guttural; that when the lower throat is partly closed, the tones are threatening and pectoral.

Singers are taught to impinge their voices against the front upper palate of the mouth, and at this place the tones are bright and beautiful. For speaking and conversing, the tones may be forward in the position just stated; or the voice may be impinged against the middle of the palate, in which case a different effect is produced; and if impinged against the soft palate, the dark or gloomy quality is made.

Then when the upper throat is open and round, another timbre follows; but when the lower throat is open and round, still another effect is produced. And so on through the entire list of changes in the voice that reflect the soul or the character of the speaker.

All these varieties of voice are known as TIMBRE QUALITIES.

As you open this lesson you ask if there can be anything more to be learned about the voice. But you will agree, ere long, that this faculty of speech is most wonderful, most amazing in its powers.

The end has not yet been reached.

Colour is a great thing; but no musical instrument can of

itself produce colour ; although the players are able to do so to some extent.

But the church organ is able to produce timbre qualities. You have heard it almost sing in the beauty and ecstasy of its tones ; then suddenly change to the heavy roll of majesty ; or again produce the liquid notes of birds at early morning ; and so on, through a multitude of qualities that are summoned by the manipulation of the many stops. The organ has timbre qualities, but lacks tone colour.

The true character or inner life of a person shows itself in the timbre that prevails in that person's voice. He who leads a gloomy, solemn life, will fall into the unconscious habit of using the dark form, and generally a low pitch. If his gloom is mingled with sorrow or suffering, the pitch is higher, and there is a mixture of the laryngeal timbre in the voice.

Although the dark form is perfectly natural, and is given to the world in fact by the world's great mother, yet everybody does not possess it. It is easily acquired by practice.

A man or woman whose life has more of happiness than of sorrow in it, will fall into an unconscious habit of using the bright form, and *vice versa*.

Daniel Webster's habitual timbre quality was orotund. He was brought up amid the giant scenery of New Hampshire and the grandeur of earth impressed itself on his mind and heart.

" TIMBRE MEANINGS "

The BRIGHT TIMBRE means happiness, brightness, or vitality. It is produced by impinging the voice forward in the mouth so that it strikes against the hard palate near the front upper teeth.

The DARK TIMBRE means gloom or solemnity. It is made by impinging the voice against the soft palate near the back of the mouth.

The PURE TIMBRE means beauty. It is made with a round shape of the throat.

The OROTUND TIMBRE means grandeur. It is made by enlarging the whole larynx and thereby increasing the volume of sound.

The GUTTURAL TIMBRE means hatred. It is made with the flat shape of the throat.

The NASAL TIMBRE means scorn. It is made by lessening the resonance of the voice which seems as if the nose intervened.

The ORAL TIMBRE means weakness. It is made by mouthing the voice, or confining the sound within the mouth with very little vitality.

The LARYNGEAL TIMBRE means suffering. It is made at the vocal cords and has no vitality elsewhere.

The ASPIRATE TIMBRE means something startling or secret. It is made by a large proportion of escaping air mixed with the voice.

The WHISPER TIMBRE means extreme secrecy or startling importance. It is made by removing all tone from the voice, and using only a whisper.

The PECTORAL TIMBRE means awe or deep malice. It is made by the flat shape of the lowest part of the throat.

Just as the player of a great church organ would suit the stops to the character of the selections played, so any person in life should suit the Timbres to the uses made of the voice.

In business conversation the Pure Timbre is the most attractive, and may be shaded with some slight changes in the Bright and Dark.

In social conversation, the Bright, Dark, Pure, Orotund and Whisper are useful, but should be tempered in good taste.

The preacher has need of the Bright, Dark, Pure, Orotund, Pectoral, and possibly the Whisper, which is very effective when rightly used.

The lawyer in his address to the jury has need of all the Timbres, as has been proved in the lives of every successful lawyer.

The actor needs exactly as many Timbres as the lawyer. Edwin Booth was past-master of Timbre tones. The difference between the actor and the lawyer is that the latter keeps more closely to the conversational Timbres except when he is depicting human character, while the actor has occasion to depart more frequently from those Timbres when he steps out of the merely conversational rôles.

The reciter, entertainer and imitator needs all the Timbres that are described in this lesson.

The lecturer is a social converser on a large scale.

The orator is an actor in part and needs in part of his work all the Timbres. John B. Gough was the most wonderful depicter of human character of modern times ; yet, without his mastery of these Timbres, he would have been a mere lecturer. The Timbres coined for him thousands of pounds, and they did the same for Dickens, the reader of his own characters.

A Timbre is the character of the tone.

A Quality is the blend in which the Timbre is employed in the voice.

We will include here those Qualities that are most useful in ordinary life.

The First Quality is Bright.—The Quotation is :

" My happy heart with rapture swells."

The Second Quality is Dark.—The Quotation is :

" Her death was sadly beautiful, and her soul was borne upon the perfume of earth's drooping lilies to the land of flowers that never fade."

The Third Quality is Neutral.—The Quotation is :

" Though they smile in vain for what once was ours, they are love's last gift."

The Fourth Quality is Half-Bright.—The Quotation is :

" The Rhine ! The Rhine ! Our own imperial river ! Be glory on thy track ! "

The Fifth Quality is Half-Dark.—The Quotation is :

" One sweetly solemn thought comes to me o'er and o'er."

All the foregoing Qualities are made in the Pure Timbre mixed with either Bright or Dark Timbres, except the Third which is neutral ; that is, without brightness or darkness.

The Sixth Quality is Bright Orotund.—The Quotation is :

" And the spent ship, tempest driven, on reef lies rent and riven."

The Seventh Quality is Half-Dark Orotund.—The Quotation is:

" Through what variety of untried being, through what new scenes and changes must we pass ! "

The Eighth Quality is Dark Orotund.—The Quotation is :

" Toll ! toll ! toll ! thou bell by billows swung ! "

The Ninth Quality is Whisper.—The Quotation is :

" Hark ! Listen ! Keep still ! Some one is coming ! "

The Tenth Quality is Aspirate.—The Quotation is :

" Thou sure and firm-set earth, hear not my steps which way they walk ! "

20

The Eleventh Quality is Bright Guttural.—The Quotation is :
" I loathe you in my bosom ! "

The Twelfth Quality is Dark Guttural.—The Quotation is :
" To-morrow, and to-morrow, and to-morrow, creeps in this petty pace from day to day, to the last syllable of recorded time."

The Thirteenth Quality is Pectoral.—The Quotation is :
" I am thy father's spirit, doomed for a certain term to walk the night."

You can make your own colours.

In a previous lesson you were taught to make the round voice and to remove its crudities. That produces the Pure Timbre. Such a Timbre you must have if you would have friends. So that much is assured, and is easy.

To produce the Orotund Timbre, merely give greater volume of sound to the Pure voice. Make the throat cavity deeper and larger, and that is all there is to it. So the Orotund will be at hand in your tones very soon.

The Bright and Dark Timbres are matters of impingement, which means that a forward throwing of the tones will brighten the voice, and a backward throwing of the voice will darken it.

The Guttural is made by the top of the flat throat. To be sure, the Guttural is a flat voice and is faulty ; but hatred is a faulty phase of character.

The Aspirate is a mixture of tone and whisper. It is a fault, but the above remarks concerning the Guttural will apply.

The Pectoral is like the Guttural, except that it is made in the lower throat, while the Guttural is made in the upper throat. Very little practice will be needed to secure it in your voice if you use the quotation given.

In fact all the quotations help very much to establish the Qualities.

MIXING BEAUTIFUL COLOURS

STILL MORE BEAUTIFUL practice is to be had in the mixing of colours ; for much of the work is left to the taste and discretion of the student, and that is always the source of the greatest progress in anything. The kind of colouring that enters the voice through the qualities is always allied with the use of tone colouring, of which we have given thirty-two examples in a preceding lesson. We advise practising them with these qualities, so that one set of values may be mixed with another set. Both are wholly natural ; and both are the result of life activities from which art gets its instruction.

All artists mix their own colours.

You will remember the historic inquiry made of one great painter by a novice who asked him what he mixed his colours with, and the great man said, " With brains."

You now have, or soon will have, thirteen basic qualities in your voice, and you have been taught how to increase the mental vitality of words by the use of glides ; in addition to which you have practised Tone Colour until you are able to put your feelings into every utterance and to harmonize the feelings of the occasion and the value of the thoughts spoken.

You can see the great need of the modulating movements, for they compel your mind to wake up and summon all others to listen to you. You know the necessity of Tone Colour, for a colourless voice is as dead as the sound of a nail scraping on glass. You do not want to present such a voice to your friends and acquaintances.

Colour may exist without the aid of Timbres ; but it will be weak and of poor material. Timbres are really the instruments through which you speak. If you had a voice like the reed notes of an organ, you would have beauty of tone, and this you could colour ; but how much better it is to have more stops to manipulate. You know how depressed the organist would feel if he found all the grand Timbres of the organ out of use some Sunday morning when the church was alive with interest in his work.

The great organ becomes a group of instruments when it employs all the Timbres which the stops bring into being. So your voice should be made into a group of instruments by the various Timbres which nature has given you for your development. Hide no talents under a bushel, for it is wrong to do so.

As soon as you have built up the Timbres and have mastered them in the Thirteen Qualities of the preceding lesson, then you have secured a group of instruments, each distinctly different from the others.

These are colour-mixers.

Mixing your own colours is the grandest and the most fascinating of all work in this world. The human voice is the sublime gift of the Creator to humanity, and lifts the race to the very pinnacle of power and supremacy. But the work of building its many instruments is the most satisfying and the most useful of all developing agencies in this realm of high art.

Because no one has done this to your knowledge, you are of the belief that it is not worth doing. But some few great men and women have accomplished these tasks, and have made fortunes in so doing.

It is a great pleasure to mix your own colours.

You are left to your own judgment and tastes in this work. Look over the selections herein given, then take account of stock of what colours and Timbres you possess already in your voice, and produce the combinations which you please. Try different combinations on each selection.

The first offering is one that will admit of many variations in colour and Timbre, but not of greatly marked degree. Remember that the meaning of the Pure Timbre is Beauty, and that the first five Qualities of the lesson devoted to them are made up of the Pure Timbre.

The mixing of the Bright and Dark Timbres with the Pure does not take away any of the beauty of the voice effect, but changes the degree of brightness or vitality into a more solemn or gloomy form of beauty.

First Selection

" NIGHT "

" How beautiful this night ! The balmiest sigh,
Which vernal zephyrs breathe in evening's ear,
Were discord to the speaking quietude
That wraps this moveless scene. Heaven's ebon vaults
Studded with stars unutterably bright,
Through which the moon's unclouded grandeur rolls,
Seems like a canopy which love has spread
To curtain her sleeping world. Yon gentle hills,
Robed in a garment of untrodden snow ;
Yon darksome rocks, whence icicles depend—
So stainless, that their white and glittering spires
Tinge not the moon's pure beam ; yon castled steep,
Whose banner hangeth o'er the time-worn tower
So idly, that rapt fancy deemeth it a metaphor of peace."

Second Selection

" MUSIC OF THE STARS "

" How sweet the moonlight sleeps upon this bank.
Here we will sit and let the sound of music
Creep in our ears ;   soft stillness and the night
Become the touches of sweet harmony.
Sit, Jessica. Look how the heaven
Is thick inlaid with patines of bright gold.
There's not the smallest orb which thou behold'st
But in his motion like an angel sings,
Still quiring to the young-eyed cherubims ;
Such harmony is in immortal souls ;
But whilst this muddy vesture of decay
Doth grossly close it in, we cannot hear it."

" GRAND MIXED COLOURS "

The Pure Timbre prevailed in the preceding lesson. We
now bring the Orotund into use. Its meaning is Grandeur.
You are to mix the colours to suit your own tastes and feelings.

THIRD SELECTION

"MOUNT BLANC"

"Hast thou a charm to stay the morning star,
In his steep course ? So long he seems to pause
On thy bald, awful head, O sovereign Blanc !
The Arve and Arveiron at thy base
Rave ceaselessly ; but thou, most awful form,
Risest from forth thy silent sea of pines
How silently ! Around thee and above
Deep is the air and dark, substantial, black,—
An ebon mass. Methinks thou piercest it,
As with a wedge ! But when I look again,
It is thine own calm home, thy crystal shrine,
Thy habitation from eternity !
O dread and silent Mount ! I gazed upon thee,
Till thou, still present to the bodily sense,
Didst vanish from my thought.
Entranced in prayer
I worshipped the invisible alone."

FOURTH SELECTION

"RICHELIEU"

"Then wakes the power which is the age of iron
Burst forth to curb the great and raise the low.
Mark where she stands ! Around her form I draw
The awful circle of our solemn church !
Set but a foot within that holy ground,
And on thy head—yea—though it wore a crown—
I'd launch the curse of Rome."

FIFTH SELECTION

"WEBSTER'S GREAT PERORATION"

"When my eyes shall be turned to behold, for the last time, the sun in heaven, may I not see him shining on the broken and dishonoured fragments of a once glorious union ; on state dissevered, discordant, belligerent ; on a land rent with civil

feuds, or drenched, it may be, with fraternal blood ! Let their
last feeble and lingering glance rather behold the gorgeous
ensign of the Republic now known and honoured throughout
the earth, still ' full high advanced ' ;—its arms and trophies
streaming in their original lustre, not a stripe erased or polluted,
nor a single star obscured ;—bearing, for its motto, no such
miserable interrogatory as ' What is all this worth ? ' nor those
other words of delusion and folly, ' Liberty first, and union
afterwards,'—but everywhere spread all over, in characters of
living light, blazing on all its ample folds as they float over the
sea and over the land, and in every wind under the whole heaven
that other sentiment, dear to every true American heart—
' Liberty and union, now and forever, one and inseparable.' "

Sixth Selection

" SHIEL'S GREAT PERORATION "

" Whose were the arms that drove your bayonets at Vimeiro
through the phalanxes that never reeled in the shock of war
before ?   What desperate valour climbed the steeps and filled
the moats at Badajos ?   All his victories should have rushed and
crowded back upon his memory,—Vimeiro, Badajos, Salamanca,
Albuera, Toulouse, and, last of all, the greatest—Tell me—for
you were there.   I appeal to the gallant soldier before me, from
whose opinions I differ, but who bears, I know, a generous heart
in an intrepid breast.   Tell me, for you must needs remember,
on that day, when the destinies of mankind were trembling in
the balance, while death fell in showers ; when the artillery of
France was levelled with a precision of the most deadly science ;
when her legions, incited by the voice, and inspired by the
example of their mighty leader, rushed again and again to the
onset ;—Tell me, if for an instant, when to hesitate for an instant
was to be lost, the ' aliens ' blanched ? "

"VITAL MIXED COLOURS "

The Guttural Timbre depicts Vitality of feeling, as well as
hatred and kindred moods, all of which are really vital.

The Pectoral is a more awful form of Guttural.

While these two Timbres originate in faulty uses of the voice, the faults in some cases are inspired by sublime censure of the evils of life, and a purpose to expose them. Thus the Guttural and Pectoral so common in the famed Indian Orators whose eloquence has been of the highest order, are grand at times in their effect on the hearers. Louis Kossuth was as great an orator as he was a General ; and the moving power of his speeches was in the Guttural and Pectoral tones, highly coloured by a fine nervous intensity.

SEVENTH SELECTION

" VICTOR HUGO'S VITAL STYLE "

" A cannon which breaks its moorings on board ship becomes abruptly some indescribable, supernatural beast. It is a machine which transforms itself into a monster.

" This mass runs on its wheels like billiard balls, inclines with the rolling, plunges with the pitching, goes, comes, stops, seems to meditate, resumes its course, shoots from one end of the ship to the other like an arrow, whirls, steals away, evades, prances, strikes, breaks, kills, exterminates."

EIGHTH SELECTION

" SHAKESPEARE'S VITAL STYLE "

" Poison be their drink,
  Gall, worse than gall, the daintiest meat they taste ;
  Their sweetest shade a grove of cypress trees,
  Their sweetest prospect murdering basilisks,
  Their softest couch as smart as lizard's stings,
  Their music frightful as the serpent's hiss,
  And boding screech-owls make the concert full ;
  All the foul terrors of dark-seated hell."

NINTH SELECTION

" THE INDIAN'S HATRED "

" Some strike for hope of booty ; some to defend their all ;
  I battle for the joy I have to see the white man fall.

I love, among the wounded, to hear his dying moan,
And catch, while chanting at his side, the music of his groan.
You've trailed me through the forest ; you've tracked me
    o'er the stream ;
And struggling through the everglades your bristling bayonets
    gleam.
But I stand as should the warrior, with his rifle and his spear,
The scalp of vengeance still is red, and warns you—come not
    here ! ''

<hr />

TENTH SELECTION

'' THE GLADIATOR ''

'' If ye are beasts, then stand here like fat oxen waiting for
the butcher's knife ? If ye are men, follow me ! Strike down
yon guard, gain the mountain passes, and there do bloody
work, as did your sires at old Thermopylæ ! Is Sparta dead ?
Is the old Grecian spirit frozen in your veins, that you do crouch
and cower like a belaboured hound beneath his master's lash ?
O comrades ! warriors ! Thracians ! if we must fight, let us
fight for ourselves, if we must slaughter, let us slaughter our
oppressors ! If we must die, let it be under the clear sky, by
the bright waters, in noble, honourable battle ! ''

The world knows more of the habits of its famous men than
it does of the manner of living of the thousands who have won
successs in the private walks of life. Thus it knows to a
certainty, by reading the biographies of such men as came before
the public in their efforts to shape the destinies of nations, that
they one and all without exception build the fires of personal
magnetism in themselves by the repeating aloud of the most
stirring thoughts they could find.

Patrick Henry developed his magnetism by practising aloud
in deserted or unused schoolhouses. Edward Everett was an
incessant practiser before a mirror, using thrilling thoughts in
potent words. In his life of Daniel Webster he tells of the
latter's practice in the deep woods where he was often overheard.

RAPID MAGNETIC ADVANCEMENT

NOTHING SO AMPLY PROVES the complex character of humanity as the varying changes of the voice, suiting themselves to all manner of moods and feelings, and all kinds of intellectual activities from the lowest to the highest adventures of speech. But there still remains a vast field of development, intended to impart to every message from the mind the highest service in efficiency ; for by such means what might possess value in ordinary form becomes a mighty force when driven home with the utmost power of physical magnetism, or muscular magnetism. This use of these words must not be confounded with the bad habit of setting the muscles for the display of mere force or noise.

"QUICK MAGNETISM"

It does not take long to develop muscular magnetism, to fire your nervous system with a new life, and to see for yourself the effects of a little practice of the right kind.

The mouth, by muscular motion, makes the checks called consonants. We wish that muscular action to be impelled with greater energy. Deal to each check a hammer blow ; then another, and so continue until you have struck many blows on one check.

If your arm is not used, it will grow soft and flabby. If you use it in the right way, it will become strong and large, and its muscles will harden and take on greater power. The same is true of the muscles of the mouth that are employed in making the vocal checks.

New energy behind them will bring development that will aid very materially in their work of executing the tasks set for them to do.

Take a little sentence to begin with : " *I will have my bond.*"

In this sentence the word *bond* is very important. Now repeat the word *bond* with intense energy ; not of voice, but of muscular touch ; and keep on repeating it. The " b " and the " nd " in the word can be given a very powerful muscular touch in the mouth, and the energy behind the utterance can be made to grow all the time.

Keep on increasing the power of the muscular touch. This implies more impelling energy in every repetition. You must have your mind on the work. You must be determined to succeed in adding more energy as you proceed. After saying the word *bond* hundreds of times, then repeat the whole sentence ; *I will have my bond*, and note the fire that comes into the brain. This is only a beginning ; but from the least beginning great achievements may follow.

Take another sentence : *I am determined.*

Take the last word and find the dams or vocal-checks in it. They are " d " in the beginning and in the end, and " t " and " m " in the middle. The " n " goes with the final " d " Just repeat these checks separately hundreds of times each before uttering the whole word ; then speak the whole word " determined " hundreds of times. Remember to impel always increasing energy in every repetition of letter or word. Do not become languid or indifferent. Keep the source of the power growing stronger and stronger always. This is the secret. Then repeat the whole sentence :

" I am determined."

If you have read this lesson and the one preceding a few times until you understand the manner of practice, you will achieve results in a very short time ; and these results will go into every word you speak to other persons. Something will begin to hold their attention and bring them to you.

Force of voice is never required.

In fact many men now of national fame have practised this method in their rooms without being heard in the next rooms. One of our students developed great magnetism in this way and never was discovered in his practice as he omitted the vocal tones, when other persons were present in the same room. He pantomimed the action. This is not the best. A low, quiet tone can be employed.

" MAGNETIC COINAGE "

It is not loudness of voice that enables a person to be heard.

It is the coinage of sound into syllables and words.

Our life sounds are known as vowels.

Our vocal-checks or dams are known as consonants.

Every life-sound should have the full variation of mouth-shape that the sound requires. It is possible to hold the mouth in one position and utter the words of a sentence, so that you think that you can hear them distinctly ; but other persons will not hear you clearly, and the voice is for others, not for yourself to hear.

If the vowels have no mouth action the utterances are not clearly made, and not easily heard. It is not sufficient that the audience hear the *sound* of the voice—they should hear *what* is said. Language consists merely of syllables ; syllables of vowels and consonants. One syllable differs from another merely in the fact that different vowels and consonants are employed, or combined differently.

If a speaker or reader with more voice than brains should endeavour merely to make himself heard, he could do it by shouting or yelling unintelligible sounds, as the street vendors do ; the voice is *heard,* and distressingly so. But a quiet tone, accompanied by clear enunciation, will carry sense, in the form of intelligible words, farther than the shouter's voice.

A strong voice is of no avail if the vowels and consonants are not well-formed and made.

" MAGNETIC CONSONANTS "

All the vocal checks or consonants that are worth practising on are given here. Simply repeat them with a hard muscular touch on each one, and with ever-increasing nervous energy behind to propel them. Each one should be repeated hundreds of times. But *saying* them will not do any good. Hammer them. Give them intense power from the nerve-centres. Make the mouth execute them with tremendous pressure. Drift always into a naturalness as you proceed.

The genius is he who thinks of what he is doing ; the mind-wanderer does things mechanically.

Bd—Cribb'd, bobb'd, robb'd.

>He *robb'd* his friend in the field.

Bdst—Cribb'dst, bobb'dst, fib'dst.

>Thou *fib'dst* to thy best friend.

Bldst—Gambl'dst, rambl'dst, fabl'dst.

>Thou *rambl'dst* over the ground.

Bst—Sobb'st, stubb'st, robb'st.

>*Sobb'st* thou at such trifles ?

Dldst—Handl'dst, fondl'dst, fiddl'dst.

>*Fiddl'dst* thou much, my friend ?

Dnd—Madd'nd, wid'nd, broad'nd.

>Study *broad'nd* and *wid'nd* his life

Fld—Stifl'd, muffl'd, baffl'd.

>He *muffl'd* the drum and *stifl'd* the sound.

Fst—Laugh'st, quaff'st, stuff'st.

>*Laugh'st* thou at this ?

Fths—Fifths, twelfths.

>They formed by *fifths*.

Gld—Smuggl'd, wrangl'd, mangl'd.

>The *smuggl'd* garments were *mangl'd*.

Gldst—gurgl'dst, struggl'dst, bungl'dst.

>Thou *bungl'dst* it.

Gst—pegg'st, flogg'st, drugg'st.

>Thou *drugg'st* and *flogg'st* him.

Kldst—Shackl'd'st, tackl'd'st, buckl'd'st.

>*Buckl'd'st* thou thy armour ?

Klst—Encircl'st, tackl'st, buckl'st.

>*Encircl'st* thou her form ?

Kndst—Heark'n'dst, lik'n'dst, black'n'dst.

>Thou *lik'n'dst* it to death.

Knst—Wak'n'st, heark'n'st, beck'n'st.

>Thou *heark'n'st* well.

Lft—Engulfed.

>The wave *engulfed* him.

Lfth—Twelfth.

>Did you witness " *Twelfth* Night ? "

Ldgbd—Indulg'd, divulg'd, bilg'd.

>They were *indulg'd* but *divulg'd* not.

Lps—Scalps, pulps, helps.

>What *helps scalps !*

Lpst—Scalp'st, help'st.

   Help'st thou not ?

Ngdst—Long'dst, wrong'dst, hang'dst.

   Hang'dst thou innocent men ?

Ngst—Bring'st, hang'st, sing'st.

   Thou *sing'st* like a lark.

Ngths—Lengths, strengths.

   He was left many *lengths* behind.

Vst—Shov'st, liv'st, prov'st.

   Thou *prov'st* thy point.

" MAGNETIC BARRIERS "

Some persons with good voices and other excellent qualities are sometimes placed in a bad position by the inability of the tongue muscles to execute the mixed variety of consonants that may intrude without warning. Many a fine address has been ruined in this way.

A young man who was trying to impress a young lady with his superior ease and polish fell into this trap that his own tongue set for him.

Conversations meant to be serious have been turned into ridicule by the same causes.

The trouble arises from the fact that some letters do not allow other letters to be sounded with them without special practice to develop flexibility of consonant muscles.

Take for example the reply made by a waiter when a young man asked him to bring two kinds of soup for himself and lady friends. The young man tried to order " Sheep soup, shoat soup and beef soup." But he never got as far as the first two. The waiter said," I understand. You want lamb soup and young hog soup."

Can *you* say, " Sheep soup, shoat soup," easily and rapidly, or at all ?

Try it aloud, and then ask your friends to try it aloud.

It will strengthen the tongue muscles.

You wish to be understood when you speak ; you cannot afford to be misunderstood.

Then pay strict attention to clearest articulation of words, for which the following is excellent practice.

If you can speak these words readily, then increase the speed of utterance to make them flexible.

Here are some others :

" She stood at the gate, welcoming him in."

" A pink trip slip."

" A million alien minions."

" Literally literary."

" A shame it is to sham so, Sam."

" Sue saw six slender saplings."

" He twists his texts."

" A peculiar pecuniary predicament."

" She thrust six thousand thistles through her thumb."

" Around the rough rocks the ragged rascals ran."

" Beef-broth." This must be said many times with great speed.

" Tie tight Dick's kite."

" Sunshine some shun."

" Six thick thistle sticks."

" Then thrust it through the thatch."

" Chaste stars are not chased tars."

" Triumphant nymphs."

" Ghastly ghosts at sixty-six Sixsmith street."

" The axe performs the acts."

" All sects, regardless of sex."

" The prow proudly plows the deep."

" He sent back the blank black ink."

" A knapsack strap." Say this rapidly many times at once.

In fact, the true test of flexible tongue muscles is in your ability to read all the foregoing examples very rapidly.

While there are many valuable methods in this series of lessons, one that should receive extra attention is that of " Magnetic Consonants." In a few minutes you can prove that this line of training will develop in you the power and fire of muscular magnetism. You will not have to wait many minutes to see the effects of it.

Then you will find that muscular magnetism is the basis of personal magnetism. It gives at first surprise ; then a glow of satisfaction ; then a realization of a new-found power ; then ambition ; then courage ; then the determination to ascertain to what ends you can carry your gifts ; and soon you are rising in the world far above your fellow-beings. This is the plan and purpose of Nature. Nor is it right to hide your talents under a bushel.

And the practice of " hammering consonants " will change the shape of the face to such a degree that a photograph taken before the work begins and another after it ends, will show a decided improvement. The lips, in a few months of constant practice, will have the fine chiseling that the sculptor aims to give to his noblest men and women. All the muscles from those at the forehead down to those at the chin, and from ear to ear, are involved in this practice. If you doubt it, watch your face in a glass when you are hammering the many consonants with energy and determination to increase the nervous power that impels them. An unused face is immobile, which is a polite term for being stupid. This practice develops excessive mobility, adds a charm to every feature, brings solidity in place of flabby skin, and lights up the features with an attractiveness which halts the attention of others.

The mind is stimulated more by the voice than by any other cause. The expressive voice lights up the face in a way that is hard to describe. The coinage of words by every great man or woman who has ever come in contact with the public has been of rare power. All the consonants used by them have been energized from the nerve centres, and found execution on muscles that, like live wires, have burned them into the minds of all who have listened to them.

When you find yourself acquiring a new power of making your ideas felt by other people, this stimulus will arouse in you a new ambition that will grow rapidly. We wish we could show you the proofs of this fact in the lives of people who were dire failures because of their inability to impress their hearers ; whose ideas could not be given living expression in their voices ; and who revolutionized their careers by the mastery of this simple system.

It is Nature itself.

THE GREAT TEST

MORE THAN A THIRD OF A CENTURY ago a Committee was organized consisting of two Politicians, one newspaper proprietor and a scientific investigator, for the purpose of determining by direct observation the actual results of the training methods employed under this system. The Committee was in charge of the Hon. Adolph Meyer, prior to the time when he became a Member of the Board of Trustees of Ralston University, which position he held for many years and up to the time of his death. He was a man of great ability.

Twelve men were selected from twelve walks of life ; chiefly because of their total lack of personal magnetism. One was an unsuccessful business man, one a lawyer who had never won a case, one a labourer, one an unskilful dentist, one a poor doctor, one a carpenter, one a teacher of whom it was said that " he would never set the world on fire," one a clerk in government service, one a salesman in a very modest store, one a clerk, one a painter, and one a photographer in failing circumstances. Of course these selections were purposely sought, with the intention of making the work as difficult as possible.

We had previously announced that every person of ordinary intelligence could be made to recognize in four weeks the fact that personal magnetism was natural to all individuals ; that it was latent in all ; and that what was needed was some instigating cause to awaken it.

We had also stated that distinct and marked evidence could be obtained in the same four weeks of the awakening of this power, and of its rank as the supreme gift of life ; that it was a part of existence ; that it nevertheless could be amply manifested in this short time ; and, finally, that the most unmagnetic men and women might be easily brought into the possession of

this gift if they earnestly desired to do so.   It was because of
the last assertion that we found ourselves about to teach this
great power to twelve really " hopeless cases " if our statements
had not been accurately made.

The Committee were told in confidence that our elementary
method by which we were able to show astounding results in a
few weeks followed our " Rule of Four," as we called it.   Bear
in mind that this " Rule of Four " is not a large part of our
System, but is a mighty one as far as it goes.   It consisted of
the following steps :

1. Kill the worst forms of Leakage at once ; for neither
magnetism nor self-control can be acquired when they exist.

2. Kill the worst forms of monotony ; for there is nothing
so repellent in human intercourse as sameness of sound, sameness of voice, sameness of pitch, and sameness of colour in
spoken words.

3. Fire the mind ; not the brain ; nor the nerves ; but the
mind ; by opening its portals to the reception of mental
pictures.

4. Turn the voice into a human dynamic energy, by sound-
dams.

These steps, as we have stated, are all elementary, but
necessary and effective in the highest degree.

The first session was devoted to the discovering and reducing
the worst forms of Leakage.   We showed that natural magnetism was all the time developing of itself, and constantly
running to waste.   In the next session we made clear the
offensive forms of monotony, such as sameness of tone, sameness of pitch, colourless voices, and one colour only when any
was used at all.   The question has often been asked, why tone
colour is taught ; and the answer is that all unmagnetic
persons have colourless voices, and these depict the character as
holding the same relation to magnetism as the spineless jelly-
fish holds to the powerful lion.   These principles were made
very clear at once, and were as quickly grasped and acted
upon.

Now came the only difficult part of the work.   The mind must
be fired by opening its portals to mental pictures.   A mental
picture is a scene that lives in the thoughts.   We selected the
historic battle between the Swiss and the Austrians at that

stage when the latter had surrounded the former and were advancing on them in a circle which projected spears from which there seemed no escape. The following quotations make the connected story when put together ; but we used them singly because each one presented a mental picture in itself. With body free from Leakages, and with voice free from sameness, each quotation was repeated fifty times, slowly and very deliberately, with the picture fully alive in the mind.

"All Switzerland is in the field."—Think of the little army completely surrounded by a vast army that is advancing with levelled spears, intent upon the complete destruction of the Swiss. As soon as the mental picture is vividly present in the mind, speak the words very firmly ; and so proceed with all the quotations :

"She cannot fly, she will not yield, she must not die."

Here are three pitches : one in the middle range ; one below it ; and one very low. Here are also three colours : hopelessness ; absolute firmness ; and solemn hope.

Be sure to give these full expression.

"Her better fate here gives her an immortal date."

This is a look into the future, full of bright hope.

"Few were the numbers she could boast, but every freeman was a host, and felt as though himself were he on whose sole arm hung victory. It did depend on one indeed ; behold him—Arnold Winkelried ! Unmarked he stood amid the throng in rumination deep and long, till you might see with sudden grace the very thought come o'er his face ; and by the motion of his form anticipate the bursting storm. 'Make way for liberty,' he cried, then ran with arms extended wide, as if his dearest friend to clasp ; ten spears he swept within his grasp. Swift to the breach his comrades fly : 'Make way for liberty,' they cry, and through the Austrian phalanx dart as rushed the spears through Arnold's heart, while, instantaneous as his fall, rout, ruin, panic seized them all ; an earthquake could not overthrow a city with a surer blow. Thus Switzerland again was free ; thus death made way for liberty."

Here are not less than eighteen mental pictures, and each one should live in the mind and be viewed as accurately as if it were beheld openly. This is the secret of opening the mind and awakening in it the fires of magnetism. As soon as the student is able to see one mental picture his success is assured. In these quotations eighteen different colours may be developed.

The fourth step in the Rule of Four is the most potent of all. It develops dynamic power in the voice by treating all vowels as sounds, and all consonants as dams. A consonant is a shutting off of a vowel prior to its utterance or as soon as uttered. A consonant may precede or end a vowel ; it cannot exist of itself. The sound-dams are all finals ; meaning they all follow vowel sounds. The firm closing off of a vowel by a consonant holds in check the magnetism of the voice. The union of two final consonants doubles this power. The union of three final consonants triples it. The union of four final consonants in one ending quadruples it. Rufus Choate, probably the most magnetic man of the last century, next possibly to Junius Brutus Booth, the actor, always before a speech spent minutes in four-consonant endings, such as KAMSKT, KAMSTK and others, which are too difficult for beginners. But Choate also practised Greek words having three consonant endings. Wilson Barrett, the most magnetic of actors, ascribed his success in this power chiefly to consonant practice.

To our class of twelve " hopeless cases " we gave the consonant combinations that attend the Department of the Magnetic Voice in this book ; and we personally drilled them every day until they mastered this part of the work. To show the value we placed on such practice, we opened each session with unison repetition of the word, IRKUTSK, fifty times very slowly and firmly ; and every ten minutes we came back to some similar practice. In a few days the muscles of the tongue of each student began to develop great flexibility and strength, which is an invincible combination.

At the end of four weeks all twelve men had acquired perfect mental pictures of the scenes stated ; had mastered their most offensive faults : had risen to the expression of great intensity of feeling held in perfect check and reserve power ; and were so clearly changed, one and all without exception, that the Committee unanimously pronounced their progress " astounding." As a result the Chairman became an official of our Ralston University ; and took great satisfaction in following the after-history of these twelve " hopeless cases." The unsuccessful business man gradually founded a large business, rising from small beginnings. The lawyer who had never won a case acquired slowly but surely a large practice. The unskilled dentist won success in his profession. The poor doctor bade farewell to his poverty. The carpenter became a contractor and builder. The teacher obtained an appointment as Inspector of Schools, after a few years. The clerk in the government service was made Superintendent in his own division. The painter became a master contractor. The salesman established a business of his own. The clerk succeeded to the ownership of the business in the course of time. The labourer became a builder and contractor. And the photographer, the last we heard from him, was at the head of a business syndicate.

The important fact that stands out in these histories is that there comes a time in the affairs of men, and women too, when failure can be combated and success secured by the development of the natural gifts that are stored away in every individual life ; and that, instead of long and weary years of practice, the maximum amount of progress can be achieved with the minimum amount of work. Of course nothing comes of itself in this world.

We depend largely on the formation of mental pictures ; but mental pictures are the glory of genius ; and the difference between the power to see mental pictures within the mind, and not to see them, is now, always has been, and always will be, the difference between common clay and the noblest human achievement.

It has always been the chief pleasure of the author to take in hand those men and women who are regarded by their fellow-beings as "worthless cases," meaning merely that they are in fixed ruts in life and are incapable of rising in the world. All that the author has required is that each one should be in earnest, and should be endowed with a fair share of good sense, or practical intelligence ; something to build on. The result has also been that every one of these cases has been successful, and such persons have risen to prominence.

DEPARTMENT OF APPLIED PERSONAL MAGNETISM

LESSON FIFTY-NINE

THE TWO MINDS

W E NOW MUST FACE LIFE itself, and enter into the myriad associations that are involved in the endeavour to make use of the teachings of this book as far as they have proceeded. There is too much teaching and too little learning in the world. Teaching pours into the mind the facts and principles of things ; learning adopts them ; education uses them. In the study of personal magnetism, when our first book appeared more than forty years ago, there were no others on the subject in existence. We were the first. Since then, there have been a few works on the same subject, but for the most part they have been books of advice ; all of which has been good.

But advice is easy to give and hard to adopt.

Such books have told their readers that in order to acquire personal magnetism, they must be pleasant, agreeable, neat, polite, generous, sympathetic, honest, truthful, on time, active, helpful, of good habits, and so on without limit. In fact nothing that was good was overlooked. While all the pleasing qualities that exist are sure to make a person attractive and useful to others ; they do not make others useful to such person. The agreeable man who is generous, is helping others to use him ; the man with personal magnetism uses others to help him ; thus reversing the situation. This is an important distinction. Of course we shall teach every good quality, but not as an agency merely for somebody else to take advantage of it ; reciprocity is fairer and always means a square deal.

Before proceeding further, let us stand face to face with the

exact purposes of this study. We will not mince words, nor
beat about the bush. We intend that our students shall be
divided into two classes :

1. Those who are willing and eager to follow our advice
to read carefully and slowly every word of the book twice.
This is Class One ; or the First Class.

2. Those who some time in the future may read the book
in the manner stated, or may not feel inclined to do so. They
include from five to fifteen per cent of the persons who receive
the book ; they read it once, and then loiter along the byways
of life.

Having separated the readers into the two classes, we then
deal with those of Class One ; and we set for them the goal
of 100 Per Cent of Progress in the acquisition of this power.

ONE HUNDRED PER CENT is reached when :

1. Financial independence is attained or assured.

2. Perfect respect and confidence from others are won.

3. Mastery over all the affairs of life in every department
of existence is acquired.

No person needs more in this world. Few have obtained as
much. But the goal is not difficult to any one who is in earnest ;
and the course is pleasant all along the way. Sugar-coated
pills are alluring to the taste. Our lessons are all sugar-coated ;
they are not only interesting, but fascinating. More than this,
every lesson is loaded to the muzzle with benefits that reach
every department of life ; and if you do not wish them for
the purposes of gain and advantage, you cannot afford to omit
them for the wonders they will accomplish in other ways.
Not one is wasted. Your improvement begins at the start,
and never ceases until you die, going on even after the last
lesson has been studied. No other line of training or instruction in the world produces such results.

Before going ahead, let us review briefly what has gone before.

The Department of Magnetic Sources is very helpful and
inspiring.

The Department of Mental Magnitude finds you facing in the
wrong direction. It turns you completely about, and faces you
forward ; after which it makes all the difference in the world
what you do or how you do it. You cannot go wrong when
you are facing right. Nor does it make so much difference

how fast or by what means you are travelling ; if you are facing right, you are going on.   The man or woman who masters Lessons 12 and 13, is already far to the front of the human throng ; and these lessons are very easy to master.

The Department of the Magnetic Eye is so valuable that, if it were possible to place a cash equivalent against it, the amount would be surprising.   We read books by interpreting their words into ideas.   Here we read faces like open books. Take this Department into your evening half-hour of thought and study ; read one lesson each evening ; think of the vast wealth of opportunity that is placed within your reach ; carry the knowledge into the affairs of the morrow ; and note your growth in self-conscious power.

The next Department, that of Instantaneous Personal Magnetism, gives you daily work to do.   You will not omit it.

The Department of Magnetic Health is of the greatest importance to every person regardless of having an interest in this study ; for it will effect changes from ill conditions to those of the perfect enjoyment of life with body, mind and nerves freed from every malady and danger that now brings weakness and loss of vitality which are serious deterrents in the efforts to win success.   These lessons have a value in excess of the cost of the book a thousand times over.

The Department of Tension Energy is the crossing of the fine from the prevailing conditions of drifting that sweep people along a common current to nowhere in particular, over to the side of aroused activity and awakened purpose.   The fires of purpose are lighted and existence begins anew.   As a method of building an enormous vitality, it has no equal, and there is nothing that can take its place.

The Department of Repose is like entering a garden in which all the beautiful attractions of Nature abound.   The calmness of still life supercharged with living power enthralls the scene with the exquisite loveliness of mind and heart.   Centuries ago there were no gentlemen, no gentle-women, no gentle folks ; all humanity were physically coarse.   Then a division was made when it was seen that here and there refinement of manner appeared, self-control asserted itself, and a calm and attractive demeanour compelled admiration and obeisance.   Now a still further advance is developing these qualities in higher degree,

This line of training alone embraces the greatest attractions in life ; and its advantages are so valuable that it should be given precedence over all others.

The Department of the Magnetic Voice is a complete world in itself. It is through the voice that most people influence their followers and associates ; for the one distinguishing endowment of humanity as the head of the animal kingdom is the power of articulative speech. The system which we present here has been taught for forty years in private schools, colleges, academies and seminaries as the best method known for the development of the voice in speech and conversation, and in all uses, where all the rich and beautiful qualities of tone and expression were sought. It has a substantial and practical value in every phase of human activities ; and especially in business, professional and social life.

While you have been developing the new wealth offered in these Departments, another process has been going on ; and one of which you will by this time have found some recognition. This process was first made evident to you when you had finished the study of Mental Magnitude and its Régime as taught in the twelfth and thirteenth lessons ; and had passed successfully through the Department of Instantaneous Personal Magnetism. It was further unfolded in the Departments of Magnetic Health, Tension, Energy and Repose ; and confirmed in the new powers of speech that were taught in the Department of Magnetic Voice where the soul spoke through the rich colourings of sound and tone in which the thoughts and feelings of other beings were engrafted on the heart and mind of the student. Then that other process became a reality and revealed the fact that in each human being there exist

TWO MINDS :

1. The Physical Mind.
2. The Magnetic Mind.

THE MAGNETIC MIND

OUR USE OF THE TERM, the Two Minds, is made applicable to this study. In other works various names are given by scientists and writers to these same minds. For many years there has been a persistent reference by scholarly investigators to what is often termed the subconscious faculty, as a mind wholly apart and entirely different from the so-called workaday mind. In all leading institutions of learning, the subject of psychology is now taught as a branch of the highest importance ; some claiming that it controls all human activities, and makes for success or failure depending on the uses derived from it. Experiments and the after-history of graduates prove that all opportunities for advancement in the world are swayed inevitably by the influence of this power ; and, to the surprise of investigators, every test has shown conclusively that there is a mind wholly different from that hitherto known as the thinking function of the brain ; that there is a life embedded in human existence that is endowed with powers that cannot be explained by any human standards.

No one name can describe properly this other mind.

It is not a faculty of a single character, but a collection of faculties ; one of which is subconscious, and hence this term has been applied to it as an inclusive one. Some years ago a very able writer issued a small book entitled a scientific demonstration of the existence of an immortal life within man, based solely on proofs of the presence of this other mind ; and to fall in with the accepted usage he employed the name subconscious faculty. In some hospitals, the same term is used by doctors and surgeons in their curative experiments ; and thousands of remarkable cures have been effected through a recognition of the powers of this faculty.[1]

The Physical Mind that is mentioned in the last page of the preceding lesson is that which is generally understood as the entire conscious thinking faculty in all its divisions, including its sensations, its intelligence, its memory, and its power of reasoning. Writers and teachers allude to it as the conscious mind ; also the working mind ; also the thinking as well as the automatic mind ; to distinguish it from the subconscious faculty.

The Magnetic Mind is connected with that other mental world of which the subconscious faculty is only a part, and with it forms a group of activities such as those of the genius, of the inventor, of the poet, of the great dramatists, of the leaders in all onward movements, and of the inspired writers of the past. History presents in countless ways the efforts of such genius to break through the wall that separates the natural from the supernatural powers of life. But that which was once supposed to belong to the realm of the supernatural has been found to be a part of the plan of Nature ; just as the belief in the occult warnings of eclipses and earthquakes has melted into modern knowledge. So in time it will be learned that there is no supernatural world ; but that all existence is wedded together.

The Magnetic Mind contains three powers :

1. The Truth-Teller.
2. The Ideal-Maker.
3. Mental Determination.

The Truth-Teller is a double-power. It is able to discern the truth of the future by applying the experiences of the past. It is also able to take advantage of its faculty of discernment by possessing the ability to accept the truth of the future as though it had actually already occurred, thus avoiding the reefs and dangerous shoals that are wrecking most lives and neutralizing the brilliant victories of personal magnetism.

The Ideal-Maker creates in fact the individual that is sought.

[1] NOTE.—Any person who wishes to be made familiar with the sources of proofs of the nature, activities and powers of this supernatural faculty, may address enquiries to the Publishers of this book.

In early youth, and sometimes far into middle life, men and women build castles in the air. Blood and brain and heart convert their inmost wishes into seeming realities ; and it has been aptly said that if these castles could only become material facts, the world would be a beautiful place in which to live. The Ideal-Maker does not deal in masonry or concrete structures, but creates a person and a personality that represent the highest type of existence on this little planet, and then leads the way to their realization. Measurements are taken, not of the individual, but of the idealized person and personality, and the power of the Magnetic Mind draws and lifts up to these standards the being for whom they are intended. We shall see.

Mental Determination furnishes the best example of the difference between the Physical Mind and the Magnetic Mind. The latter is able to accomplish anything ; but the Physical Mind succeeds only as far as it has free advance or can break down the barriers that stand in its way. In the Department of Tension Energy we saw that the habit of setting the muscles was a detriment to the cultivation of magnetism. So the habit of setting the mind is a detriment in another form. Luckily the Magnetic Mind cannot act in that way ; for what is known herein as Mental Determination is the opposite of setness ; it is movement.

This is the greatest force in life.

There is power in a locomotive that stands on the track of a great artery of travel, but that does not move. In like manner there is power in the obstinate person who conceives a fixed idea, and who stands by it with all steam up. But he does not get anywhere. The world moves past him. Progress finds him there still, and still there. When the great machine is given the open valve, it moves and goes on into the world of action. It sees life, participates in it, and becomes a part of it. In like manner, Mental Determination is power in motion.

It has a goal, and it moves towards it by the process of action, not of belief or fixedness of position.

All sorts of causes operate to set the Physical Mind or working consciousness in fixed positions or fixed ideas. Disease is a frequent cause. Old age, in which the brain cells ossify or harden and destroy their flexibility, is a very frequent cause, and does not wait for the arrival of decrepitude in a majority of cases ; for this organ may begin to lose its flexibility even when a person is in the teens or twenties. One-way thinking and one-way believing partly paralyse its powers to see or accept anything that challenges such thinking or belief.

The non-flexible or set mind is rarely ever able to attain that fullness of magnetism that wins success or draws friends or worthy companions.

In our journeys among people of all ranks and grades of achievement in life, we have never yet found any man or woman whose mind had become set in lines of thinking or believing who was magnetic, or who had any genuine friends. Some there were who had acquired wealth and power, before whom others fawned to their faces, and sneered behind their backs ; and whose so-called closest friends were posers of convenience.

Obstinacy is merely an acute form of the set mind.

As long as the majority of the people are fools, so long will the world be full of setness of minds and setness of existence ; of friendless and unpitied men and women barricading their miserable selves within the hides of mules and waiting for death to make somebody sorry. They cannot help themselves, nor their condition. All we can say is that if you belong to the class of persons who cannot extricate themselves from the inability of flexible thinking, or if you are of the kind that grip an idea and hang to it like a dog to a rag, you can make no progress in this study beyond what you have already attained.

The Magnetic Mind is open ; wide open ; open always to the Truth ; it never closes itself against facts ; it never sets itself to an unalterable belief, for it believes what it knows and experiences. It, however, gets nearer the truth, for it is always nearer the sources of the truth, than the Physical Mind. The latter is the accumulation of earthly experiences beginning at birth, and including all that can be remembered since then. The Magnetic Mind has its sources of knowledge from the opposite direction.

It cannot be said that persons who set their minds in a fixed belief and purpose, although as a rule devoid of magnetism, cannot acquire some of this power ; but they cannot reach the heights. They, in the first place, do not understand the difference between setting their minds to a fixed purpose, which is always praiseworthy if the purpose is worthy, and setting it to a flexible purpose which bends always to the Truth and to the presentation of facts. This distinction is hard to grasp. But it is the alternative of no magnetism and failure on the one hand, and uniform success on the other hand.

A flexible purpose that moves in the right direction is magnetic.

A fixed purpose that closes the mind is never magnetic.

Take the old illustration of the college seeking to impress on the intellects of its law students the methods of getting proper testimony before a jury when balked by the laws of evidence. The professor speaks of a table that is to be moved through a doorway to the next room. The first attempt is to force it through lengthwise ; but as the door is less than three feet in the opening and the table is four feet long, the task seems impossible. Having seen the futility of the effort in this way, the table is then turned so that the end may be pushed through the doorway ; but as the width is a full three feet, and the opening at the door slightly less, the table still remains in the first room. Now comes the application of the law of flexibility. The table is laid on its side ; two legs are worked through, then the body, and finally the two remaining legs, and it is in the next room.

Taking this example only as an illustration, the obstinate mind in life would persist in trying to force the table through the doorway with the broadside facing it ; and would sit down and stay there set in mind and purpose. Life is made up of countless such cases. The Magnetic Mind retains its flexibility in all things ; suits all the activities of existence to conditions that must be met, and meets them in the best way possible. In other words, it moulds its efforts to the necessities that arise, changes its methods without changing its direction, and often stoops to conquer without abandoning its purpose.

One of the most beautiful characteristics of the Magnetic Mind is its habit of sending out tentacles of thought in order to draw in new influences that arise from contact with other persons, analysing them, and, if found to possess new values, to absorb them ; otherwise to discard them as having been found wanting.

THE TRUTH-TELLER

A REVIEW OF THE PRECEDING LESSON will disclose the following summary of that power of the Magnetic Mind that is called the Truth-Teller. It is double. On the one hand it is able to discern the truth of the future by applying the experiences of the past. On the other hand it is able to take advantage of its faculty of discernment by possessing the ability to accept the truth of the future as though it had actually already occurred; thus avoiding the reefs and dangerous shoals that are wrecking most lives, and neutralizing the brilliant victories of personal magnetism.

There are more reefs and dangerous shoals in marriage than in any other institution of life ; yet, despite opinions to the contrary, they are not hidden, but lie in full sight just below the surface of the shining waters. The victims look afar off and do not see them ; or, being told of them, they say, " Even if so, in our case they will not bring harm." The Physical Mind is swayed by the Four Appetites, or one or more of them. In Lesson Sixty, just preceding this, there will be found a summary of the processes that develop the Magnetic Mind. Those processes, aided largely by the Régime of Mental Magnitude which is found in Lesson Thirteen, will overcome the influence exerted by the appetites.

If, however, the Physical Mind holds sway, the appetites will bring ruin in ninety per cent of marriages. A very large majority of people are or have been married ; and the wrecking of this alliance will in nearly every instance result in harm to those who make the mistake of entering into it ill-advisedly. A mistake avoided is worth a thousand corrected.

We have seen that when ill-health brings pain, suffering and physical torture, magnetism is never possible. In like manner mental ill-health, such as must attend the wrecking of married life, brings worries, suffering, anguish, hopeless drifting for years, and loss of ambition to get on in the world until there is the legal separation and the new start at a point far back of that where the first course began. As we have said, a mistake avoided is worth a thousand corrected.

With the Magnetic Mind in control, mistakes need not be corrected ; they are avoided. The Truth-Teller has charge of affairs. He shows you facts by asking you questions :

1. You are thinking of marrying a woman whom you say you love. Do you know that love begins at puberty in response to the sexual appetite ? That it exists solely as a partner with that condition, is born with it, and cannot live without it ? That love is a fever of the nerves tortured by the same appetite ? That there is really in fact but the shortest conceivable step from loving and hating ? That countless thousands of wives have loved intensely, and suddenly have hated bitterly ? That ninety-nine per cent of married people have awakened after marriage to find their mistake, all of whom, if forewarned, would have said, " Oh, we know there have been wrecks in millions of other cases, but with us it will be different ; we are perfectly mated, and will love each other as long as life shall last and ever after."

2. You are marrying in order to meet the demands of your sexual appetite, and the foregoing enquiries do not deter you, then you will go on to the wreckage we have described in the early part of this lesson. But if you are marrying in order to possess a mate as a loving and sympathetic companion, then let the Truth-Teller analyse the prospects for you, and see if you will take the step. We are discussing the man side first. You have found the one woman in this world who was created for you. She is pretty. Is she ? Beauty is skin deep. Have you seen her with the " make-up " off ? But supposing that in her natural skin, her face is fair, its texture is velvety, and the lines are yet absent, what of those mornings when, after her stomach and liver are upset by indigestion, she is sallow, yellow, jaundiced, of sour breath and fishy eyes, drawn features and sagging jaw, are you then enamoured of her beauty ? There must be something more than a doll face of velvety texture and smooth surface to hold your love.

3. How about the housework ? Can you afford to pay for help ? If you can, have you the means to pay for them, to feed them and to house them ? If, after paying all your bills as estimated before marriage, and as many more that will arise without being estimated, will you find yourself in debt at the end of each year, or will you come out about even ? And are you prepared to meet the cost of emergencies, exigencies and unexpected liabilities that come in flocks to all married couples ? If you are in debt, where will you be when old age arrives ? If you come out even, where will you be when the same old age arrives ? If you save one hundred pounds each year, how many years of smooth financial sailing will be required for you to save up sufficient money to invest so that when you are too old to work you can live on the income ? Safe investments do not average much over four per cent. Four thousand pounds placed at such interest would yield only one hundred and sixty pounds a year ; and saving at the rate of one hundred pounds a year would require forty years to provide this sum, with, of course, a slightly larger income from invested interest ; but compounding it would not produce enough to enable you to live decently after you are superannuated. Hence the saving of one hundred pounds a year during marriage will not be enough ; and the chances are a thousand to one that you will start saving as the man started planting his land, as soon as he caught up with the end of the rainbow. You will be getting ready to start the next year. But if you do not start some time, woe to you and your old age !

4. If you are thinking of building your own house, the Truth-Teller wishes to say that the cost of material is about three hundred per cent above normal ; and the cost of labour from three hundred to four hundred per cent above normal. If you use electric light, or have other conveniences, and especially are compelled to pay for the services of plumbers, or painters and carpenters for repairs, or even in constructing a house, the wages charged in addition to the swollen prices of material are pro-hibitive. What is normal ? It is argued that if all wage earners and business men and women receive these abnormal prices, then one line of charges will balance the others. But the only test of what is normal comes from dividends from the bonds of the nation, and from stocks and shares of the great typical

22

corporations, such as the steel companies, the railways, the industries and the banking institutions. Taking as the basis the purchase price of such bonds and stocks to-day, and the dividends that are distributed to owners of them, the average income from these sources is nearer four per cent per annum than five ; and, while all material and wages have risen from three hundred to four hundred per cent over the figures of thirty years ago, the returns from bonds and stocks have been standing still. Yet people may be surprised to learn that a very big percentage of all income on which people pay their living expenses comes from these investments ; and, when those who now depend on their earnings in other ways are too old to remain active in business, employment or professional life, ALL their income then must come from similar investments. This is the only way of determining what is normal ; and possible bankruptcy must be foreseen as the most dangerous reef of married life until the cost of material and labour shall again become normal. If it requires to-day four times the earnings of labour or business to equal the value received, excessively high wages and charges bring no advantage, and stand in the way of purchasing living investments as a sufficient protection against old-age demands.

We present these abnormal figures because the mental worry that attends the struggle to finance marriage, with the years passing and nothing being laid by against old age, frets husbands and wives until they become nervous and irritable and lose both magnetism and ambition.

5. If you think that two persons can live as cheaply as one by marrying, you should first make estimates of every possible expense that you can think of as pertaining to marriage, and multiply these by four. The Physical Mind cannot be made to believe this ; but the Magnetic Mind knows it to be true. We are discussing the average families, not those that are of very limited means. The husband may be in business, or may be employed in a high-salaried position, or may be building up some profession ; he is quite sure to be in one of these three vocations. The only point we make in this lesson is that he should know the cost of marriage as it affects him ; should every year establish a margin between his income and his expenditures ; and should have the solid satisfaction of knowing that

he is living within his means, and providing for the future. His exact financial situation should be made known to his wife, for if she is worthy of being a wife she will help him to establish this margin and will glory in their united efforts to succeed.

This is genuine personal magnetism applied to the greatest institution of all time, marriage, and it tends to hold husbands and wives together.

Let them read this lesson together and study its meaning.

Every person should possess a Truth-Teller. It is a section of the mind that is lighted by the highest candle-power known to science ; it lights up the past, collects the unvarying facts from that direction, and throws them forward on the screen of the coming years. If these facts have been unvarying in the past, they are sure to remain permanent guides for the future.

In addition to these facts it reveals the processes of life as they are being unfolded in the present, and shows their infallible control of the future ; for it is a law of action that no coming event can originate itself, but must be brought on by a chain of causation from preceding conditions.

The Truth-Teller divides the future of each man and woman into three parts : Possibilities, Probabilities and Certainties on the bright side ; and into three other parts on the dark side : Impossibilities, Improbabilities and Certainties, the last being certainties of failure.

LESSON SIXTY-TWO

DISCERNING THE TRUTH

STILL GIVING HEED to the Truth-Teller, we look
into the homes of those people who have weathered
the storms of wedlock and are still united in the same
bonds that first made them mates, and that still hold them
together. In one village of about two thousand inhabitants,
whose history we have known personally for over thirty years,
there has not been a single divorce, nor a single separation
except by death. In this village, less than ten houses are
rented in each hundred, the others being owned, some by
labourers, some by professional people, some by business men,
and some by persons who are employed in offices or otherwise.

In every family during the first years of wedlock, there were
no servants, the wife doing the housework except the laundry
and occasional cleaning, and the husband attending to his
duties. In later years a few of the families employed help,
but we do not know of a single case where the wife gave up
the cooking or superintending it. Eighty per cent of these
families were affiliated with some church, but less than half
of them attended regularly.

In another town of nearly ten thousand inhabitants, whose
history we have known personally for over thirty years, the
same general conditions prevail, and divorce has been almost
unknown. Some of the families were well-to-do, and employed
servants ; but not until later years never more than one
regularly. There was a large proportion of church-going
people in this town.

From records made in a number of villages, small towns and
large towns, grading through small cities up to those of middle
size, it has been learned that three factors have tended to
keep married people together : the influence of openly observed
methods of living, the fact that the wives have been workers

340

in their homes, and the general custom of attending church at least some of the time. We have a list of seven thousand or more small towns where, during a quarter of a century, less than one couple in two hundred have been divorced or separated, where women work in their own homes, and where church influence is active. As the towns become cities, the divorce evil grows with the growth of the latter ; we mean pro rata. Thus in any large city the proportion of divorces to those of marriages is the largest of all.

When we come to the study of VALUES we shall see the reason of this increase.

We are now taking a stroll with the Truth-Teller, and will deal with the wrecks that are made in city life among marriages that occur there. For this purpose we will not include wedlock among the poorer classes, as they have wholly different problems to face. We will step up a grade or two higher from the classes which we discussed in the preceding lesson, and find ourselves among the middle ranks of the well-to-do, and also among the rich. The Truth-Teller wishes to call attention to the following varieties of wedded couples :

1. Here is a wealthy merchant who has married a young woman, the latter vowing that she was attracted by her love for him, and not by his wealth. He is still in business, but spends his evenings with her when she is at home or goes to the opera, the theatre, or visiting. During the day she loafs, as he can afford to employ servants. On an average they go out two evenings each week, but are at home with each other the remaining five evenings. He sits in the library, reads his paper and falls asleep. She does fancy-work or reads a novel, and eventually retires. The opera bores them both. The theatre is barely endurable. Visiting is irksome, because it is filled with flattery and insincerity, and is always perfunctory. There are occasional outings and short holidays. The husband feels that he owns the woman, and she takes advantage of her freedom during the day to form indiscreet acquaintances in order to make tolerable the dull evenings. There is no magnetism ; and all VALUES are lacking.

2. In another case a rich broker marries a woman for her extraordinary beauty. He must devote his time during office hours to his work ; so she is left to herself, and becomes a loafer.

She rises late in the forenoons, after a lazy breakfast in bed, gets through some tedious hours until she can call at her beauty parlour, fills in more hours playing bridge, is at home in time for the evening meal, drags her husband to some lascivious dance or cabaret, drinks liquor and smokes cigarettes to excess despite the well-proved fact that these things are responsible for the rapidly increasing spread of cancer among her kind and class, and gets home in the small hours of the morning or later, having spent her vitality and lowered her character in a round of excitements not one of which is wholesome or productive of enjoyment, but all of which are pulling her down to the level of their own origin. When these wives do not die early of cancer they drift into the lives of libertines, and the history of such women confirms the fact that a big percentage of them either are divorced sooner or later, or openly defy the law. Taking at random the cases of five hundred marriages between men of wealth and women of beauty that occurred in a large city, we find that in exactly four hundred and three of them the end came in the manner described.

All VALUES are lacking, and magnetism never existed. There was nothing to hold those couples together. They all regretted the marriage after it was too late.

The Truth-Teller is able to discern the truth of the future by the experiences of the past. The Physical Mind will not accept the truth of the future. The Magnetic Mind is endowed with the power to take advantage of its discernment, and to avoid the reefs and dangerous shoals that are wrecking most lives and neutralizing the brilliant victories of personal magnetism.

3. In another variety of cases which we will represent by a sample only, the wife is decent, she does not drink liquor nor smoke cigarettes to excess, nor submit herself to the arms of dancing libertines, nor hang around cabarets, nor cultivate indiscreet friendships with other men. Her husband is wealthy. He must be at his office during the hours of the day, and she is left to herself, and becomes unwillingly a loafer. But she is honourable. She is true to her marriage vows. She has but little to interest her. He takes her to the opera at times, but she feels that it is done to enable her to exhibit her fine clothes. A few other diversions fall to her lot. He desires to spend some even-

ings at home ; otherwise home life to him would be narrowed by his absence at his office in the day and his drifting out at night. So they sit together in a pleasant room. He smokes and reads the papers. She either does some fancy-work or reads a novel. They rarely speak, for there is nothing to say. In their individual absorption they do not always remember that they are in each other's presence. Many thousands of moral, decent couples drift their lives away in this dull routine.

In this case all VALUES are lacking, and there is no personal magnetism. In a subsequent lesson we shall see what these values are, and shall note their great influence over the lives of married people.

The Truth-Teller makes known the fact that men who, prior to marriage, are free to come and go as they please, night or day, are forced to the humiliation of having to invent explanations to offer their wives in order to account for their wanderings especially after the early morning hours, and are continually in hot water in failing to make their explanations convincing ; while, on the other hand, wives are expected to account to their husbands for absences and adventures. Evasions and the humiliation of being compelled to explain one's doings are destructive of magnetism, because they make independence impossible without warfare, which becomes despicable in wedlock.

The Magnetic Mind meets all such contingencies.

The fact that the greatest undertakings in life are totally lacking in VALUES is due to the substitutes for magnetism that we are trying to expose and avoid by Lessons Twelve and Thirteen of this book. When men and women are influenced in the right direction and for their actual benefit, the influencing power is magnetism ; but when they are lured to the shoals of ruin by the power of their appetites, then they find that the enterprise lacks the VALUES which alone bring success and triumph. This failure brings emptiness of hope, and an ever haunting despair.

INTRODUCING PHYSICAL VALUES

PERSONAL MAGNETISM is an exchange of values. There are as many values as there are activities and things in life. An exchange is not one-sided ; it takes but gives at the same time. A one-sided transaction is either robbery, cheating or fraud ; and the world is full of these episodes. Hypnotism is the opposite of magnetism ; it may dull the mind so that any intelligent transaction is impossible. Magnetism gives the mind its full powers of operation and discernment and endows it with its best qualities.

VALUES are of three kinds :

1. Physical.
2. Plebeian.
3. Patrician.

Physical values proceed from the Physical Mind, appeal to it, and proceed to it. They are in the lowest stratum of personal magnetism, and in the opinion of some teachers they do not in any sense involve any phase of that power ; yet they rule ninety-nine per cent of all human affairs outside of the actual realm of personal magnetism. Here are some instances :

1. A woman is passing out of her youth, is not able to more than support herself from year to year, and saves nothing against old age. Her only hope when she is no longer able to earn a living is a place in some home for old ladies. A man whom she does not love, for she is not capable of the tender emotion, offers to marry her, and she accepts. This is an example of physical values. In most cases, such a marriage is permanent.

2. A man who is boarding, and does not like the food and treatment he is getting, finds a woman who is a good cook and a neat housekeeper. He offers her his name, procures a

humble home, and enters into an alliance that is abiding. We have learned of countless thousands of such cases. If the wife is asked if it is a love affair, she generally says, " Oh, pshaw ! no ; just a mutual arrangement," or something similar.

3. A man of more than ordinary means is trapped by a widow of unusual beauty and more than average avoirdupois. She fascinates him. He marries her without an exchange of Values. Soon after the wedding, he finds that she is a loafer ; all the housework must be done and even looked after by servants who are strangers. The cooking leads to indigestion ; this to irritability ; this to a sudden awakening ; followed by quarrels, and violent outbursts of temper on the part of the wife who hurls dishes and other missiles at the head of her husband ; and they end their troubles in the divorce courts, the husband fighting like a warrior and proving that the woman was a mere beauty, a loafer in her home, a bridge-fiend, and brutal in her assaults on him. She had anticipated sufficient alimony to enable her to live in comfort for the rest of her years, but got nothing. The Judge said, " In my thirty years' experience I have known of hundreds of cases of such marriages where the wives have been mere seekers after leisure and support, giving nothing in return, and resorting to violence and physical attack on their husbands when they were not successful in their schemes. In a matter of life importance like marriage, men should have a sufficiently long period of acquaintance with the women they wish to make their wives to enable them to know who they are and what they are."

False appeals lead to disaster.

Many a man has been swung off his mental moorings by a pair of legs, and finds himself fettered to a girl or woman who can offer in return no Values whatever, for the surfeiting of his animal appetite only palls on him. These are the marriages that, in every case, are broken either by divorce or by separation ; and in every instance, when the man is forewarned, he says, " Oh, we are going to prove to the world that we are an exception to the usual cases." They all say that.

Since it is true that unhappy married life hurts if not ruins the victims of it, the fact should be hammered home to every person, whether now married or not, that there must be an exchange of Values, and these Values are never magnetic if merely physical.

4. A widower of wealth with residences, cars, yacht and leisure, marries a woman who gives him nothing in return but some of her leisure, some of her display of clothing, some of her association, her companionship in travel, and her ability to arouse interest among her flatterers by receptions, parties and dinners ; all of which bore him and leave her discontented and surfeited with life. This same couple could secure from their conditions and opportunities, aided by their wealth, a genuine enjoyment of existence ; and it need not compel them to seek ease of conscience by slumming and ill-directed charities, which are forms of repentance of mis-spent lives. But this match, like thousands of the same kind, ended in divorce. There was no exchange of Values.

5. A woman of wealth married a poet, and regretted it. Her idea was that she should bask in the sunlight of genius. Another woman of wealth married a military officer, and regretted it. She was attracted by his uniform and the straight manner in which he walked or strutted. These became monotonous. A young woman of wealth married a chauffeur because he was handsome, of fine build, of lovely face, lovely eyes and soft-spoken voice. She found soon after that there was no exchange of Values, and they were divorced. In almost every such case, as in marriages of wealthy girls to poor young men, or to rich young rakes, after weathering the storms for a few weeks, months or even years, divorce follows. An observer of three thousand such cases arising in the past fifteen years states that every one of these three thousand were divorced or separated ; all unhappy ; all regretful ; all bitter at life ; and all because the Physical Mind was unable to discern the truth, and the Magnetic Mind did not send the Truth-Teller to disclose the certainties of the future.

Any transaction that is not founded on an exchange of Values is a failure, and will be laid bare to the storms of life that must follow. Fair-weather success is like a wisp of a boat with filmy sails floating idly in summer zephyrs and collapsing at the first angry gust of the heavens. The existence of Magnetic Values will carry any one through any storm to any port.

It is a fact that most girls and women prefer to wed a man

of means rather than one of poverty ; yet if both are poor and work for a competence, the chances for happiness and permanency are increased. Prospective suitors do not know generally that their financial rating is investigated, or their money worth is ascertained in advance of a proposal, so that they may be accepted if satisfactory, or let down easily if not wanted. Thus we see that the gentler sex is after physical values, and has none to offer in return. Such marriages are failures.

A young man works for his employer the number of hours agreed upon and does the kind of work for which he is paid. This is an exchange of physical values ; work and faithfulness on the one hand, and compensation on the other. There is nothing magnetic about it. Let either value fail to meet the other, and discontent follows. If the work done is not well enough done, or the remuneration too little, the whole arrangement is likely to collapse. Long years of service faithfully performed may be rewarded specially, but still the matter is physical. In order to make it magnetic, these values should change to those that are either plebeian or patrician, as will be seen later on. An exchange of wages for work with nothing else involved is the lowest form of human association.

In sales, the delivery of goods or property for an equivalent in money or other value is crude and primitive ; but if each sale sends out a drawing influence looking to future transactions, it becomes magnetic.

The same law runs through all the affairs of life.

The monotony of exchanging something physical for some thing physical is merely dry, vaporized barter and sale, whether of property, services or cash. We call a marriage a success if the parties remain together until death, following a humdrum existence, securing a living and escaping poverty. Yet it is colourless, for it is only an exchange of Physical Values. On the other hand the attempt to avoid this humdrum existence leads to separation. The solution is the exchange of Magnetic Values.

MAGNETIC VALUES

FROM THE BEGINNING of human intercourse there have been exchanges of Values, but probably they have all been of a physical nature. Once there was no money, and other things had to be used for payment in sales and trades. In the material world, it sometimes happens that payment is made in equivalents that are neither money nor property. At a charitable affair fair kisses are sold at so much each to raise money for a good cause. This may be classed as a service or a favour. The husband who gave up his liberty for the joy of possessing a wife, and who remains out so late at night that he cannot adequately explain his absence, finds a way to buy peace and reconciliation by gifts of jewellery, or a fur coat ; this being an exchange of material value for a smile, a kiss and forgiveness. Some wives handle these situations skilfully. But the real worth of marriage will have departed. with wedlock that rich old fools purchase when they gifts to maidens fair in exchange for their consent to marry. Animal appetites destroy the judgment, and there is no magnetism to guide them off the shoals.

We have seen in the preceding lesson that there are three kinds of Values ; the Physical, the Plebeian, and the Patrician. The first of these was disposed of in that lesson. When it succeeds it is because policy is the ruling power. The husband who provides a home and support in exchange for the services of a woman who is a good cook and housekeeper is following the law of policy ; and she is doing the same. It is a very important exchange of Values ; and there is no denying the great fact that any kind of Values that are fairly exchanged are nearly always fruitful in permanent content ; while the lack of mutual Values even of a magnetic character is one-sided and permanency is threatened.

The Magnetic Values are :

1. Plebeian ; or
2. Patrician.

In this division we do not intend to present the plebeian values as unworthy. On the other hand they are all of them of the utmost worth in their class. Let us look at some of them :

1. A married man who furnishes home and support to the woman whom he has married in exchange for her cooking and housework is following out the law of policy in a very equitable bargain. But both he and she may be totally lacking in Magnetic Values.

This principle is valuable.

To possess these Values of the plebeian class, he should be :

Neat, well-dressed even in his lounging hours, clean, polite, considerate, generous, sympathetic, helpful, good-dispositioned, cheerful, of proper taste in most things if not in all, observant of the rules of good form and etiquette as far as his mode of life demands, decent in his language, free from profane or obscene talk or suggestion, dignified when he should be, and respectful of the views and beliefs of others. His breath should not be foul ; his teeth should have no ulcerated roots or rotten cavities ; his nose and throat should be free from catarrh ; his tonsils should not be discharging pus ; and he should not be suffering from intestinal poisoning which is sure to find its way to his breath and skin.

These are just practical suggestions of the Values that make a man personally desirable to a woman.

Refinement in life has no limit.

Good taste need not drive a man into classical music or classical literature ; but the man that invented certain jazz music, the man that plays it, the man that dances to it and the man that willingly listens to it, in many instances belong to that hopeless class of vapid minds that are never capable of possessing Magnetic Values in any department of life ; for they are skim-coated thinkers that lack the basic elements of greatness in any degree. You never see the solid sense of any respected man or woman jigging itself away to such semi-crazy contortions of music.

2. A married woman should be all that the man should be,

as far as we have described his plebeian values. We call them plebeian because they may be adopted, assumed, worn for a day or on special occasions ; yet when so exhibited they do exert a most powerful magnetic influence towards winning success. Of course the abiding kinds are the patrician, for they grow into a person and are not taken on or dropped as convenience and policy may decree. These we shall discuss later.

It is claimed that marriage and employment are the two greatest influences in the world. It is because of marriage that the race remains on earth ; and this institution includes home and home support, raising and furnishing supplies for home ; also it includes the blood relationships of all kinds, with endless ties. Employment involves the employer and the employee ; but in the sense in which we use it, the services of professional skill, as of the lawyer, the doctor and the dentist are not included. They belong to their own class. Business and industrial enterprises require the employing of many millions of people in this country, and of millions in any other large country.

Employment is divided into several grades : that of the common labourer being the lowest ; that of the skilled artisan next higher ; that of the expert still higher. In business the employees are generally those of common labour, and clerks or salesmen. Then come office employees, and a variety of others in countless lines. Railway, industrial and other corporations offer employment to men and women ; but mostly to men.

In every kind of employment there is *a large magnet*, invisible but felt and recognized by magnetic employees, which is hung at the top of the whole system, and which exerts a great drawing power over all who are below it ; seeking to draw them up, up, always up. This drawing power possesses the highest magnetic value in human existence.

An employee who meets in a perfunctory manner the duties of his work, who gets through the hours from start to finish each day, who does no more than he needs do in order to keep his position may be said to be exchanging physical values for physical values. But if he seeks to better himself by a genuine faithfulness to his work and takes an interest in it, he is exchanging plebeian values for the hope of betterment.

But this is not all that he can do. The great magnet that hangs overhead *is* not drawing him up.

The merely perfunctory employee, who gets through the hours with the least wear and tear on his energies, is too numerous to be described. Sometimes he is a heavy cigarette smoker. The habit that is now so common among the labouring classes of lighting from ten to twenty cigarettes every hour is gradually working against their interests. A construction concern that employs twelve hundred carpenters, when there is a slackening of their work, always dismisses the cigarette smokers first, and retains those that do not indulge in this habit ; and in hiring others later on as business gets better, avoids employing those who are addicted to this habit.

A construction company that hired over sixteen hundred men, by observation ascertained that those who spent time enough each hour to light a dozen or more cigarettes, required nearly half their time to accomplish this perpetual feat ; and in these days when labour is demanding three hundred per cent more than normal wages, if half the time is wasted in lighting cigarettes, then the wages are doubled by that condition beyond the price demanded.

Similar reports show that with each cessation of activity in business or construction, the men who will be the first to lose their jobs are the cigarette smokers. There is now a growing understanding among great employing concerns that the non-smokers will be retained even when there is not enough work for them to do rather than lose them.

We looked three years ago into a vast office building where on one floor a large number of men were employed. Recently we again looked there and made the following enquiry : " Where are the cigarette smokers ? " The answer came, " Hunting jobs elsewhere. We have no rule against smoking, but we found that the mistakes and the slow work were chargeable to the men who used cigarettes. Instead of discharging them, we gradually let them go as the work slackened, and put on non-smokers as it became brisk again. All other offices that we know about are doing the same thing. The cigarette is sapping brain, blood and vitality out of strong men and making them slaves to the habit ; and we do not wish to have slaves work for us."

There are thousands of men employed in retail stores and in places of retail business ; and the cigarette smoker is barred from them ; and, where he refrains during working hours, but is known to indulge in the habit outside, he is in many instances the first to lose his position when a change is made.

Magnetism is the opposite of slavery ; and a habit that makes a slave of a man is a barrier to the attainment of magnetism.

Addicts of any bad habit make the specious claim that, at least outside the hours and places of employment they may do as they please ; so they make themselves unfit for day work by night orgies of various kinds. We cited the case of a large number of young women employees in a great office, many of whom were yawning while trying to work ; indicating that they were wasting their physical, mental and nervous energies by late hours at night. These women were gradually eliminated from their positions, although many of them were helping to support dependent parents. The question arose, did it pay to sacrifice golden opportunity for the greed of exhausting pleasures ?

Employers now have a way of learning how those who work for them spend their time outside the employment ; not intending to spy on their help, but to be able to advance those whose habits are good ; for it is the fairest scheme in the world to help those who are trying to help themselves.

True character can bear being watched.

The head of one of the great corporations of this country told us that it was their policy to advance their employees who were of good habits and were efficient, and were enabled to do so because their private lives were investigated and given consideration in connection with their faithfulness as employees. Magnetic values always win success.

SPIRIT OF PERSONAL IMPROVEMENT

LEAVING THE LESSER POWERS to the brief accounts already given, we hurry on to the real climax of applied magnetism, as we take up the study of greater things. When we speak of values we do not refer to money or property, but to qualities and evidences of worth. Money and property are agencies of the blessings they are charged with bringing to people ; and are not the final goal of ambition in any true life. We have shown that Values of the physical kind may, if exchanged evenly, serve as imitations or substitutes of those that are magnetic. The latter we have divided into two classes : one plebeian and the other patrician. Plebeian Values are those that are higher and nobler than the physical kind, yet are not engrafted on the life of the individual, but may be put on and laid off at will. Despite this limitation they are magnetic in a moderate degree.

To understand the enormously high worth of Patrician Values, or those that cannot be assumed and cast aside at will, but that are made a part of the individual, we should note the status of the Plebeian Values by way of review, which will be very brief. Thus some embryo book of personal magnetism teaches that politeness develops this power, among many other things. Politeness is something that can be put on and laid off at will. At home you assume no specially kind or attractive tones, but use your commonplace voice. A caller comes to see you whom you wish to impress favourably, and at once you put on what is called your " Sunday voice." Everybody does this. When the visitor departs, you lay aside your assumed tones and come back to the common style of talking. The difference is marked to any observer who studies you. So with your manners, your graciousness and your attentiveness.

All these are Plebeian Values ; they all lead to a moderate

degree of personal magnetism ; but they never ascend the heights, for anything that can be put on and taken off at will is transient and not deep enough to have become inherent.

The same thing might be said of the Patrician Values. It is true that they can be assumed ; but only by an effort great enough to make them permanent. Experience shows that once they are engrafted on the personality of the individual, they remain for life. Employment, marriage and business together with the professions, embrace nearly all the activities of humanity. It is in these departments of existence that the power of personal magnetism finds its opportunities of achieving their victories ; and these we must consider as we unfold the present lesson.

The Spirit of Personal Improvement is one of the Patrician Values.

This spirit itself is magnetic. It is not a state or condition but a movement ; it goes forward, never backward, and never stands still ; for all of which reasons it is bound to exert unusual power over the life of the individual. If it once acquires momentum it does not stop. But it will not operate through the physical mind. A higher faculty is necessary to set it going. This is the whole trouble. The physical mind cannot be convinced that every step in the personal improvement of mind and body adds value to every department of life, and by building a better general individual builds a better man or woman in some special line of activity. The instances of the usefulness of this law are numerous. Take the case of Lawrence Barrett that we have mentioned in some former lesson ; when a lad he was not only poor but uneducated. When he became an actor, he did not stop with that profession, but became a scholar in all general lines of mental growth ; and his scholarship was reflected in his dramatic career.

In law it is well known that the higher a man rises in his general knowledge of history, literature, rhetoric, language and the biographies of great men and women, as well as in many of the college branches, the better lawyer he will become. A one-sided mentality is not attractive. Every great lawyer has been highly educated in other lines, or he could not have been great. The value of this all-round knowledge is recognized by the requirements now made when applicants are examined for admission to the bar.

But we know of a young lawyer who, instead of sitting with his feet on the table waiting for clients to call, utilized his time collecting forms, copying written pleadings in other cases on file in clerks' offices, learning how to carry cases up to higher courts on appeal, saving exceptions, making bills in chancery or equity, preparing unusual papers by studying those that had been drawn for past trials, copying contracts and recorded deeds, leases, wills and countless other documents ; all of which he kept at hand in his office so that during his otherwise idle hours he could make himself familiar with them. Clients employ lawyers because of their experience ; this line of experience consists in having had contact with such writings. The result was that the young lawyer rose rapidly in his profession and was often called into consultation by older attorneys in important cases where technical knowledge was needed. Evenings he read and studied books that made him a finely educated man.

The young and ambitious artist, if guided by his physical mind, will devote his many idle hours to reading novels, thus weakening the artistic temperament. His theory is that all he needs, after graduating from an art school is to go out and paint when the weather is fit, send his work to shows or dealers, and wonder why the cheques never appear. If he would lay aside his novel and absorb the history of mankind instead ; and, as companion to such study, master the finer phases of rhetoric, of grammar, of the forgotten matters of his earlier schooling ; read the biographies of great men and women ; and inform himself about the lives and characteristics of other peoples the world over ; he would be adding true values to the little that Nature has bestowed upon him ; for artists are not made by art schools. There never was a real artist who was not a poet by inclination ; he may never have written a line, but he has caught the sacred fire by absorbing the spirit of the geniuses of the past. If he can arouse this fire in himself by reading and being thrilled by the fancies of such geniuses, he may find himself an artist some day. Novel-reading dries up the fancy, shrivels the imagination, and lowers the mental tone so that all he has left is the inclination to go out on days when the weather is fit and try his hand at painting something.

The poetry that is necessary in the life of the artist is seen working its charms when it leads the painter out where Nature has preceded him in her works of art. The man or woman who goes out for miles to try a hand at painting something sees nothing worth painting until some attractive scene is reached. The true artist sees values everywhere ; he passes countless wealth in landscape, the sky, the river, the fields, the forests, the drooping foliage, the flowering roadside ; to him there are "sermons in stones, books in the running brooks, and good in everything." He is alert. He sees. He feels. He will succeed.

The Spirit of Personal Improvement is at work in him.

It goes with him through life.

Drop into some retail shop, and note the assistants that have nothing to do while waiting for patrons. They discuss all the gossip of the times. They idle away many valuable hours every day of their lives. In one group of assistants was a young man who sought the Spirit of Personal Improvement. One day he brought a small pocket dictionary, and consulted it during the periods when little demand was made on his services. A customer entered the shop. Other assistants who were absorbed in some news, emerged slowly from behind their counters, but the assistant with the dictionary put it quickly in his pocket, and was the first to greet the customer. This was always the case. The manager eventually noticed this fact. One day the head of the firm said to the manager, "Can you find out what kind of a book that assistant is reading when he has nothing to do ? " He did find out. It was a dictionary. On another day the assistant had a different looking book ; it was about grammar. On still another day he brought a third book ; it was about rhetoric. Later on, when the head of the firm knew these things, he instructed his manager to see that the assistant's wages were raised under an agreement that nothing was to be said to the other employees, and with the impression that no one but the manager was to know of the increase.

In the course of time the head of the firm called the assistant into his private office and said to him :

"Young man, you have been in my employ three years. Is that so ? "

The sternness of the enquiry alarmed the youth, who replied timidly, " It is true, sir."

" Well, during that period do you know how much of my time has been used by you reading books that you have concealed in your pockets ? "

" I was not reading exactly, but studying. I thought I might improve myself in that way. Besides I did not encroach on any of your time, as I always was ready to wait on customers."

" You had your evenings to yourself. Why use my time at the shop doing what you could do at home in the evenings ? Was that right ? "

" I have always had work to do at home helping my mother who is not well ; and besides, when I did have any spare time in the evenings I read history and literature and other things from books too big to bring to the shop."

" Well, as you admit that you have used my time for three years for which you have been paid by the firm, what adjustment do you propose to make ? "

" I will leave that to you, sir."

" Well, I do not wish to be hard on you. I am starting a large branch in another part of the city nearer to your mother's home. I will offer you the position of manager at double the salary you are now receiving, in addition to which I will admit you to a limited partnership, so that while your income will be assured, it may be largely increased by the profits from the branch. You know we do not do business without profits."

The assistant was astonished, and remained silent for a time, his employer watching him closely. When he was able to express himself, he enquired :

" Why are you so kind to me, sir ? "

" I am kind to myself," said the employer. " Your private life is known to me. It is exemplary. Your habits are clean. My other assistants are time-wasters. You will never be poor. They will never be worth any more than they are now. Mark me, you will never be poor."

You, who are reading these pages, do you know that you and countless thousands of other employees have exactly the same opportunity for advancement, if you are working at a salary ? Your physical mind will say, " Oh, what's the use ? " If you proceed far enough to awaken your Magnetic Mind, its Truth-

Teller will convey to you the information that there hangs above you in your employment a magnet which is there to draw you up, up, up!

The process is easy.

Just let the Spirit of Personal Improvement enter your life and begin to do its work.

The Unseen Magnet is hanging over the head of each and every man and woman who adopts this Spirit of Personal Improvement ; and it affects every phase of human life everywhere. It appears not only in the results of each line of business, but in all employment, and also in the larger work of those who conduct the great affairs of the world, no matter what they may be.

We are greatly pleased to have learned that our efforts on behalf of employees and employers in this one line alone have been wonderfully rewarded, and we have been informed that wherever there has been a sincere attempt to put into practice this Spirit of Personal Improvement, the most remarkable success has resulted. We have inspired thousands of young men and women to add values to themselves in this way, and we know of no case where they have not risen rapidly and to great heights compared with the prospects that confronted them before they undertook this method of betterment.

A fertile mind is necessarily magnetic ; and such a mind is able to find ways and means of self-improvement. It may be in one direction, or in another ; but the great fact must be met that, on the one hand, there is the inclination to waste minutes and hours, to get through the day with the least effort possible, to even be on time and to remain until the last minute attending to the absolutely necessary duties, yet doing so in a perfunctory manner ; while, on the other hand, there are countless little ways in which human values may be acquired and added to every person who seeks the higher and better things of life. We have cited a few examples only ; but a book might be written on those that remain.

We are proud of the fact that large business concerns and other employers are making use of these lessons in order to encourage their employees to improve themselves.

MAGNETIC INITIATIVES

WHATEVER MAKES A PERSON more valuable to himself will make him more valuable to others ; and the reverse of this proposition is true. There is another reverse condition that is not given much attention. It is this : Personal improvement lifts the individual up because of the power of its influence ; and a person is improved and lifted up by associating with thoughts, ideas, impulses and individuals that are higher in life than the person. To seek one's associates among those of a lower level draws downward the whole character ; to seek them among those on the same level maintains the same level ; but to seek them among those of a high level draws upward the character and the individual.

These are all magnetic forces ; and they are at work in millions of lives every day.

Ideals and ambitions also are magnetic ; they may be born in the appetites which we have discussed in the Second Department of this book ; and if so they draw downward. They may seek only the physical levels of life, and so carry people through the monotony of existence to the grave. But if they are born of great and noble desires, they draw upward. It is not at all difficult to find these high levels ; and even to find associates among people who occupy higher stations in life. In your friendships and affiliations do not stoop ; but rather rise.

Out of this habit of looking upward and forward comes the Spirit of Initiative. This seems on its face like some fanciful dream. But it is just as practical as the Spirit of Personal improvement that we discussed in the preceding lesson. Let us look at what it can do, by again visiting the place of employment where young men may choose their own fate by their determination to add magnetic values to themselves. We will cite two little histories that came to our personal attention many years ago.

A young man who had risen to the position of a salesman, and who was given by his employer full power to allow credit to buyers, or to deny credit, or after having allowed it, to cut it off, found that the country was on the verge of a widespread business panic. He did what no other salesman did as far as his thoroughness went. He had a list of all the concerns and individuals who sought credit of his employer. The great mercantile agency that was employed at a yearly cost at that time of twenty pounds, had not been called upon to furnish reports outside of its general publication and occasional bulletins. This young man asked private reports on each and every debtor of his employer ; and followed this request every month ; paying the extra cost when it was incurred.

The result was that he was enabled to eliminate every debtor who was verging on bankruptcy, to deny further credit, to collect what was due, and to close their accounts. When the full blast of the panic struck the business of the nation, which occurred in less than a year, not a shilling was lost through bad debts to this employer. The young man had carried on his investigations without being told to do so, without informing his employer what he was doing, and with the utmost discretion from beginning to end. When the employer came through unscathed, he learned of the long and very tedious campaign of the young salesman, and in time made him a partner, when the business assumed its normal prosperity.

This is the Spirit of Initiative.

It was the right thing to do. But no other salesman did it. It was taking the initiative. Even the employer would not have thought of doing it or of ordering it to be done.

Another instance of the same spirit came to our attention many years ago. In a certain city, the business of which was largely devoted to one kind of manufacture, namely, the making of shoes, there were a number of goat and kid concerns engaged competitively in supplying their goods to the shoe concerns. The salesrooms were piled up with great supplies, from which the buyers from the shoe factories were enabled to select the kinds and quantities they desired. In order to meet with the exact demands of these buyers, a large assortment of goat and kid skins were carried in stock that were not saleable in the dull years.

A young man who had risen to the position of head salesman of one of these leather concerns, seeing the loss entailed by the practice of carrying many thousands of skins for which there was no steady demand, adopted the following course without the knowledge of his employer : He made a tour of enquiry among all the shoe manufacturers, noting in a book the information he obtained, which included the number of skins generally required each year, the kinds, the grades, the styles of finish and other details of importance. He also learned the time of year each of these would be needed. He then made a monthly tour of these places in order to keep in touch with them. It so happened that a large majority of the concerns visited were the regular customers of his competitors, and were not inclined to deal with him on that account. He met this objection by arranging with the factories which he represented to produce the grades, kinds and finishes that were to be required by the shoe manufacturers ; so that when they could not find exactly what they needed elsewhere, they were compelled to buy of him.

The result of this method was that his employer no longer carried useless stocks ; and was able to dispose of all the goods that his factories could produce. More than this, the business grew steadily and became very profitable. The employer asked his salesman how he happened to think of the plan that had proved so successful. The latter said, " I found myself idling away hours of time daily with a very dull business. I had time to slip out and visit the offices of the buyers. I had to choose between doing this or really doing nothing. What moved me most was the fact that so many grades were being carried in order to meet the requirements of the trade ; and I thought if we could know what the coming demands were to be, we could make our goods for such demands. It succeeded."

Some years ago we put the question to a large number of business men, asking them how many kinds of initiative of the true kind they could think of as possible in their business, and they admitted that they had never thought of such efforts in the right way ; but the result of the enquiry was that they could see at least five hundred important steps could be taken in advancing their interests. Some mentioned one or two ; others many more ; and a few as many as fifty different methods of betterment. Once their minds were started thinking in the right direction, they made great progress.

All employees hold in their own hands their fate and their future ; but initiatives are not confined to this class. Employers have come to see a great light. Professional men and women have done the same. The whole secret consists in waking up to begin with, and in looking present conditions in the face ; then matching every present condition with what it would be if it were made better. Some persons are rather favoured by a spirit of insight into possibilities that escapes others. Henry Clay Frick rose from a boyhood of poverty to become Carnegie's most valuable assistant, solely by his insight into the possibilities of initiative activity.

It is a splendid training, this habit of looking for ways of betterment. It is valuable in home life and in personal self-improvement. But whenever started, it sheds an influence on all departments of daily existence, and reaches out in many directions. It is magnetic because it leads the way to success. Millions of minds are apparently dead to-day in lives that are stagnant, that might be aroused by this spirit, and become tremendous factors in building new hopes.

We have in this lesson dealt with business matters, but the same principle of magnetic initiatives will apply with equal force and value to all the relationships of life. The most inviting field for such endeavour is in the home. There is too much routine there ; too many days of constantly repeated humdrum existence ; too little real home-interest by the husband, and a consequent loss of interest by the wife. A sweeping improvement may be made if one or both will adopt the magnetic initiatives, and awaken a vital desire to make the home mean all that its name should imply and inspire. Then a new world will be discovered.

MAGNETIC MARGINS

THE STUDY OF LIFE is as endless as are the activities of life. We come now to a different line of practice, which may be summed up in a few words. Always retain some margin in everything. There are other meanings for the same word, but in our study we refer solely to progress or distance in what we do. There are other ways of stating it, that do not convey all that is intended. Thus we might say, never reach the limit. Or, keep back some power. Or, display a reserved and repressed energy. There are still other ways of saying some part of the same thing. But the fact is that no person remains magnetic who does not leave some margin in everything.

Examples are very numerous, and only a few can be given.

If you rise from the table with your appetite fully satisfied, you are weaker than if you had risen slightly hungry. In any physical effort, if you use the last ounce of your strength, you weaken yourself. In making an address, as where the inexperienced lawyer speaks to the court, if he throws into it all his vitality, he soon tires those who hear him. We once had the pleasure of studying the methods of a great advocate who was struggling to win a case in which his client was entitled to victory, but which was combated by almost insurmountable opposition aided by a combination of influences that seemed too great to be overcome. This lawyer in his final address seemed to have reached his limit of power, but a reserved force was apparent; this he drew upon, and again seemed to have reached his limit, when a new degree of energy was apparent, and so on step by step until he reached heights of magnetism that towered above all opposition; and he won. He afterwards told us that at no time did he reach a limit; and that accounted for his constant increase of power.

Satiety in any form is not only not magnetic, but it is destructive of what magnetism has already been acquired. In a life of ambition there is always the zest of striving for victory; but let one's ambitions be fully realized, then the zest is gone. Wealth won after a struggle is stale. A life of ease is wholly devoid of magnetism. The greatest form of happiness is the striving after something not yet attained.

In courtship and marriage this law runs true at all times and in many ways. A margin is always magnetic here; and marriage is the greatest and most extensive institution in the world. Courtship is supposed to consist of the effort of the man to win the consent of the woman to marry him. When this phase of it is true, as long as the prize has not been attained, it is highly valued; but when attained and a sense of ownership follows, the value is lessened. On the other hand, the general fact is that the man is sought by the woman where he is above the average of his sex; but it is not always the case that he knows it. She may lead him on by an appeal to his appetite of one kind or another. If no margin is left in the winning of him, then as soon as he realizes that satiation has been reached, he loses his interest.

It is an old philosophy that teaches women to keep suitors far enough away to prevent reaching the limit. A courtship that reaches the climax before marriage generally falls to pieces. It is the lure of the unattainable that draws a man towards a woman; never the satiety of the attainable. By following this rule, many a woman has exerted a substitute for magnetism that has won a good husband; whereas had she given herself unreservedly to the man, he would have tired of her; and if he tired of her before marriage he would have done so most decidedly afterwards. There is a great fascination which a man has for a woman whom he cannot approach to the limit, which is wholly lost when she permits him to approach her prior to wedlock.

In displays of affection whether before or after marriage, satiety kills the desire or lessens it. Too much personal handling of a woman by a man leads her to ask either orally or silently if he will not please stop pawing her over. She thinks it, if she does not speak it. Too much kissing or embracing may reach satiety and cease to be desired keenly. It is better to leave a margin. After marriage, satiety in the sexual appetite which is reached by the man more readily than by the woman, kills the magnetism of love more quickly than any other influence in life. The man at once becomes unattractive, seems selfish, sluggish, irritable, exhausted, and not the same being who once told her that she was the most adorable woman in the world and he could not exist without her. In his state of satiety he seems to bristle all over with the thought of don't touch me, I'm tired of the sight of you. This satiety is the cause of nearly all the quarrels of marriage ; for it opens the way to ill-natured discussions in which the man thinks himself free to say what he pleases to hurt his wife's feelings, since now he owns her and can let loose his natural self, which he concealed in the glare of courtship.

The wife is always attractive to the husband as long as he desires her companionship ; and he can keep her attractive for a lifetime by learning the simple lesson of so mastering himself as never to reach the point of satiation. He then becomes a different being ; and to him she is far different. It is a self-apparent fact that sexual satiety completely expels magnetism from the individual. If it preceded any great effort as where a public speaker sought to sway a vast audience, failure of the most dismal kind would be the result. By the same process, the keen edge of love and the joy of companionship are lost in married life.

Desire is magnetic when there are true values to exchange.

The unmagnetic people of the world always seek to reach every limit in matters in which they engage. If they enjoy dancing, they must overdo it and carry it into the early hours of the morning. Many a woman who is seeking her living by employment, instead of trying to improve herself for higher stations in life, runs her vitality to shreds by late hours at night, and yawns away the following days in a mental condition unfit for genuine work. Married couples waste too many night hours in excess of card-playing, stopping only when the limit of time is reached ; not knowing that a reasonable attention to any pleasure is better than such excess.

Margins may become very magnetic by reason of their fascinating power of arousing the keenest interest in life. Take for instance the argument made by a man and his wife that all money that comes in shall be subjected to a regular budget, by which the expenses shall be kept less than the receipts.   Both know at the end of every month how much has come in, how much has gone out, what remains, and the plan of saving this margin between the receipts and the expenditures.   Then things that he would otherwise have bought will be found not needed ; and the same with her.   Where such margins have been secured in married life, if reports that have come to us may be said to indicate the general facts, there have been none of the mis-understandings and consequent ill-feelings that occur when husband and wife are not fully cognizant of the financial conditions that prevail in their home.

We have in mind a cottage built twenty-five years ago, planned by husband and wife the year before they were married, a little six-room house, with a small garden in front and a good-sized garden in the rear, in which both took part when the land needed to be cultivated ; and six neat little rooms inside the house, bright and attractive ; being gradually paid for as the husband's business prospered, until all debts were paid, and a goodly sum now is invested in bonds and mortgages ; the result of severe struggles and self-denial in their first years of wedlock, in which the wife made as many sacrifices as the husband, all the while seeking firmly to preserve the margin that made this success possible.   They have a married daughter who with her husband is following this same law of margin ; not flippantly wasting all they receive, but building for the happiness of the future.

These cases are not rare.   Thanks to the study of magnetism they are becoming more and more numerous.   There is a solidity and permanency to all marriages that are brought under the influence of the margins to which we have referred.

The result is the solidity of the home institution, and the permanency of home life and happiness.   By consultation with the Truth-Teller which is described a few lessons prior to this, the countless mistakes that make all living wretched are avoided ; for all future possibilities and certainties are made clear.

THE VANISHING ILLUSION

ARRIED LIFE, as has been said, is the most extensive and most numerous institution in the world. For this reason it should be made the basis of the greatest uses of personal magnetism. Centuries ago when wives did not often leave their husbands, they were not held to marriage by love any more than to-day, but by compulsion. There are some tribes and castes of peoples even in these times that require the death of the wife as the necessary fulfilment of her marriage vows in case her husband should die. Gradually going backward in time in our own history we drift to the same tendency in spirit at least ; and the placing of the woman on the same level of freedom with the husband to-day is the newest phase of human progress.

This equality and perfect freedom of the sexes are gradually changing all the old standards of marriage. Wives may now work in offices and places of business, and support themselves if they so choose ; and in the large cities the ties of wedlock are so very thin and attenuated that a wife is at liberty to associate in almost any way she pleases with the husband of some other woman. The result of this ultra freedom is that almost all marriages are either falling apart, or the parties drift away by the law of counter attractions. Years ago the motive for marriage was the desire of the wife for a home and support, and the wish of the man for a housekeeper. Now the woman is able to support herself, and the man finds that his wife is not willing to cook or keep house, or manage his home for him.

No other magnet is active in bringing men and women together except the sexual appetite ; young men and women are rapidly learning that this magnet need not lead to wedlock.

The question then arises, why should a man and woman marry. One other magnet remains, and that is what is called love.   But as it is an emotion that is born of an illusion as to the super-wonders of the party who is loved, as soon as this illusion vanishes, love flees, especially in this age of freedom, equality of the sexes, and easy divorce.   Of every one hundred love-marriages, not more than two remain love-marriages, even where the couples live together.   The question still pursues us, why marry ?

The answer is : Do not allow the illusion to vanish.

Of what is the illusion composed ?   Take the case of the man who has been placed on a high pedestal during courtship, because his fiancée believes him to be what he has seemed to her to be.   She was led to believe that he was neat, clean, attractive in body and mind, and of good disposition.   These are not impractical dreams ; for they might have been what they purported to be.   What poorer investment is there in wedlock than the easy readiness to cast off neatness, cleanliness, physical attractiveness, mental attractiveness and a winning disposition ?   The husband may not think it matters much that he has not visited a dentist for months, that his teeth are decaying and give out a terribly offensive odour, that they are infected at the roots by ulcers that poison the blood, and that his tonsils are emitting pus that flows forward in the mouth and lubricates his kisses.   It is said by dentists that nine in every ten men who are married to refined women are afflicted in the manner just stated.   How can it be possible that women retain any love or even respect for such husbands ?   The woman is equally guilty, but not in so large a number of cases.

Then comes the bad breath odour that attends men and women who are suffering from intestinal poisoning ; which malady also causes all catarrhs and all forms of body odour.   Nor is the bath visited often enough.   Neglect in dressing and in personal refinement plays a large part in the losing of love.

Men and women were not made equal in the sense of being like each other in qualities and attributes.   The man who is mentally virile and morally upright, is the best ideal ; and the woman who is morally upright and mentally beautiful is the best ideal in her sex.   Masculinity in women is not Nature.   By birth she is a creature of refinement, daintiness, purity and sweetness ; and only her hard struggles in life or her inherent wantonness can estrange her from these qualities.   The husband who maintains his status as virile and upright, is never likely to lose the love of his wife if she is normal morally; provided he gives due attention to the matters we have discussed on the previous page. The wife who maintains her status as refined, dainty, pure and sweet, who cultivates a beautiful mind and is morally upright, is secure in her husband's love, provided she gives attention to the matters to which we have referred.

But magnetism includes an exchange of Values in marriage; and these are not appeals to the Appetites. One Patrician Value on the part of the wife requires that she shall retain her place in Nature in all respects. Another Value of this order is her willingness to prove a real helpmate to her husband; to offer him her aid in all things; and to be a real partner in the contract. He should never leave home in the mornings without having laid aside all selfishness, all disinclination to assist her in her duties, all hasty disregard of the things that interest her. Mutual interests are Values, and these should be interchanged. The least little thing that absorbs the attention of the wife should not be too small to attract the attention of the husband. Mutual consultations are useful. When he comes to the home at noon, or especially at the close of the day, her work should be his work; her weariness should be lifted by his assistance, for it is gross selfishness on his part to lounge around reading a paper that yields him no mental value, while she plods through the evening finishing her work.

The best test of magnetism and continued interest is the readiness of husband and wife to devote their spare time to each other; or, if to others, then in each other's companionship. We know of a couple who were married fifty years and who in all that time were never separated any evening. They had all the pleasures of society, friends, parties, theatre, opera, travel and holidays; but never found it necessary to spend any evening or night apart. And they were supremely happy. Loyalty in marriage is a Patrician Value. It is magnetic. It also stands as the noblest of virtues. If a man must continually go out night after night after marriage, he should have remained single. Affiliations between married men and men who are not married are antagonistic to those higher affiliations that should exist between husband and wife. The moment a

24

married woman forms a close personal and confidential friendship with some other woman, with her husband in the background of her affection, she becomes disloyal to him.

Husband and wife should be good friends with each other, perpetual associates, steady pals, with openness of mind and exchange of confidence, making all their plans together, hunting in each other's thoughts for the themes that are dominant and the interests that are most alive ; never saying or doing anything that shall in the least hurt the feelings of the other ; never taking umbrage at any remark or incident ; forgiving freely ; yielding gracefully ; refusing to antagonize ; never becoming morose, silent or stubbornly diffident ; cultivating sympathy, brightness, hopefulness and optimism under all circumstances ; and forming the mental determination to place loyalty to each other above all other considerations in life. There have been such marriages, and they have been magnetic ; they have been blessed in the highest degree ; and have served as stepping-stones through the journey of earthly existence, on, on to a world of unending rewards.

The first two pages of this lesson teach matters that cannot be neglected ; for even if all the finer qualities exist, and there are evidences of the presence of the coarser ones, the latter will submerge the former.

In the preceding paragraph we have mentioned a phase of personal magnetism called mental determination ; and as this is the key to all accomplishment in life, we will devote the next lesson to its consideration.

In bringing the present theme to a close, we will recall the old saying that a chain is no stronger than its weakest link. Whether in marriage or in other forms of human association, if there is a weak link in the character of the individual, the whole structure is likely to fall. Thus if either husband or wife exhibit a single serious fault, the illusion may vanish in a flash. The prevention of this disaster may be secured by forming the mental habit of self-study at all times. This is the most valuable asset in the life of any person.

LESSON SIXTY-NINE

MENTAL DETERMINATION

A S THIS COURSE OF INSTRUCTION approaches its
end, the two most important themes are to be considered. In a book of this size it is not possible to
include the analysis of the mental powers with which humanity
has been endowed. For centuries preceding our era, in the
old Greek ascendency, the existence of a mental power beyond
that of the ordinary faculty of reasoning was taught and
exemplified. Then the idea slept until a few decades ago
when many evidences arose to set savants thinking and in-
vestigating. The result was the claim that a subconscious
mind was a part of the mental equipment of humanity.

To-day this claim is universally approved.

In other works the distinction between the physical mind
which operates through the cerebrum, and the psychic mind
which operates through the meninges or brain membranes, is
fully discussed and proved. But it has always been our belief
that, whatever this distinction may be, the only facts that
matter are those that appear as results, not processes ; and
that names and theories are of less value than actualities. In
any event it is this distinction that now interests us, as we
approach the study of mental determination. We have seen
in the early part of this book that a setness of the muscles is
non-magnetic ; and that a setness of the physical mind, or
process of reasoning that operates through the cerebrum, is
obstinacy, and is therefore non-magnetic.

It is a common trait of teachers and advisers to tell ambitious
men and women that whatever they make up their minds to do,
they will do ; and what they will to accomplish, they will accomplish. This sounds all right, but has rarely ever succeeded.
It is true that persistent hammering at one object sooner or
later brings the desired results, if no obstacles of an insurmount-

371

able nature interfere. Yet, on the other hand, if the will-power is operating through the subconscious faculty it rarely fails. To generals who lived in the centuries preceding the time of Napoleon, there were Alps, and they were obstacles that could not be overcome. To him there were no Alps ; his keener mind saw the way to pass them.

When the mind is set through the operation of the physical processes of thinking, and this setness persists for a time, it becomes an obsession, or disease. Setness means fixed position. Thus obstinacy is a disease, for it is a fixed attitude of the mind. Thinking always on one leading subject is a disease. Unchanging belief founded on nothing but belief, or blind faith, is an obsession, and is most repellent, driving away friends and admirers. Political fixedness in place of statesmanship is likewise an obsession and non-magnetic.

The difference between a set purpose of the physical mind working through the cerebrum, and mental determination working through the subconscious faculty, is that the former is fixed and immovable, while the latter always progresses or goes forward. The mule stands still when he is obstinate. His brain is set, determined, but makes no headway.

The only absolutely certain method by which the subconscious faculty may be recognized is that which takes the conscious mind into the last stage of wakefulness at night ; for every psychologist and physician who has experimented along these lines knows that the subconscious mind is always alert and on the verge of recognition at that moment when the conscious or working mind is lapsing into unconsciousness, which occurs at the time stated, or when sleep is coming on. It is then that the most remarkable cures have been made through therapeutic suggestion in hospitals and sanatariums.

It has been proved many times that any form of mental determination that invites progressive action and not fixedness, that is given expression in the mind during the last moments of wakefulness at night, if founded on a careful development of the power of magnetism as taught in this book, will bring the results desired. The best preparation for this practice, which should be made a habit, is to read this book through twice slowly and with great attention to all that it teaches. Following such reading, the most powerful method that can be adopted is to memorize the thirteenth lesson, which deals with Mental Magnitude Régime.

After these steps have been taken, and after all the advice and suggestions of that lesson have been carried into effect, the next thing to do is to take into the subconscious mind at night the full determination to achieve some great work, or to win some great end ; or, if minor matters are important, work them out by the same process. We can assure every student who follows this plan that success will be attained. Not many years ago a great French psychologist came to this country and performed some remarkable cures by this process. He made the statement that where a certain mental belief was given oral expression, the sound of the voice reflected in the brain would be taken up and be given actual life in the entire nervous system. But this method failed a hundred times where it succeeded once ; the fault being that the physical mind alone operated. Tests were made with the subconscious mind in the manner we have stated herein, and there were one hundred victories for every single failure ; just reversing the ratio. Thus if a person who has mastered this course of instruction will form some purpose in his mind, and give it utterance in spoken words, no matter how faintly they are uttered, at the moment of falling asleep at night, the several natural laws that we have described will operate to bring results.

The only way of knowing for a fact whether this method will succeed is to give it a thorough trial. When physicians, hospital doctors and psychological scientists put such methods to the test and follow them up to get results, and do actually get results of the highest importance to the world, no sensible person will treat them lightly.

It, however, is not merely in the use of the last waking moments at night that this power is employed. That is only a developing practice. As soon as the faculty is recognized, it may be used at any time of the day or anywhere, and in any way. But it must be kept moving. Avoid fixedness. We have seen a little lawyer, weighing less than nine stone, drive out of a building a bailiff who had a legal right there ; and no force was used. He started and kept moving, like a stampede limited to one objective. It was mental determination. We have recently concluded the history of a couple who had been

unhappily married, both of whom took up this study in order
to find a remedy for their marital failure ; and both developed
in the highest degree this power of mental determination and
applied it to the suggestions and matters contained in the preceding lesson, which is entitled The Vanishing Illusion.   The
success has been one of the most pleasing and complete we have
ever known.   They were too proud to live apart, and too
honourable to seek a divorce that would have brought a lifetime of unhappiness to their children ;   so they suffered in
secret as far as the outside world was concerned, and now they
have no more anxieties.

We know of more than one hundred recent cases of employees
who have bettered themselves by the same power of mental
determination ;   and scores of business men who were drifting
down grade but who have since begun to win success.

Many requests have reached us as to what are the best themes
on which to practise mental determination ;   and invariably
we advise those that are contained in the seventy-three lessons
of this book.   But Mental Magnitude Régime stands in the
most important of all positions in this regard.   It is contained
in Lesson Thirteen ;   and that lesson is a magnet in itself.

Charles Spurgeon, who claimed that his prayers were always
answered, said that he never prayed with his brain, nor with
his physical thoughts ;   at that time very little had been discovered of the subconscious mind, so that he made no reference
to that faculty ;   but he stated his firm belief that he possessed
an inner self that outranked his thinking brain ;   and it was with
this inner self that he prayed, and won answers to his prayers.

Faith when genuine, which is rarely the case, dwells in this
inner self which to-day is fully recognized as the subconscious
faculty.   There is a kind of faith that emanates from the thinking mind, which is the reasoning power of the brain ;   but such
faith never rises higher than firm belief ;   and all belief, if true,
is founded on facts that are apparent to the conscious mind.
No normal person says that he believes something unless he has
some basis of fact for such credence.   Faith, when genuine, is
never founded on facts, but on subconscious knowledge ;   and
as such is far more likely to be well founded than the usual
conclusions called belief.   Mental determination, when using
the mind of faith, carries its results into far realms.   Those

who heard Spurgeon pray felt that he was demanding an answer by the strong assertiveness of his voice.

Cures have been wrought by mental determination in the form of faith emanating from the subconscious mind ; but this faith has generally been exercised by the person causing the cure. Occasionally it is true that the patient is able to cure himself by faith, but it must be accompanied by mental determination, not by belief coming from the reasoning mind.

We have knowledge of many cases where unruly children, who could not be controlled by nurses and governesses, have been effectively managed by those who have developed mental determination. Some years ago we recorded the case of a country school, the bullying boys of which had caused several teachers to leave until a young man who had developed this power took charge ; and during his several years of teaching there, not one attempt was ever made to annoy him. In explaining the circumstance, a boy who has since become a successful merchant says : " The first moment our new teacher entered the school, he walked among us, looked at us, talked kindly but very firmly to us, and we liked him because we felt and seemed to know that he would not permit any fooling. So we stopped it, and began to learn our lessons." The teacher told us his account in a few words : " I went there with the firm resolve, no matter what happened, to be master first, last and always ; and I was."

Mental determination always wins.

But this power is most effective in making a man or woman supreme over the influences that lead them into mistakes and disasters through an appeal to their appetites, or their inclinations. It is said that the greatest evil in the life of a person is the willingness to drift along from day to day aimlessly. They let matters take care of themselves ; and this is something that never happens in the right way ; otherwise life would not be crowded with failures and disappointments. The mind is the engineer of the body ; and it is the duty of every engineer to direct and control the power that is placed in his charge. The directing and controlling agency must hold sway at all times.

DEPARTMENT OF MAGNETIC HEALING

LESSON SEVENTY

METHODS OF HEALING

A BRIEF BUT IMPORTANT department will close this extended study of personal magnetism. Because our title seems familiar it must not be assumed that old methods are to be presented here. Too much of the imagination has been brought into play by the kind of healing that has been called mental and sometimes magnetic. In our system we do not leave anything to the flights of fancy or to the beliefs that have been fed by the suggestions of others ; but each and every step in this line is scientifically demonstrated as practical and useful for the purposes for which it is intended ; and has a basis as exact as any proposition in mathematics.

There are two sides to the question of healing ; one relates to the efforts of the patient to heal himself. There are many cases of extraordinary weakness where the sick man may give up, or may assist in effecting a cure. There are plenty of instances where the desire to die is rewarded by such an end. On the other hand the incentive to live is furnished by some great love, some reciprocated affection, or some material advantage. These experiences show that the patient holds some of the power of a cure in his disposition to help. There are many familiar cases where the exercise of great will-power has prolonged life, and even effected a final cure. We recall the recent episode of a mother who, on seeing her little child, said, " I must live for her sake." This experience has been repeated many times, as shown by the reports of doctors.

It is said of a well-known Queen that, on learning of the

sacrifice of her troops in a certain war, she took to her room and expressed a desire to die, and her death followed very soon. History indicates that Queen Elizabeth, on ascertaining that her lover had been executed by reason of the treachery of a rival, lost the desire to live and died almost immediately. Edison, in a published statement, recites the fact that his grandfather, after passing the age of a hundred, declared that he was tired of living, went to his room, undressed, got into bed, and died by act of his will-power. " There was nothing the matter with him," said the inventor.

These facts being accepted as true, it is the duty of those in charge of patients to study what purposes and desires are at work in the minds of those who are critically ill; for they often swing the scales one way or the other.

Our present study relates rather to the influences of the doctor or attendant over the case, and not so often in fatal instances as in ordinary sickness where recovery may be hastened. There are professional healers who call themselves faith doctors, meaning that if they can arouse sufficient belief in the minds of patients they can effect a cure; but they must be able to exert a positive influence in themselves and transfer such power to the patients in order to prove magnetic. There are others who are known as mental healers who make use of their own faculties in efforts to bring about cures; and others who seek to arouse a mutual mental effort in patient and healer. With these we have nothing to do.

We seek to enhance and increase the natural, everyday powers of doctors, nurses, attendants and members of the family by the practical use of those gifts that Nature bestows on every one in more or less degree. These values appear in the voice, in the eyes, in the touch, in the face, and in the presence of the person who will be referred to here as the healer, although there is no intention of educating any one for the profession of doctor or healer. It simply comes down to this: There are endless opportunities for all persons to assist in saving others when the crises arise. The presence of a person is magnetic when it follows the laws of the Sixth and Seventh Departments of this book. The face is magnetic when it follows the laws of Mental Magnitude and of Mental Determination; the one in the Second Department, and the other in the Ninth Department of this book. The eyes are magnetic when they follow the laws of the Third Department.

This leaves for our consideration only the voice and the touch.

Every great teacher of singing knows of and employs the law of mental placement of the voice in developing it. In ordinary Nature the placing or impinging of the voice in the throat is animal, coarse, rough, ugly, repellent and non-magnetic. These facts we have taught fully in the Eighth Department. Great teachers, especially in Europe where they are the most thorough, insist upon the forward placing of all tones, which means the impinging of the voice against the front upper palate ; and this they accomplish by a double method ; one that drops the back of the tongue, lowers the larynx and raises the soft palate ; the other solely by the action or attention of the mind, for which reason it is called the mental tone as distinguished from the animal or physical tone in the throat.

Mentality of this kind is located in the forward brain, the cerebrum, so that the voice that is cultivated is controlled by this organ ; while the animal or physical tones are controlled by the animal brain or cerebellum.

The subconscious mind is known not to be located or controlled by either brain ; but the character and activities of the meninges or brain linings account for the presence there or control by that part of the subconscious mind. It is an accepted fact that all organs of the body are governed by their membranes, on the health of which the normal functioning of such organs depends. It is also known that disordered meninges or brain membranes will cause insanity, crime, low moral practices, and all manner of evil ; while the perfect health of these membranes will lead to exactly opposite conditions ; and the building up of great magnetic powers in these membranes will induce the activities of genius, inspiration and the most extraordinary control over all persons. Experiments made and being made in hospitals and by experts show results that are pronounced marvellous.

Luther Burbank, after receiving instruction or aid from one of the greatest of European psychologists, made the public statement that he had accomplished cures among others that were almost unbelievable, and which if seen would astound the world. He was not only exceedingly magnetic, but had used his higher faculties in his wizardry of the plant world. Other persons are doing fully as much as he had done, but without making their work public.

As the mental voice is impinged forward against the front upper palate, and the animal voice against the throat, so the subconscious voice is impinged against the soft palate, which is high up, or should be, in the upper throat. This is the dark quality taught in the Eighth Department. It is a dark, smooth tone, made softly as if imitating distant thunder, using the word "Roll" for the purpose. When established it is called the subconscious voice ; and this fact is verified by the practice of doctors who employ therapeutic suggestion as a means of cure. An expert says that—

"The voice in healing must be *low, cultured* and *caressing*."

Such a voice is easily acquired especially by a person who is magnetic. Doctors, nurses, attendants and friends should develop tones that are *low, cultured* and *caressing* ; and these are readily acquired in our Eighth Department. No one would for a moment think of using the coarse, repellent and ugly throat tones ; nor the mentally bright and metallic forward tones ; which leaves nothing but the subconscious voice that impinges on the soft palate and is controlled by the operations of that faculty.

Such a voice when used by a person on himself, accomplishes all the results that have been claimed for self-suggestion ; but when directed on behalf of another it is even more helpful ; but should be charged with a message directed by a living, moving purpose, and impelled by the full force of mental determination. It must not be empty of ideas, nor a drifting, purposeless proceeding.

DEATH AND LIFE

THE SYSTEM OF HEALING is completely interwoven in all the lessons of this book, for which reason all we can advance is a suggestion or two concerning the methods by which it may be applied ; and the lesson just preceding this tells in a few words the whole story of procedure. But the matter of the magnetic touch remains for discussion. Almost invariably when a man or woman discovers the possession of the natural power of magnetic healing, the attempt is made to use it in a vigorous manner, which involves great tensing of the muscles and nerves. There is no magnetism in a set condition of the muscles or of the nerves. Setness of mind, as has been shown in Lesson Sixty-Nine on Mental Determination, is non-magnetic. The results are as wide apart as the poles between tensed set nerves, and moving tensed nervous flow. The magnetic touch is of the latter character.

In the Sixth Department we have shown the difference between setness in tensing and flow in tensing ; and the best of all tests is the ability to tense slowly and gradually the whole arm from the shoulder to the wrist, and while the hand hangs limp and the fingers can be shaken about like so many ends of rags. One of the finest and best of all habits is that which employs this method of slowly tensing the arm with the hand limp, and then stroking some part of the body of a patient who is suffering from pain, as of a headache, by passing the limp hand very gently over the part, all the while allowing the flow of nervous energy that is checked at the wrist to come into the hand, and gradually into the finger-tips. In this instance there is an actual magnetic current passing from one person to the other ; and when accompanied by the voice of healing which is " *low, cultured* and *caressing*," the effect is instantaneous ; although we have been informed of many cases where only the magnetic touch has been employed ; and in our own experience in the past forty-five years such cases are too numerous to be even counted. In the development of the voice that is " low, cultured and caressing," full attention should be given to the preceding lesson which contains a vast amount of help in the fewest words possible.

The battle of life must be fought against setness in all its forms, for any thinking person can readily see that there is no flow of a magnetic current unless there is a movement of it.

In magnetic healing the power of Mental Determination, if it is kept a moving power, and not a set condition of the will, is almost invincible. When this power is allied with the full system of personal magnetism as taught in this book, the combination means all that can be wished for by mind or heart, and has no human limitations. For these reasons we strongly advise every student of these pages to make this book the one greatest companion of his or her life ; to know it perfectly in each and every one of its lessons ; to become familiar with all its teachings ; to go through life with it closer to the activities of daily existence than any other agency or influence ; and to never part with it or its aid.

When founded on such a basic structure, the employment of the power of Mental Determination interwoven with all the teachings of this book becomes a giant force in the life of the individual. There have been many cases of the use of this power when health, through carelessness, has brought some strong man or woman to the verge of the grave. We have seen desire to live whip this power into an almost unbelievable energy. In one case which has been recorded in medical works, a woman who was dying, but who did not know it, overheard arrangements being made in an adjoining room for her funeral. From a bed of supposed helplessness, she arose, rushed to the next room, demanded the facts, was told that she was dying, hurled the lie in the faces of those present, and proceeded to dress. Twenty years afterwards, she was doing her own housework.

Doctors enjoy reciting among themselves, and keeping from the public, many extraordinary cases in which it is claimed that the dead have arisen under the stress of the mental determination of others, generally of loved ones and close friends;

but there are two kinds of death in the body. The engine of the automobile " goes dead " when the machinery stops. When a person dies solely because the machinery stops, as when he is the victim of acute indigestion, drowning, shock, anæsthesia, heart failure, asphyxia, neurasthenia and other causes, he is called dead enough to bury although all that is needed is some power to set in motion again the machinery of his life ; yet in fact he is not dead enough to bury until the autopsy is begun or the untimely activity of the embalmer is started on its course.

Doctors say that fully thirty-three per cent of all burials are of persons whose life machinery has merely stopped, but who need only some power to set it going again.

Just think of it !

Yet this is the fact. And humanity is apparently helpless. The remedy is in the establishing and endowment of a school of healers, legalized and genuinely equipped for the practice of a new profession, discarding the old pretences of the so-called mental and magnetic healers, and coming down to the actual science of Nature, tested and verified with mathematical certainty, knowing the real processes required, and applying them in a rational and effective manner. We are not teaching that the actually dead person may be raised from the dead ; but we do know that a person whose life machinery is in good condition, but who is called dead because it has stopped its activity, may be revived ; and you may call it raising the dead, or give it its proper name, reviving a living person before the embalmer makes it a hopeless case.

Human beings, like plants, depend on vitality for their existence. It has been said that one person who possesses an excess of vitality, may impart much of that excess to another person. By the law of electrical flow, the weaker may draw in the stronger current.

The accounts of remarkable cases of reviving the apparent dead that are told by doctors among themselves are, as far as we have had the privilege of learning the facts, which is not often, seemingly true. At least some physicians who are sincere and trustworthy seem satisfied that they are true. A case that is referred to by doctors as " typical," because it has many similar cases to sustain its claims, is that of a man who learned that his son was dying. By swift journeys he hurried to the scene, but arrived too late. The embalmer was there about to begin his work of actual death. The first thing the father did was to knock the undertaker down and out, and throw his apparatus into the yard. He said afterwards, "I do not know why I did this ; but I did know that my son was not dead. When I learned of his critical condition I was fully determined that he should NOT DIE. A glow of light seemed to shine in and around my body. Wherever I went, it kept about me. When I came into the house and saw what was about to be done, it was not frenzy but mental determination that compelled me to take full charge of the matter. I do not know why I knocked the undertaker down and kicked his apparatus into the yard. I knew I must act quickly. I had but one idea, that my son was alive, and that all he needed was the strong force that I was enabled to exercise to arouse him."

It seems that the father stripped the body of his son, and, stripping all clothing from his own body, that he took the son into his warm, glowing embrace, and held him there, saying over and over again that he was alive, he was alive, he was not dead, he was not dead, he must begin to breathe, his heart must begin to beat, the blood must begin to flow, the skin must begin to get warm, life must come back for it lingered close at hand ready to come back when given the opportunity ; and so he continued without ever losing hope or lessening his determination to win back the child of his love. It required time, but he had no knowledge of the passing of the minutes. Nor did he know how long he was there. Time was marked off, not by the ticking of the clock but by the process of events ; each event was an epoch ; and each epoch the enacting of a fate that came to him because he deserved it.

Soon the body of the son displayed returning warmth in its surface ; this was an epoch. Then the father knew that victory was assured. The glow of the living organism passed into the dead. It reached the heart, and then the lungs. The eyes opened. The lips spoke,

"FATHER!"

DOCTORS OF MAGNETISM

SOME DAY all doctors and medical people will depend on Nature as nearly as can possibly be done; and discard the use of chemicals to fight out one poison with another, as the saying goes. It is remarkable, even in this slightly advanced era in changing the methods of treatment, to note the tendency to adopt the services of the source of all magnetism, which is the sun.

At a certain Institution doctors are using split rays of the sun in order to extract out of the most vital portion of those rays the magnetism that Nature intends for bringing the spark of life into human bodies. As is well known the sunbeam consists of a series of rays. It was once supposed that the heat of the sun furnished not only warmth but vitality. This has been disproved. At one end of the spectrum is the red ray, and beyond this is what is called the infra-red ray, which carries the sun heat through glass; while at the other end of the spectrum is the violet ray, beyond which is the invisible ultra-violet ray, which carries all the magnetism from the sun, all the vitality for plant life and for human life. This will not pass through window glass.

Between the heat of the red ray and the vitality of the violet ray are the destructive forces of the sun which, when too greatly exposed, do injury. Doctors and governments, as well as great hospitals, are now splitting the violet rays and making use of its magnetism; for this is the source of all power both of vitality and magnetism. The latter come from the ultra-violet or invisible portion of the violet rays; while we look for heat from the infra-red rays. This does not imply that there is no warmth in the other parts of the sunbeam, but that other forces come from the other rays, some of which are destructive, some the sources of energy, and all capable of great activity that is akin to heat.

In another way, but without realizing the fact, doctors have for many years employed the magnetism of the sun in the use of cod-liver oil. The codfish feeds at great depths in the sea, rarely coming into contact with the sunlight at the surface. As a recompense, Nature provides for the storing in the liver of great relative quantities of magnetism that is exactly like that from the sun, but that is self-generated. It does not come from the sunlight, but does come from the effects of the sun in an indirect way.

IT IS SELF-GENERATED.

Poultry that are kept in the outdoor sun during the egg-forming period, lay eggs that are charged and super-charged, like cod-liver oil, with the same kind of magnetism, but get it directly from the sun rays. Here are two results, both the same, one from the sun itself, and one from self-generation in a living creature ; and both kinds of food furnish a curative treatment in disease.

In a great hospital they are able to bring the ultra-violet or magnetic rays of the sun through windows, but they make use of panes of quartz-crystal that are worth almost their weight in gold. This enables the doctors to treat patients indoors, for the clothing must be removed for the body to absorb this magnetism. Then arose the question, how can these magnetic rays be obtained when the sun is not shining, and during the night ? The answer was the invention of the quartz-mercury lamp, which delivers the desired rays in unvarying and reliable quantity. It is made of a tube containing mercury vapour, through which an electric current is passed. It emits light that is extraordinarily rich in the ultra-violet or magnetism rays. The tube is made of pure quartz-crystal melted at a very high temperature with an oxy-acetylene flame.

Thus we see that, while all magnetism comes originally from the sun, it can be generated by a living creature, as we have shown ; and it can be summoned by the inventive genius of man. If one living creature is given the power to self-generate magnetism, it stands to reason that humanity should be able to do likewise. A certain Clinic for the cure of children not only brings these little patients into the direct rays of the sun, but includes in their medical diet a certain quantity of cod-liver oil daily ; thus making use of the same magnetic vitality in two ways : first, that which comes directly from the sun ; and, second, that which Nature had provided the fish as compensation for being deprived of the direct rays of light, and the compensation, in this case, overran the needs. It was one of Nature's excesses.

We have said at the beginning of this lesson that doctors will some day depend on Nature. The letters that now read M.D., and that mean Doctor of Medicine, will some day read still M.D., and indicate a new meaning—Doctor of Magnetism.

The change has begun. The use of cod-liver oil is making magnetism take part in many cures. The use of eggs, milk and other foods that have come from the influence of the ultra-violet or magnetic rays is feeding magnetism to the body ; and this practice is spreading everywhere very rapidly. Exposing the body to the sun rays is another form of magnetic healing. Drawing the sun-magnetism through quartz-crystal windows is another form. And the use of the quartz-mercury lamp, without reference to the sunlight, but by the " made-light " of the mercury-vapour tube, shows still another advance.

We have shown that this same form of magnetism is self-generated in a living creature, and in great abundance, owing to Nature's proneness to run to excess in some of her processes.

That almost every human being is endowed with the same power of generating the kind of magnetism that brings life to the body, and increases life in others, has been proved by the teachings of this entire system, including every page of this book. More than this, we will state that any student of this work may readily acquire the power of helping others who are deficient in vitality or who are suffering from disease.

The death of Luther Burbank called attention to his statement that was published far and wide a few weeks before his demise. He said :

" I am frank to state that I have successfully applied this power in from 200 to 300 cases, effecting cures constantly. The result of these cures would make your hair stand on end, if known." He refused to draw his patients into the light of publicity, as some persons might misinterpret his motives. He said his usual method in effecting cures was to take the sufferer by one hand and place his other hand on the patient's back. His work and results were vouched for by the scientist and physician who probably stands at the head of his branch of the medical profession of to-day, Dr. Konradi Leitner, Swiss specialist. Dr. Leitner says of his first meeting with Burbank : " When I clasped his hand we both felt the flow of magnetism ; and each one of us mentioned the thrill that we received at the time."

A young woman, not thirty years of age, but surrounded with all the luxuries that great wealth could bring her, refused to marry a man who loved her ; stating as the excuse that she was too frail for marriage, and probably was not long for this world. It was a case of low vitality, not only of body but of the entire system, accompanied by mental discouragement. Being a church member, and entering into the social activities, she took part one evening in a gathering, one of the festivities of which placed her next to a young man, whose hand she was to clasp. In so doing she felt a steady flow of vitality enter her arm and travel through her body. The following statement comes from the young man who had been an eager student of this system of magnetism, and whose version was confirmed by the lady herself :

" When her hand clasped mine," he said, " I felt a strong quiver of her arm, and a tightening of her hold. We were strangers to each other until that time, although I had seen her often. As soon as the game, as they called it, was over, although the evening was very young, she asked me to take her and her mother home. Arriving there, she made me the surprising request that I act as her doctor, telling me that my vitality or magnetism could alone restore her health. Her mother joined in the request. The result can be surmised. We grew to care for each other ; and, although I was poor and she was rich, we were married ; and neither has regretted it."

We were at one time teaching a large class in personal magnetism and made the statement that each and every one of our students would acquire by self-generation such a volume of magnetism that it would have a decided curative power. One lady asked the privilege of bringing a lady friend to the next session, saying that this friend was very low in vitality and was said to be hopelessly ill from nervous prostration.

No doctor was able to cure her, although she was amply able to employ the best specialists. The friend came to the next session. Among the students were some who were beginners, some who had made partial progress, and some who were well advanced. This friend was not told these facts, but supposed all were of the same status in their progress.

As an experiment she took the hand of one who had developed a high degree of magnetism, and at once reported the passing of a decided current from him to her body. Then she took the hand of one who had not advanced far, and reported that she felt but little effect. Next she took the hand of a beginner and stated that she felt nothing whatever. " Now," it was stated to her, " you will take the hand of a novice who may some day be very magnetic, but you will feel nothing now." She was given the hand of the most advanced pupil in the class, and said with alacrity, " You have made a mistake. This gentleman is full of magnetism." Without detailing the history of subsequent events, we need only say that she found a way to fully recover her health, and one of our students found a beautiful wife.

The world is entering upon the era of magnetism.

This is true of the curative systems of civilisation. All life, all health, all vitality, come from the sun by one of two processes : either from direct contact with the rays of that orb, which cannot be had on cloudy days, or during the nights, or in climes where the sun shines but little, and which, in other climes where the sunlight is destructive, is too severe.

We have cited Nature's compensation in one case ; and we find a similar compensation in the case of humanity. To one form of life she gave the power of self-generation of magnetism ; to every man and woman she has given, in much higher form, the same power of self-generation of magnetism ; and it has been the mission of this book to set forth that great gift, and the natural and practical ways of acquiring it and of using it.

Any exhibition of power is magnetism.

To win success in any department of life is one of the goals of magnetism, and that quality is taught in this work.

To rise above want, achieve financial independence, and live in old age free from worry on account of reverses, is clearly a mission of this power. In fact, most people believe they have achieved the only real success in life when they place themselves beyond want.

Yet every person should strive to win the perfect respect and confidence of all others who are worth knowing. This also is a valuable result of the practice of this power.

Still further in the struggle of existence is the mastery over all the affairs of life in every department of one's being. Thus we round out a successful career.

Thus far the battle has been fought against adversity and failure ; yet, if we were to close this study without carrying the struggle far enough to combat the one greatest of life, which is disease, we would be remiss in our duty.

It is gratifying to know that the student of this system never need seek help against sickness in person ; as the very essence of this training is automatically self-curing. This means that, no matter how weak in vitality, or how deficient in health you may be when beginning this study, as you proceed you will find all traces of illness, all weakness, all ailments, even those that are chronic, gradually disappearing. They pass away even as the snows of the plains melt before the advance of spring. In a history of forty-five years, we have never had an exception ; so it may be taken for granted that your case will not be a failure in this respect.

Nor is failure possible. The power that we invoke by our plan of self-generation of magnetism is life itself, coming from the great orb of life, and building in the human body the very life that it draws into itself.

There have been so-called magnetic healers in the past ; but we know of none who have possessed this genuine power unless they have also developed this gift of self-generation just as it is taught herein.

The real healers are yet to appear. Burbank was one, but he played with the gift only to test its reality ; and he laid down his life in a fever of overwork in his experiments ; and, as some say, because of misunderstanding of his views on life and death he worried himself into the grave. Dr. Leitner is one of a large number who have come to use this power in its highest sense ; not as mere healers. Coué effected cures by the laying on of hands ; but failed in teaching his system to others who were not magnetic.

In the old days there was one great medical school, the allopathic. In after years it had a competitor in another large school, the homœopathic. These are called the regulars. Later on came the osteopaths ; and still later the chiropractics. A great religion that numbers a million or more followers practises religious cures but avoids medicines. We are stating history, and are not passing judgment on any of these. But it stands to reason that when life can be traced to the magnetism that comes from the sun, and when this magnetism can be self-generated by any man or woman owing to the compensation of Nature, then the drift of civilized progress must of necessity turn to the only original form of natural cures, magnetism.

We have shown that this power acts automatically in bringing perfect health to any student of this system.

In order to use it in a public or professional way in curing others, it is probable that some legal recognition may be necessary. But this does not stand in the way of helping friends and acquaintances ; and it is a very pleasing test of one's powers to employ them in such a cause. The principle that is at work is seen in the comparative funds of vitality in youth and age. The young man can run faster than the old man ; he can endure greater tasks, more severity of strain, and more hardships. He can eat foods that would injure an old person. While he is taking on growth, as in the years of development and young manhood, he draws into his body daily more vitality than one who has passed those stages.

It is this excess of vitality that magnetism brings into the body of one who is frail or ill. The contact of the hands is not always sufficient ; it is better that one hand of the patient should be placed in one hand of the curer, while the other hand of the latter is placed on the bare flesh at the back of the body between the shoulder blades. Tests have been made in a number of ways ; but this seems the most effective. During this effort the curer should tense the body in the manner taught in this book, and should fire the mind with the purpose of mental determination. But these measures are not required where there is a great difference between the two vitalities. The clasping of the hand is sufficient.

A physician who gave full attention to this system, and who became very magnetic, stated that he helped all his patients by merely coming among them ; as he entered the room of one who was ill, the effect was noticeable. He stated that on one occasion when he was spending a brief period at the mountains in summer, where he was wholly unknown, and where no one even suspected that he was a doctor, he was introduced by a newly made friend to several ladies, with each of whom he shook hands in response to their proffered greetings, and one of these ladies claimed at once that he was charged full to the brim, as she put it, with magnetism. She said that she felt a great flow or current pass through her hand into her body. It was a case of great disparity of two vitalities ; his very strong, and hers very weak. Later on he was met by a friend who called him doctor, with the result that this lady insisted on receiving magnetic treatment from him. She said that she had come to the mountains for her health ; that she could not get well under any treatment she had tried ; and all she asked was that he make the effort to help her by merely the laying on of hands. This method required nothing more than contact in that way ; and she fully recovered her health ; not under his care after the holiday was over, but through the assistance of another doctor who was selected by this physician because he lived in the same city with the patient. So that any doctor is able to self-generate magnetism, it does not matter who he is, in effecting cures.

But as the body is built of material that comes from the lap of Nature, it is always wise to supply it with the elements that enter into its perfect making, and avoid those foods that destroy magnetism. Several lessons are devoted to this diet. It is magnetic. We recommend the following combination as invincible :

1. Make use of a magnetic diet for your patients, assuming that you seek the opportunity to help your friends and acquaintances to get well.

2. Aid them to understand the value and the methods of securing the magnetic ultra-violet rays direct from the sun when that can be done.

3. Direct them to the use of such foods as, under the latest progress in growing or obtaining them, will furnish the magnetic vitality that comes from the influence of the ultra-violet rays, such as we have discussed in the early part of this lesson.

4. Cultivate in yourself the practice of imparting magnetic currents in contact with your patients ; using any of the methods that have been described in the preceding page, such as contact of the hands, or the contact of one hand with the hand of the patient, and placing the other hand on the back in the manner stated.

5. Build up great funds of magnetism in your own body for such uses, and for the value it imparts to your own life ; so that you may be instrumental in saving others from illness and disease.

Since writing the preceding lesson of this book we have had reports from several persons following the tests we have been making ; and there is a unanimity of statement that this combination as suggested herein has never met with a failure. Some cases go further than the limited contact stated. Thus a mother whose little girl was pronounced dead by a doctor, took the bare body of the child into her own disrobed body, and, as she said, "enveloped it with her magnetism in a position whereby the surcharged vitality of her body entered the child, and it breathed and lived." A number of very conservative doctors have expressed a firm belief in the power of a magnetic person to bring life into a body whose life is merely suspended.

The whole study is of vast importance in an age when methods are changing rapidly ; and humanity is coming closer to the source of life.

THE PERSONAL MAGNETISM CLUB

THE WORLD-WIDE MAGNETISM CLUB is an organization carried on by correspondence in a general way, and by local meetings in a special way, that came into existence in the year 1888, with the avowed purpose of turning into practical use in daily life the newly formed habits and valuable principles of this system of personal development. Human association and intercourse are necessary parts of every normal and successful life. It is not good for man to be alone. It is not good for woman to be alone. Nor is it good for human beings to segregate themselves and live selfishly apart from other human beings.

Of course it is possible for a hermit to develop the gift of personal magnetism, but he would have no use for it except to ennoble his own character which, in his opinion, might be worth while.

But the pleasure, the enjoyment, the triumphs and the great achievements of existence require the intermingling of humanity in multiform ways, with as much variety of intercourse as is possible ; and in and through all these interwoven interests this power has its greatest opportunities.

The International Magnetism Club has never advertised its existence, and has never sought members. When local meetings are held they are composed of persons of close acquaintance with each other. The general organization seeks to help its members solve all the problems of this system as far as they desire such help and, in turn, gathers a great fund of new knowledge from experiments and experiences occurring in the lives of its members, which of necessity becomes enormously valuable to future students.

There exists a widely held belief that the International Magnetism Club is exclusive, and that only certain persons are

allowed to join it. This is not so. In using the term
" MAGNETISM CLUB " we have in mind two meanings.
First, all men and women, wherever they may be located,
who are students and followers of the Edmund Shaftesbury
lessons in Personal Magnetism, are considered members of
the Personal Magnetism Club.

Second, the term also refers to the group or series of instruction books on the various phases of Magnetic Power written by
Shaftesbury. Magnetism is a subject and study as vast as life
itself. Magnetism permeates all life from the least to the
greatest. So extensive and important a power cannot be
adequately analysèd and completely taught in a single volume.

This explains why the Personal Magnetism Club embraces
the books mentioned at the end of this book. There are some
people who want to study all the known methods of magnetic
development, and for them were some of these private " Magnetism Books " prepared. We call them " private " because
they are seldom found in any public place ; our students buy
them and cling to them jealously as prized personal possessions.
The book you are now reading is the foundation or exercise
book of the Magnetism Club. It is the vital—the " key "—
book. Upon its teachings success in using all other phases of
magnetic power rests.

The Magnetism Club was organized for its students to exemplify in public and private life the principles of Personal
Power as taught by Edmund Shaftesbury. Its slogan for
many years has been : " Personal Magnetism can accomplish
anything which is in the realms of possibility."

The books of the Personal Magnetism Club, in the early
editions, were the first to be issued on the subject, when there
were no other systems in existence. { Imitators arose—but fell
by the wayside.' To-day the new and enlarged systems are the
standard method and are so recognized everywhere. To the
best of our knowledge Shaftesbury's books represent THE
ONLY LIBRARY OF PERSONAL MAGNETISM SECRETS
IN THE WORLD.

Magnetism is a double power : aggressive and protective—
the best friend of man or woman, and their best defence. But
Magnetism is not hypnotism. The latter deadens the faculties,
while magnetism gives them life and energy. Hypnotism puts

into a cataleptic sleep ; while magnetism inspires, thrills, enthuses, awakens and enlivens.

If you possess personal magnetism, you can wield some power over every man, woman and child ; you will also be safe against the influence of others. Men and women who have never done much for themselves in the way of success, or who had never reaped the full reward of living, have taken up the study of the instruction books of the Magnetism Club and re-made their lives.

Magnetism and success are synonymous terms ; and progress in life is proof that they are moving onward. The best progress is that which is practical, and that can be turned to actual uses. The individual who never goes to bed at night unless he has in some degree added to his self-improvement during the day is moving onward to success ; and that person who at the end of each year has laid aside some part of his earnings or gains is moving onward to success. All others are stagnant, and are treading the road to failure.

What you have accomplished you should turn to account among your fellow-beings. In that way you will find your pleasure in life, your enjoyment of existence and your only real triumphs in this world. As far as this earth is concerned, there is no greater goal. But in order to do this you must participate in multiform ways in the intermingling of humanity. And this must be done without waste of time and opportunity. Here is the greatest field for the uses of magnetism.

How to accomplish all these things is, and has been for many years, the work of the Magnetism Club.

This Club inspires the inventor to solve his problems, and to win recognition in the world. This Club paves the way for the minister to build up a great following. This Club discloses the secrets of success in business and in the financial world. This Club makes it possible for every employee to better himself, and better his income each and every year of his active life. This Club shows the way to the lawyer to win many cases ; to the doctor to do the greatest good in his profession ; to the teacher to develop all that is possible and worth while in the minds of scholars ; and to all persons it imparts the gift of establishing true and lifelong friendships and the power to destroy all enmities.

You may organize a Local Magnetism Club by bringing together five others besides yourself, to meet from time to time to discuss and practise the teachings of this book. Any six persons may effect such an organization; or may depend solely on membership in the General Group, known as International Magnetism Club which, for nearly forty years, has achieved the most wonderful results for its Members. We begin, as stated, with the most practical as well as the most effective acquisitions in life; and these are first to be sought by discussion and advice, as well as planning, in order to find the best way of adding each day some degree of self-improvement, no matter how slight, and of saving every month out of one's gains or earnings something against the future. Such problems are readily solved by mutual discussion and advice among half a dozen persons who are in earnest.

These basic achievements prove that you are going in the right direction; neither drifting aimlessly, nor being lured blindly to a heart-breaking failure.

We have said that a half-dozen persons may, by discussion and advice, suggest exactly the best methods to be adopted to this end, and for other uses of magnetism. By this plan many thousands of men and women have been given the new start in life that they needed. Nothing is more pleasing than to see a prospective failure turned into a grand success. This book has been purposely written so as to become of itself an uplifting and personal power from merely the reading of it.

In its helpfulness to others at certain crises in their lives, and at turning-points where one of two roads must be chosen, either of success or of failure, this book has come at the right moment and has been found to be most urgently needed. Its main distribution comes, not from public advertising of its merits, but from being recommended or presented by people who see the vast good it can do when placed in the hands of others. Charity is becoming universal, and is failing because it teaches people to become dependent. A wealthy woman whose life is devoted to charity says, " The best help we can give to those who might become successful is to show them the way to help themselves; and for this reason I give to many intelligent men and women a copy of the book of personal magnetism."

There are many business executives who keep themselves

informed of the progress, character and value of certain employees, and who find it has paid them to give to the latter copies of this book. There are others who find that their employees need some real awakening of ambition and power in order to become more useful, who adopt as a business method the habit of giving this book to those in whom they take an interest.

In bringing this work to a conclusion, the author wishes to send to each and every one of his numerous students the greeting that is not a farewell, but a wish and a hope that all may find these studies pleasant and inspiring ; that they may become influences that shall work great changes in all the conditions and prospects of life ; that they may take the place of careless and trivial reading and do away with wasted hours, by substituting the most useful and valuable things for those that are useless, and that each reader and student of these pages shall reach a standing of one hundred per cent in personal magnetism, by the following acquisitions :

1. Financial independence for all the rest of life.

2. The perfect respect and confidence of others.

3. Mastery over all the affairs of life and in every department of earthly existence.

PRINTED BY MORRISON AND GIBB LTD., LONDON AND EDINBURGH

Made in the USA
San Bernardino, CA
10 July 2017